KAWASHITA

河下水希

I sometimes wonder what I'll be doing ten years from now.
I hope I'll still be writing manga, and that I'll have calluses on
my fingers from pushing my pen around. On the other hand, it's
interesting to imagine myself doing something entirely different.
Anyway, today is New Year's Day, so I should be thinking about
a resolution for the coming year, not worrying about what I'll be
doing ten years down the road...

Mizuki Kawashita's best-known series is the 19-volume
Ichigo 100% (Strawberry 100%), which was serialized in Japan's
Weekly Shonen Jump from 2002 to 2005. The huge success of the
series inspired a 24-episode animated TV show and a game for the
PS2 (***Ichigo 100%—Strawberry Diary***), both of which were released
in Japan in 2005. Kawashita's other works include the two-volume
comedy ***Lilim Kiss***, which ran in ***Weekly Shonen Jump*** from 2000 to
2001, and the one-shot stories ***Natsuiro Graffiti*** and ***Koorihime Kitan***.

STRAWBERRY 100%
3

The SHONEN JUMP ADVANCED Manga Edition

STORY & ART BY
MIZUKI KAWASHITA

Translation/Yuko Sawada
Touch-up Art & Lettering/James Gaubatz
Cover & Interior Design/Hidemi Dunn
Editor/Annette Roman

Editor in Chief, Books/Alvin Lu
Editor in Chief, Magazines/Marc Weidenbaum
VP, Publishing Licensing/Rika Inouye
VP, Sales & Product Marketing/Gonzalo Ferreyra
VP, Creative/Linda Espinosa
Publisher/Hyoe Narita

Printed in the U.S.A.

Published by VIZ Media, LLC
P.O. Box 77010
San Francisco, CA 94107

10 9 8 7 6 5 4 3 2
First printing, January 2008
Second printing, September 2008

THE WORLD'S MOST CUTTING-EDGE MANGA

www.viz.com

www.shonenjump.com

PARENTAL ADVISORY
STRAWBERRY 100% is rated T+ for Older Teen and is recommended for ages 16 and up. It contains suggestive situations.

ratings.viz.com

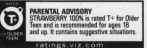

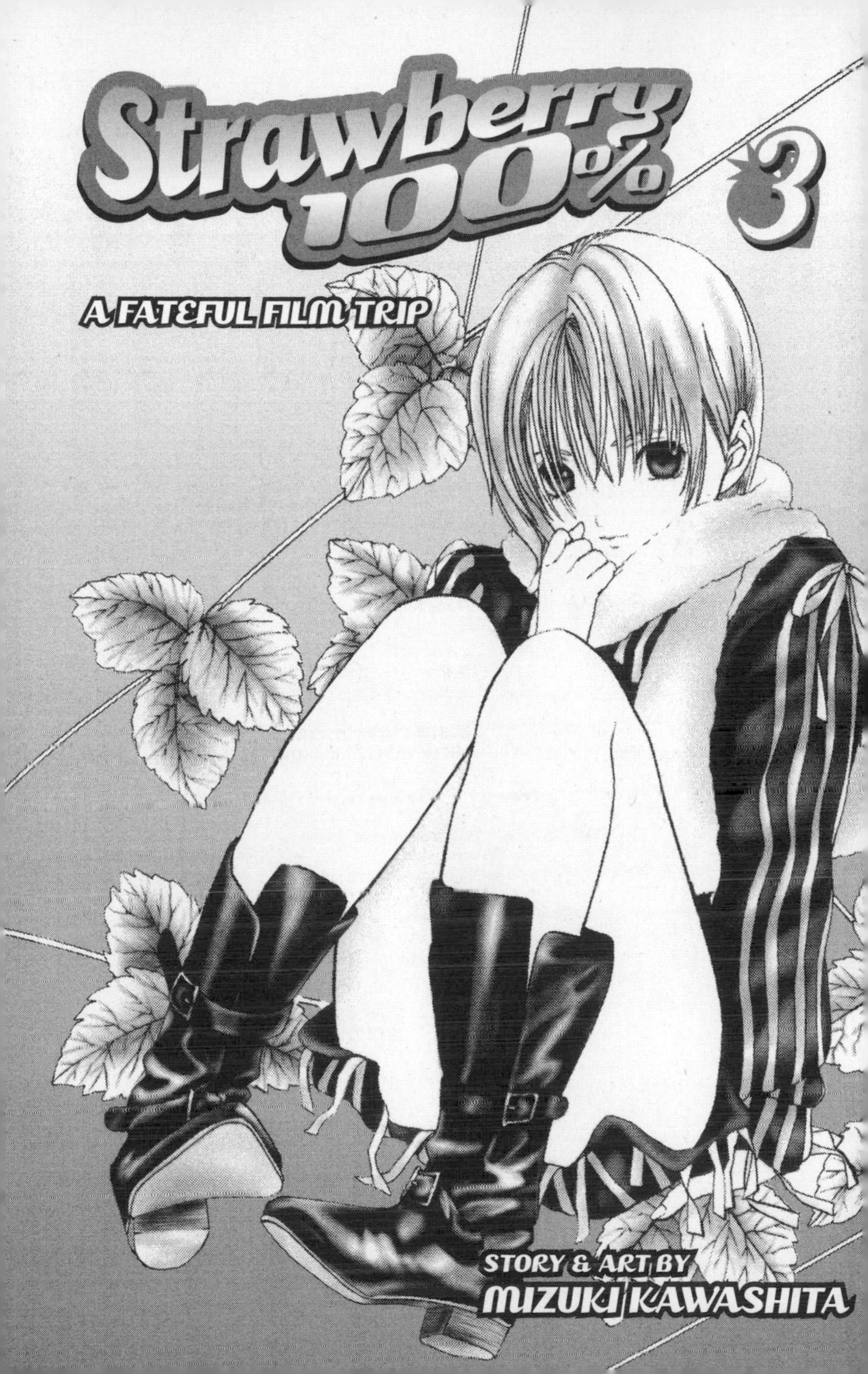
Strawberry 100%
3
A FATEFUL FILM TRIP
STORY & ART BY
MIZUKI KAWASHITA

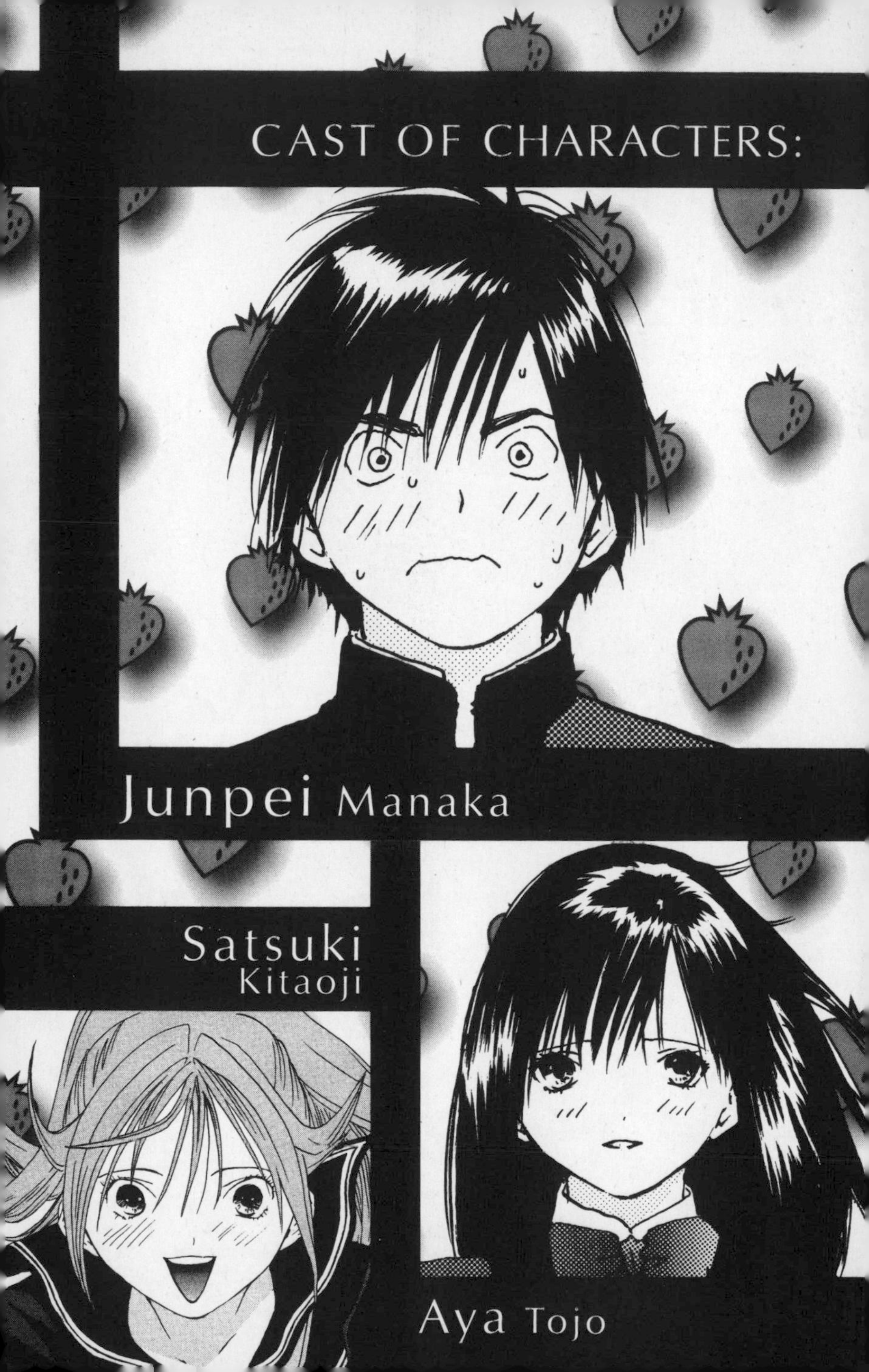
CAST OF CHARACTERS:
Junpei Manaka
Satsuki Kitaoji
Aya Tojo

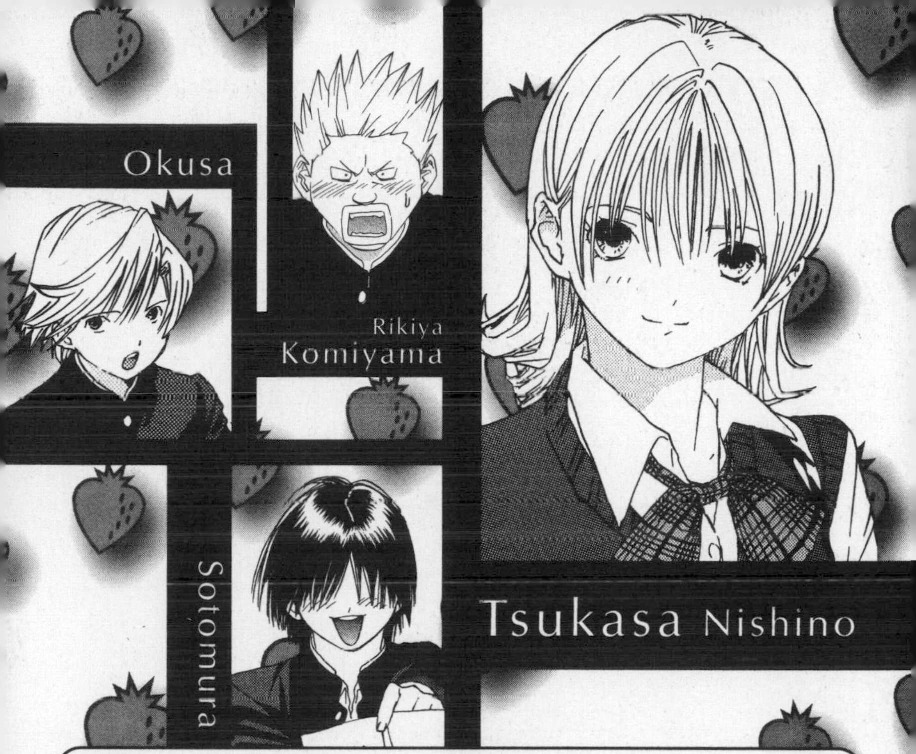
Tsukasa Nishino
Rikiya Komiyama
Okusa
Sotomura

THE PURSUIT THUS FAR...

Ordinary ninth grader Junpei Manaka spots a beautiful girl lying on the roof of his school one afternoon, her skirt accidentally flipped up to reveal strawberry-patterned underwear. He is struck by how beautiful she looks with the sun setting behind her. After this apparition jumps to her feet and flees, Junpei finds a notebook. His hopes are dashed when he learns that it belongs to his nerdy classmate Aya Tojo.

Junpei's buddies, Okusa and Komiyama, assure him that the girl he glimpsed on the roof can only be Tsukasa Nishino, the most popular girl at their school. Without questioning their assumption, Junpei decides to go for broke and ask Tsukasa out.

That night, Junpei opens the notebook and discovers that it contains a novel Aya is working on. Junpei is amazed by her writing. When he returns the notebook to Aya, he tells her something he has never told anyone before—that he dreams of becoming a movie director. As they talk about their ambitions for the future, the two become friends.

The following day, Junpei asks Tsukasa to meet him in the schoolyard after school. When Tsukasa arrives, Junpei, acting on Aya's advice, shows off by doing chin-ups and asks Tsukasa to go out with him. To everyone's astonishment, Tsukasa agrees to be Junpei's girlfriend. As Junpei contemplates his unexpected success, he catches sight of a pretty girl wearing strawberry panties running off. It occurs to him that maybe the girl he saw the other day on the roof wasn't Tsukasa after all...

Unable to focus on his studies, Junpei is not best prepared when the day of the Izumizaka High School entrance exam arrives. Worse, in the exam room, Junpei makes a startling discovery—it turns out that Aya is in fact the mysterious girl with the strawberry panties. Junpei is so shocked by this stunning revelation that the exam is over before he can pull himself together.

A few days later, the test results are announced. Tsukasa and Aya passed, but Junpei and Komiyama are only wait-listed.

On the way home, Tsukasa startles Junpei and her other friends by revealing that she has decided not to go to Izumizaka after all... She gives two contradictory reasons: she doesn't want her love life to take priority over other opportunities, and she believes she has a better chance of winning Junpei's heart from a distance...

CONTENTS
vol. 3

ICHIGO 100%

CRUSH 18: THANKS FOR THE MEMORIES

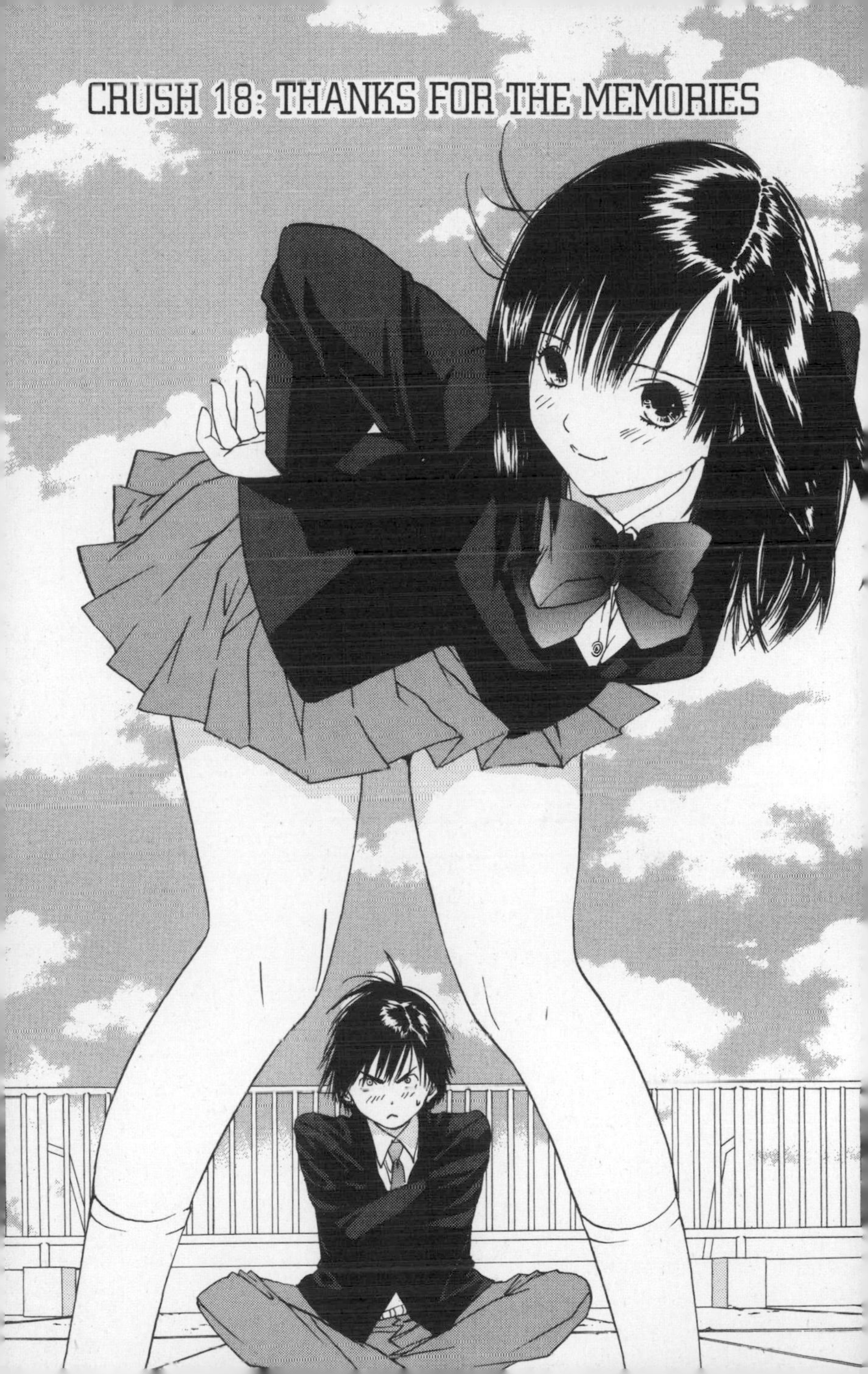

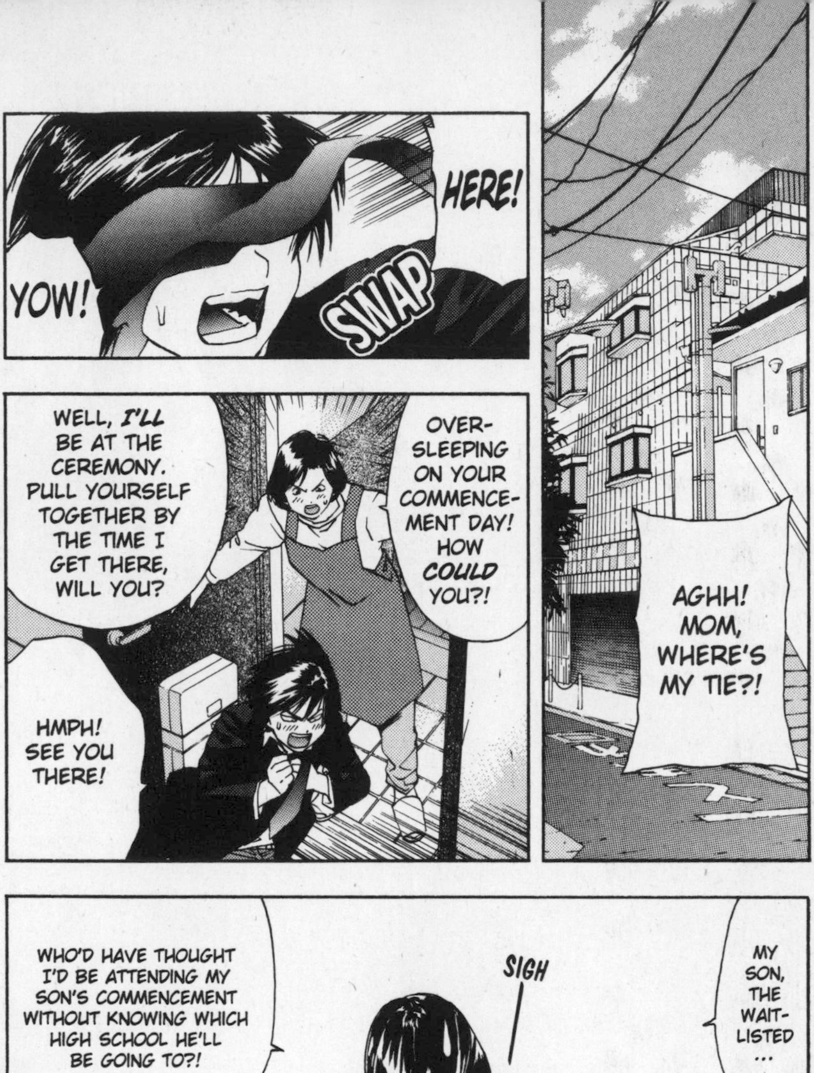
AGHH! MOM, WHERE'S MY TIE?!
HERE!
SWAP
YOW!
OVER-SLEEPING ON YOUR COMMENCE-MENT DAY! HOW *COULD* YOU?!
WELL, *I'LL* BE AT THE CEREMONY. PULL YOURSELF TOGETHER BY THE TIME I GET THERE, WILL YOU?
HMPH! SEE YOU THERE!
MY SON, THE WAIT-LISTED...
SIGH
WHO'D HAVE THOUGHT I'D BE ATTENDING MY SON'S COMMENCEMENT WITHOUT KNOWING WHICH HIGH SCHOOL HE'LL BE GOING TO?!

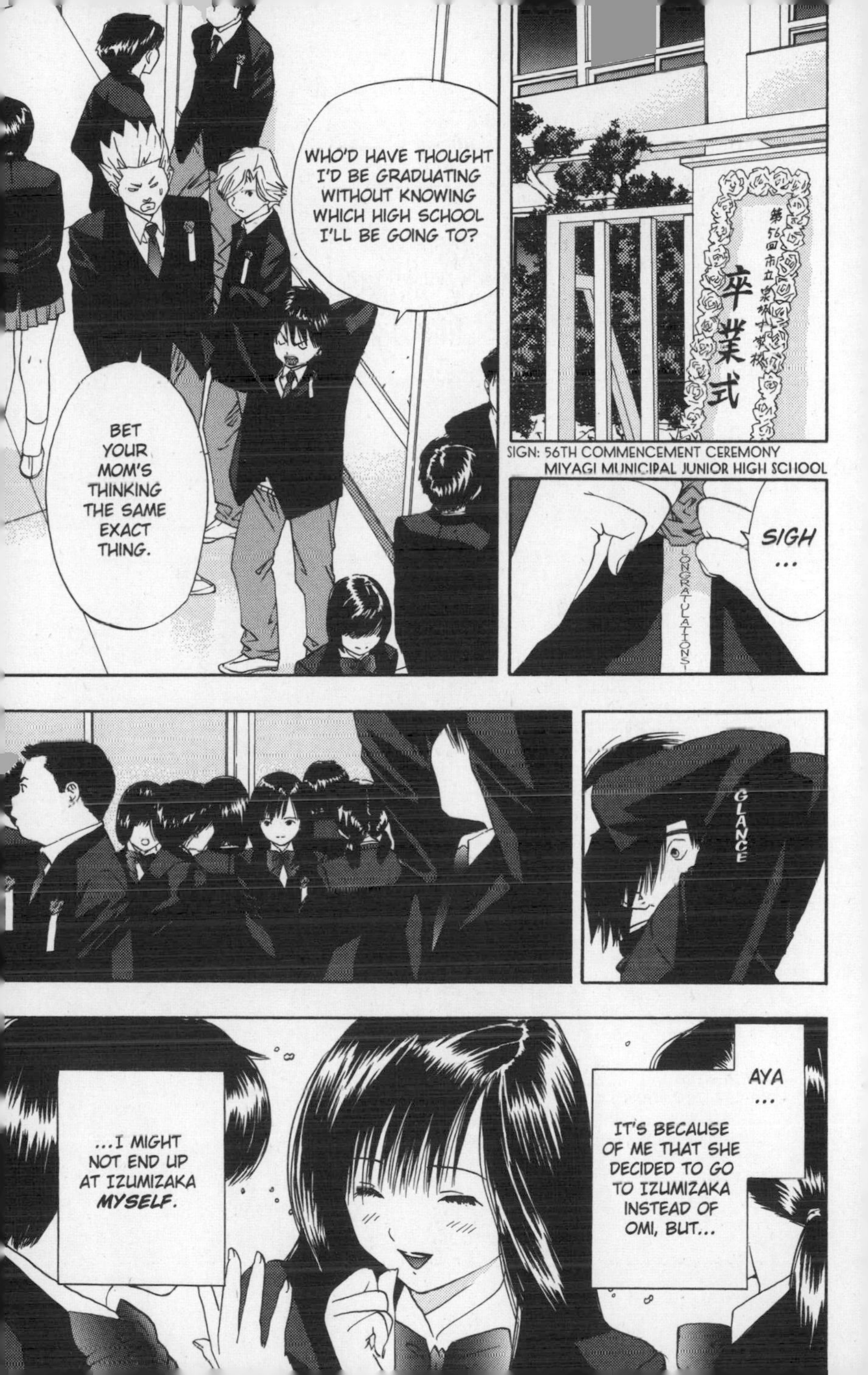
卒業式
SIGN: 56TH COMMENCEMENT CEREMONY
MIYAGI MUNICIPAL JUNIOR HIGH SCHOOL
SIGH ...
CONGRATULATIONS!
WHO'D HAVE THOUGHT I'D BE GRADUATING WITHOUT KNOWING WHICH HIGH SCHOOL I'LL BE GOING TO?
BET YOUR MOM'S THINKING THE SAME EXACT THING.
GLANCE
AYA ...
IT'S BECAUSE OF ME THAT SHE DECIDED TO GO TO IZUMIZAKA INSTEAD OF OMI, BUT...
...I MIGHT NOT END UP AT IZUMIZAKA *MYSELF*.

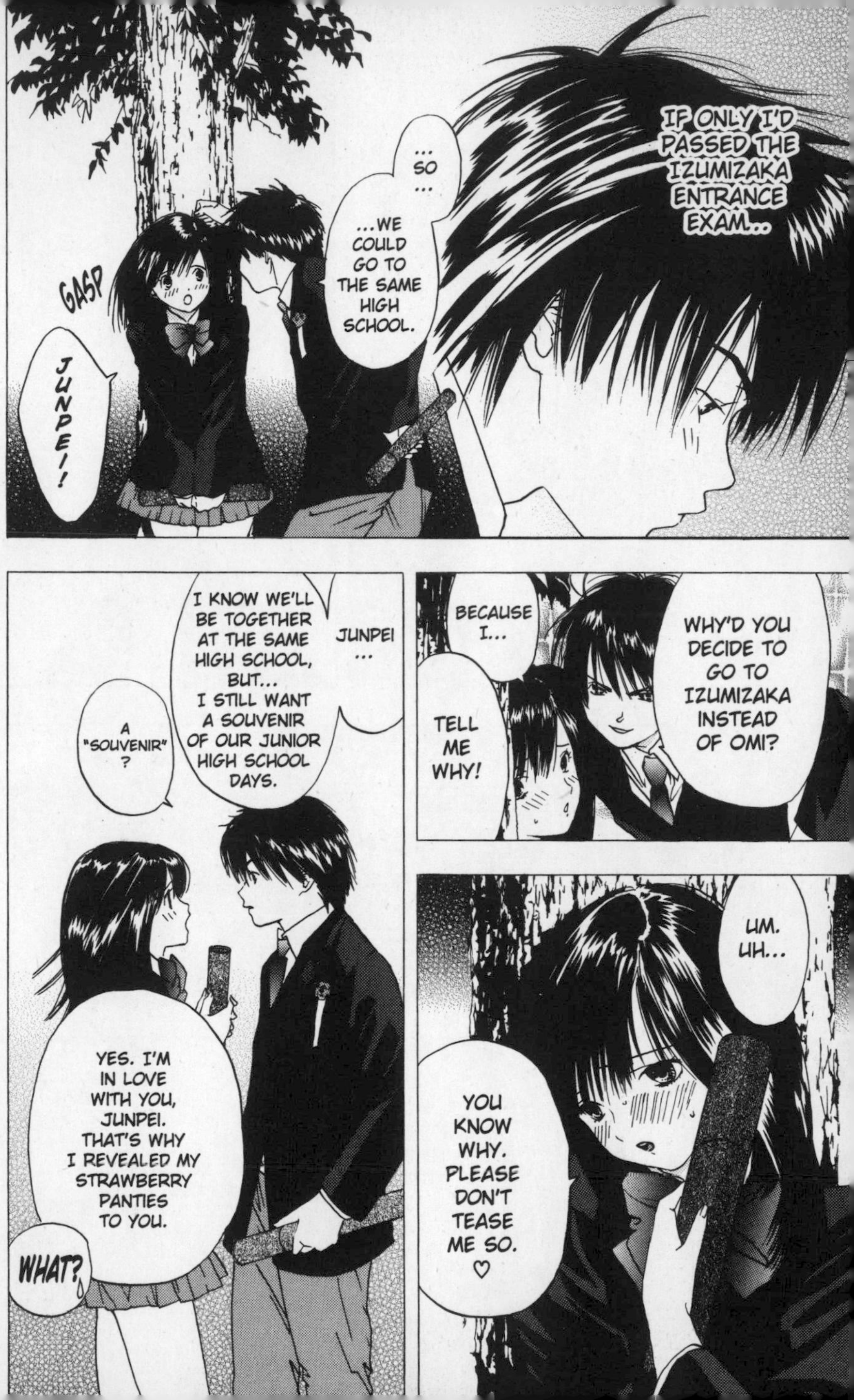
IF ONLY I'D PASSED THE IZUMIZAKA ENTRANCE EXAM...
...SO...
...WE COULD GO TO THE SAME HIGH SCHOOL.
GASP
JUNPEI!
WHY'D YOU DECIDE TO GO TO IZUMIZAKA INSTEAD OF OMI?
BECAUSE I...
TELL ME WHY!
UM. UH...
YOU KNOW WHY. PLEASE DON'T TEASE ME SO. ♡
JUNPEI...
I KNOW WE'LL BE TOGETHER AT THE SAME HIGH SCHOOL, BUT... I STILL WANT A SOUVENIR OF OUR JUNIOR HIGH SCHOOL DAYS.
A "SOUVENIR"?
YES. I'M IN LOVE WITH YOU, JUNPEI. THAT'S WHY I REVEALED MY STRAWBERRY PANTIES TO YOU.
WHAT?

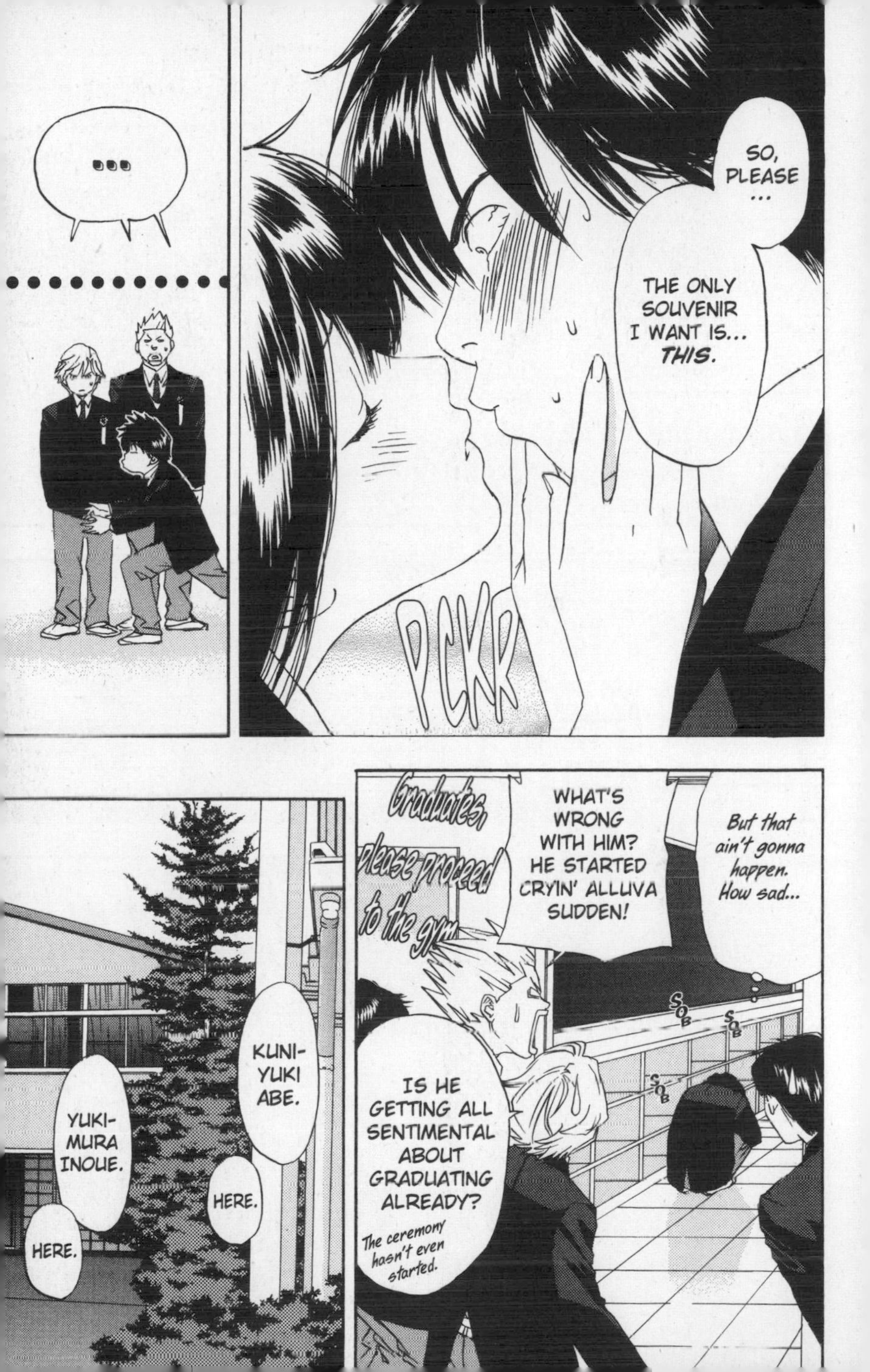
SO, PLEASE ...
THE ONLY SOUVENIR I WANT IS... THIS.
PCKR
...
But that ain't gonna happen. How sad...
WHAT'S WRONG WITH HIM? HE STARTED CRYIN' ALLUVA SUDDEN!
Graduates, please proceed to the gym
SOB
SOB
SOB
IS HE GETTING ALL SENTIMENTAL ABOUT GRADUATING ALREADY?
The ceremony hasn't even started.
KUNI-YUKI ABE.
HERE.
YUKI-MURA INOUE.
HERE.

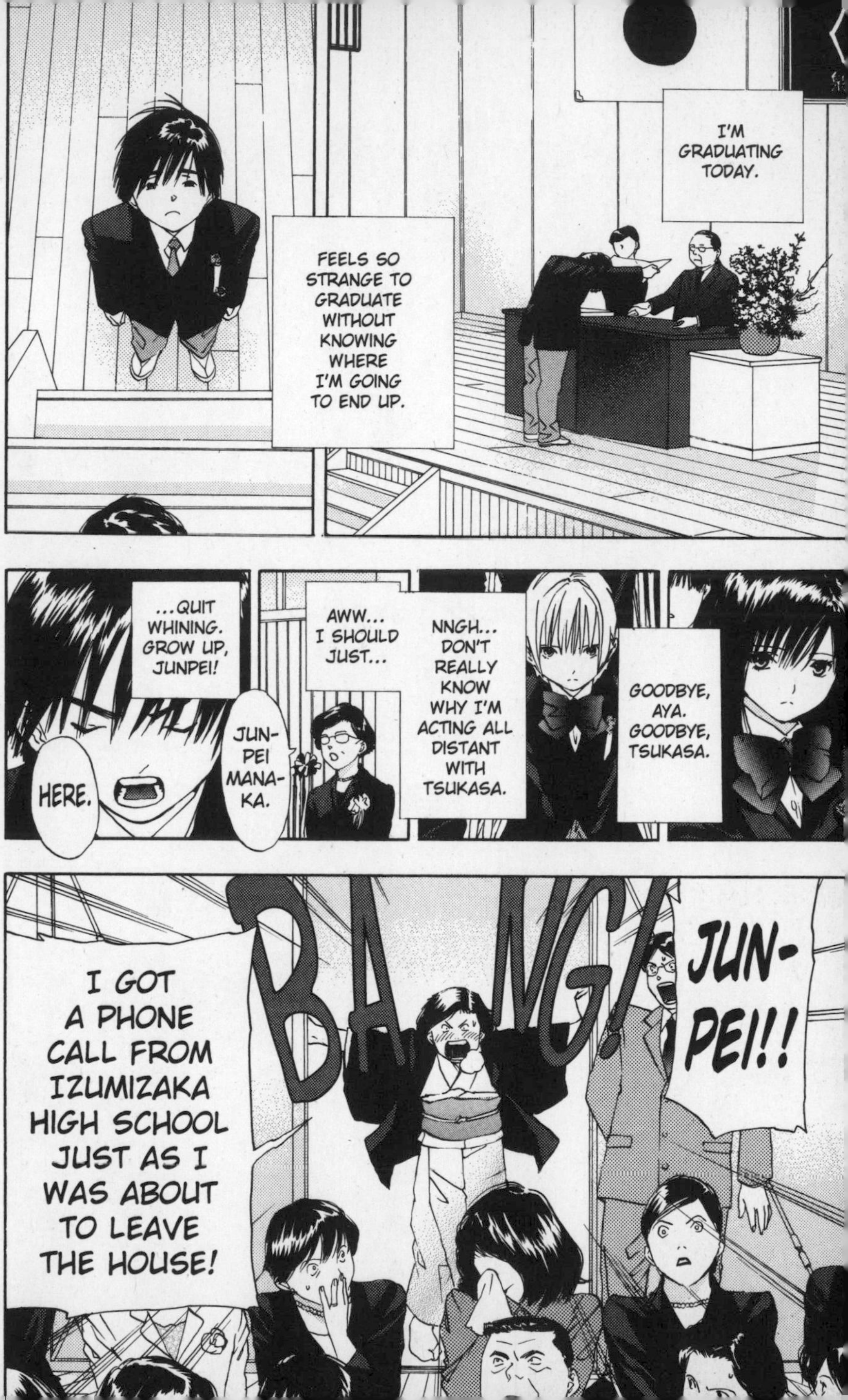

I'M GRADUATING TODAY.
FEELS SO STRANGE TO GRADUATE WITHOUT KNOWING WHERE I'M GOING TO END UP.
GOODBYE, AYA. GOODBYE, TSUKASA.
NNGH... DON'T REALLY KNOW WHY I'M ACTING ALL DISTANT WITH TSUKASA.
AWW... I SHOULD JUST...
JUN-PEI MANA-KA.
...QUIT WHINING. GROW UP, JUNPEI!
HERE.
JUN-PEI!!
BANG!
I GOT A PHONE CALL FROM IZUMIZAKA HIGH SCHOOL JUST AS I WAS ABOUT TO LEAVE THE HOUSE!

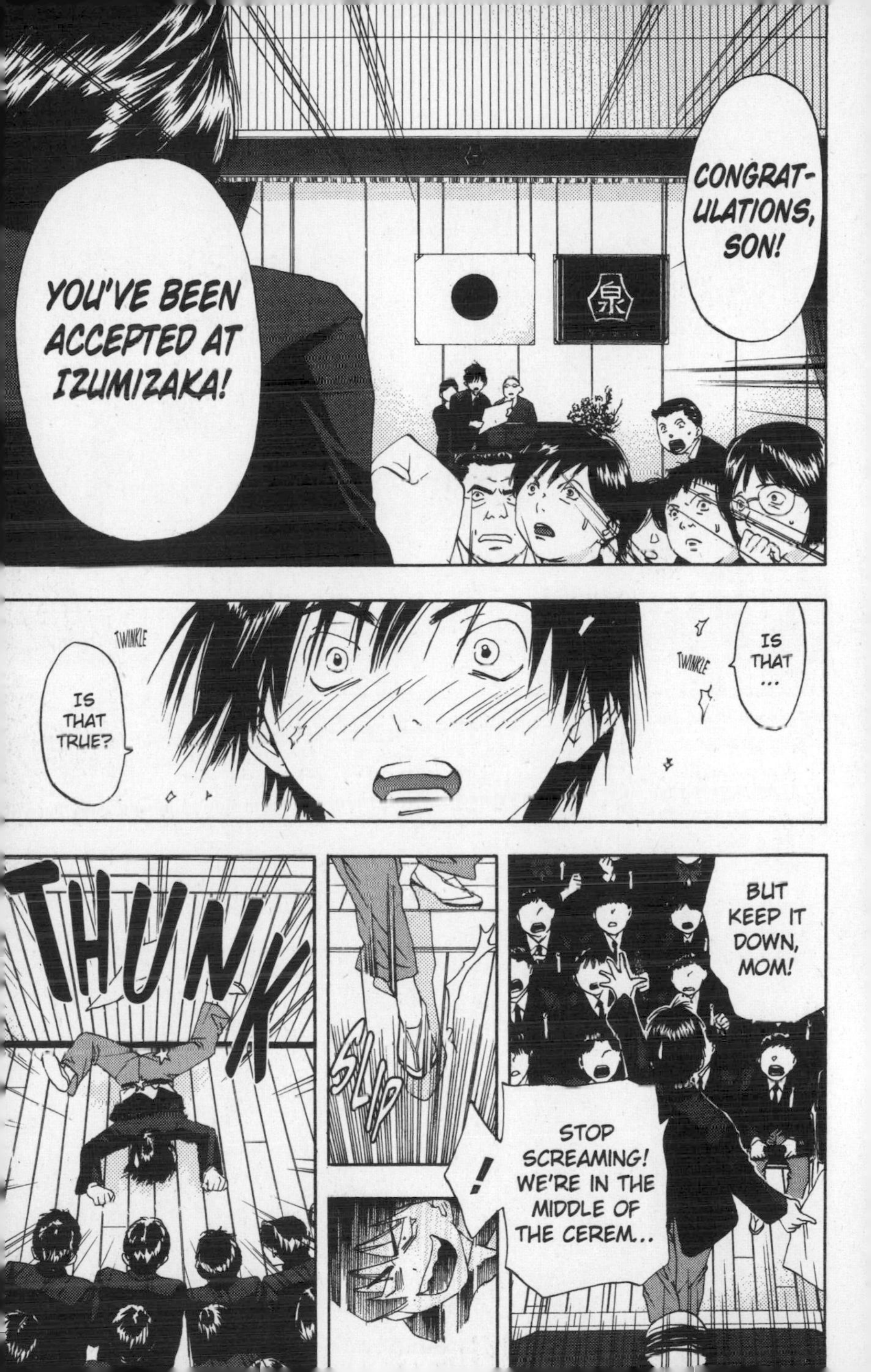
CONGRAT-
ULATIONS,
SON!
YOU'VE BEEN ACCEPTED AT IZUMIZAKA!
TWINKLE
IS THAT...
TWINKLE
IS THAT TRUE?
BUT KEEP IT DOWN, MOM!
STOP SCREAMING! WE'RE IN THE MIDDLE OF THE CEREM...
SLIP
!
THUNK

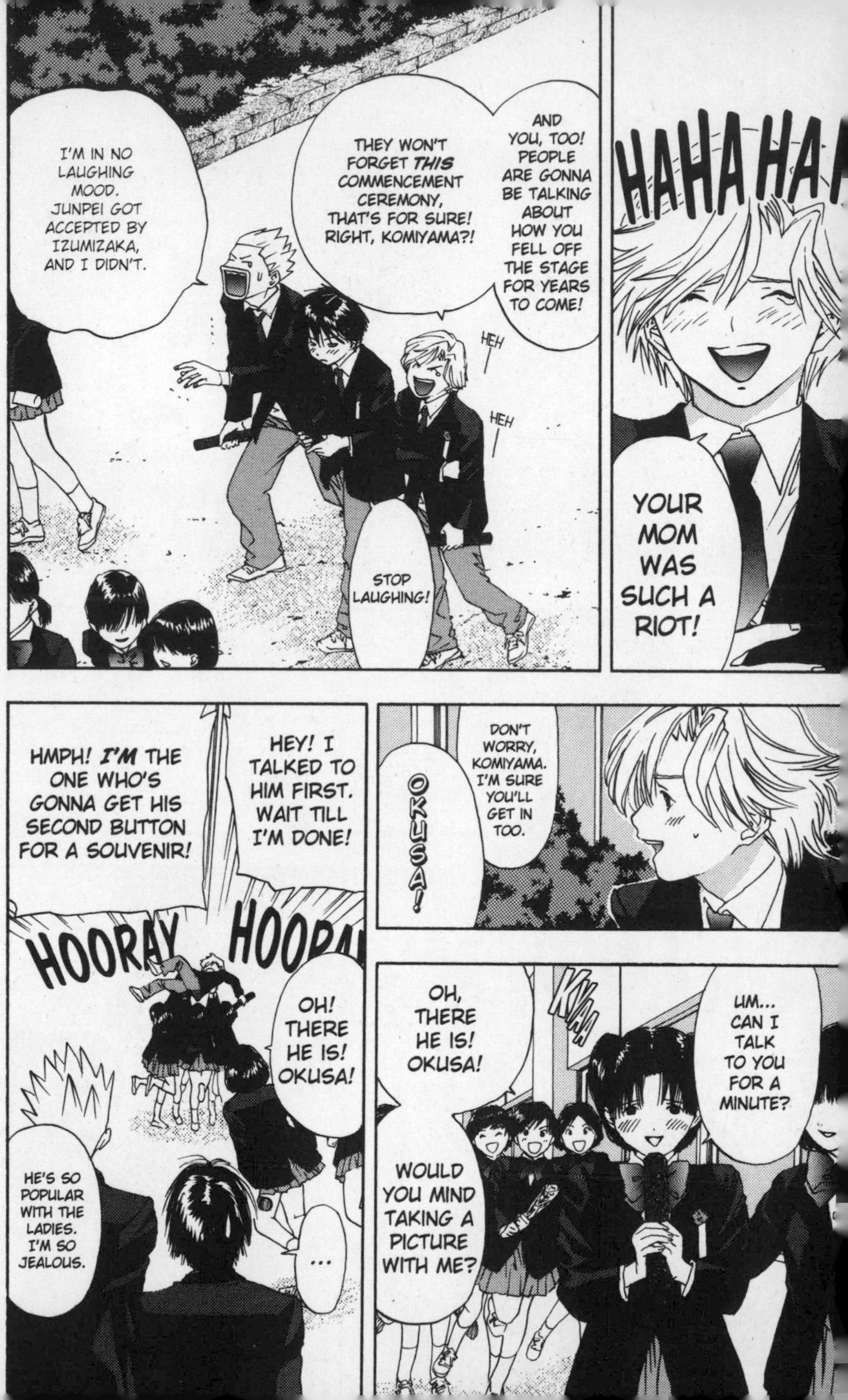
HAHA HA
YOUR MOM WAS SUCH A RIOT!
AND YOU, TOO! PEOPLE ARE GONNA BE TALKING ABOUT HOW YOU FELL OFF THE STAGE FOR YEARS TO COME!
THEY WON'T FORGET *THIS* COMMENCEMENT CEREMONY, THAT'S FOR SURE! RIGHT, KOMIYAMA?!
HEH
HEH
I'M IN NO LAUGHING MOOD. JUNPEI GOT ACCEPTED BY IZUMIZAKA, AND I DIDN'T.
STOP LAUGHING!
DON'T WORRY, KOMIYAMA. I'M SURE YOU'LL GET IN TOO.
OKUSA!
KYAA
UM... CAN I TALK TO YOU FOR A MINUTE?
OH, THERE HE IS! OKUSA!
WOULD YOU MIND TAKING A PICTURE WITH ME?
HEY! I TALKED TO HIM FIRST. WAIT TILL I'M DONE!
HMPH! *I'M* THE ONE WHO'S GONNA GET HIS SECOND BUTTON FOR A SOUVENIR!
HOORAY
HOORA
OH! THERE HE IS! OKUSA!
HE'S SO POPULAR WITH THE LADIES. I'M SO JEALOUS.
...

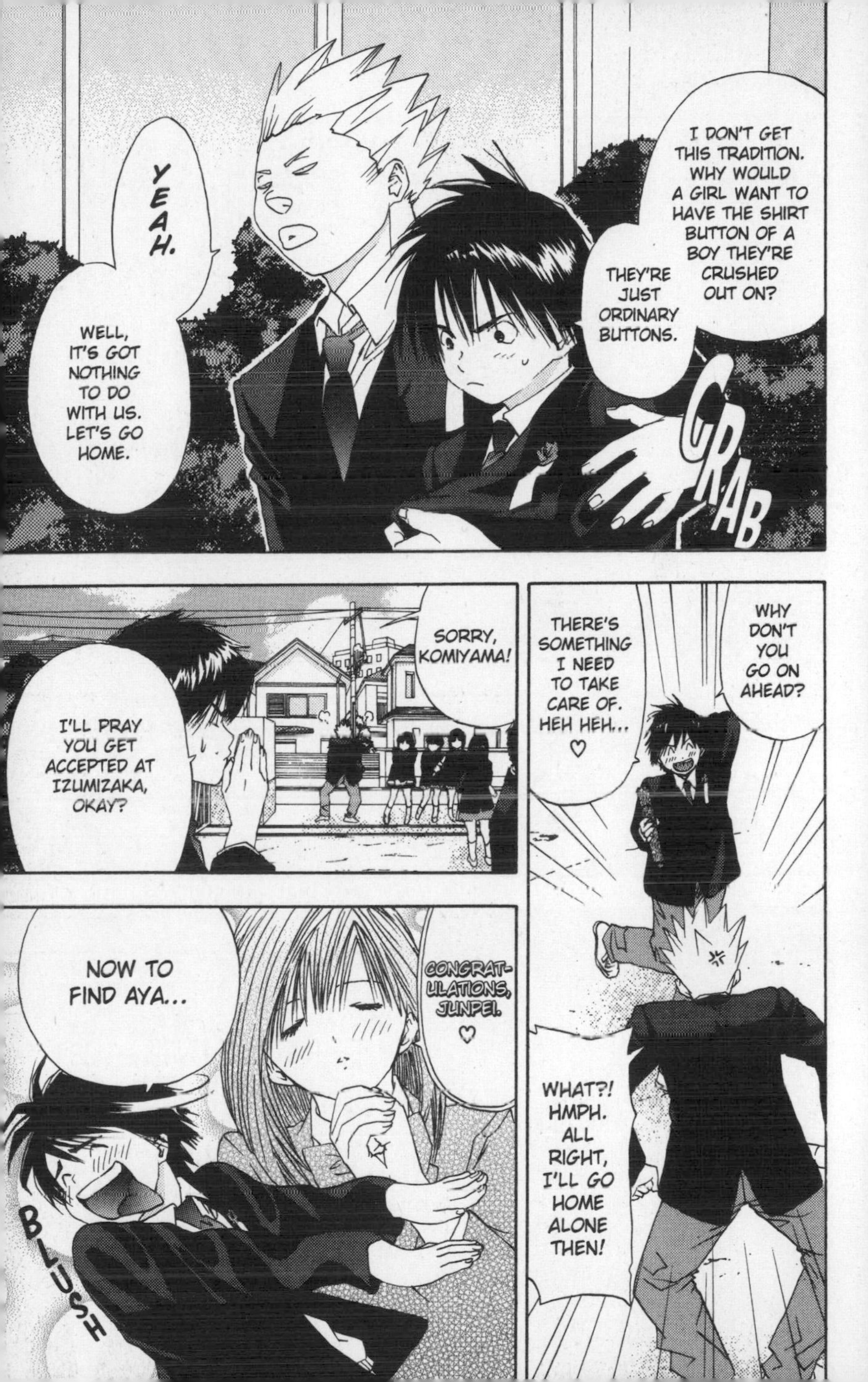
I DON'T GET THIS TRADITION. WHY WOULD A GIRL WANT TO HAVE THE SHIRT BUTTON OF A BOY THEY'RE CRUSHED OUT ON?
THEY'RE JUST ORDINARY BUTTONS.
YEAH.
WELL, IT'S GOT NOTHING TO DO WITH US. LET'S GO HOME.
GRAB
WHY DON'T YOU GO ON AHEAD?
THERE'S SOMETHING I NEED TO TAKE CARE OF. HEH HEH... ♡
WHAT?! HMPH. ALL RIGHT, I'LL GO HOME ALONE THEN!
SORRY, KOMIYAMA!
I'LL PRAY YOU GET ACCEPTED AT IZUMIZAKA, OKAY?
CONGRAT-ULATIONS, JUNPEI. ♡
NOW TO FIND AYA...
BLUSH

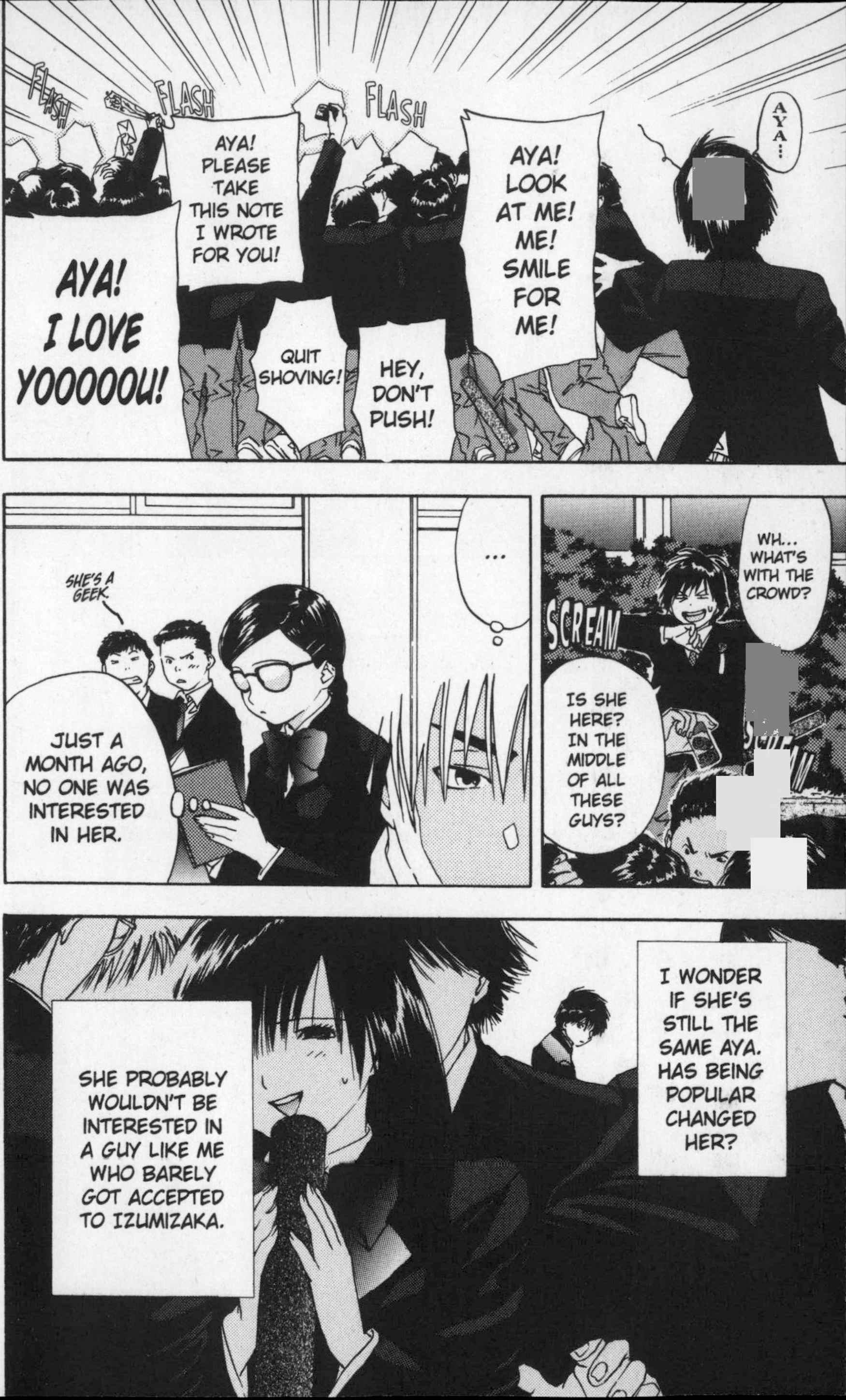
AYA...
AYA! LOOK AT ME! ME! SMILE FOR ME!
FLASH
AYA! PLEASE TAKE THIS NOTE I WROTE FOR YOU!
FLASH
FLASH
HEY, DON'T PUSH!
QUIT SHOVING!
AYA! I LOVE YOOOOOU!
WH... WHAT'S WITH THE CROWD?
SCREAM
IS SHE HERE? IN THE MIDDLE OF ALL THESE GUYS?
...
SHE'S A GEEK.
JUST A MONTH AGO, NO ONE WAS INTERESTED IN HER.
I WONDER IF SHE'S STILL THE SAME AYA. HAS BEING POPULAR CHANGED HER?
SHE PROBABLY WOULDN'T BE INTERESTED IN A GUY LIKE ME WHO BARELY GOT ACCEPTED TO IZUMIZAKA.

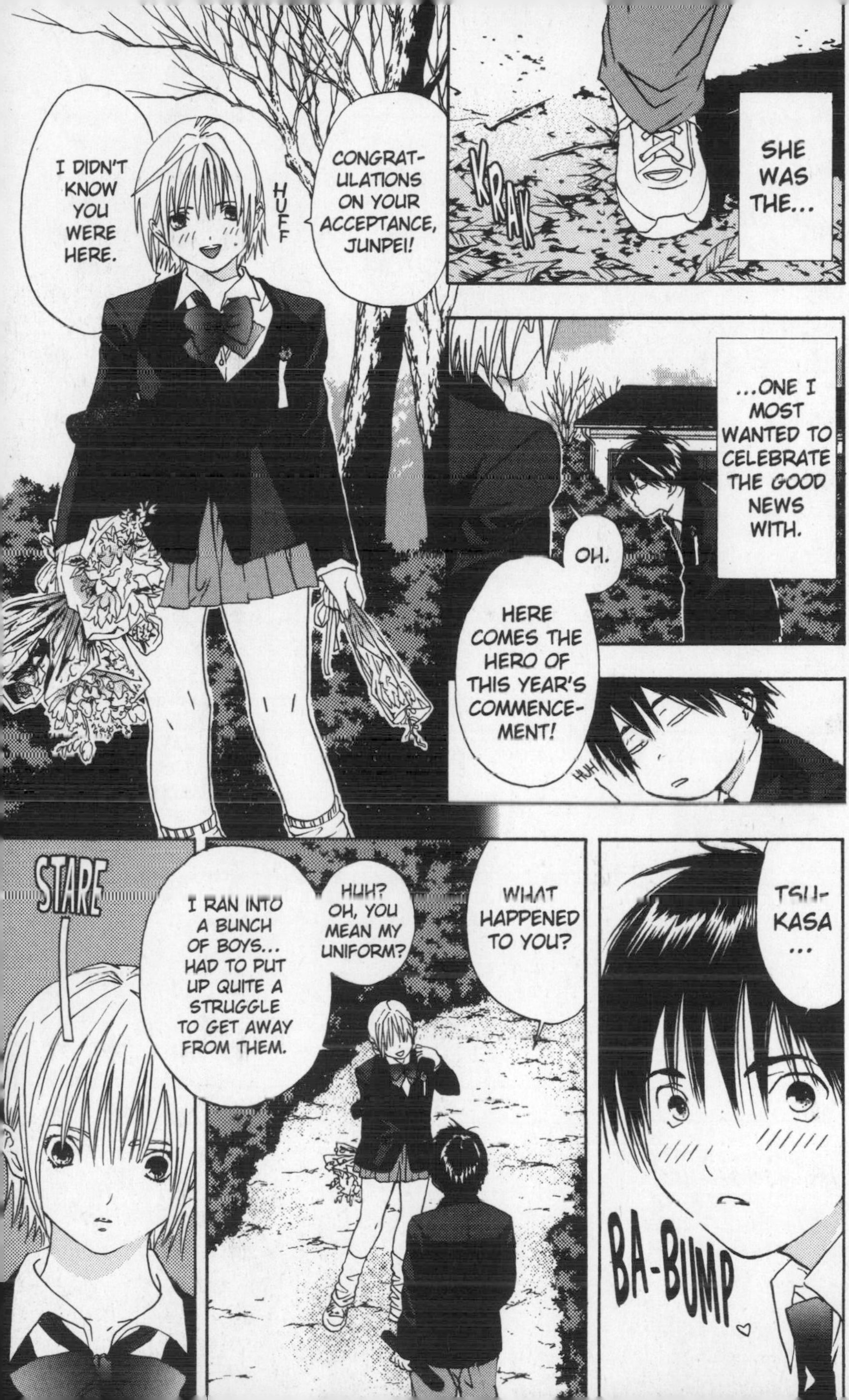
KRAK
SHE WAS THE...
...ONE I MOST WANTED TO CELEBRATE THE GOOD NEWS WITH.
OH.
HERE COMES THE HERO OF THIS YEAR'S COMMENCEMENT!
HUH
CONGRAT-ULATIONS ON YOUR ACCEPTANCE, JUNPEI!
HUFF
I DIDN'T KNOW YOU WERE HERE.
TSU-KASA...
BA-BUMP
WHAT HAPPENED TO YOU?
HUH? OH, YOU MEAN MY UNIFORM?
I RAN INTO A BUNCH OF BOYS... HAD TO PUT UP QUITE A STRUGGLE TO GET AWAY FROM THEM.
STARE

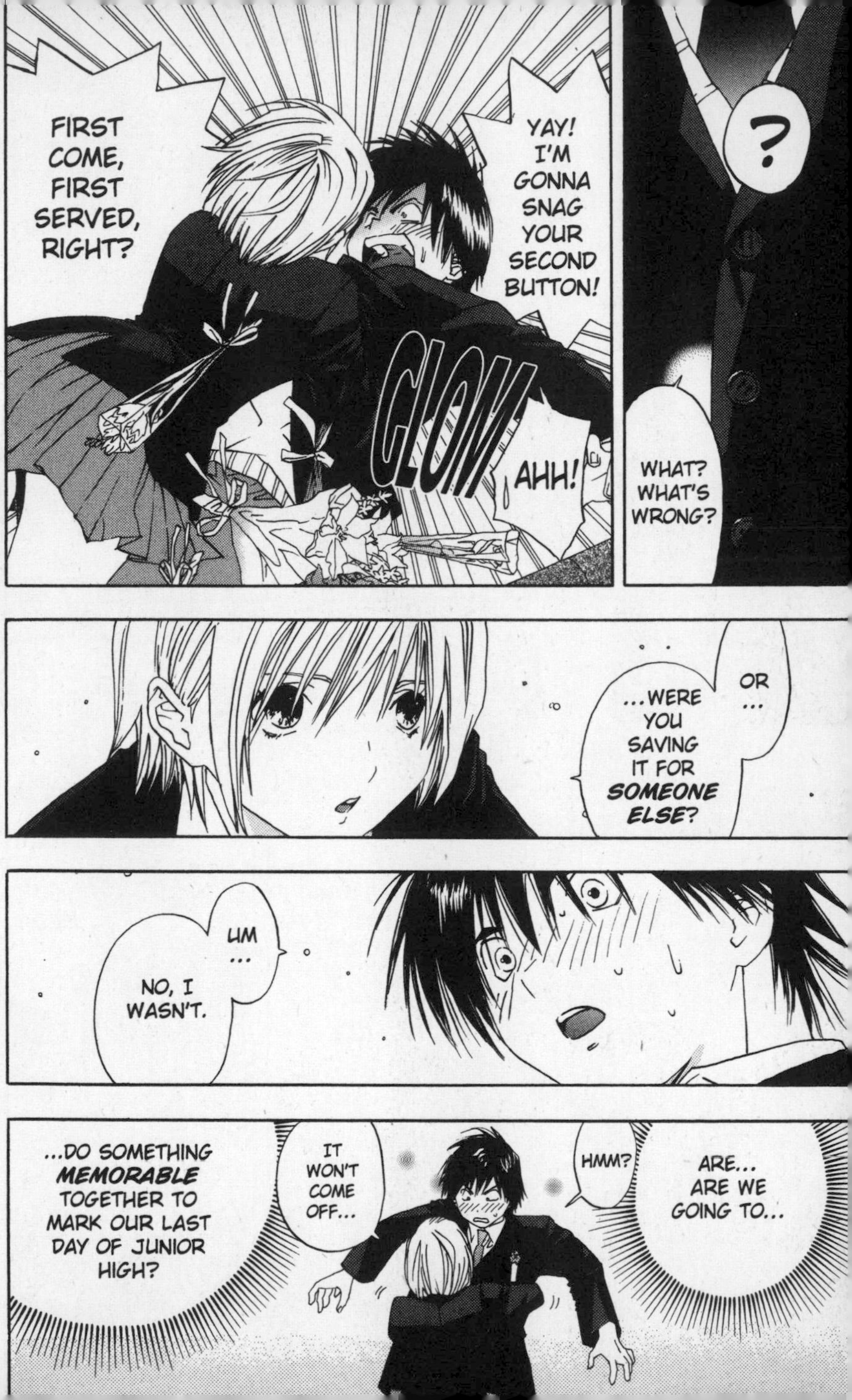
?
WHAT? WHAT'S WRONG?
YAY! I'M GONNA SNAG YOUR SECOND BUTTON!
FIRST COME, FIRST SERVED, RIGHT?
GLOM
AHH!
OR...
...WERE YOU SAVING IT FOR *SOMEONE ELSE*?
UM...
NO, I WASN'T.
ARE... ARE WE GOING TO...
HMM?
IT WON'T COME OFF...
...DO SOMETHING *MEMORABLE* TOGETHER TO MARK OUR LAST DAY OF JUNIOR HIGH?

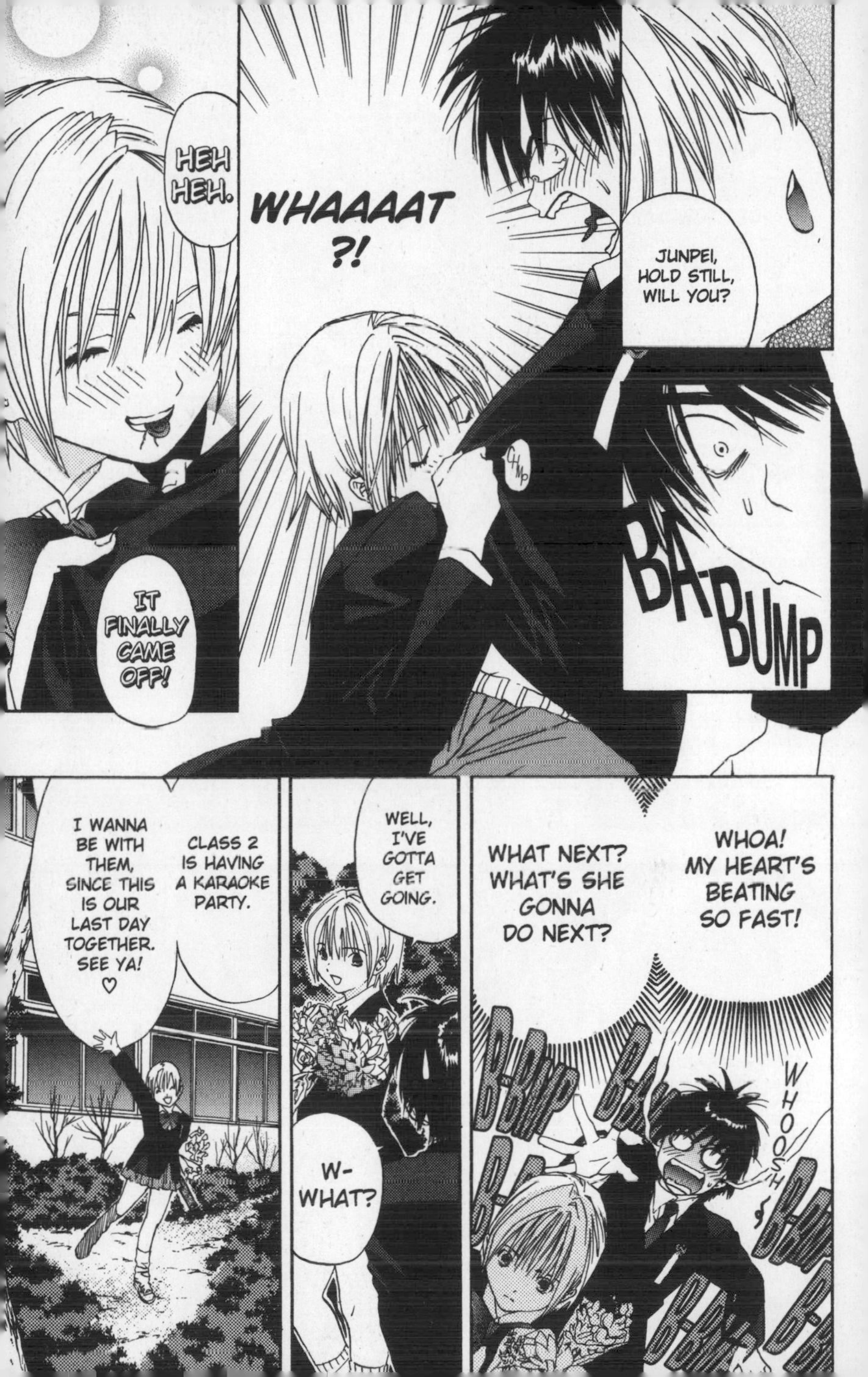
JUNPEI, HOLD STILL, WILL YOU?
BA-BUMP
WHAAAAT ?!
CHMP
HEH HEH.
IT FINALLY CAME OFF!
WHOA! MY HEART'S BEATING SO FAST!
WHAT NEXT? WHAT'S SHE GONNA DO NEXT?
WHOOSH
WELL, I'VE GOTTA GET GOING.
W- WHAT?
CLASS 2 IS HAVING A KARAOKE PARTY.
I WANNA BE WITH THEM, SINCE THIS IS OUR LAST DAY TOGETHER. SEE YA! ♡

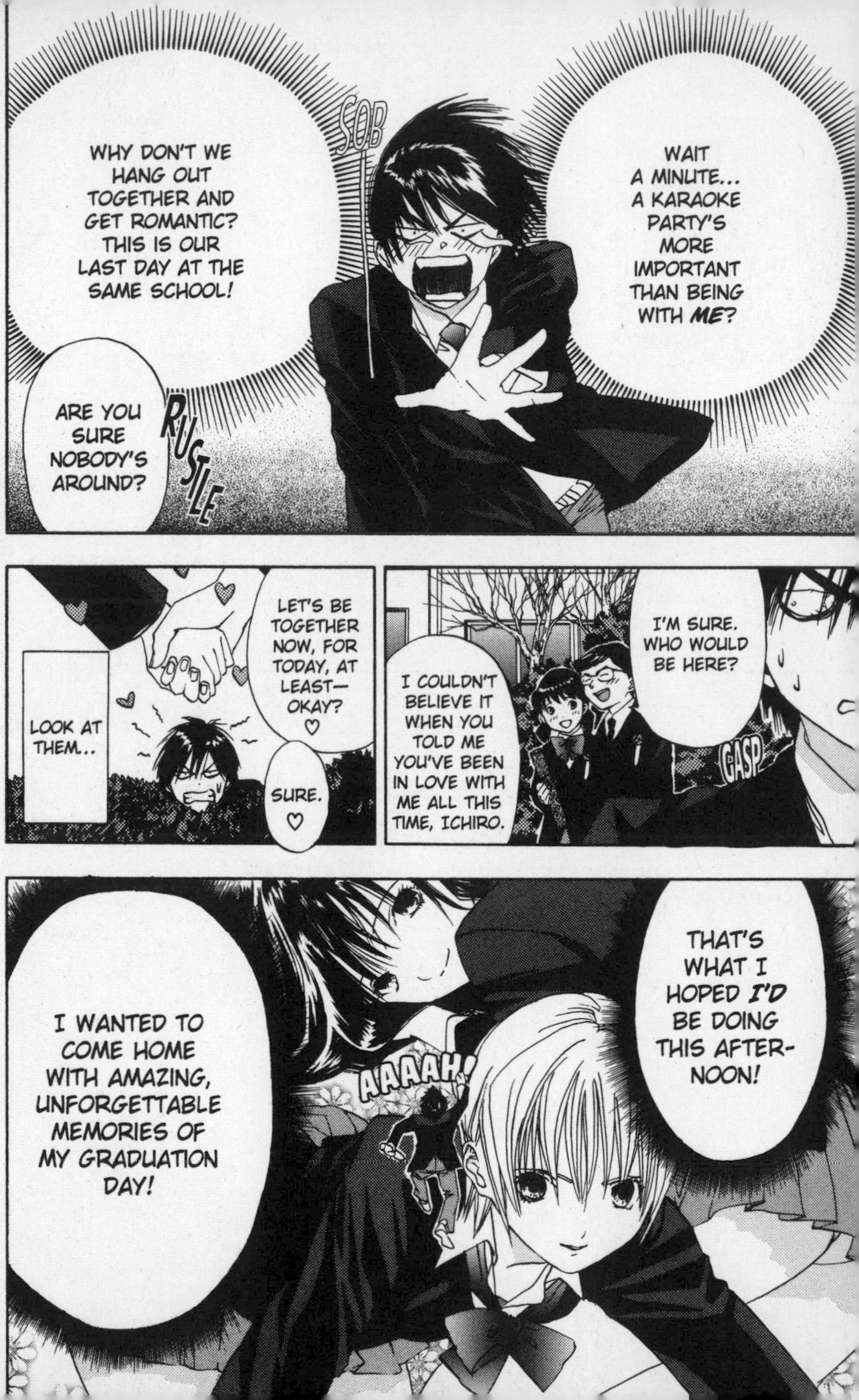
WAIT A MINUTE... A KARAOKE PARTY'S MORE IMPORTANT THAN BEING WITH *ME*?
SOB
WHY DON'T WE HANG OUT TOGETHER AND GET ROMANTIC? THIS IS OUR LAST DAY AT THE SAME SCHOOL!
RUSTLE
ARE YOU SURE NOBODY'S AROUND?
I'M SURE. WHO WOULD BE HERE?
GASP
I COULDN'T BELIEVE IT WHEN YOU TOLD ME YOU'VE BEEN IN LOVE WITH ME ALL THIS TIME, ICHIRO.
LET'S BE TOGETHER NOW, FOR TODAY, AT LEAST—OKAY? ♡
SURE. ♡
LOOK AT THEM...
THAT'S WHAT I HOPED *I'D* BE DOING THIS AFTERNOON!
AAAAH!
I WANTED TO COME HOME WITH AMAZING, UNFORGETTABLE MEMORIES OF MY GRADUATION DAY!

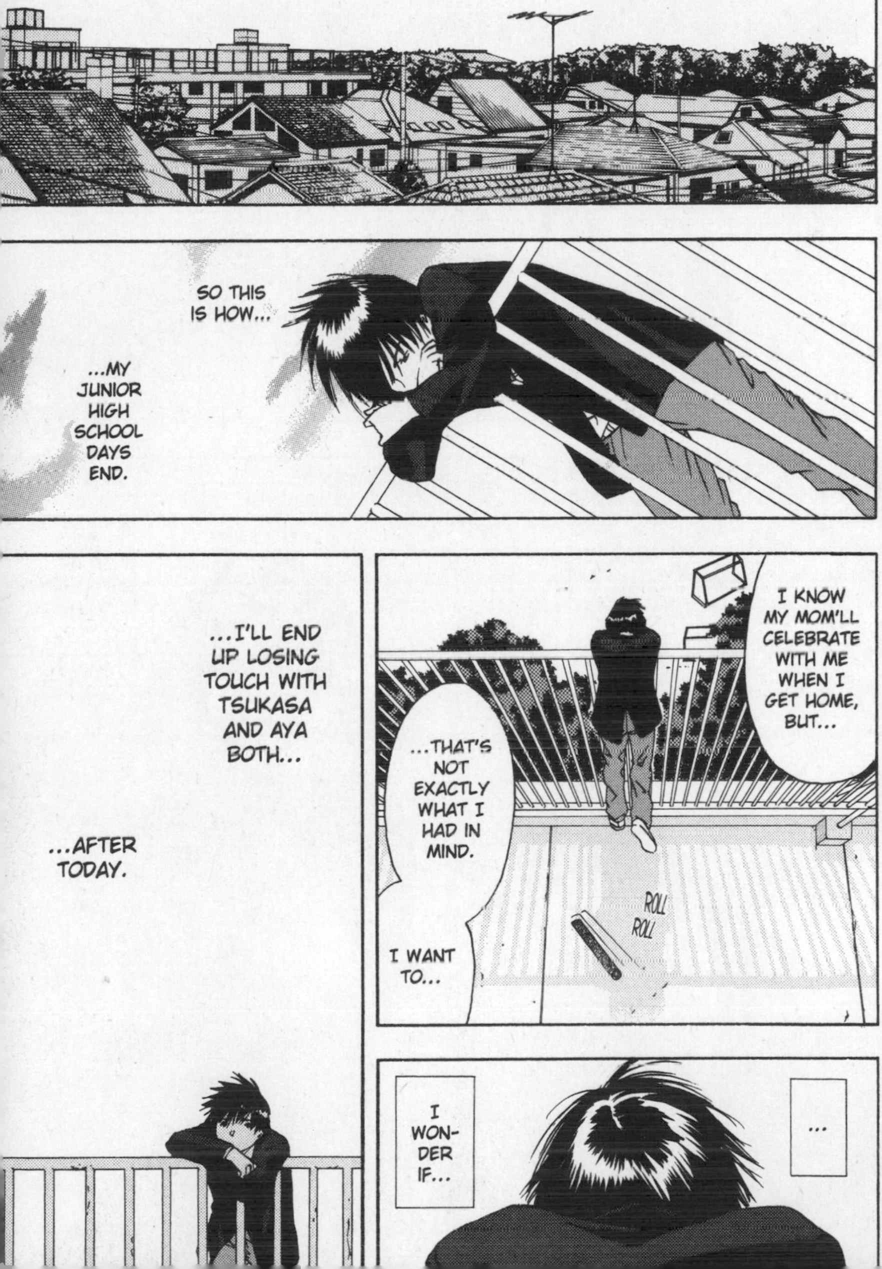

SO THIS IS HOW...
...MY JUNIOR HIGH SCHOOL DAYS END.
I KNOW MY MOM'LL CELEBRATE WITH ME WHEN I GET HOME, BUT...
...THAT'S NOT EXACTLY WHAT I HAD IN MIND.
ROLL ROLL
I WANT TO...
...
I WON-DER IF...
...I'LL END UP LOSING TOUCH WITH TSUKASA AND AYA BOTH...
...AFTER TODAY.

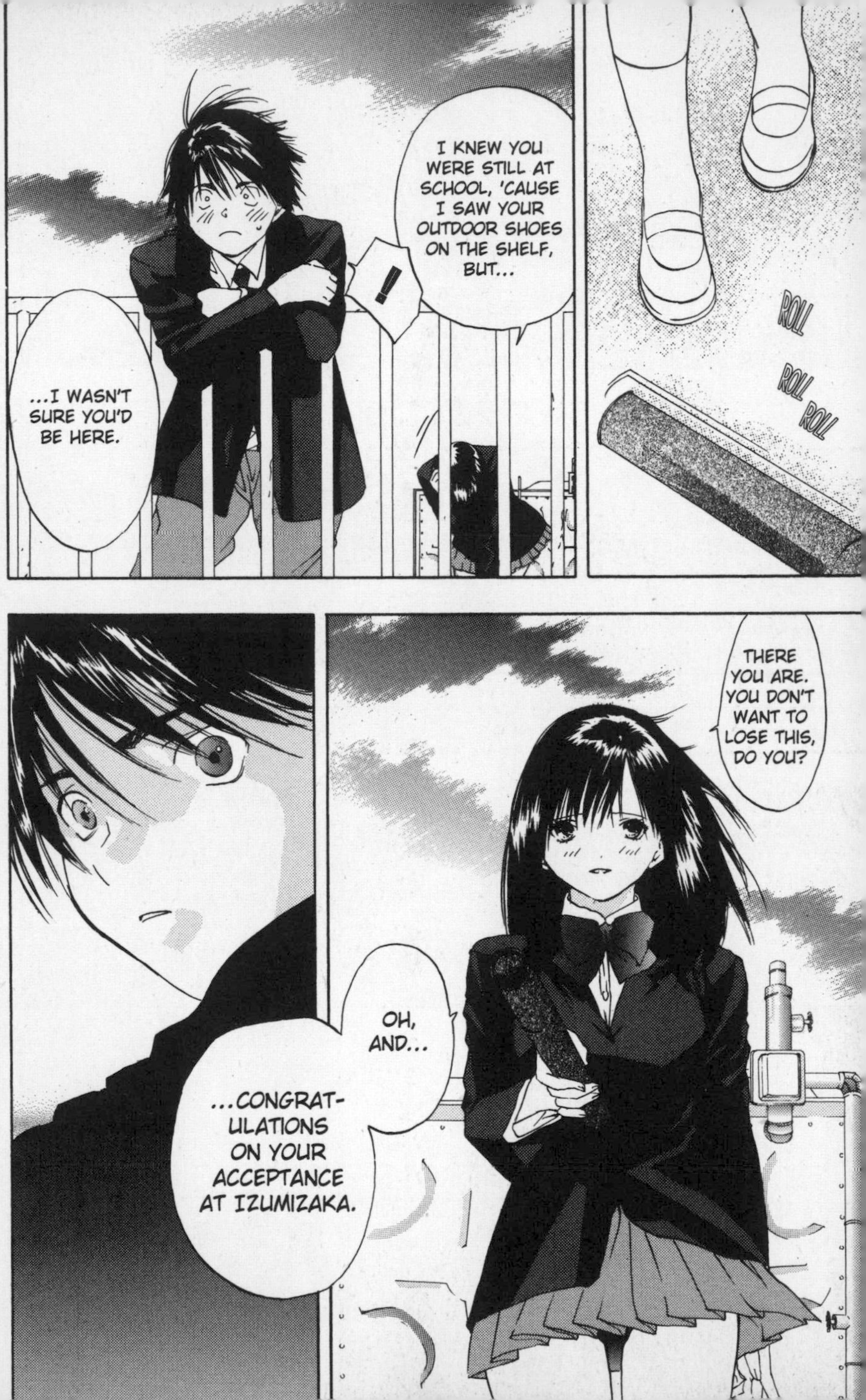
ROLL
ROLL
ROLL
I KNEW YOU WERE STILL AT SCHOOL, 'CAUSE I SAW YOUR OUTDOOR SHOES ON THE SHELF, BUT...
!
...I WASN'T SURE YOU'D BE HERE.
THERE YOU ARE. YOU DON'T WANT TO LOSE THIS, DO YOU?
OH, AND...
...CONGRAT-ULATIONS ON YOUR ACCEPTANCE AT IZUMIZAKA.

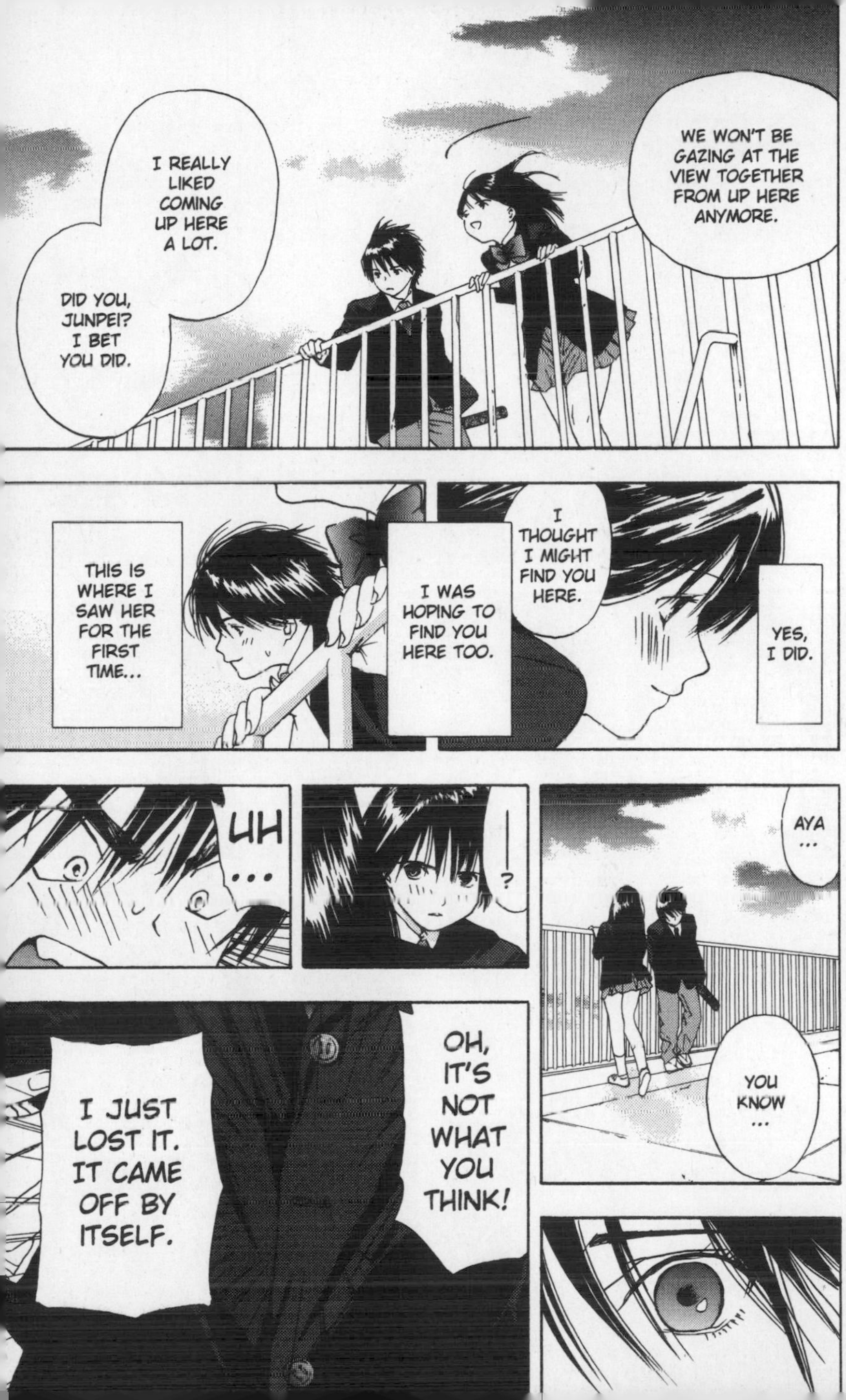
WE WON'T BE GAZING AT THE VIEW TOGETHER FROM UP HERE ANYMORE.
I REALLY LIKED COMING UP HERE A LOT.
DID YOU, JUNPEI? I BET YOU DID.
YES, I DID.
I THOUGHT I MIGHT FIND YOU HERE.
I WAS HOPING TO FIND YOU HERE TOO.
THIS IS WHERE I SAW HER FOR THE FIRST TIME...
AYA...
YOU KNOW...
!?
UH...
OH, IT'S NOT WHAT YOU THINK!
I JUST LOST IT. IT CAME OFF BY ITSELF.

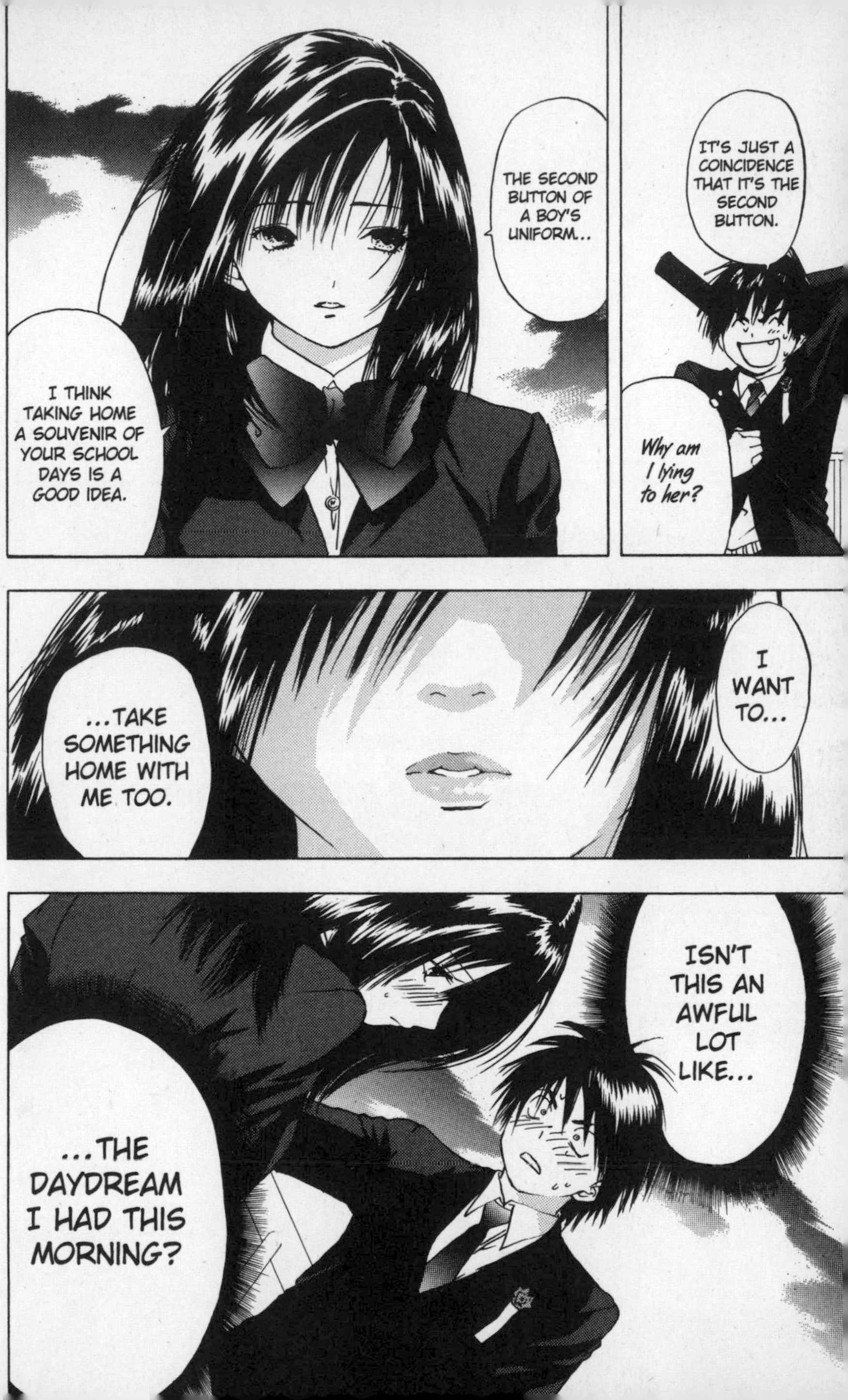
IT'S JUST A COINCIDENCE THAT IT'S THE SECOND BUTTON.
Why am I lying to her?
THE SECOND BUTTON OF A BOY'S UNIFORM...
I THINK TAKING HOME A SOUVENIR OF YOUR SCHOOL DAYS IS A GOOD IDEA.
I WANT TO...
...TAKE SOMETHING HOME WITH ME TOO.
ISN'T THIS AN AWFUL LOT LIKE...
...THE DAYDREAM I HAD THIS MORNING?

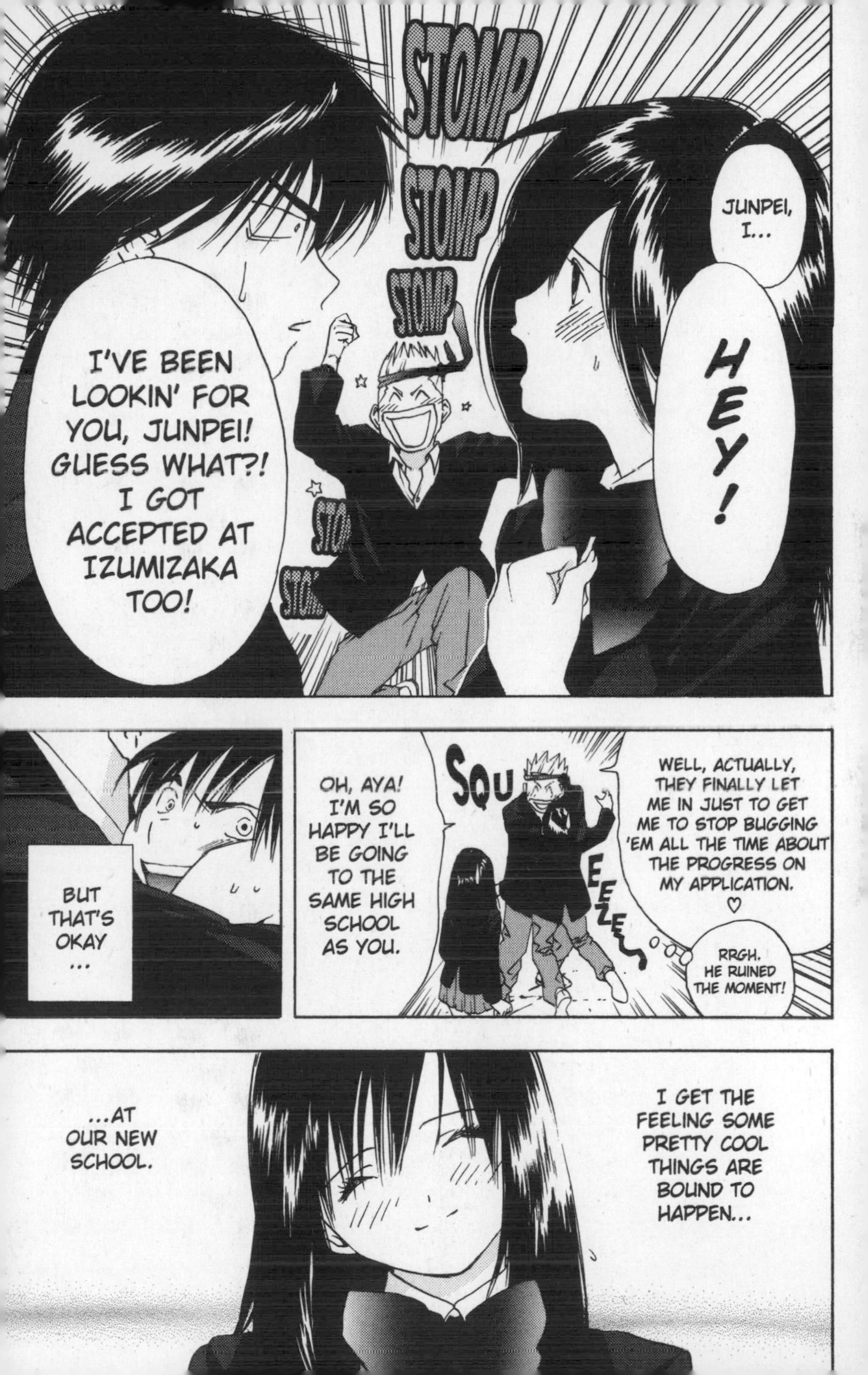
JUNPEI, I...
STOMP
STOMP
STOMP
HEY!
I'VE BEEN LOOKIN' FOR YOU, JUNPEI! GUESS WHAT?! I GOT ACCEPTED AT IZUMIZAKA TOO!
WELL, ACTUALLY, THEY FINALLY LET ME IN JUST TO GET ME TO STOP BUGGING 'EM ALL THE TIME ABOUT THE PROGRESS ON MY APPLICATION. ♡
SQUEEZE
OH, AYA! I'M SO HAPPY I'LL BE GOING TO THE SAME HIGH SCHOOL AS YOU.
RRGH. HE RUINED THE MOMENT!
BUT THAT'S OKAY ...
I GET THE FEELING SOME PRETTY COOL THINGS ARE BOUND TO HAPPEN...
...AT OUR NEW SCHOOL.

Long time no see.
Here's the third volume of
Strawberry 100%.

HI, EVERYONE!
I'M SOTOMURA,
A NEW CHARACTER
IN THE STORY.
IT'S MY PLEASURE TO
SHOW PORTIONS OF MY
HOMEPAGE *EXCLUSIVELY*
TO YOU, JUST BECAUSE
YOU'RE READING
THIS MANGA!

JUMP!

CRUSH 19:

A FATEFUL FILM TRIP

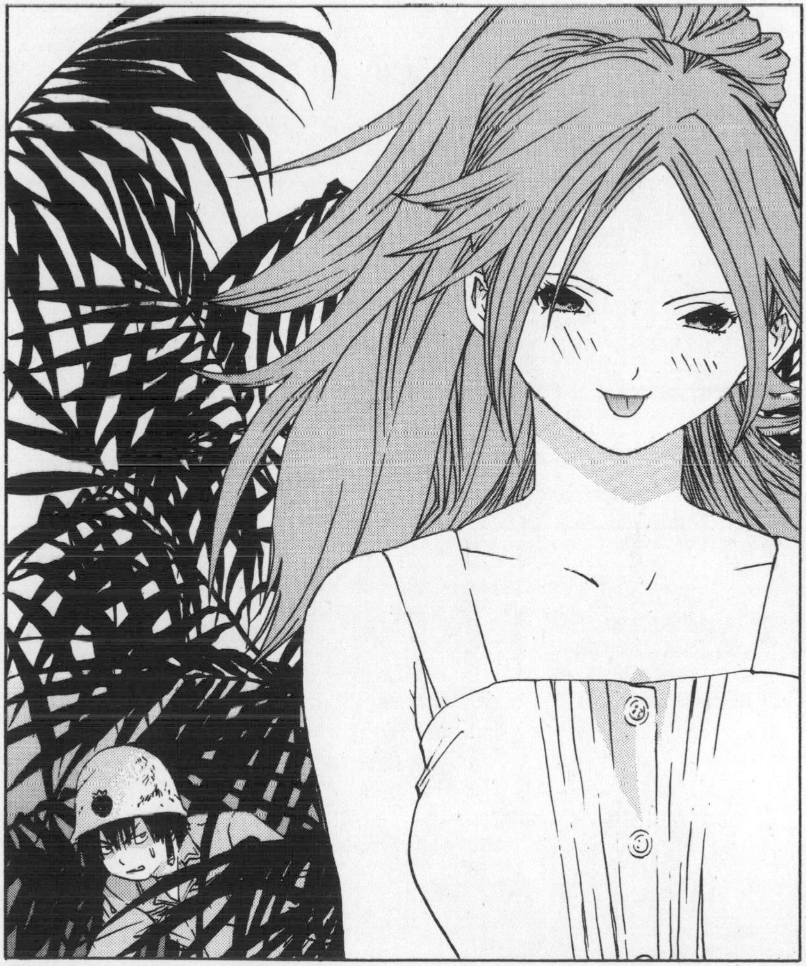

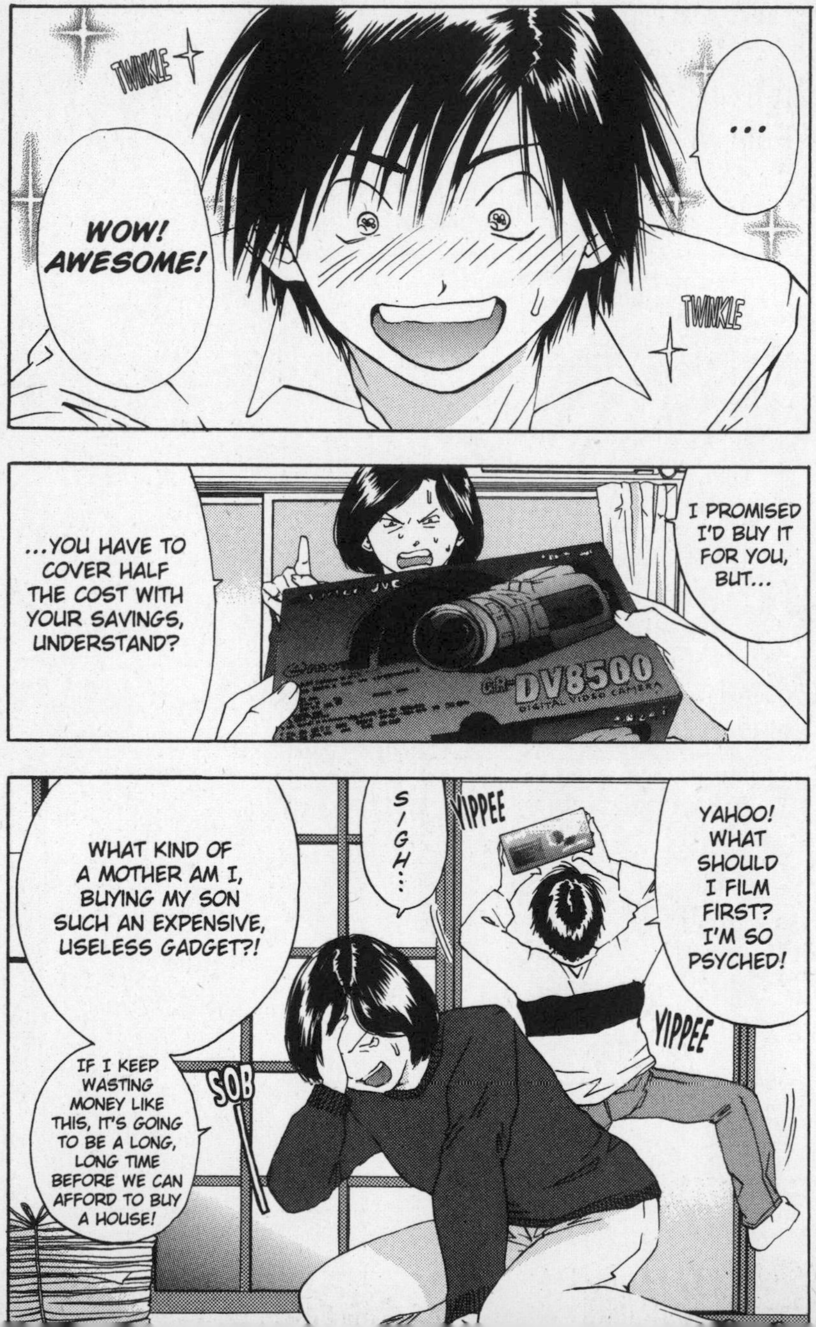
...
TWINKLE
TWINKLE
WOW! AWESOME!
I PROMISED I'D BUY IT FOR YOU, BUT...
DV8500
DIGITAL VIDEO CAMERA
...YOU HAVE TO COVER HALF THE COST WITH YOUR SAVINGS, UNDERSTAND?
YAHOO! WHAT SHOULD I FILM FIRST? I'M SO PSYCHED!
YIPPEE
YIPPEE
SIGH...
WHAT KIND OF A MOTHER AM I, BUYING MY SON SUCH AN EXPENSIVE, USELESS GADGET?!
SOB
IF I KEEP WASTING MONEY LIKE THIS, IT'S GOING TO BE A LONG, LONG TIME BEFORE WE CAN AFFORD TO BUY A HOUSE!

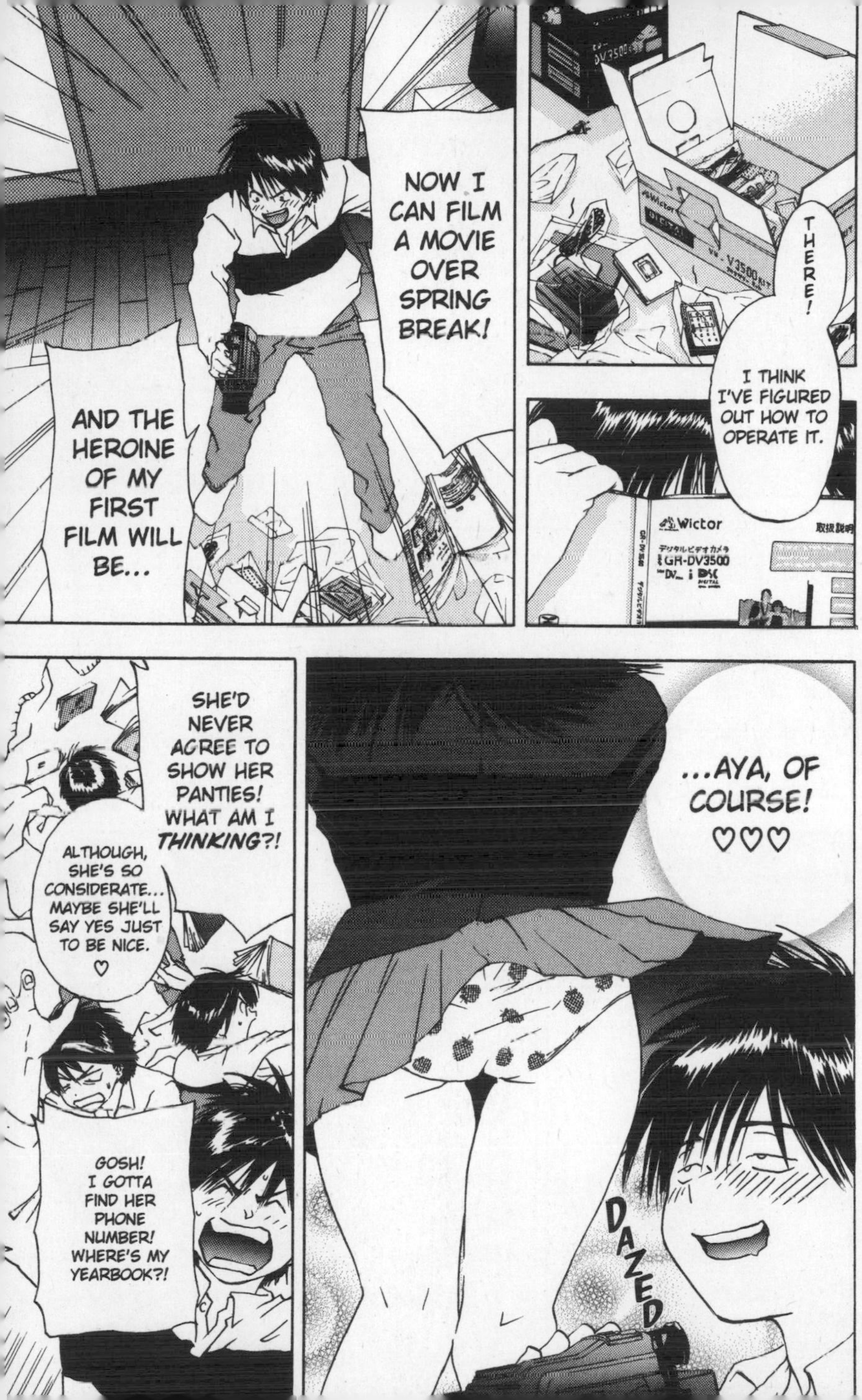
THERE!
I THINK I'VE FIGURED OUT HOW TO OPERATE IT.
NOW I CAN FILM A MOVIE OVER SPRING BREAK!
AND THE HEROINE OF MY FIRST FILM WILL BE...
...AYA, OF COURSE! ♡♡♡
DAZED
SHE'D NEVER AGREE TO SHOW HER PANTIES! WHAT AM I *THINKING*?!
ALTHOUGH, SHE'S SO CONSIDERATE... MAYBE SHE'LL SAY YES JUST TO BE NICE. ♡
GOSH! I GOTTA FIND HER PHONE NUMBER! WHERE'S MY YEARBOOK?!

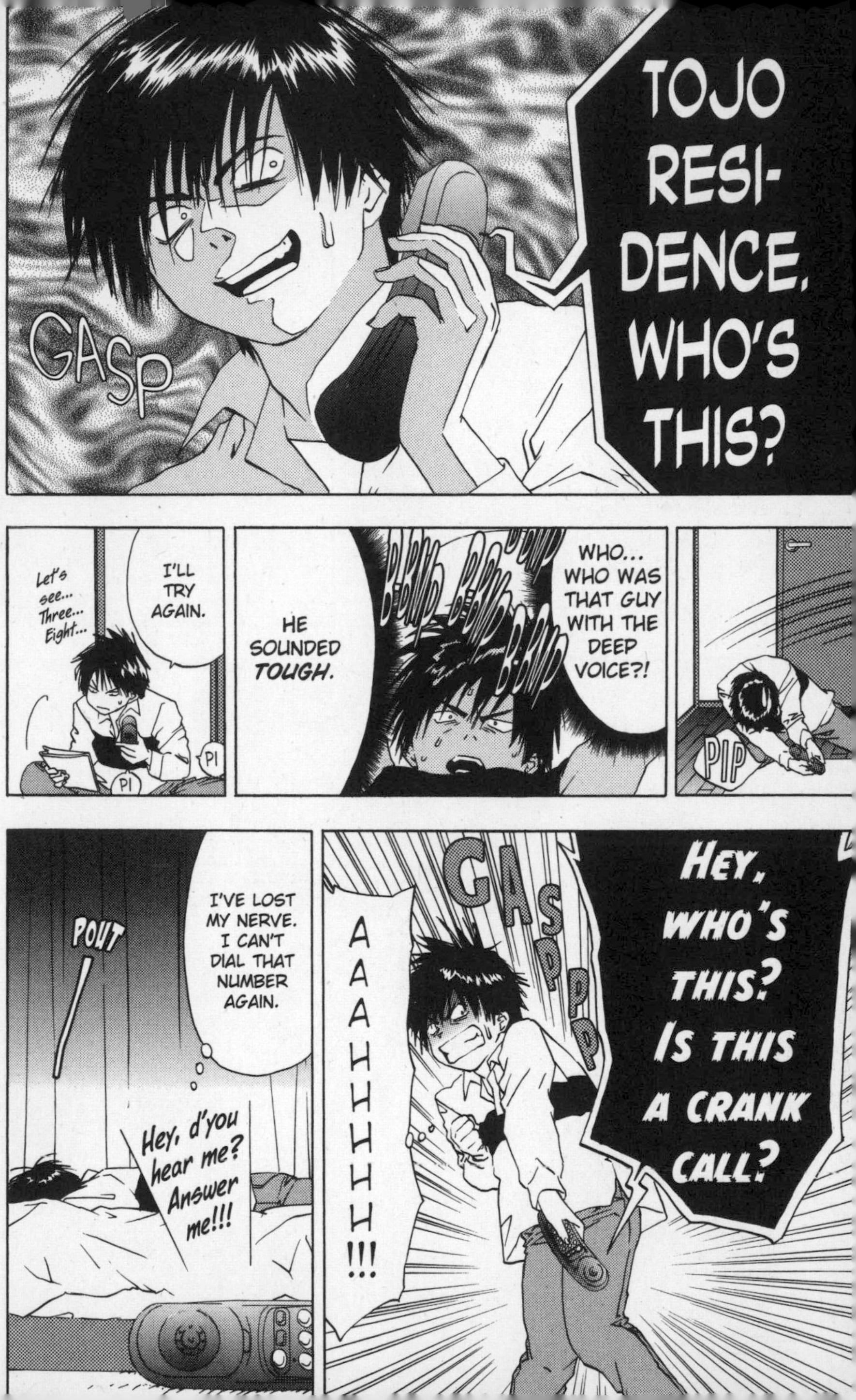
TOJO RESI-DENCE. WHO'S THIS?
GASP
PIP
WHO... WHO WAS THAT GUY WITH THE DEEP VOICE?!
HE SOUNDED TOUGH.
I'LL TRY AGAIN.
Let's see... Three... Eight...
PI
PI
Hey, who's this? Is this a crank call?
GASPPP
AAAHHHHH!!!
I'VE LOST MY NERVE. I CAN'T DIAL THAT NUMBER AGAIN.
POUT
Hey, d'you hear me? Answer me!!!

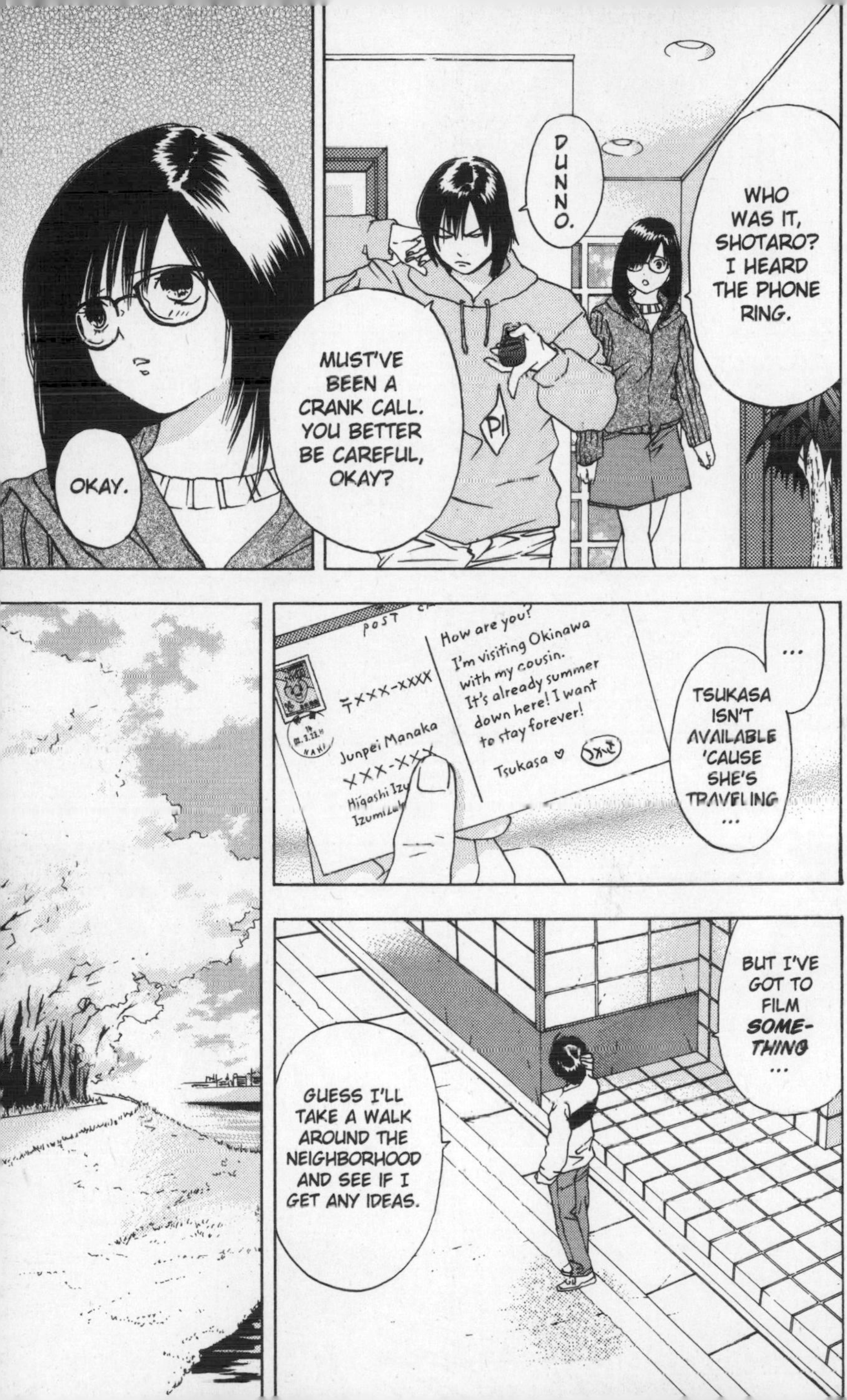
WHO WAS IT, SHOTARO? I HEARD THE PHONE RING.
DUNNO.
MUST'VE BEEN A CRANK CALL. YOU BETTER BE CAREFUL, OKAY?
OKAY.
...
TSUKASA ISN'T AVAILABLE 'CAUSE SHE'S TRAVELING ...
POST
〒XXX-XXXX
Junpei Manaka
How are you? I'm visiting Okinawa with my cousin. It's already summer down here! I want to stay forever!
Tsukasa ♡
BUT I'VE GOT TO FILM SOMETHING ...
GUESS I'LL TAKE A WALK AROUND THE NEIGHBORHOOD AND SEE IF I GET ANY IDEAS.

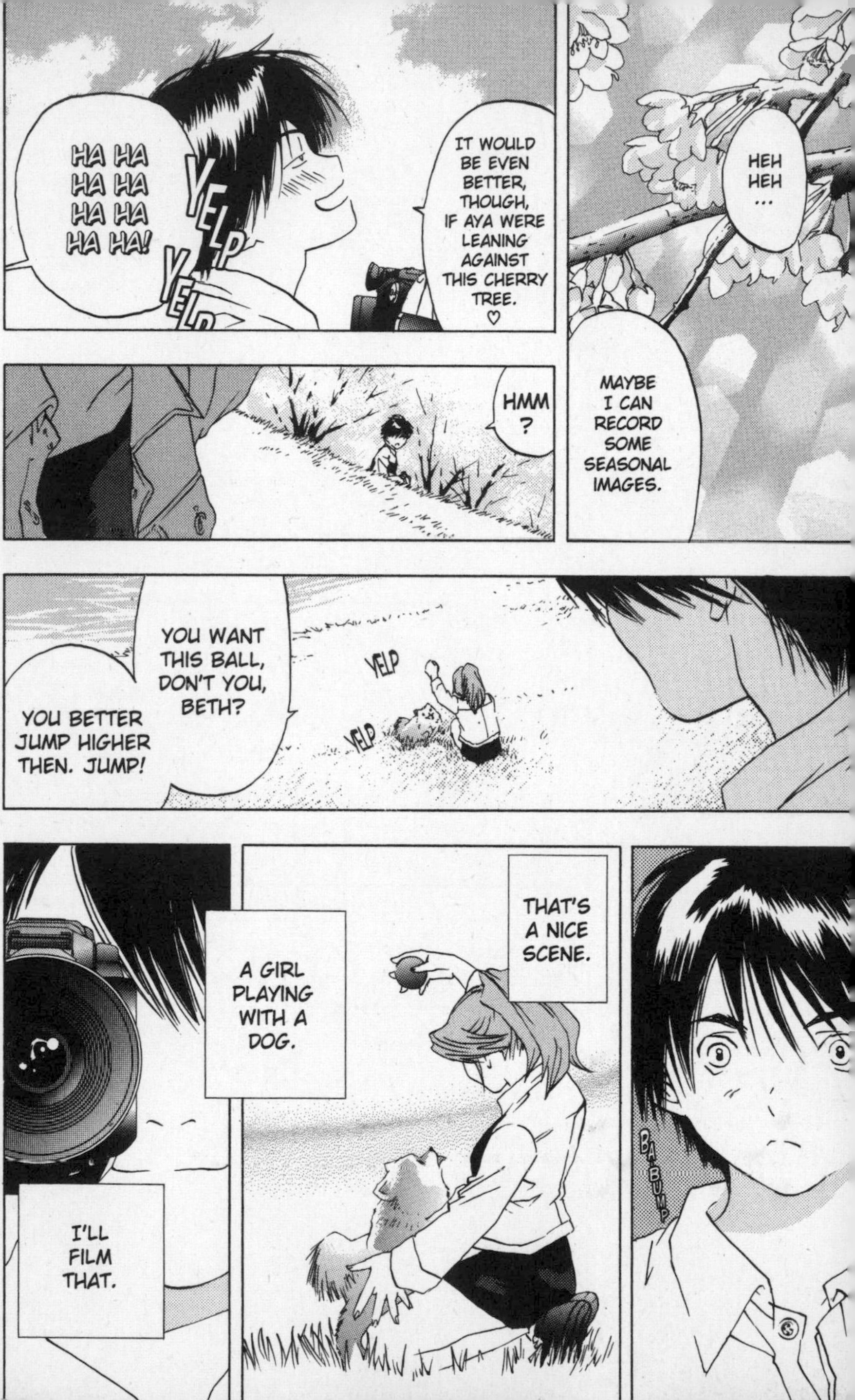
HEH HEH ...
MAYBE I CAN RECORD SOME SEASONAL IMAGES.
IT WOULD BE EVEN BETTER, THOUGH, IF AYA WERE LEANING AGAINST THIS CHERRY TREE. ♡
HA HA HA HA HA HA HA HA!
YELP
YELP
HMM?
YOU WANT THIS BALL, DON'T YOU, BETH?
YOU BETTER JUMP HIGHER THEN. JUMP!
YELP
YELP
BA-BUMP
THAT'S A NICE SCENE.
A GIRL PLAYING WITH A DOG.
I'LL FILM THAT.

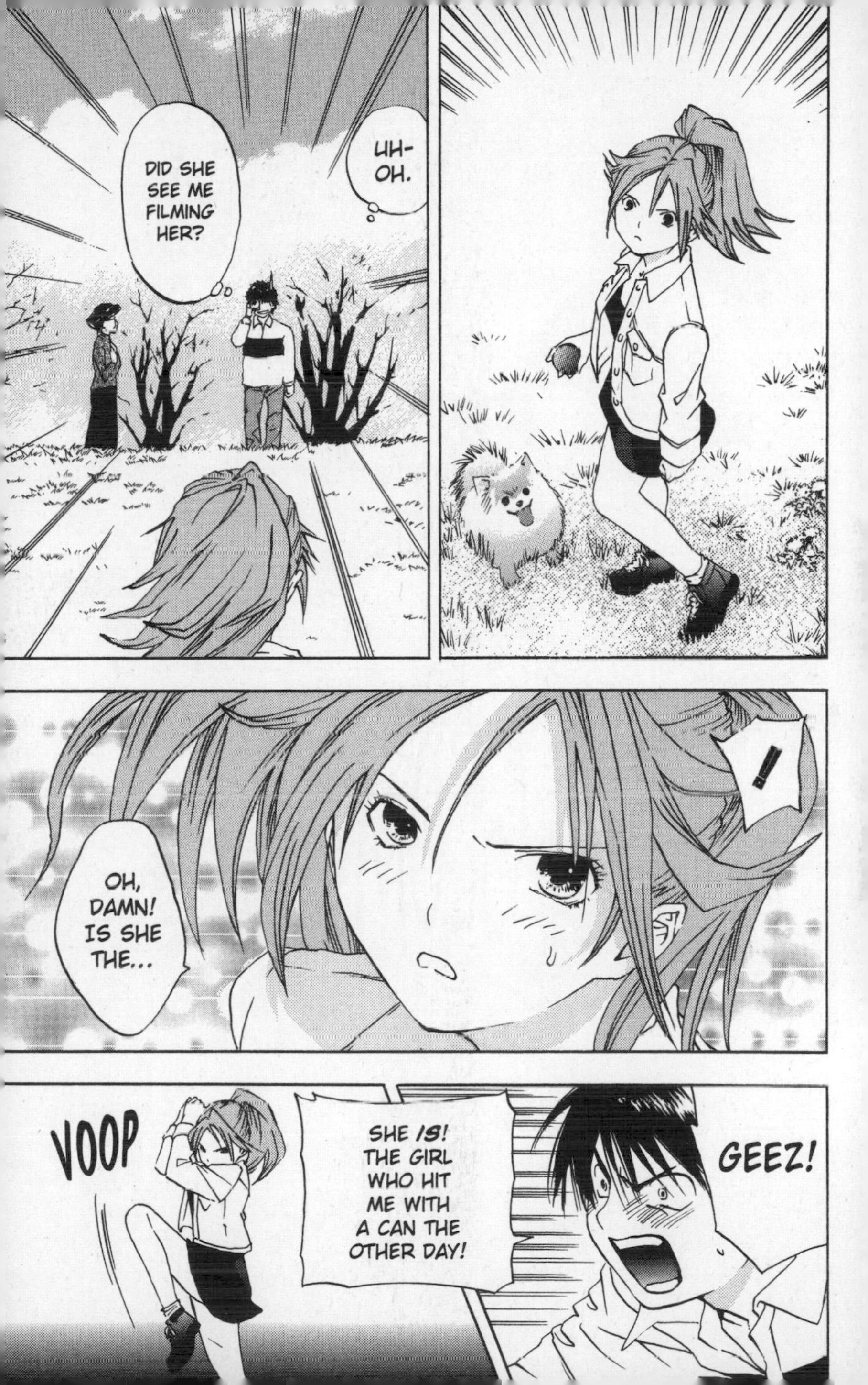
UH-OH.
DID SHE SEE ME FILMING HER?
!
OH, DAMN! IS SHE THE...
GEEZ!
SHE *IS*! THE GIRL WHO HIT ME WITH A CAN THE OTHER DAY!
VOOP

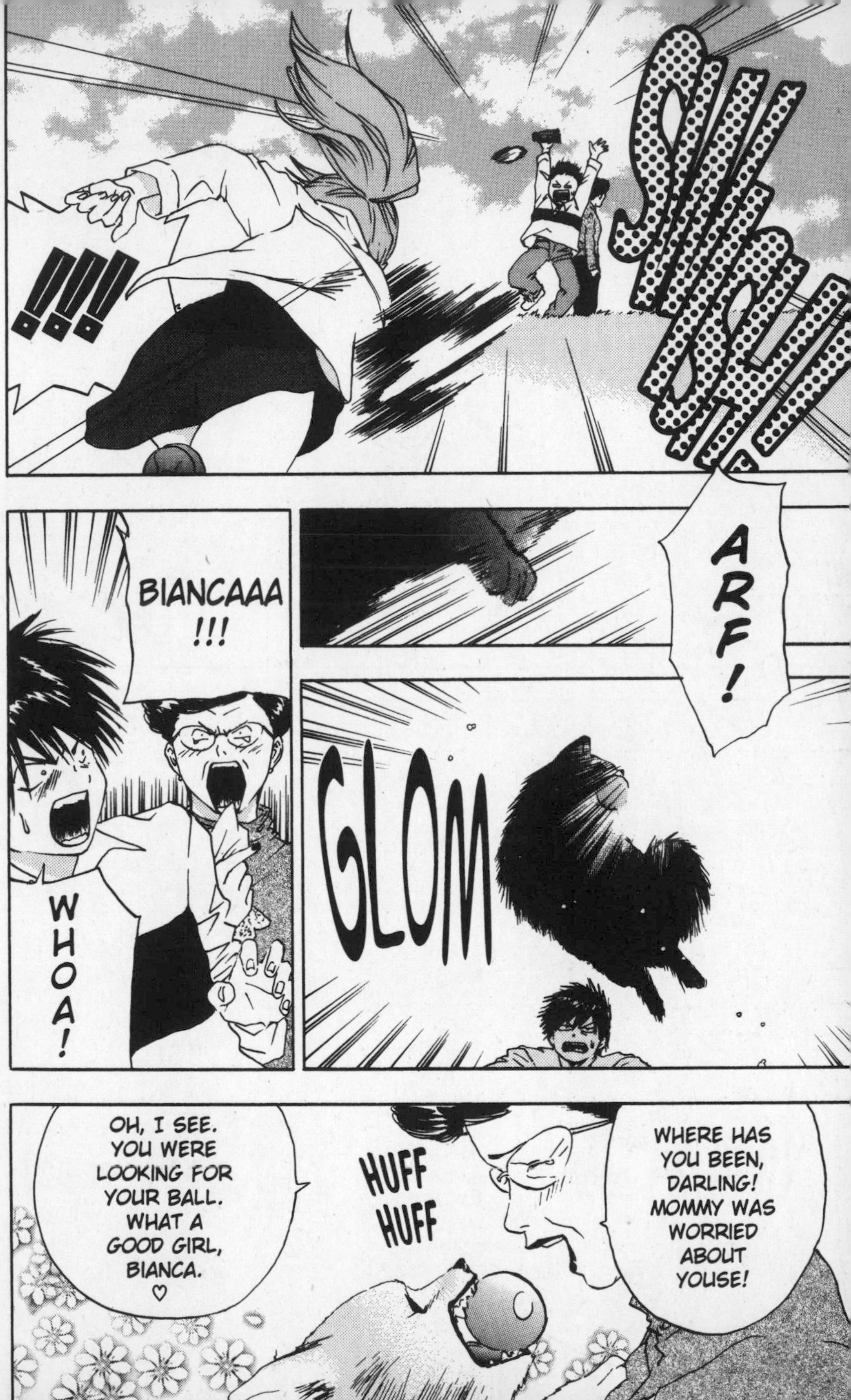
!!!
ARF!
GLOM
BIANCAAA !!!
WHOA!
WHERE HAS YOU BEEN, DARLING! MOMMY WAS WORRIED ABOUT YOUSE!
HUFF HUFF
OH, I SEE. YOU WERE LOOKING FOR YOUR BALL. WHAT A GOOD GIRL, BIANCA. ♡

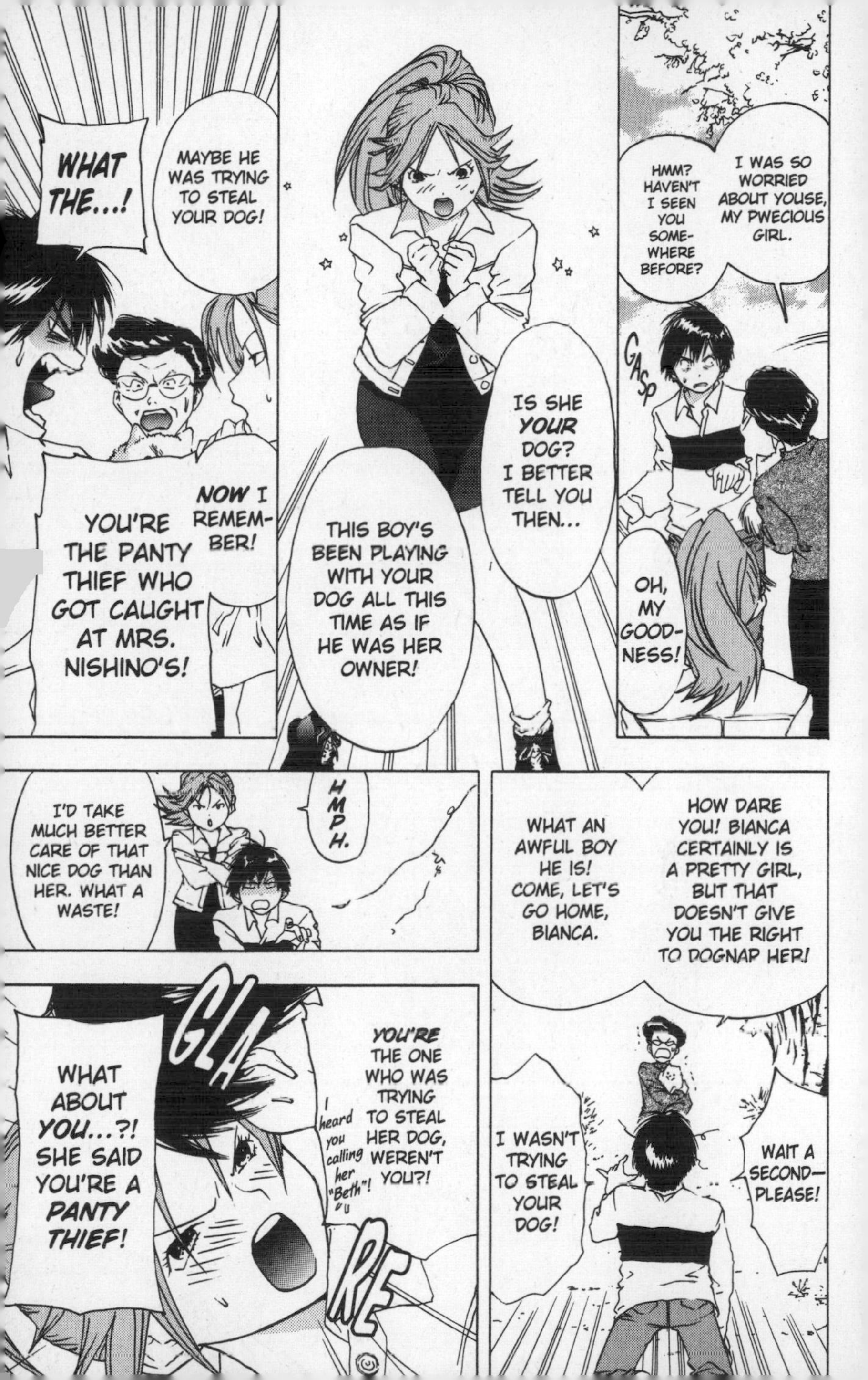
I WAS SO WORRIED ABOUT YOUSE, MY PWECIOUS GIRL.
HMM? HAVEN'T I SEEN YOU SOME-WHERE BEFORE?
GASP
OH, MY GOODNESS!
IS SHE YOUR DOG? I BETTER TELL YOU THEN...
THIS BOY'S BEEN PLAYING WITH YOUR DOG ALL THIS TIME AS IF HE WAS HER OWNER!
MAYBE HE WAS TRYING TO STEAL YOUR DOG!
WHAT THE...!
NOW I REMEMBER!
YOU'RE THE PANTY THIEF WHO GOT CAUGHT AT MRS. NISHINO'S!
HOW DARE YOU! BIANCA CERTAINLY IS A PRETTY GIRL, BUT THAT DOESN'T GIVE YOU THE RIGHT TO DOGNAP HER!
WHAT AN AWFUL BOY HE IS! COME, LET'S GO HOME, BIANCA.
WAIT A SECOND—PLEASE!
I WASN'T TRYING TO STEAL YOUR DOG!
HMPH.
I'D TAKE MUCH BETTER CARE OF THAT NICE DOG THAN HER. WHAT A WASTE!
YOU'RE THE ONE WHO WAS TRYING TO STEAL HER DOG, WEREN'T YOU?!
I heard you calling her "Beth"!
GLARE
WHAT ABOUT YOU...?! SHE SAID YOU'RE A PANTY THIEF!

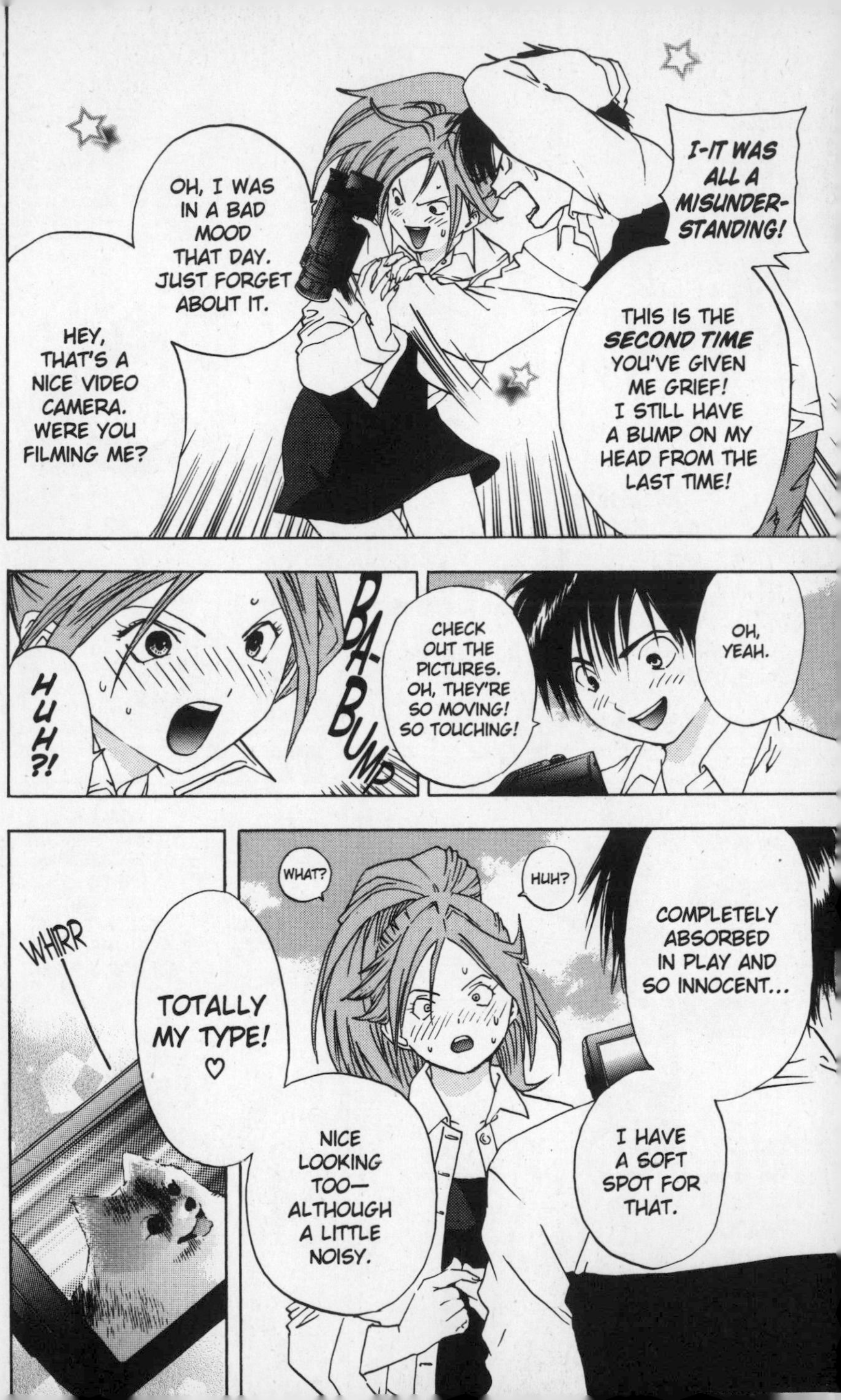
I-IT WAS ALL A MISUNDERSTANDING!
THIS IS THE ***SECOND TIME*** YOU'VE GIVEN ME GRIEF! I STILL HAVE A BUMP ON MY HEAD FROM THE LAST TIME!
OH, I WAS IN A BAD MOOD THAT DAY. JUST FORGET ABOUT IT.
HEY, THAT'S A NICE VIDEO CAMERA. WERE YOU FILMING ME?
OH, YEAH.
CHECK OUT THE PICTURES. OH, THEY'RE SO MOVING! SO TOUCHING!
BA-BUMP
HUH?!
COMPLETELY ABSORBED IN PLAY AND SO INNOCENT...
HUH?
WHAT?
I HAVE A SOFT SPOT FOR THAT.
TOTALLY MY TYPE! ♡
NICE LOOKING TOO—ALTHOUGH A LITTLE NOISY.
WHIRR

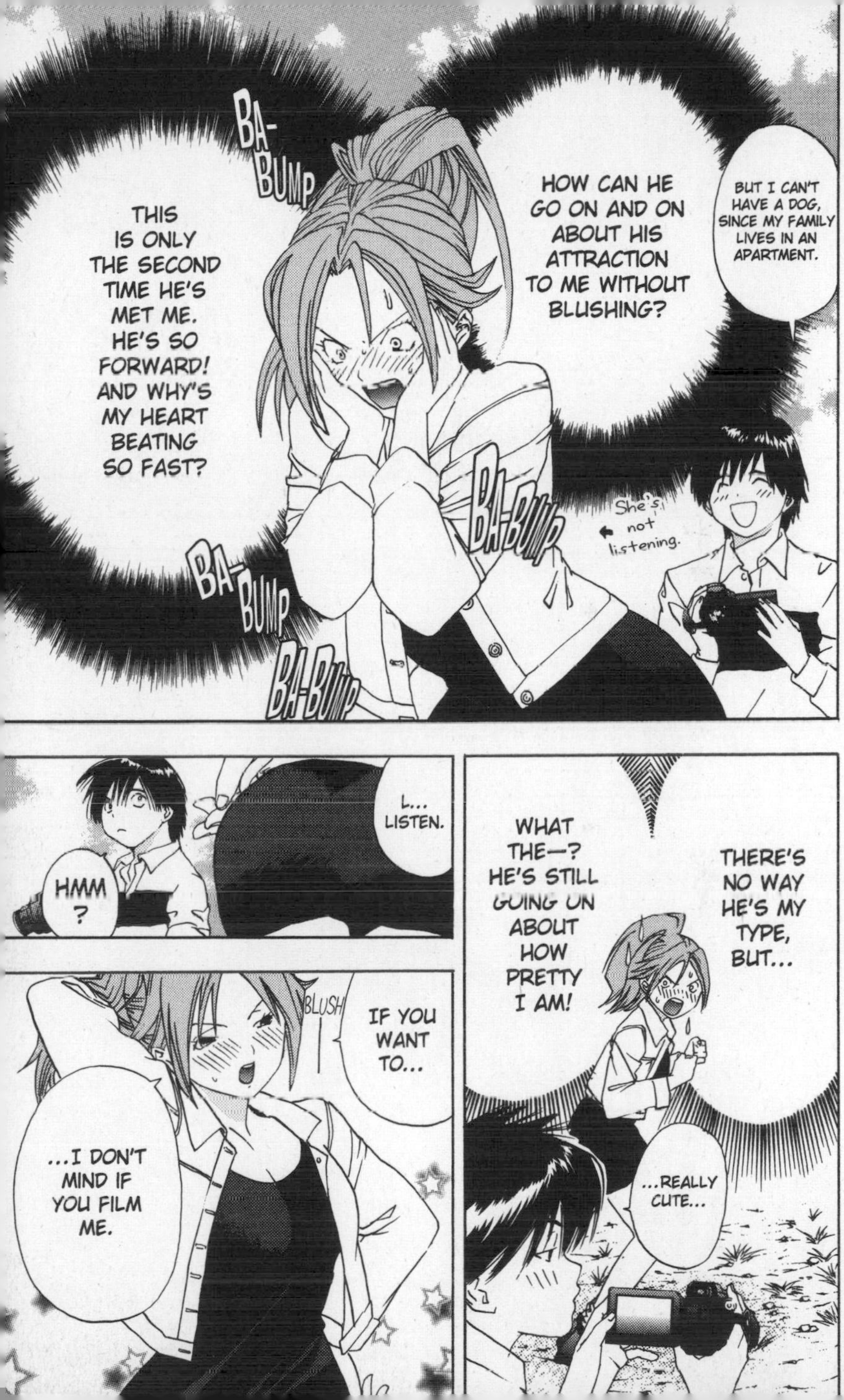
BUT I CAN'T HAVE A DOG, SINCE MY FAMILY LIVES IN AN APARTMENT.
HOW CAN HE GO ON AND ON ABOUT HIS ATTRACTION TO ME WITHOUT BLUSHING?
She's not listening.
BA-BUMP
BA-BUMP
THIS IS ONLY THE SECOND TIME HE'S MET ME. HE'S SO FORWARD! AND WHY'S MY HEART BEATING SO FAST?
BA-BUMP
BA-BUMP
THERE'S NO WAY HE'S MY TYPE, BUT...
WHAT THE—? HE'S STILL GOING ON ABOUT HOW PRETTY I AM!
...REALLY CUTE...
L... LISTEN.
HMM?
BLUSH
IF YOU WANT TO...
...I DON'T MIND IF YOU FILM ME.

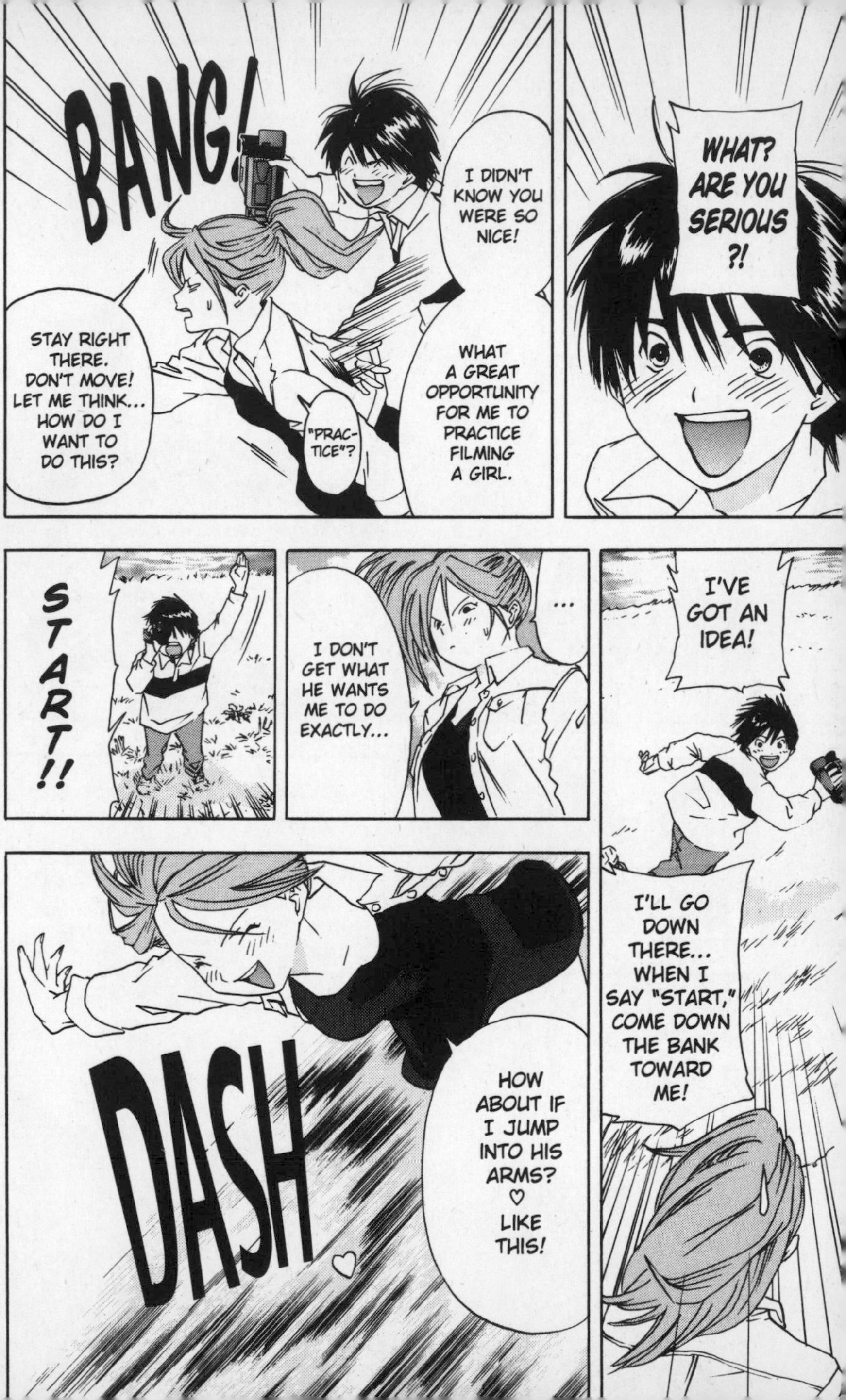
WHAT? ARE YOU SERIOUS ?!
I DIDN'T KNOW YOU WERE SO NICE!
BANG!
WHAT A GREAT OPPORTUNITY FOR ME TO PRACTICE FILMING A GIRL.
"PRAC-TICE"?
STAY RIGHT THERE. DON'T MOVE! LET ME THINK... HOW DO I WANT TO DO THIS?
I'VE GOT AN IDEA!
I'LL GO DOWN THERE... WHEN I SAY "START," COME DOWN THE BANK TOWARD ME!
...
I DON'T GET WHAT HE WANTS ME TO DO EXACTLY...
START!!
HOW ABOUT IF I JUMP INTO HIS ARMS? ♡ LIKE THIS!
DASH

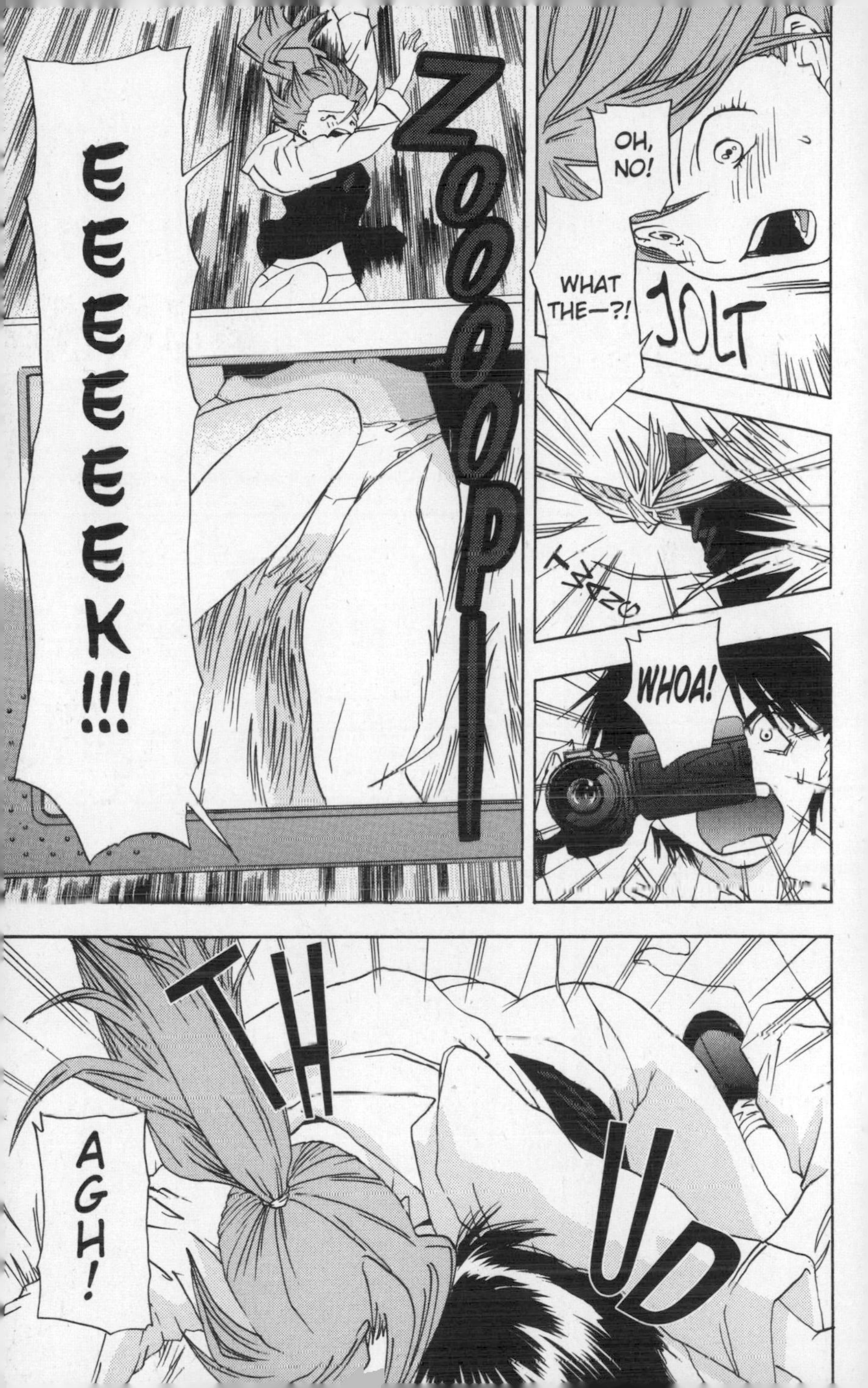
OH, NO!
WHAT THE—?!
JOLT
WHOA!
ZOOOOOP!
EEEEEEEK!!!
THUD
AGH!

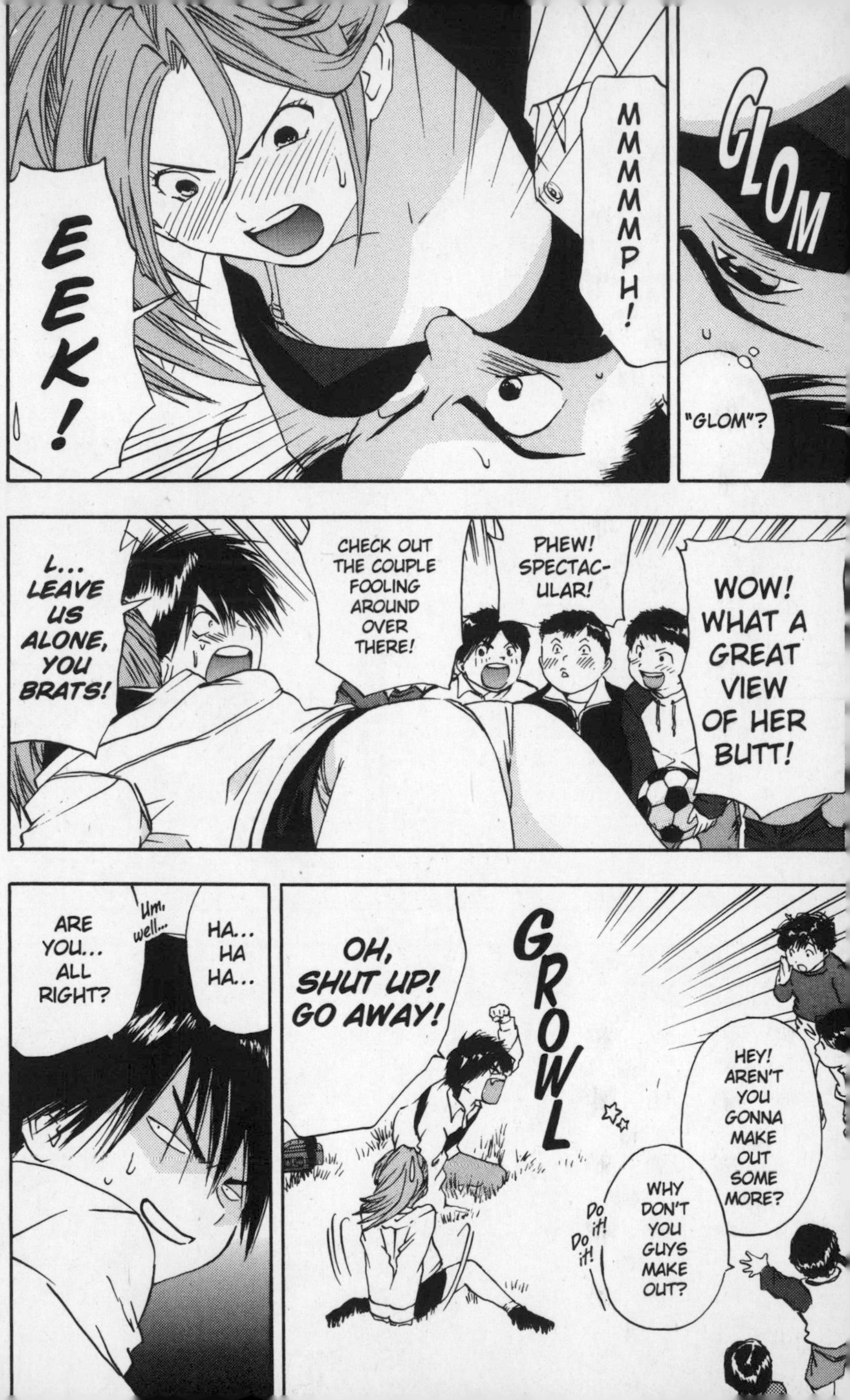
GLOM
"GLOM"?
MMMMMPH!
EEK!
WOW! WHAT A GREAT VIEW OF HER BUTT!
PHEW! SPECTACULAR!
CHECK OUT THE COUPLE FOOLING AROUND OVER THERE!
L... LEAVE US ALONE, YOU BRATS!
HEY! AREN'T YOU GONNA MAKE OUT SOME MORE?
WHY DON'T YOU GUYS MAKE OUT?
Do it! Do it!
OH, SHUT UP! GO AWAY!
GROWL
HA... HA HA...
Um, well...
ARE YOU... ALL RIGHT?

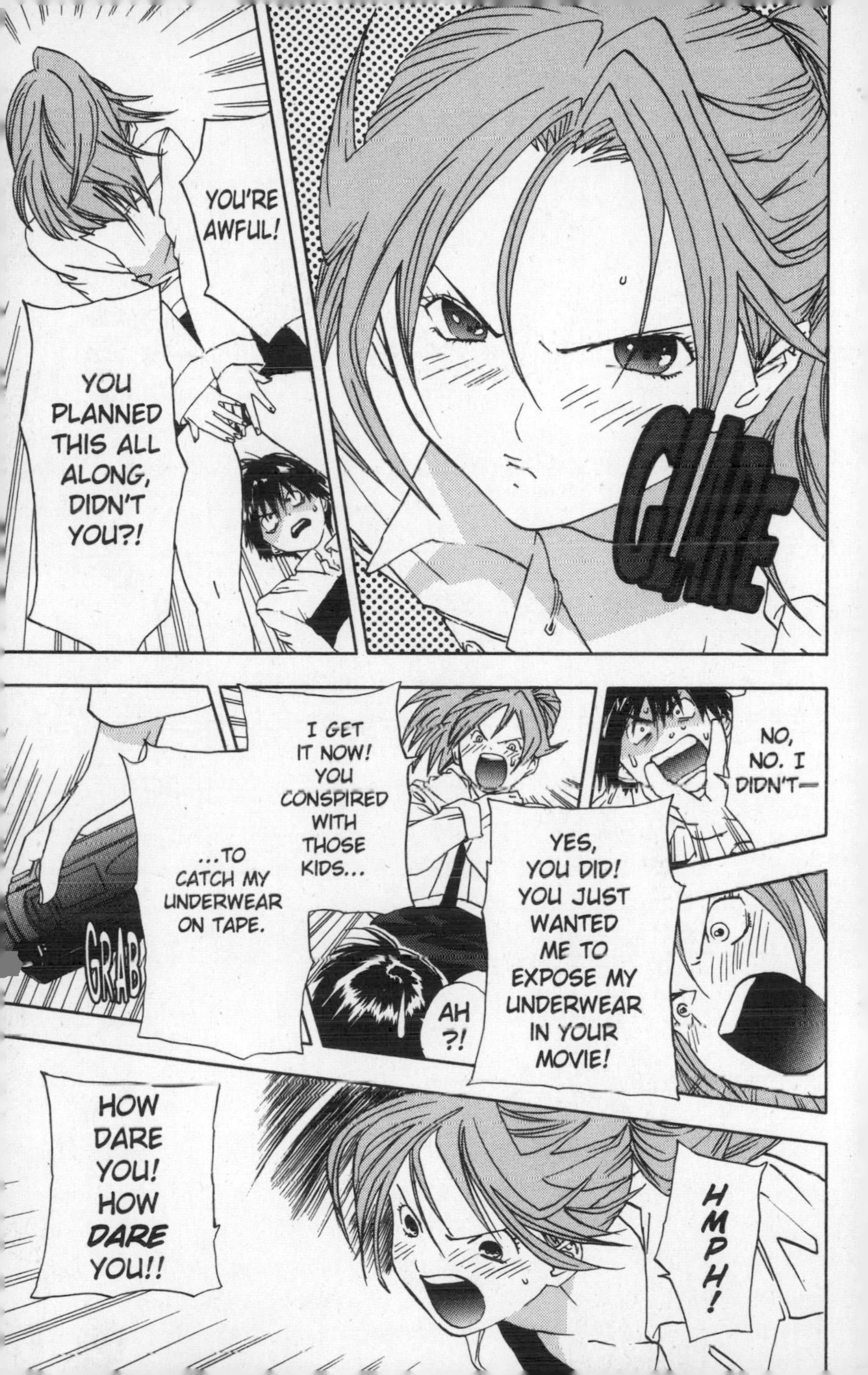
GLARE
YOU'RE AWFUL!
YOU PLANNED THIS ALL ALONG, DIDN'T YOU?!
NO, NO. I DIDN'T—
I GET IT NOW! YOU CONSPIRED WITH THOSE KIDS...
...TO CATCH MY UNDERWEAR ON TAPE.
GRAB
YES, YOU DID! YOU JUST WANTED ME TO EXPOSE MY UNDERWEAR IN YOUR MOVIE!
AH ?!
HMPH!
HOW DARE YOU! HOW DARE YOU!!

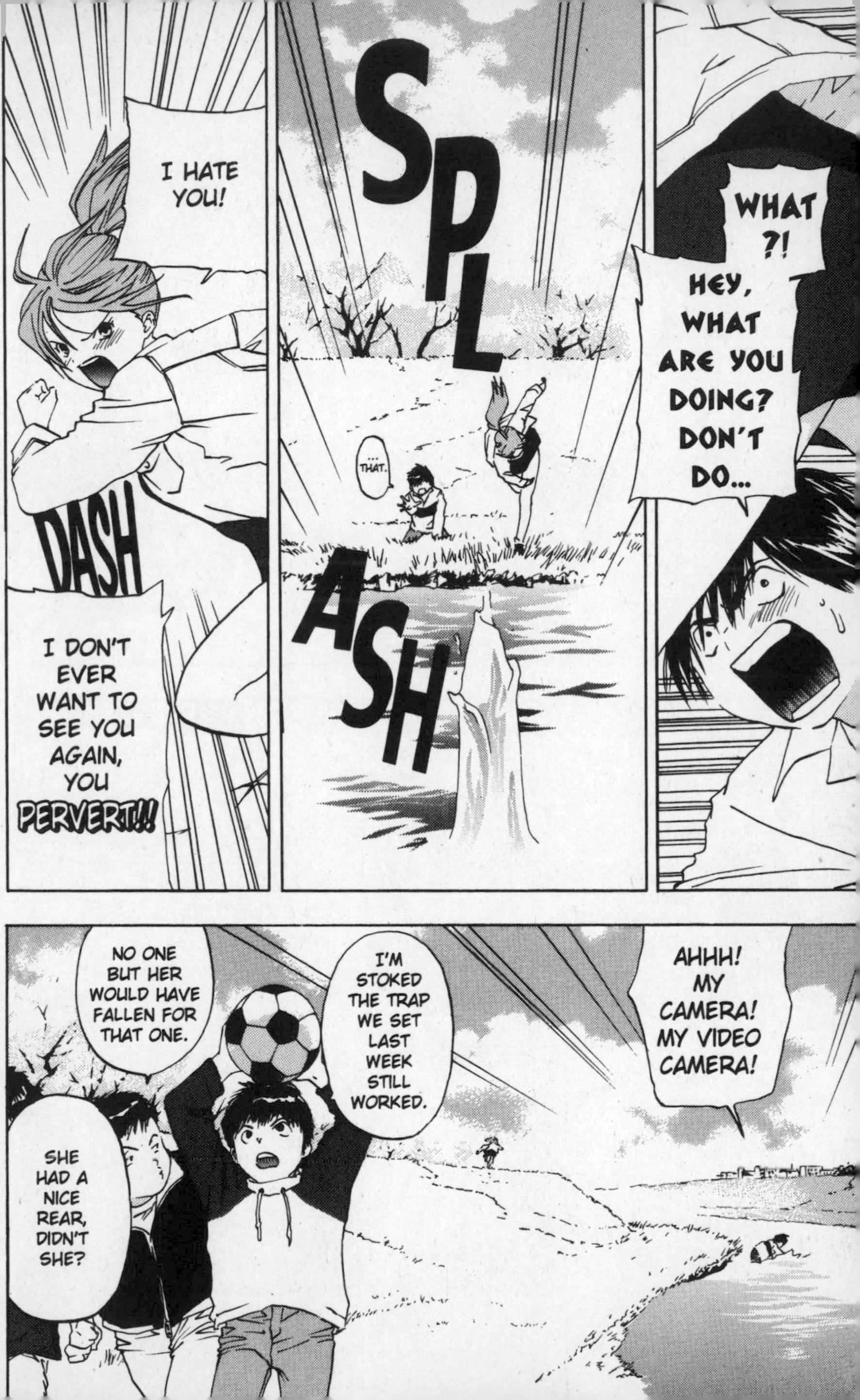
WHAT ?!
HEY, WHAT ARE YOU DOING? DON'T DO...
SPL
...THAT.
ASH
I HATE YOU!
DASH
I DON'T EVER WANT TO SEE YOU AGAIN, YOU PERVERT!!!
AHHH! MY CAMERA! MY VIDEO CAMERA!
I'M STOKED THE TRAP WE SET LAST WEEK STILL WORKED.
NO ONE BUT HER WOULD HAVE FALLEN FOR THAT ONE.
SHE HAD A NICE REAR, DIDN'T SHE?

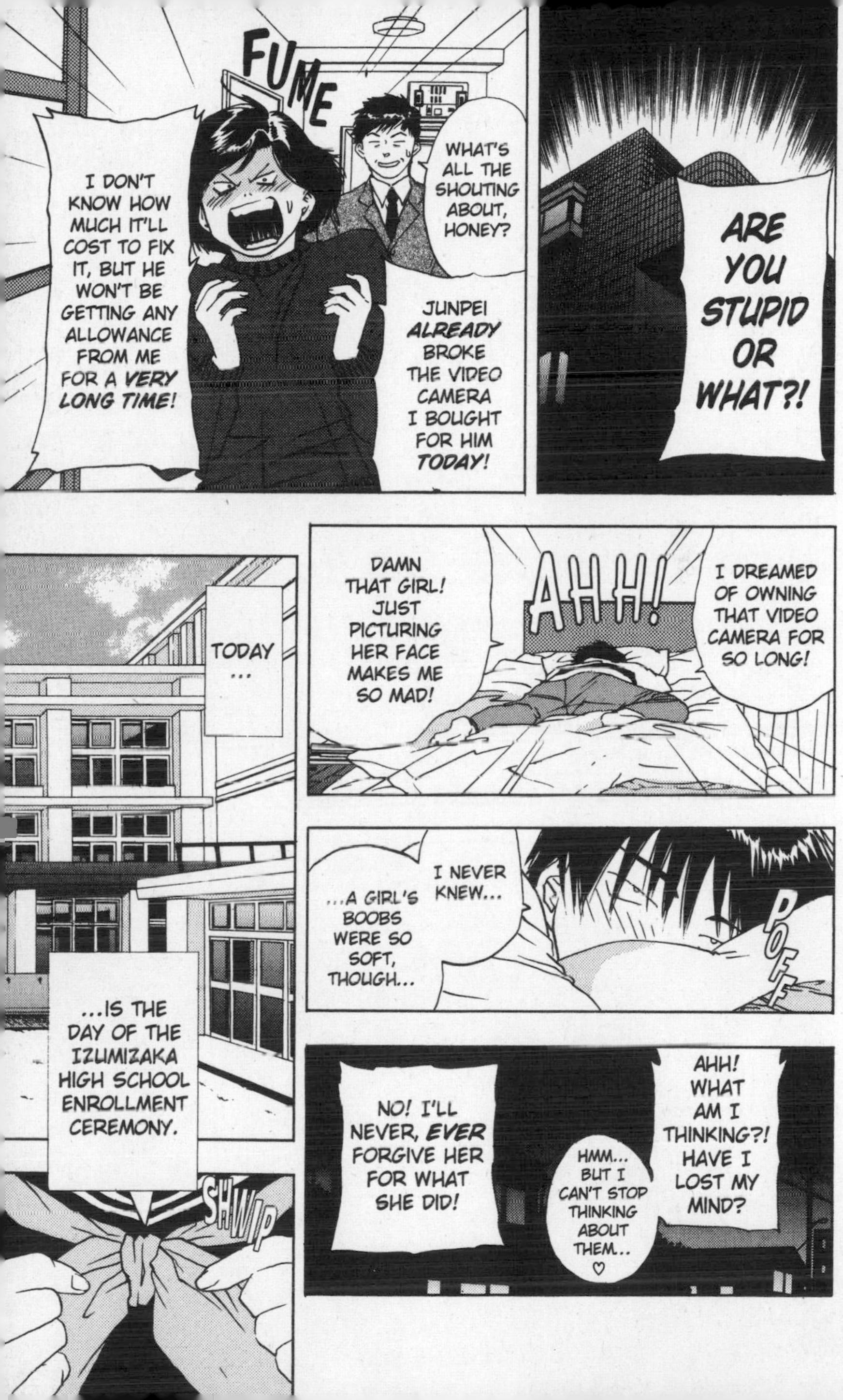
ARE YOU STUPID OR WHAT?!
WHAT'S ALL THE SHOUTING ABOUT, HONEY?
FUME
JUNPEI *ALREADY* BROKE THE VIDEO CAMERA I BOUGHT FOR HIM *TODAY*!
I DON'T KNOW HOW MUCH IT'LL COST TO FIX IT, BUT HE WON'T BE GETTING ANY ALLOWANCE FROM ME FOR A *VERY LONG TIME*!
I DREAMED OF OWNING THAT VIDEO CAMERA FOR SO LONG!
AHH!
DAMN THAT GIRL! JUST PICTURING HER FACE MAKES ME SO MAD!
POFF
I NEVER KNEW...
...A GIRL'S BOOBS WERE SO SOFT, THOUGH...
AHH! WHAT AM I THINKING?! HAVE I LOST MY MIND?
HMM... BUT I CAN'T STOP THINKING ABOUT THEM.. ♡
NO! I'LL NEVER, *EVER* FORGIVE HER FOR WHAT SHE DID!
TODAY...
...IS THE DAY OF THE IZUMIZAKA HIGH SCHOOL ENROLLMENT CEREMONY.
SHWIP

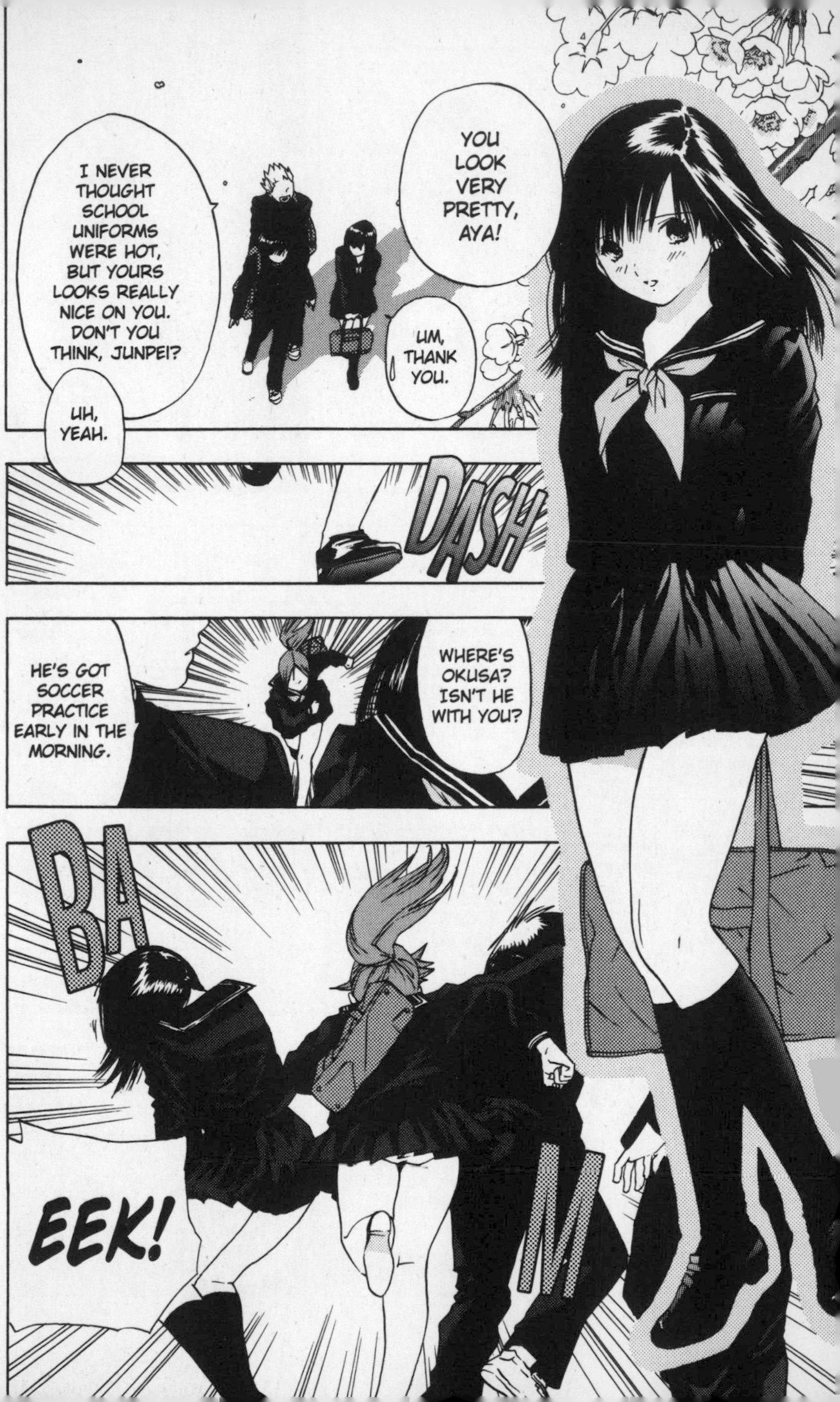
YOU LOOK VERY PRETTY, AYA!
I NEVER THOUGHT SCHOOL UNIFORMS WERE HOT, BUT YOURS LOOKS REALLY NICE ON YOU. DON'T YOU THINK, JUNPEI?
UM, THANK YOU.
UH, YEAH.
DASH
WHERE'S OKUSA? ISN'T HE WITH YOU?
HE'S GOT SOCCER PRACTICE EARLY IN THE MORNING.
BA
M
EEK!

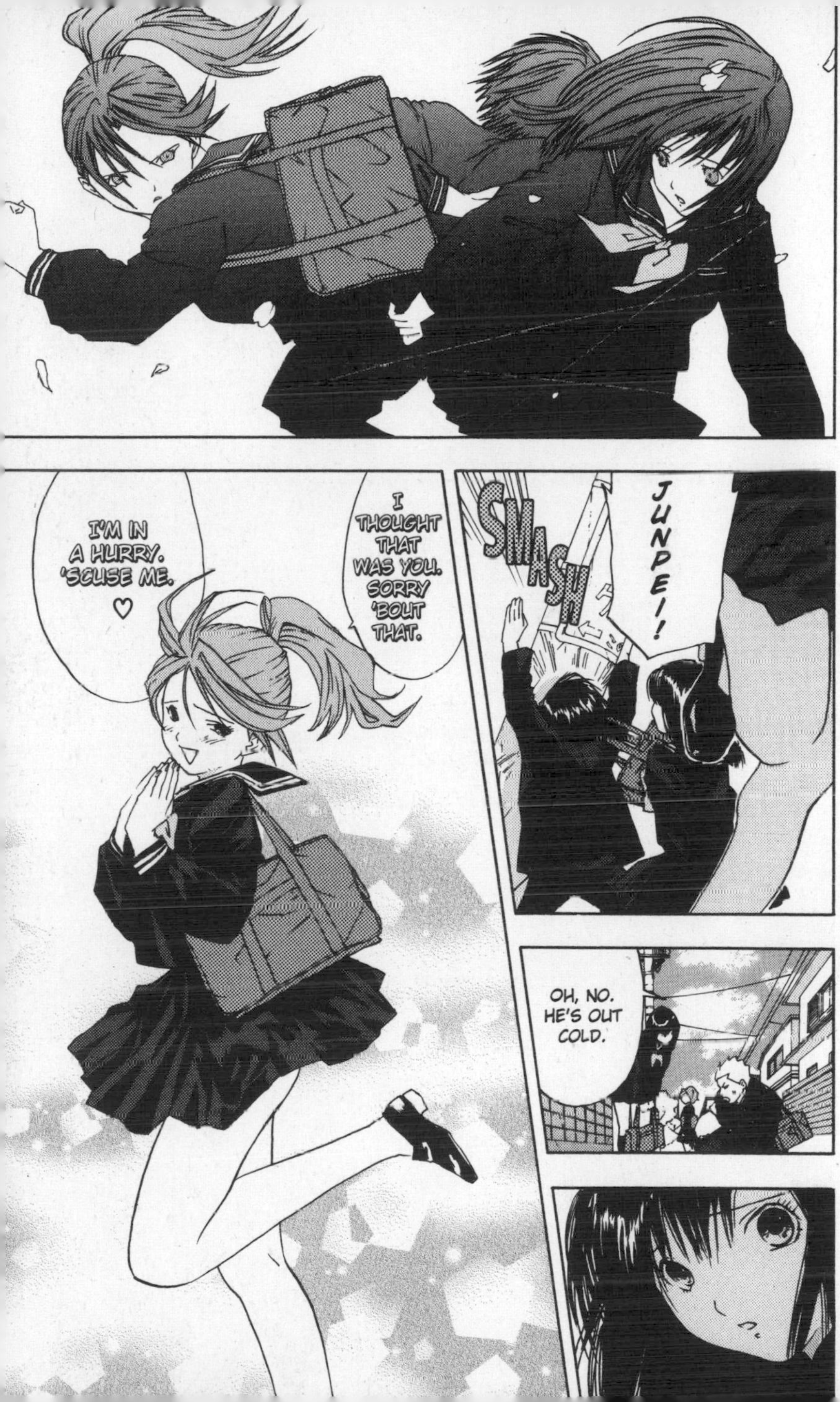
JUNPEI!!
SMASH
OH, NO. HE'S OUT COLD.
I THOUGHT THAT WAS YOU. SORRY 'BOUT THAT.
I'M IN A HURRY. 'SCUSE ME. ♡

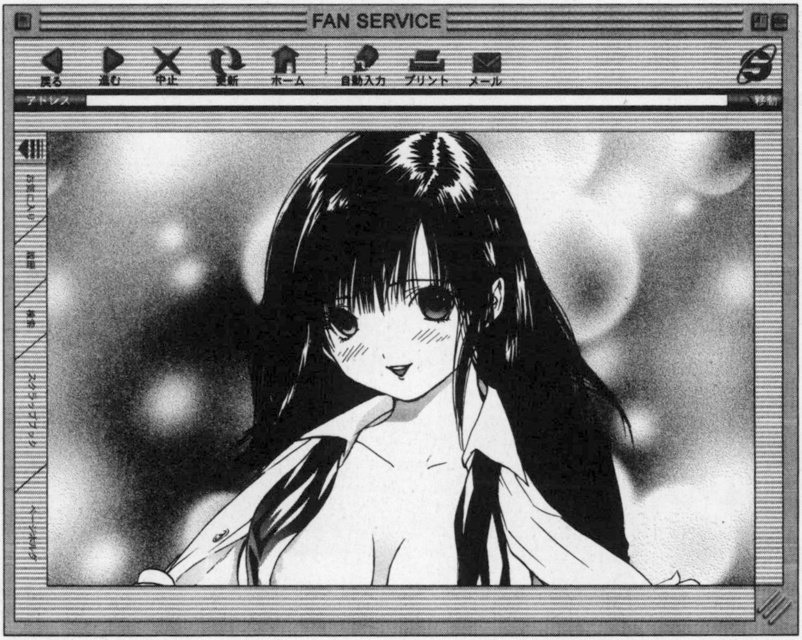
FAN SERVICE
戻る
進む
中止
更新
ホーム
自動入力
プリント
メール
アドレス
移動

NOTE: THIS IS A COMPOSITE PHOTOGRAPH.

CRUSH 20: LOVE BLOOMS AT DIVING HEAD

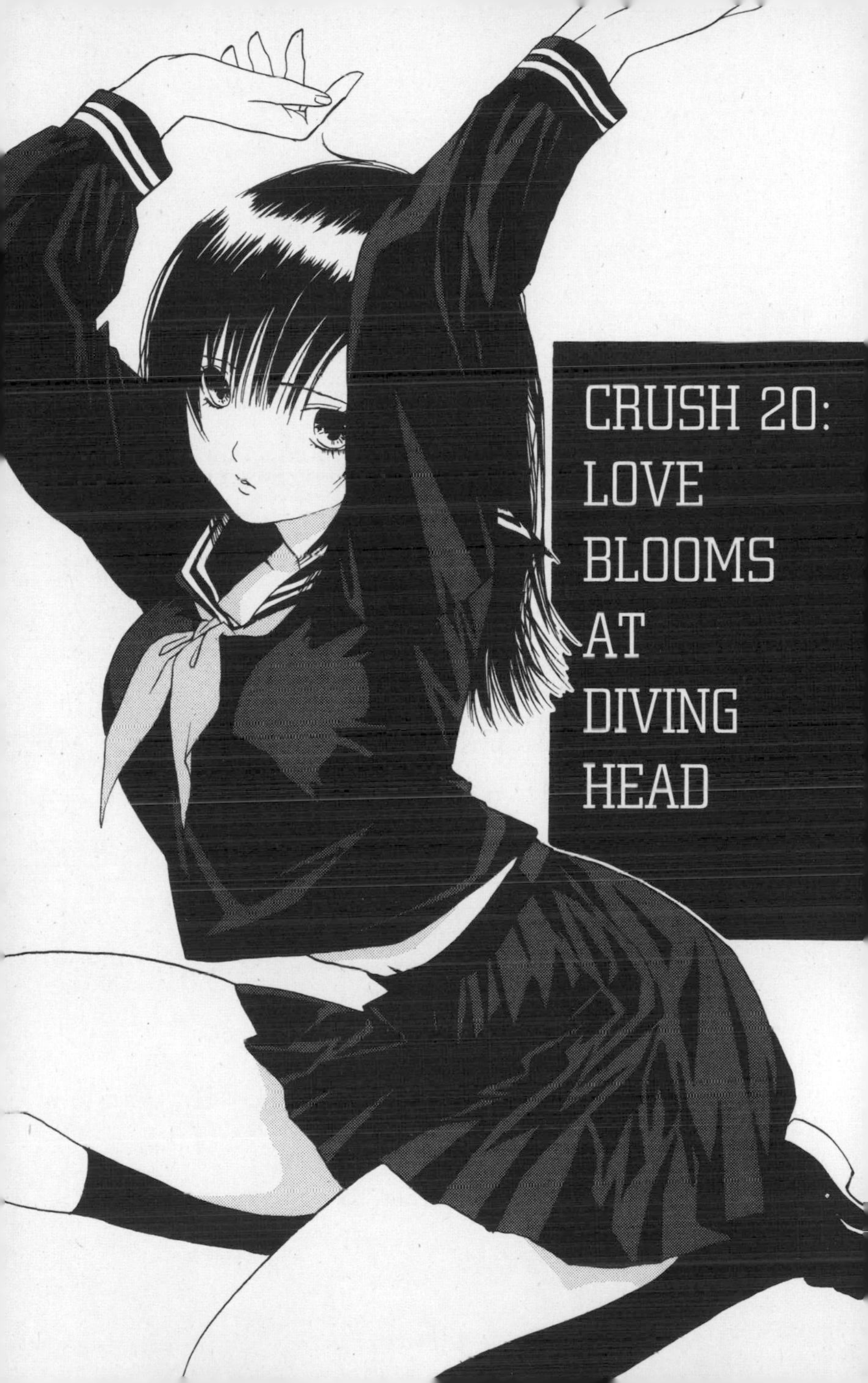

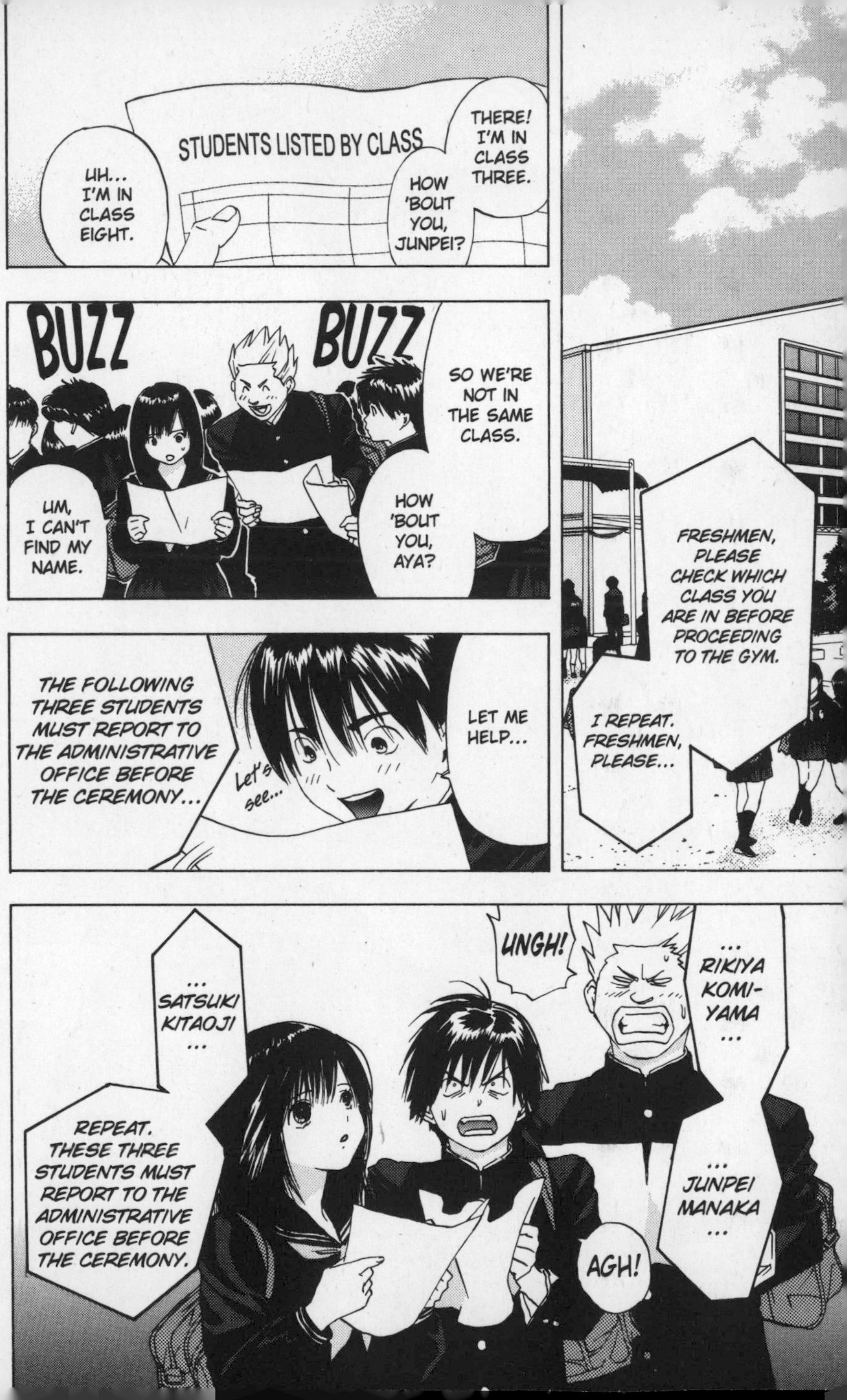
FRESHMEN, PLEASE CHECK WHICH CLASS YOU ARE IN BEFORE PROCEEDING TO THE GYM.
I REPEAT. FRESHMEN, PLEASE...
THERE! I'M IN CLASS THREE.
HOW 'BOUT YOU, JUNPEI?
STUDENTS LISTED BY CLASS
UH... I'M IN CLASS EIGHT.
BUZZ
SO WE'RE NOT IN THE SAME CLASS.
HOW 'BOUT YOU, AYA?
BUZZ
UM, I CAN'T FIND MY NAME.
LET ME HELP...
Let's see...
THE FOLLOWING THREE STUDENTS MUST REPORT TO THE ADMINISTRATIVE OFFICE BEFORE THE CEREMONY...
... RIKIYA KOMI-YAMA ...
UNGH!
... JUNPEI MANAKA ...
AGH!
... SATSUKI KITAOJI ...
REPEAT. THESE THREE STUDENTS MUST REPORT TO THE ADMINISTRATIVE OFFICE BEFORE THE CEREMONY.

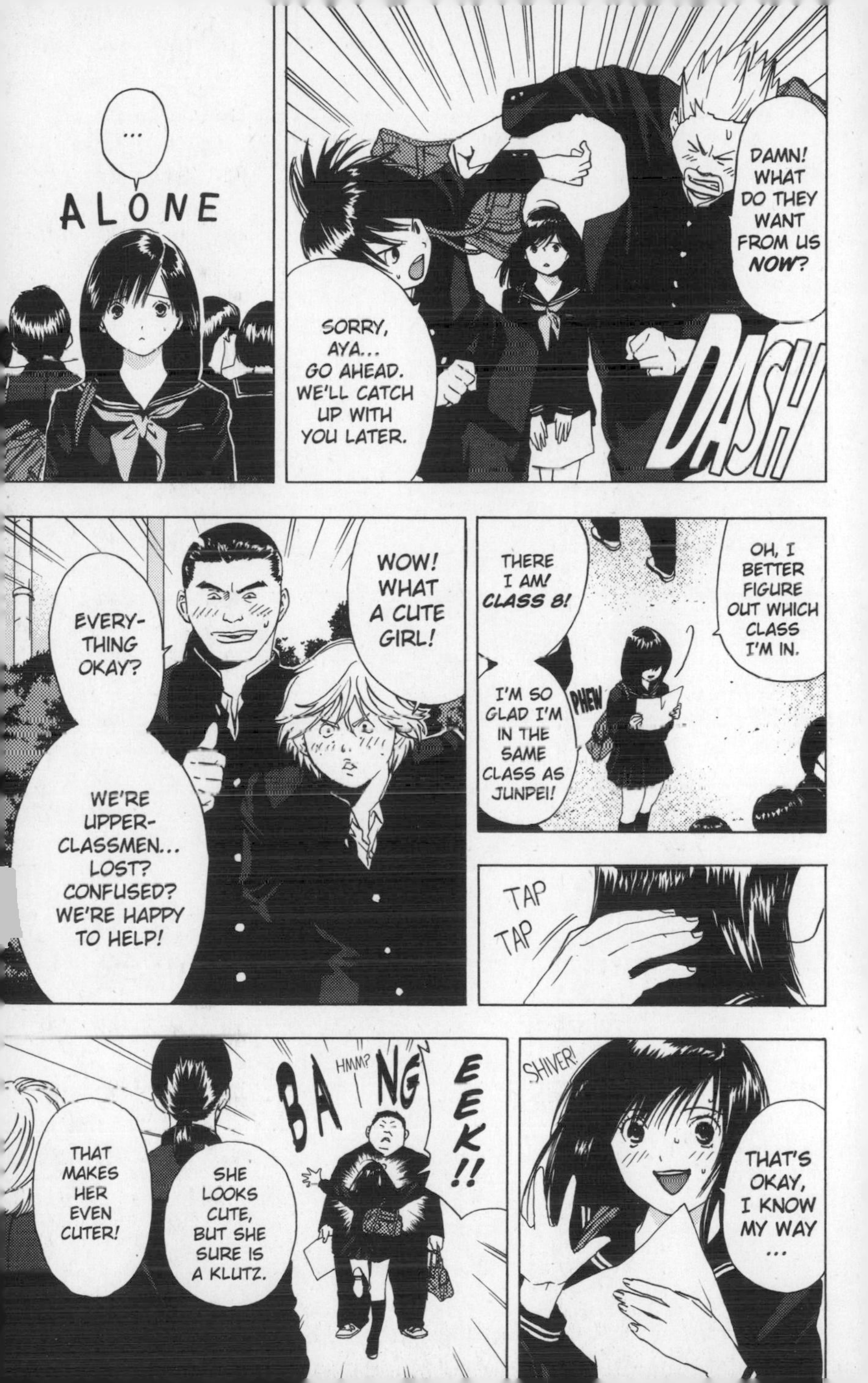
DAMN! WHAT DO THEY WANT FROM US *NOW*?
DASH
SORRY, AYA... GO AHEAD. WE'LL CATCH UP WITH YOU LATER.
...
ALONE
OH, I BETTER FIGURE OUT WHICH CLASS I'M IN.
THERE I AM! *CLASS 8!*
I'M SO GLAD I'M IN THE SAME CLASS AS JUNPEI!
PHEW
TAP
TAP
WOW! WHAT A CUTE GIRL!
EVERY-THING OKAY?
WE'RE UPPER-CLASSMEN... LOST? CONFUSED? WE'RE HAPPY TO HELP!
SHIVER!
THAT'S OKAY, I KNOW MY WAY ...
EEK!!
BANG
HMM?
SHE LOOKS CUTE, BUT SHE SURE IS A KLUTZ.
THAT MAKES HER EVEN CUTER!

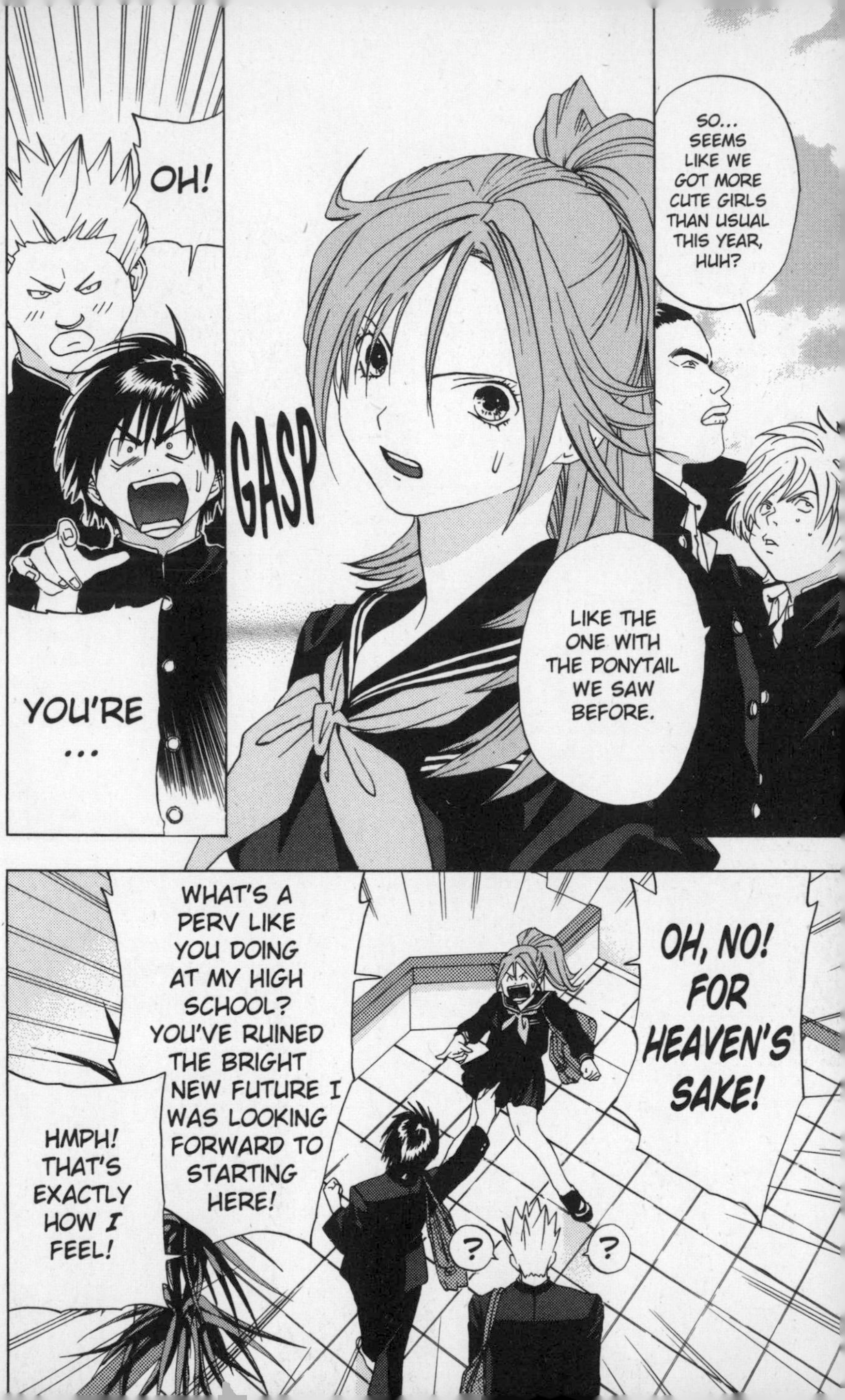
SO... SEEMS LIKE WE GOT MORE CUTE GIRLS THAN USUAL THIS YEAR, HUH?
LIKE THE ONE WITH THE PONYTAIL WE SAW BEFORE.
GASP
OH!
YOU'RE ...
OH, NO! FOR HEAVEN'S SAKE!
WHAT'S A PERV LIKE YOU DOING AT MY HIGH SCHOOL? YOU'VE RUINED THE BRIGHT NEW FUTURE I WAS LOOKING FORWARD TO STARTING HERE!
?
?
HMPH! THAT'S EXACTLY HOW *I* FEEL!

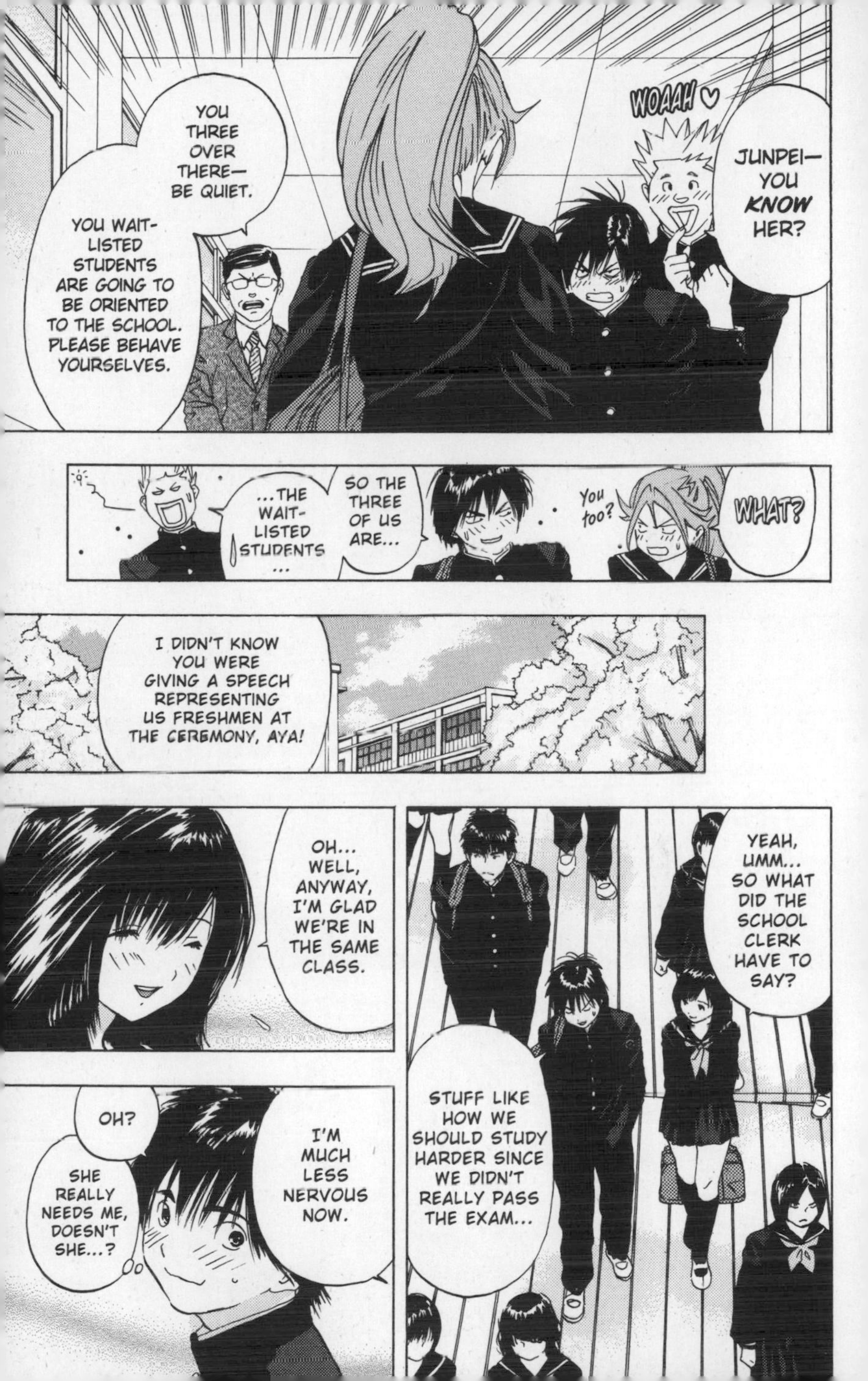
WOAAH ♥
JUNPEI— YOU *KNOW* HER?
YOU THREE OVER THERE— BE QUIET.
YOU WAIT-LISTED STUDENTS ARE GOING TO BE ORIENTED TO THE SCHOOL. PLEASE BEHAVE YOURSELVES.
WHAT?
You too?
SO THE THREE OF US ARE...
...THE WAIT-LISTED STUDENTS...
I DIDN'T KNOW YOU WERE GIVING A SPEECH REPRESENTING US FRESHMEN AT THE CEREMONY, AYA!
YEAH, UMM... SO WHAT DID THE SCHOOL CLERK HAVE TO SAY?
STUFF LIKE HOW WE SHOULD STUDY HARDER SINCE WE DIDN'T REALLY PASS THE EXAM...
OH... WELL, ANYWAY, I'M GLAD WE'RE IN THE SAME CLASS.
I'M MUCH LESS NERVOUS NOW.
OH?
SHE REALLY NEEDS ME, DOESN'T SHE...?

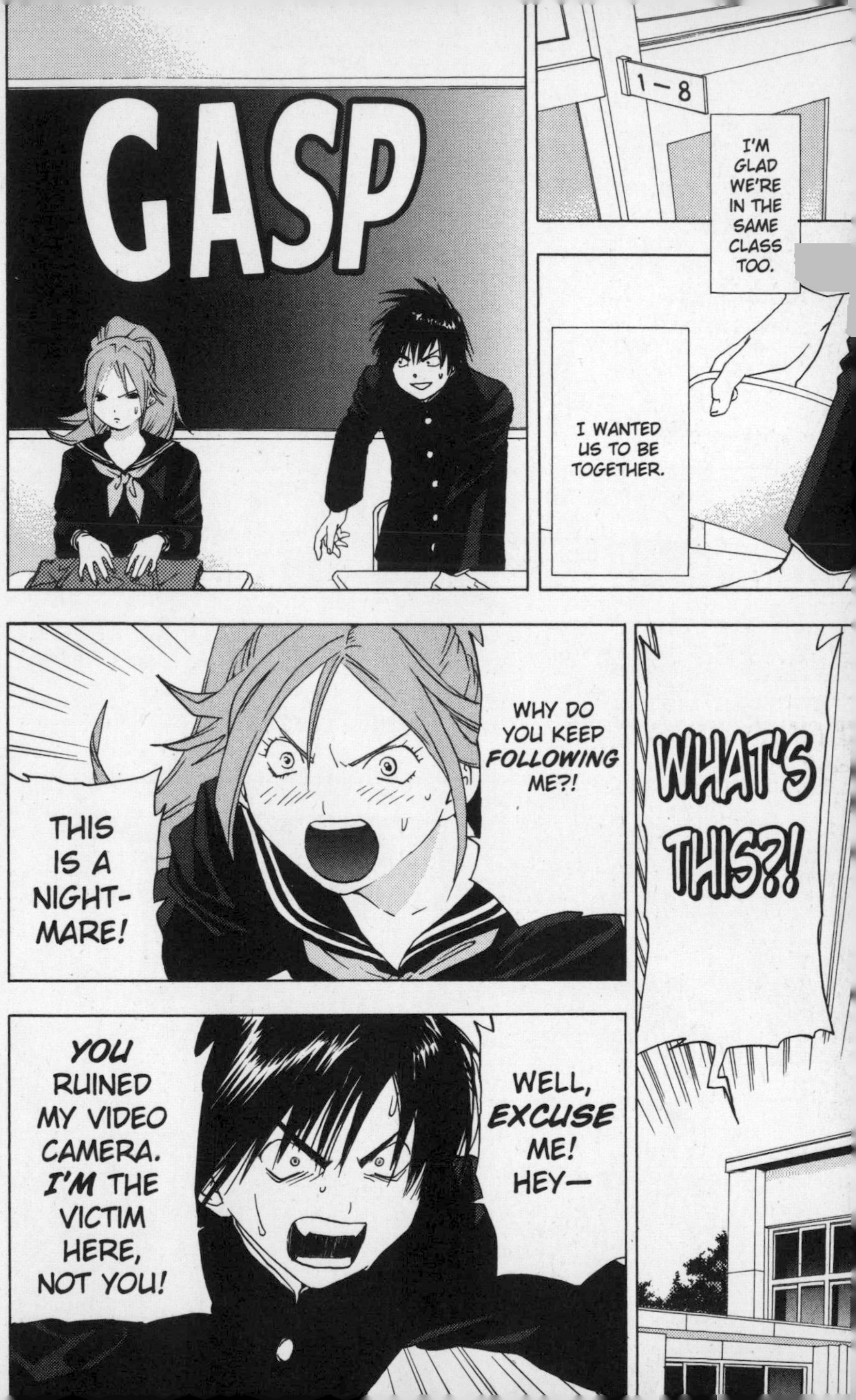
1—8
I'M GLAD WE'RE IN THE SAME CLASS TOO.
I WANTED US TO BE TOGETHER.
GASP
WHAT'S THIS?!
WHY DO YOU KEEP FOLLOWING ME?!
THIS IS A NIGHTMARE!
WELL, EXCUSE ME! HEY—
YOU RUINED MY VIDEO CAMERA. I'M THE VICTIM HERE, NOT YOU!

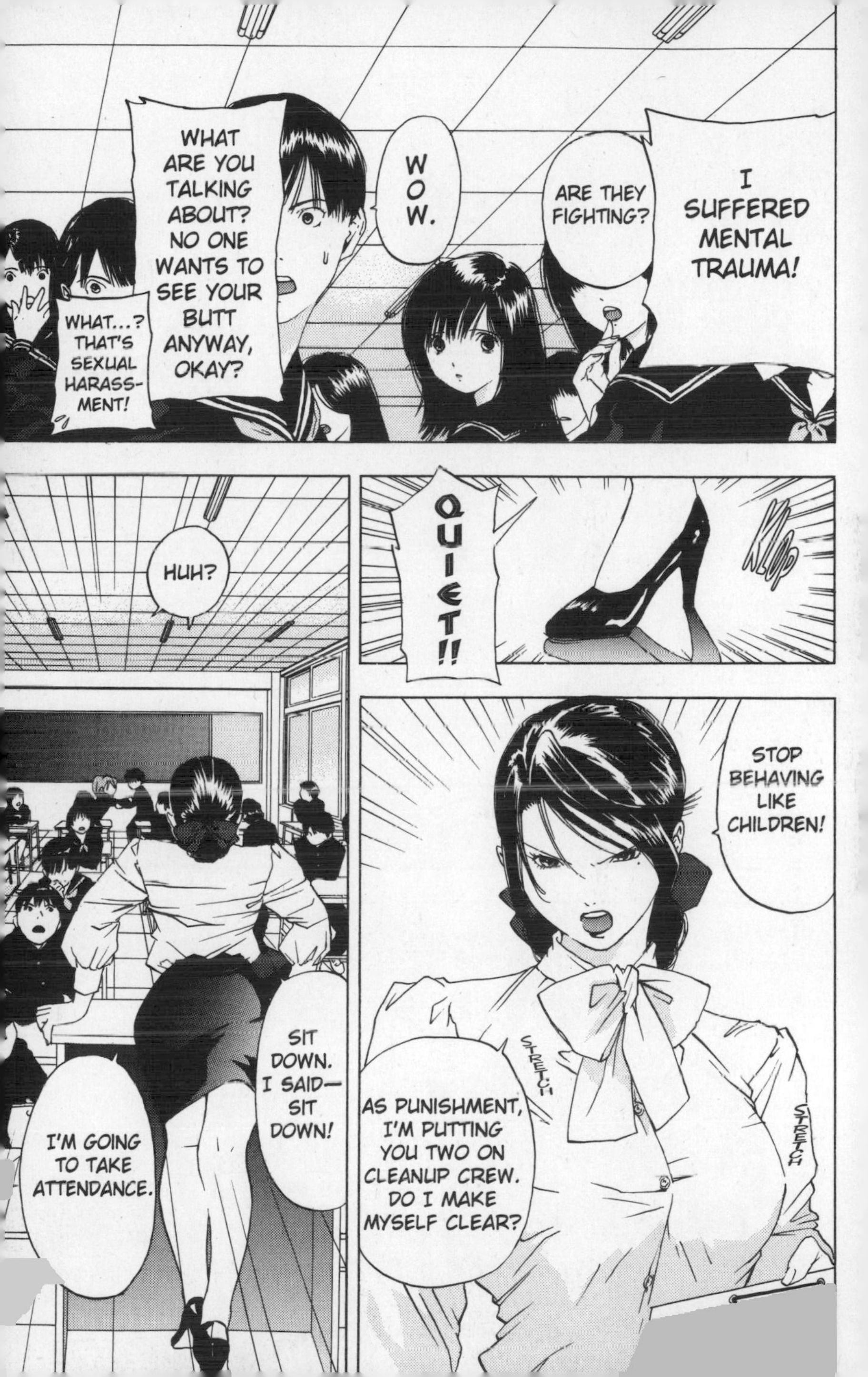
I SUFFERED MENTAL TRAUMA!
ARE THEY FIGHTING?
WOW.
WHAT ARE YOU TALKING ABOUT? NO ONE WANTS TO SEE YOUR BUTT ANYWAY, OKAY?
WHAT...? THAT'S SEXUAL HARASS-MENT!
KLOP
QUIET!!
HUH?
STOP BEHAVING LIKE CHILDREN!
STRETCH
STRETCH
AS PUNISHMENT, I'M PUTTING YOU TWO ON CLEANUP CREW. DO I MAKE MYSELF CLEAR?
SIT DOWN. I SAID— SIT DOWN!
I'M GOING TO TAKE ATTENDANCE.

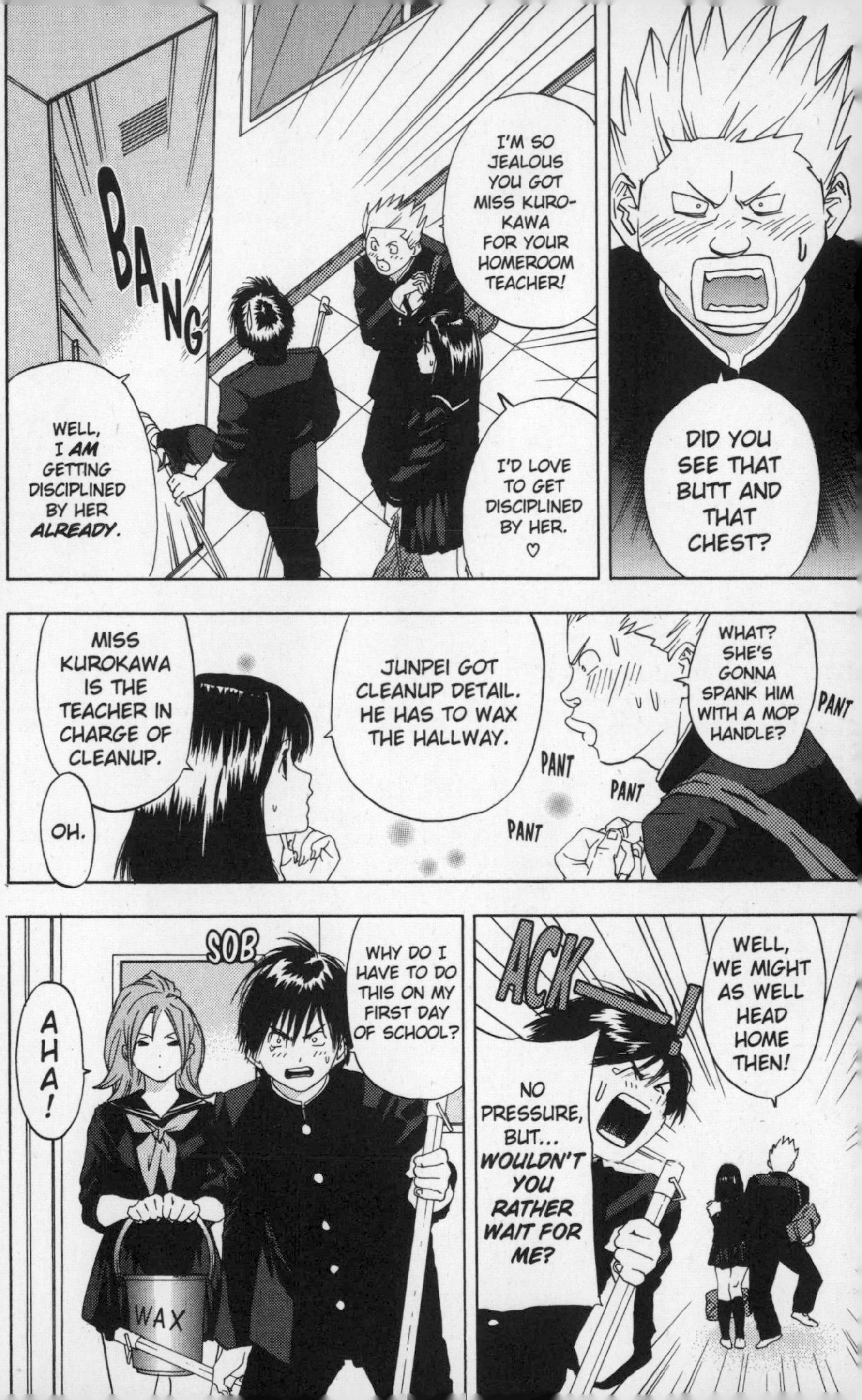
DID YOU SEE THAT BUTT AND THAT CHEST?
I'M SO JEALOUS YOU GOT MISS KURO-KAWA FOR YOUR HOMEROOM TEACHER!
I'D LOVE TO GET DISCIPLINED BY HER. ♡
BANG
WELL, I *AM* GETTING DISCIPLINED BY HER *ALREADY*.
WHAT? SHE'S GONNA SPANK HIM WITH A MOP HANDLE?
PANT
PANT
PANT
PANT
JUNPEI GOT CLEANUP DETAIL. HE HAS TO WAX THE HALLWAY.
MISS KUROKAWA IS THE TEACHER IN CHARGE OF CLEANUP.
OH.
WELL, WE MIGHT AS WELL HEAD HOME THEN!
ACK
NO PRESSURE, BUT... *WOULDN'T YOU RATHER WAIT FOR ME?*
WHY DO I HAVE TO DO THIS ON MY FIRST DAY OF SCHOOL?
SOB
AHA!
WAX

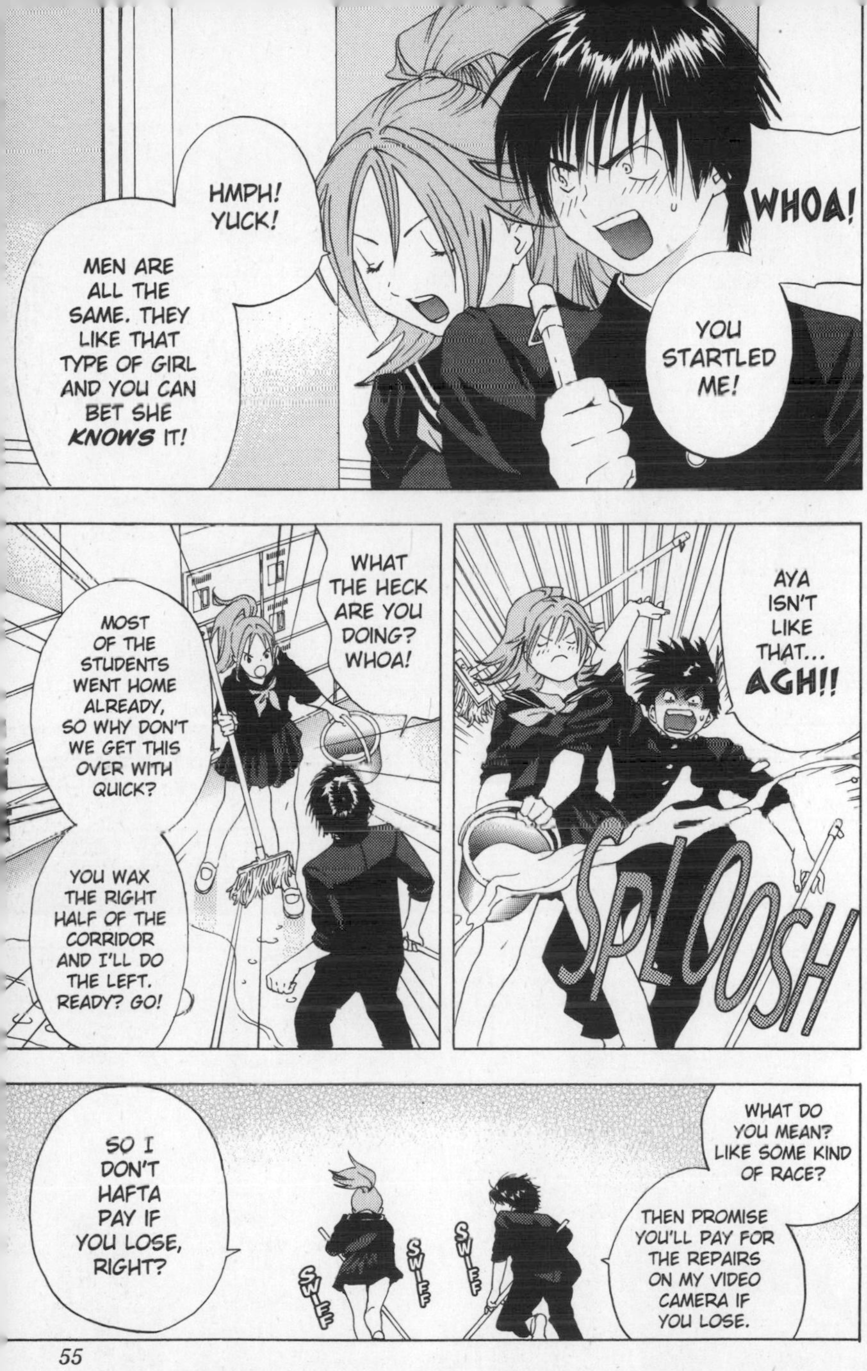
WHOA!
YOU STARTLED ME!
HMPH! YUCK!
MEN ARE ALL THE SAME. THEY LIKE THAT TYPE OF GIRL AND YOU CAN BET SHE ***KNOWS*** IT!
AYA ISN'T LIKE THAT... **AGH!!**
SPLOOSH
WHAT THE HECK ARE YOU DOING? WHOA!
MOST OF THE STUDENTS WENT HOME ALREADY, SO WHY DON'T WE GET THIS OVER WITH QUICK?
YOU WAX THE RIGHT HALF OF THE CORRIDOR AND I'LL DO THE LEFT. READY? GO!
WHAT DO YOU MEAN? LIKE SOME KIND OF RACE?
THEN PROMISE YOU'LL PAY FOR THE REPAIRS ON MY VIDEO CAMERA IF YOU LOSE.
SWIFF
SWIFF
SWIFF
SO I DON'T HAFTA PAY IF YOU LOSE, RIGHT?

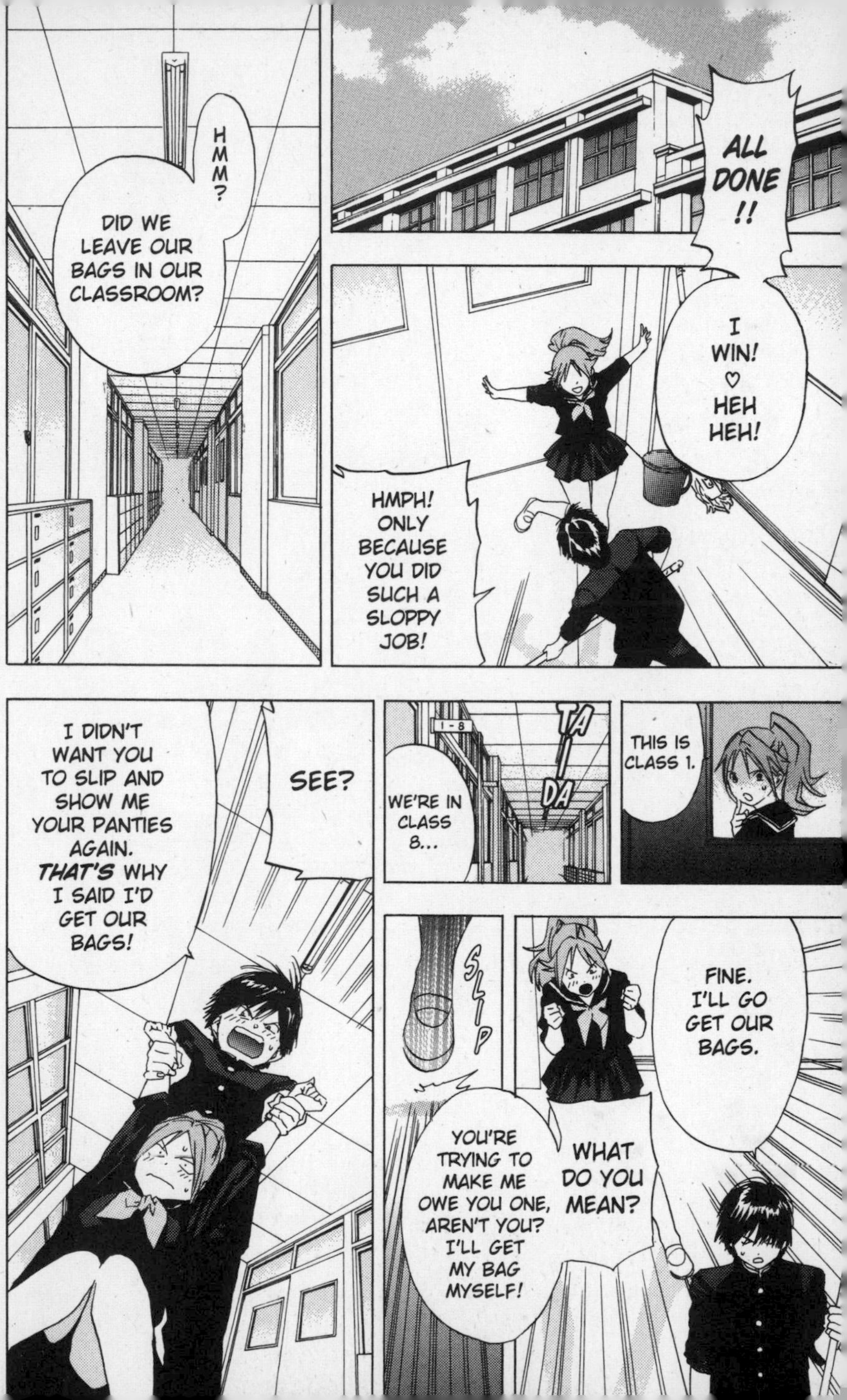
ALL DONE !!
I WIN! ♡ HEH HEH!
HMPH! ONLY BECAUSE YOU DID SUCH A SLOPPY JOB!
HMM?
DID WE LEAVE OUR BAGS IN OUR CLASSROOM?
THIS IS CLASS 1.
TA I DA
WE'RE IN CLASS 8...
1-8
FINE. I'LL GO GET OUR BAGS.
WHAT DO YOU MEAN?
YOU'RE TRYING TO MAKE ME OWE YOU ONE, AREN'T YOU? I'LL GET MY BAG MYSELF!
SLIP
SEE?
I DIDN'T WANT YOU TO SLIP AND SHOW ME YOUR PANTIES AGAIN. *THAT'S* WHY I SAID I'D GET OUR BAGS!

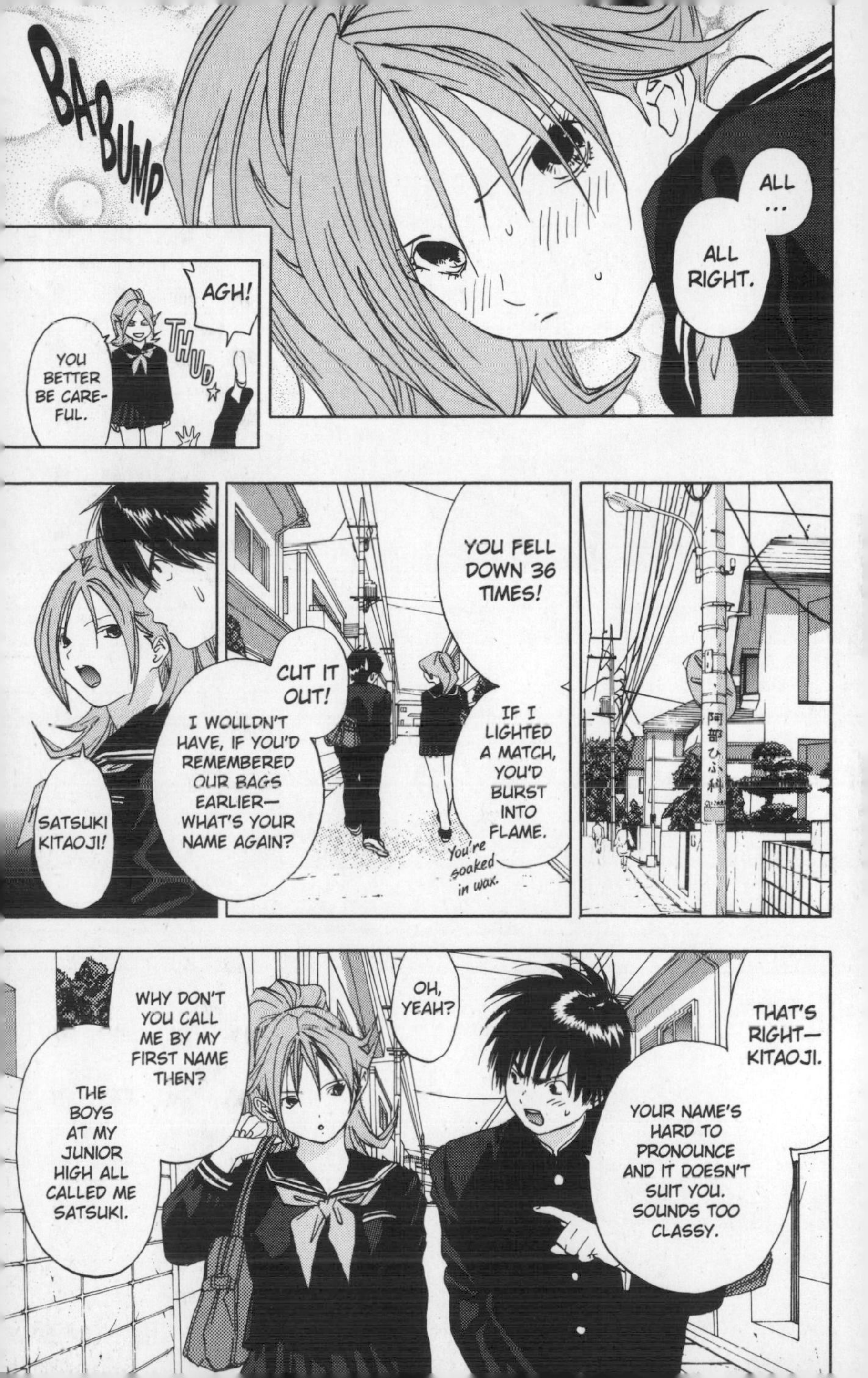
BABUMP
ALL...
ALL RIGHT.
AGH!
THUD☆
YOU BETTER BE CAREFUL.
阿部ひふ科
YOU FELL DOWN 36 TIMES!
IF I LIGHTED A MATCH, YOU'D BURST INTO FLAME.
You're soaked in wax.
CUT IT OUT!
I WOULDN'T HAVE, IF YOU'D REMEMBERED OUR BAGS EARLIER—WHAT'S YOUR NAME AGAIN?
SATSUKI KITAOJI!
THAT'S RIGHT—KITAOJI.
YOUR NAME'S HARD TO PRONOUNCE AND IT DOESN'T SUIT YOU. SOUNDS TOO CLASSY.
OH, YEAH?
WHY DON'T YOU CALL ME BY MY FIRST NAME THEN?
THE BOYS AT MY JUNIOR HIGH ALL CALLED ME SATSUKI.

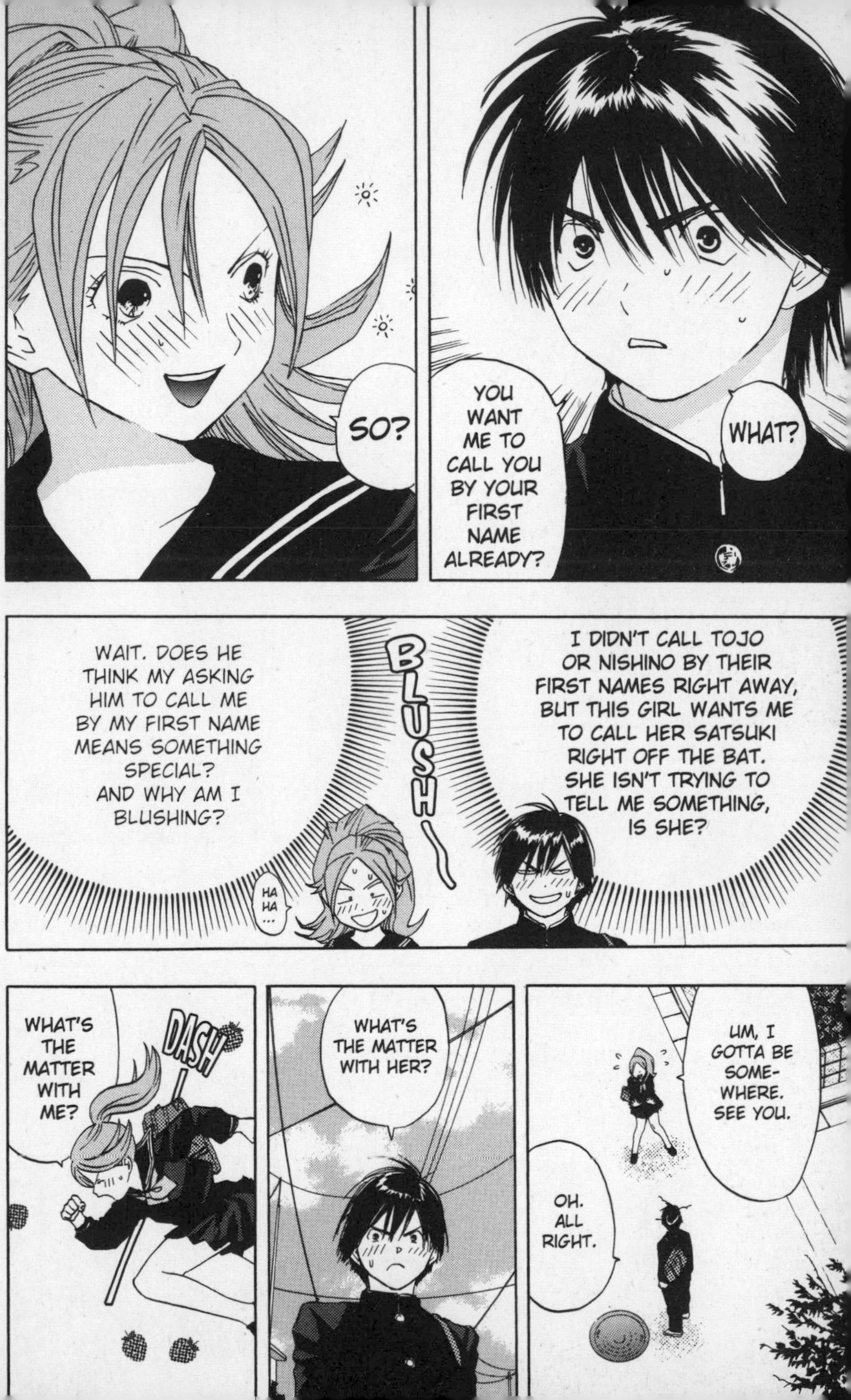
WHAT?
YOU WANT ME TO CALL YOU BY YOUR FIRST NAME ALREADY?
SO?
I DIDN'T CALL TOJO OR NISHINO BY THEIR FIRST NAMES RIGHT AWAY, BUT THIS GIRL WANTS ME TO CALL HER SATSUKI RIGHT OFF THE BAT. SHE ISN'T TRYING TO TELL ME SOMETHING, IS SHE?
BLUSH
WAIT. DOES HE THINK MY ASKING HIM TO CALL ME BY MY FIRST NAME MEANS SOMETHING SPECIAL? AND WHY AM I BLUSHING?
HA HA ...
UM, I GOTTA BE SOME-WHERE. SEE YOU.
OH. ALL RIGHT.
WHAT'S THE MATTER WITH HER?
DASH
WHAT'S THE MATTER WITH ME?

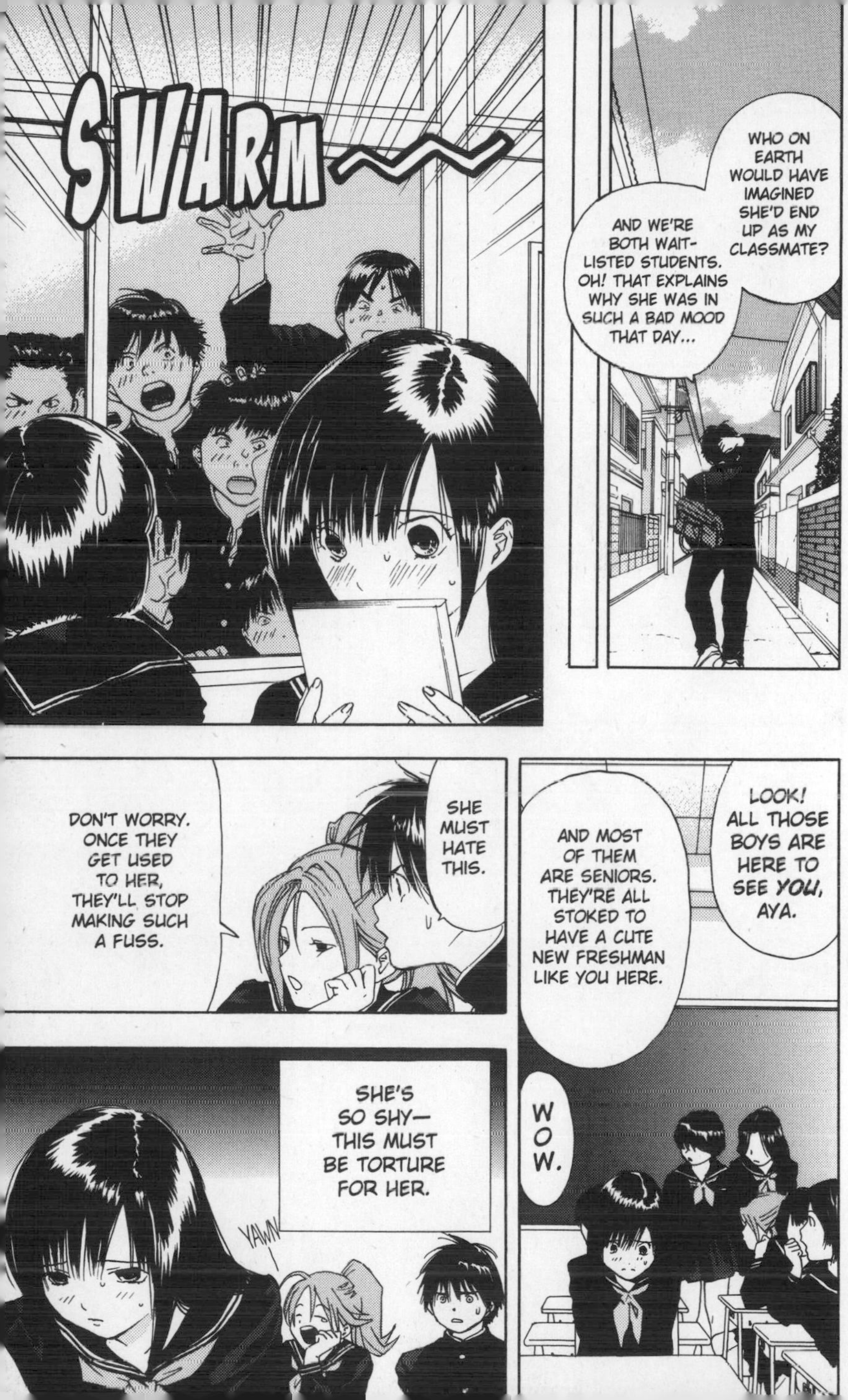
WHO ON EARTH WOULD HAVE IMAGINED SHE'D END UP AS MY CLASSMATE?
AND WE'RE BOTH WAIT-LISTED STUDENTS. OH! THAT EXPLAINS WHY SHE WAS IN SUCH A BAD MOOD THAT DAY...
SWARM
LOOK! ALL THOSE BOYS ARE HERE TO SEE *YOU*, AYA.
AND MOST OF THEM ARE SENIORS. THEY'RE ALL STOKED TO HAVE A CUTE NEW FRESHMAN LIKE YOU HERE.
WOW.
SHE MUST HATE THIS.
DON'T WORRY. ONCE THEY GET USED TO HER, THEY'LL STOP MAKING SUCH A FUSS.
SHE'S SO SHY—THIS MUST BE TORTURE FOR HER.
YAWN

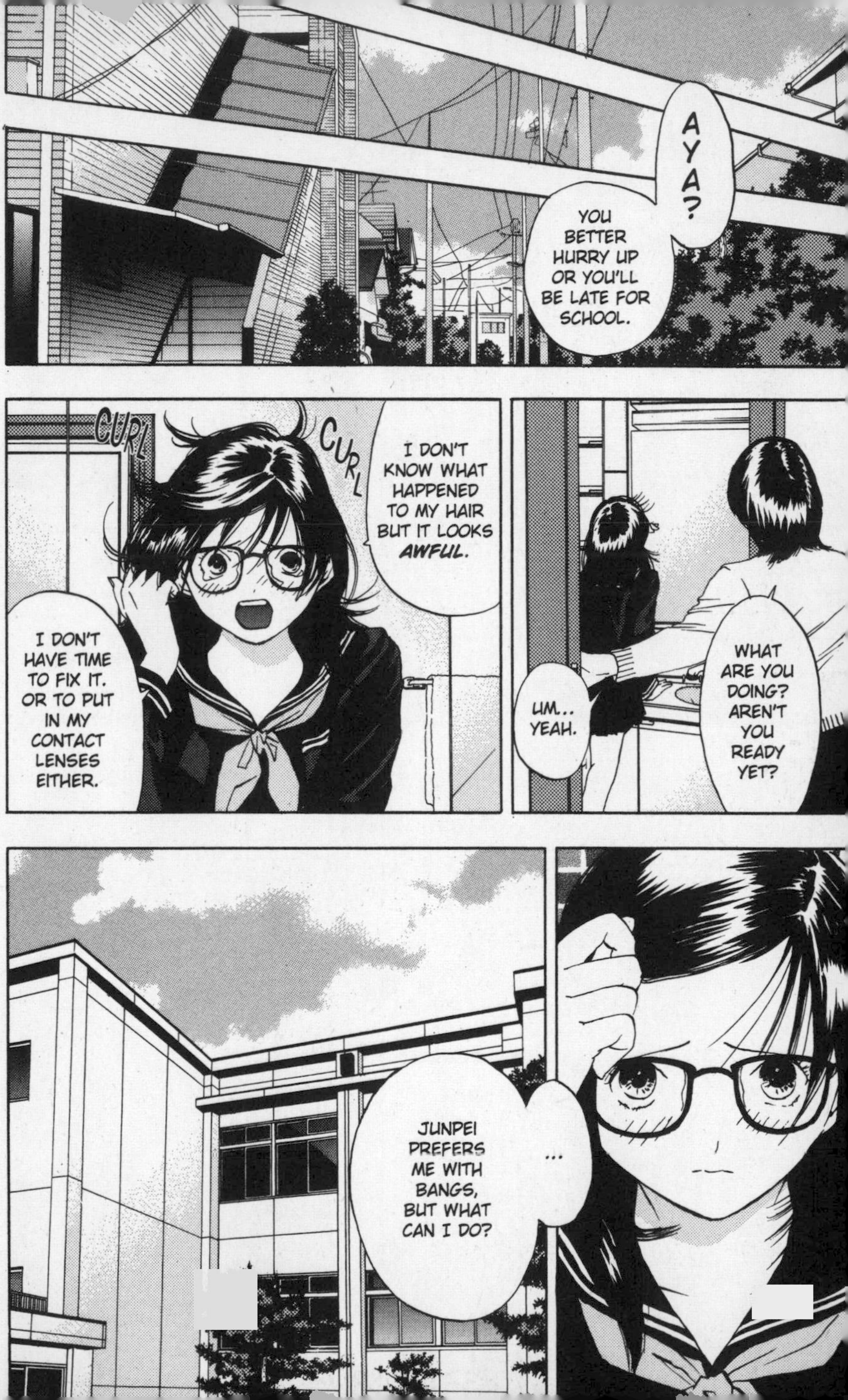
AYA?
YOU BETTER HURRY UP OR YOU'LL BE LATE FOR SCHOOL.
WHAT ARE YOU DOING? AREN'T YOU READY YET?
UM.. YEAH.
CURL
CURL
I DON'T KNOW WHAT HAPPENED TO MY HAIR BUT IT LOOKS **AWFUL**.
I DON'T HAVE TIME TO FIX IT. OR TO PUT IN MY CONTACT LENSES EITHER.
...
JUNPEI PREFERS ME WITH BANGS, BUT WHAT CAN I DO?

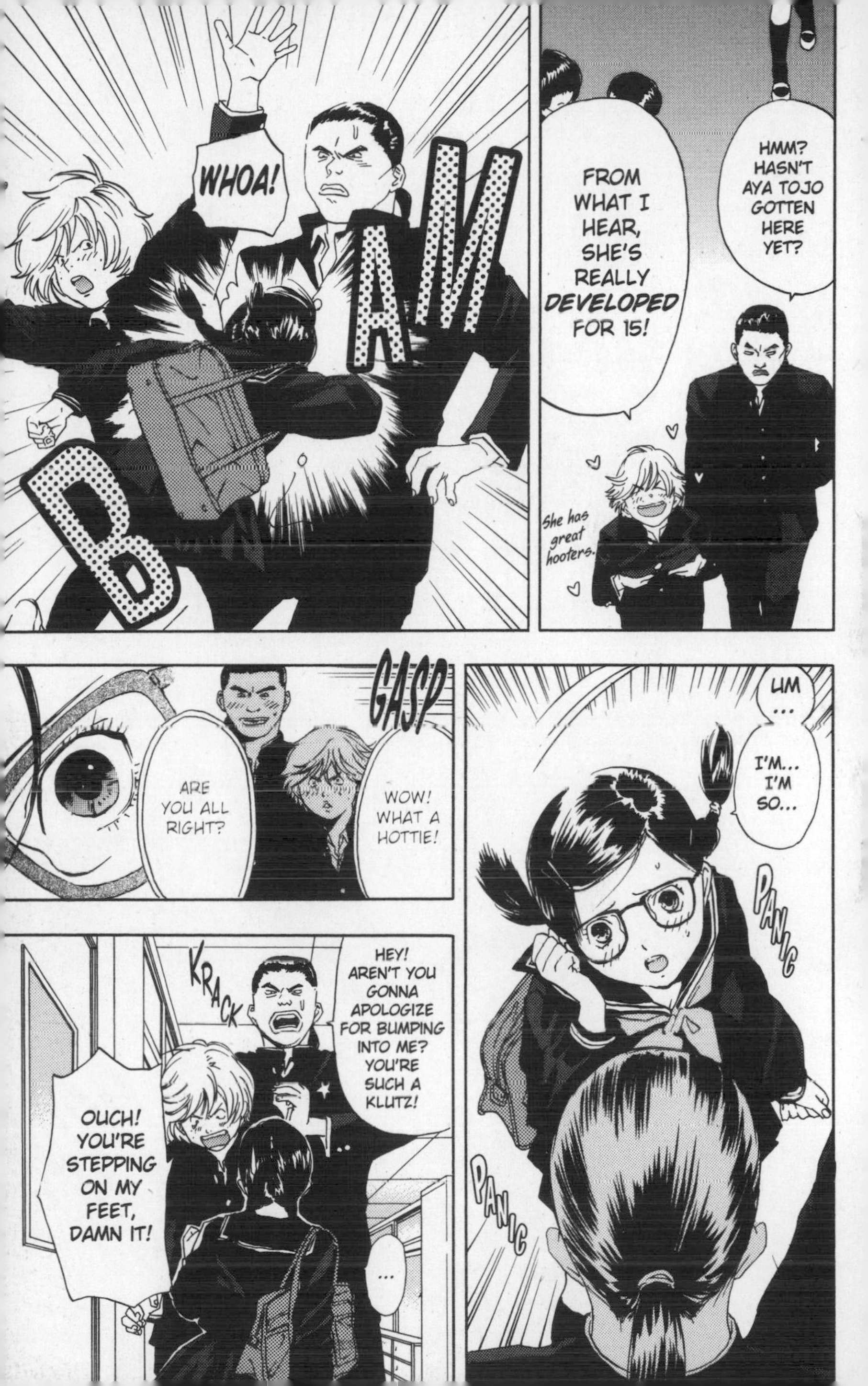
HMM? HASN'T AYA TOJO GOTTEN HERE YET?
FROM WHAT I HEAR, SHE'S REALLY DEVELOPED FOR 15!
She has great hooters.
BAM
WHOA!
UM...
I'M... I'M SO...
PANIC
PANIC
GASP
WOW! WHAT A HOTTIE!
ARE YOU ALL RIGHT?
HEY! AREN'T YOU GONNA APOLOGIZE FOR BUMPING INTO ME? YOU'RE SUCH A KLUTZ!
KRACK
OUCH! YOU'RE STEPPING ON MY FEET, DAMN IT!
...

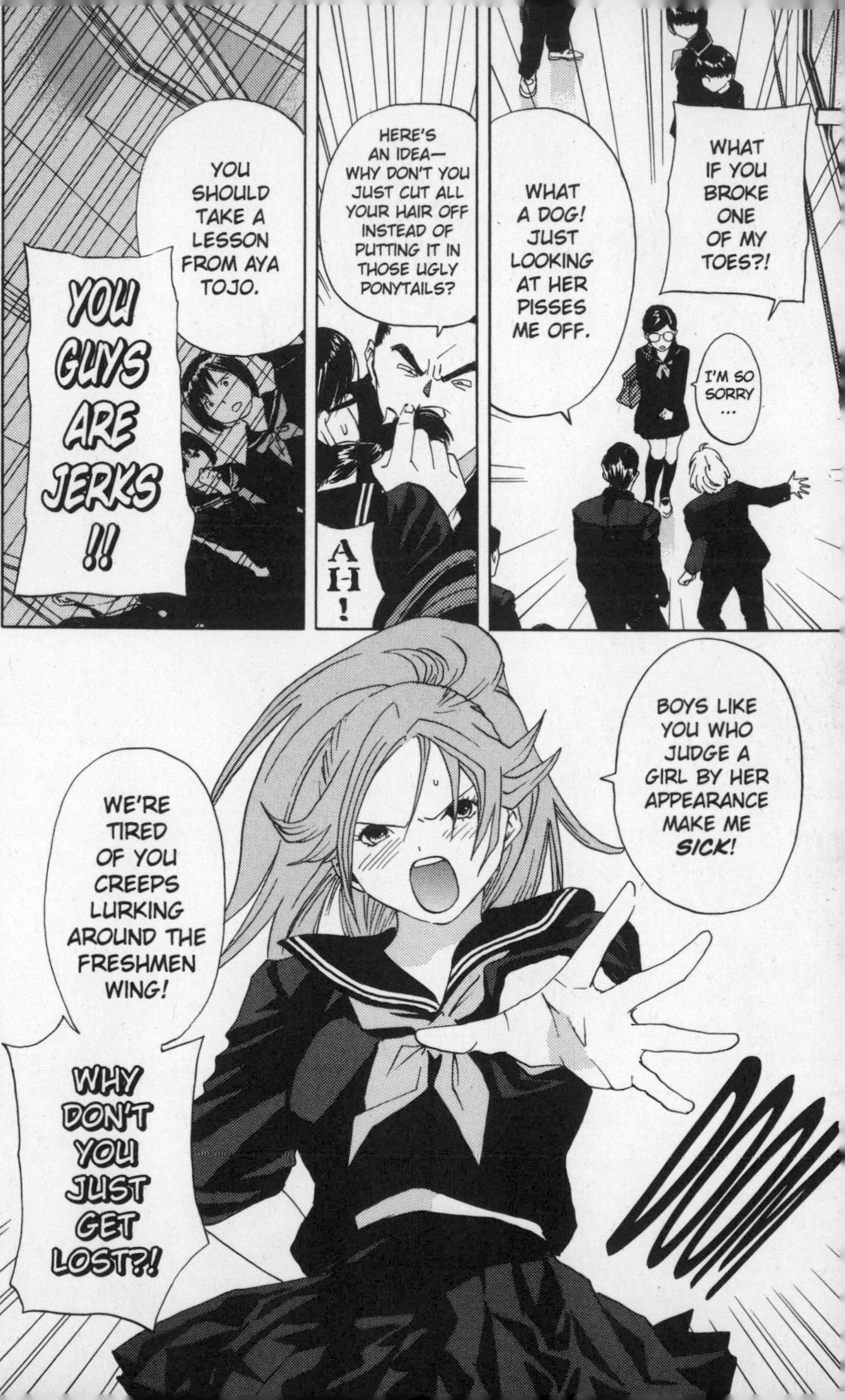
WHAT IF YOU BROKE ONE OF MY TOES?!
WHAT A DOG! JUST LOOKING AT HER PISSES ME OFF.
I'M SO SORRY ...
HERE'S AN IDEA— WHY DON'T YOU JUST CUT ALL YOUR HAIR OFF INSTEAD OF PUTTING IT IN THOSE UGLY PONYTAILS?
AH!
YOU SHOULD TAKE A LESSON FROM AYA TOJO.
YOU GUYS ARE JERKS!!
BOYS LIKE YOU WHO JUDGE A GIRL BY HER APPEARANCE MAKE ME SICK!
WE'RE TIRED OF YOU CREEPS LURKING AROUND THE FRESHMEN WING!
WHY DON'T YOU JUST GET LOST?!

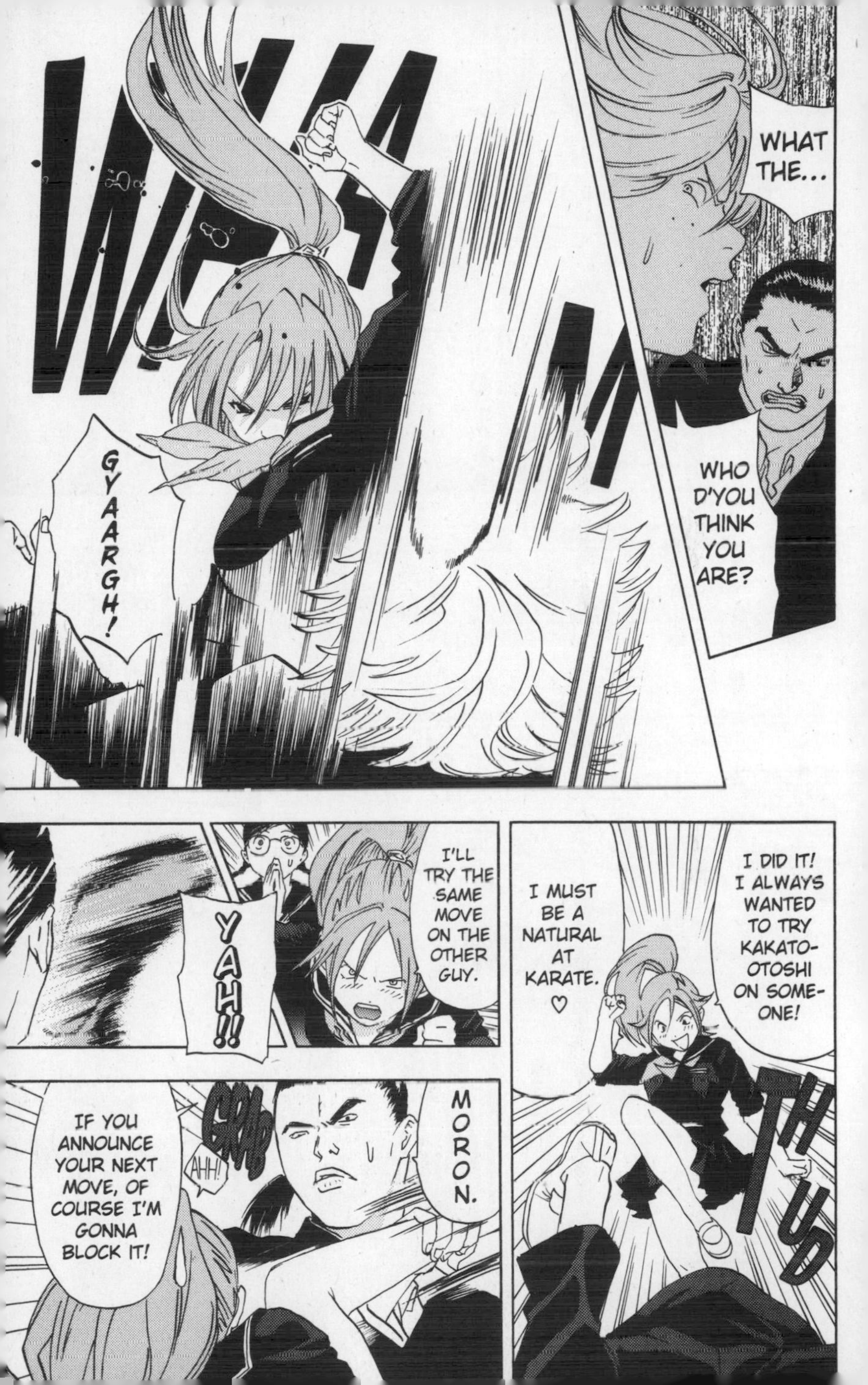
WHAT THE...
WHO D'YOU THINK YOU ARE?
WHAM
GYAARGH!
I DID IT! I ALWAYS WANTED TO TRY KAKATO-OTOSHI ON SOME-ONE!
I MUST BE A NATURAL AT KARATE. ♡
THUD
I'LL TRY THE SAME MOVE ON THE OTHER GUY.
YAH!!
MORON.
GRAB
AHH!
IF YOU ANNOUNCE YOUR NEXT MOVE, OF COURSE I'M GONNA BLOCK IT!

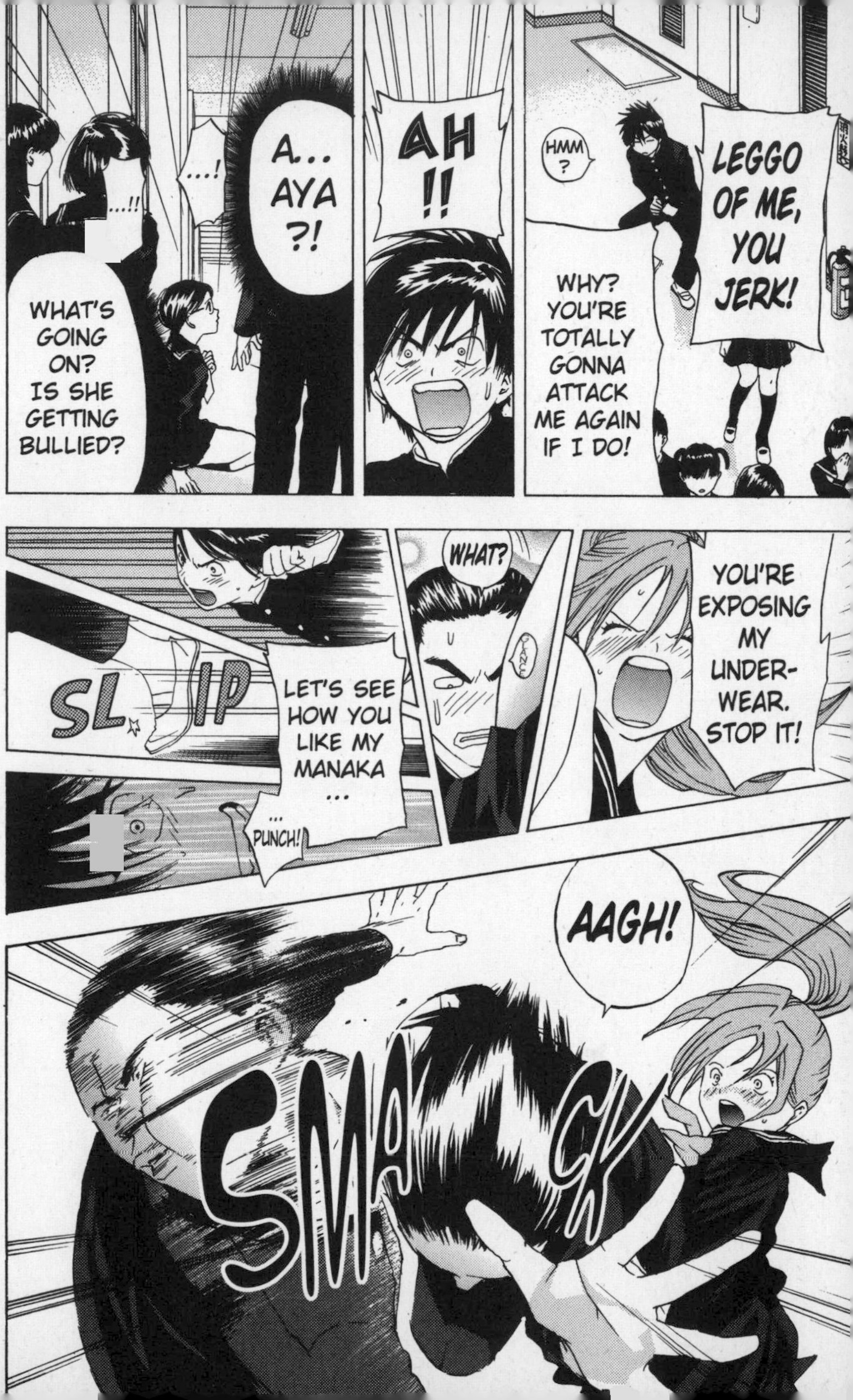
LEGGO OF ME, YOU JERK!
HMM ?
WHY? YOU'RE TOTALLY GONNA ATTACK ME AGAIN IF I DO!
AH !!
A... AYA ?!
...!
...!!
WHAT'S GOING ON? IS SHE GETTING BULLIED?
YOU'RE EXPOSING MY UNDER-WEAR. STOP IT!
WHAT?
GLANCE
LET'S SEE HOW YOU LIKE MY MANAKA ...
... PUNCH!
SL IP
AAGH!
SMACK

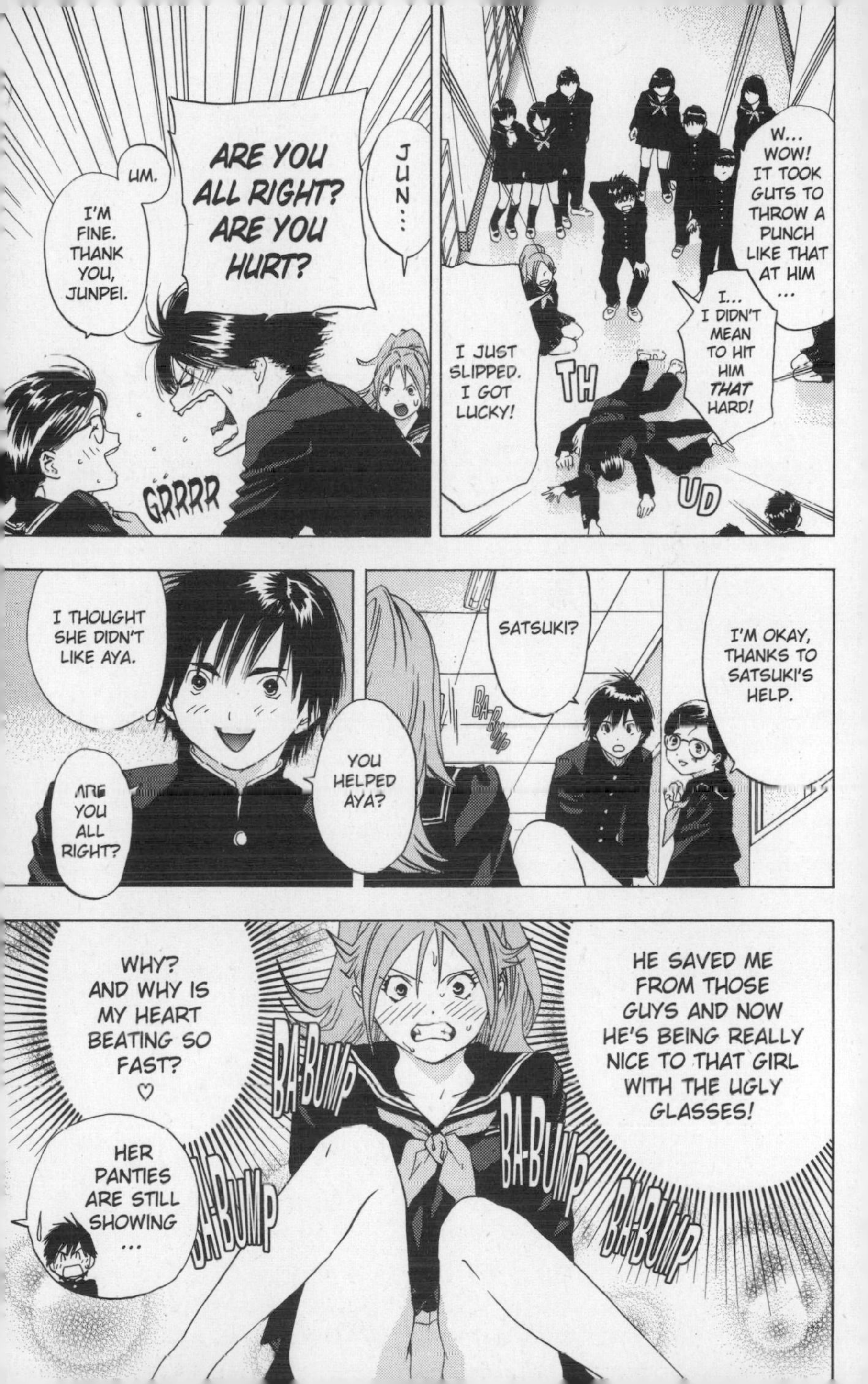
W... WOW! IT TOOK GUTS TO THROW A PUNCH LIKE THAT AT HIM...
I... I DIDN'T MEAN TO HIT HIM *THAT* HARD!
I JUST SLIPPED. I GOT LUCKY!
TH
UD
JUN...
ARE YOU ALL RIGHT? ARE YOU HURT?
UM.
I'M FINE. THANK YOU, JUNPEI.
GRRRR
I'M OKAY, THANKS TO SATSUKI'S HELP.
SATSUKI?
BA-BUMP
YOU HELPED AYA?
I THOUGHT SHE DIDN'T LIKE AYA.
ARE YOU ALL RIGHT?
HE SAVED ME FROM THOSE GUYS AND NOW HE'S BEING REALLY NICE TO THAT GIRL WITH THE UGLY GLASSES!
WHY? AND WHY IS MY HEART BEATING SO FAST? ♡
BA-BUMP
BA-BUMP
BA-BUMP
BA-BUMP
BA-BUMP
HER PANTIES ARE STILL SHOWING...

FAN SERVICE
戻る
進む
中止
更新
ホーム
自動入力
プリント
メール
アドレス
移動

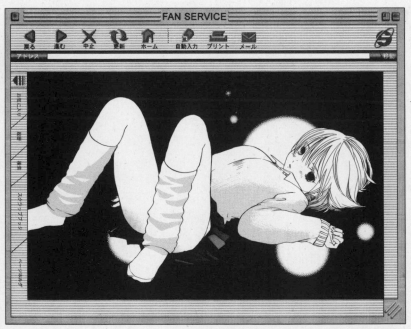

NOTE: THIS IS A COMPOSITE PHOTOGRAPH.

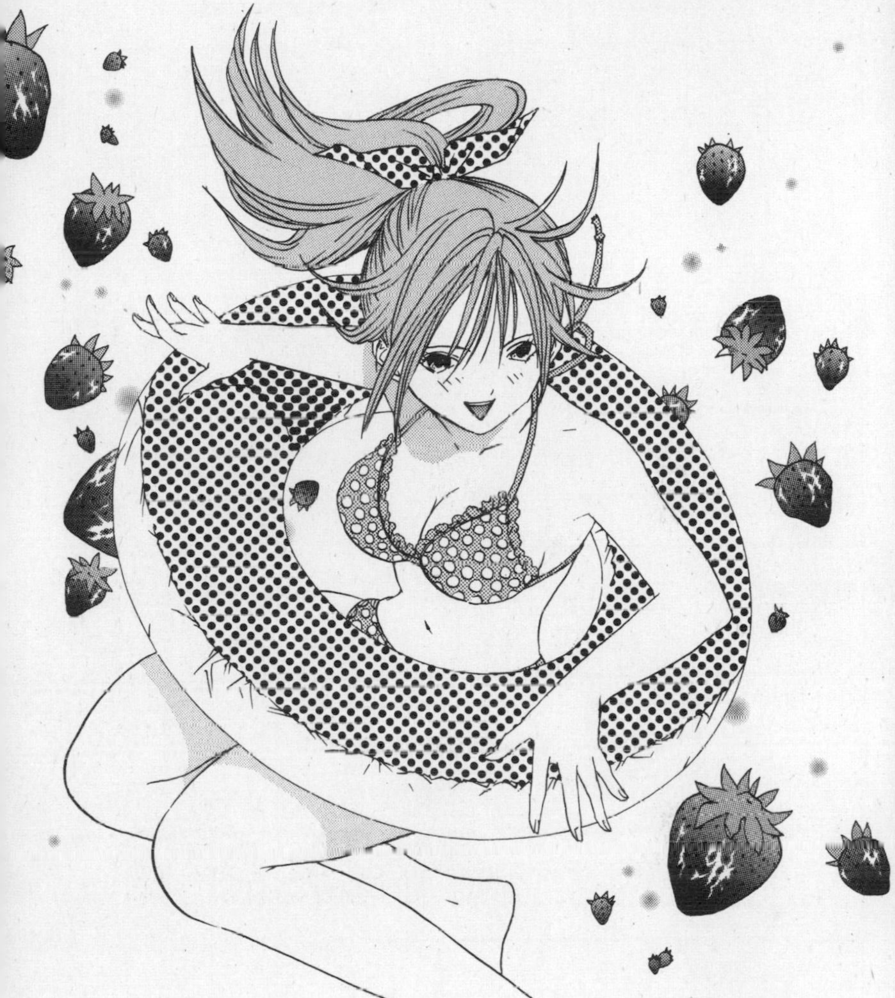

CRUSH 21:
A BETTER MAN THAN MANAKA

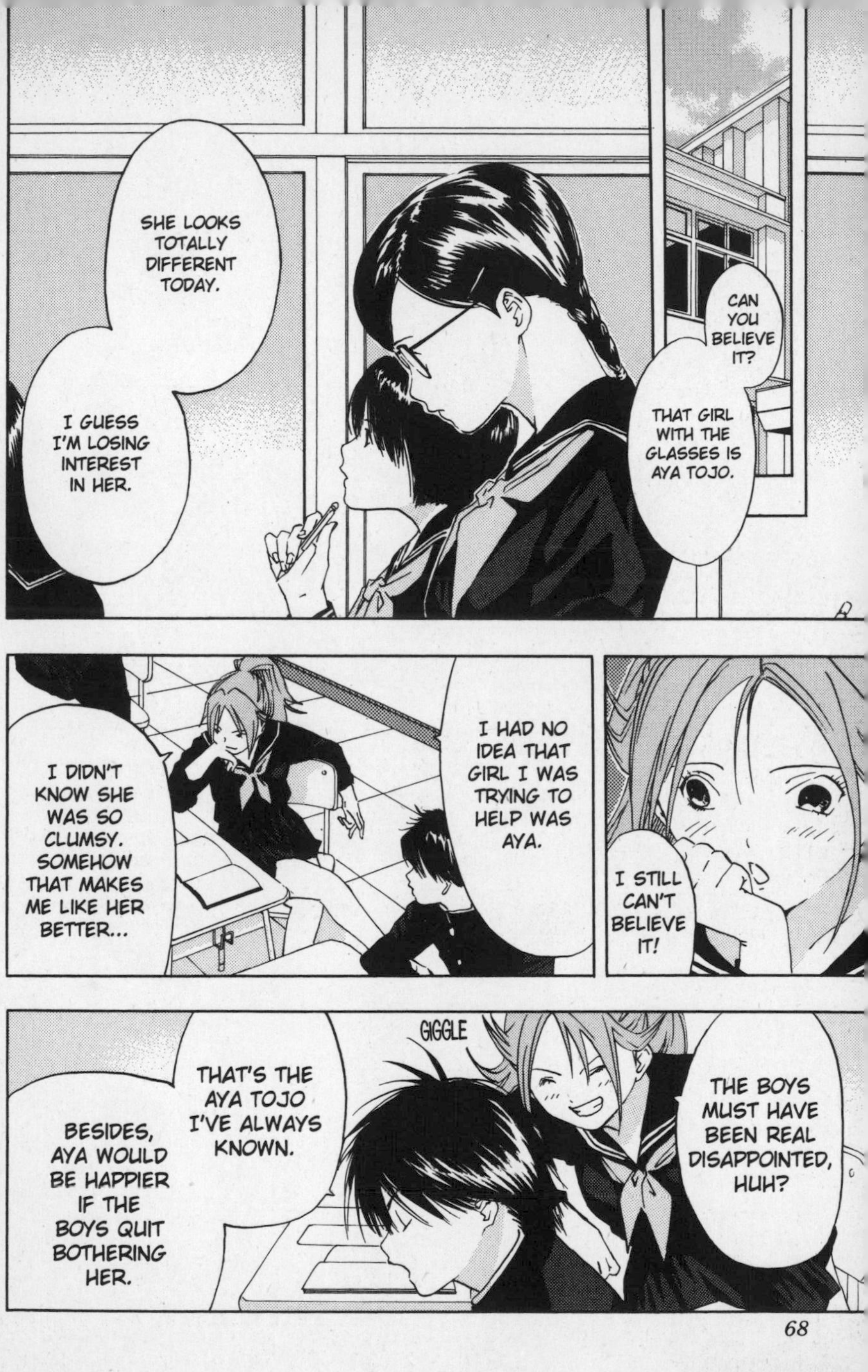
CAN YOU BELIEVE IT?
THAT GIRL WITH THE GLASSES IS AYA TOJO.
SHE LOOKS TOTALLY DIFFERENT TODAY.
I GUESS I'M LOSING INTEREST IN HER.
I STILL CAN'T BELIEVE IT!
I HAD NO IDEA THAT GIRL I WAS TRYING TO HELP WAS AYA.
I DIDN'T KNOW SHE WAS SO CLUMSY. SOMEHOW THAT MAKES ME LIKE HER BETTER...
THE BOYS MUST HAVE BEEN REAL DISAPPOINTED, HUH?
GIGGLE
THAT'S THE AYA TOJO I'VE ALWAYS KNOWN.
BESIDES, AYA WOULD BE HAPPIER IF THE BOYS QUIT BOTHERING HER.

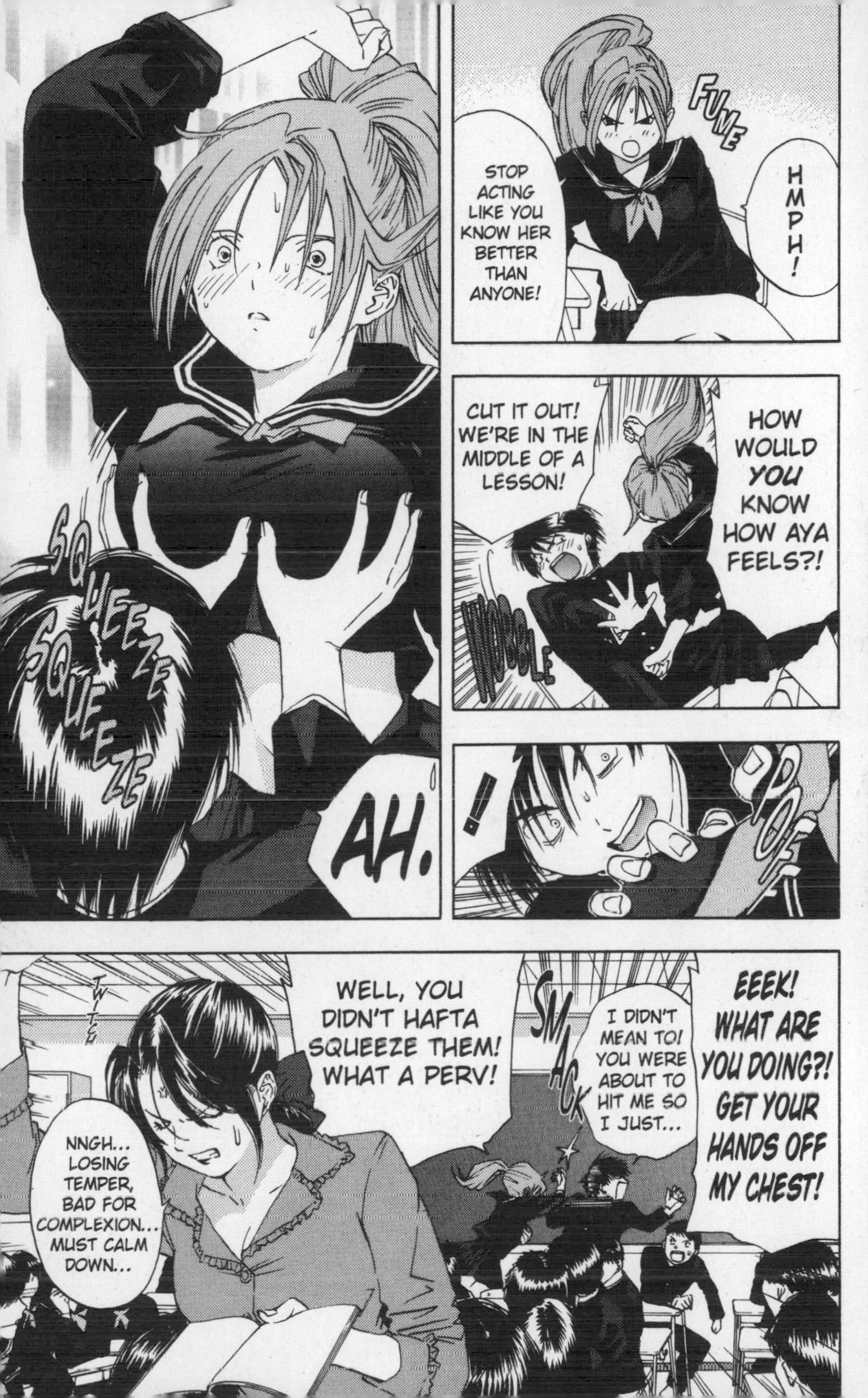
FUME
HMPH!
STOP ACTING LIKE YOU KNOW HER BETTER THAN ANYONE!
HOW WOULD YOU KNOW HOW AYA FEELS?!
CUT IT OUT! WE'RE IN THE MIDDLE OF A LESSON!
WOBBLE
POF
!
AH.
SQUEEZE
SQUEEZE
EEEK! WHAT ARE YOU DOING?! GET YOUR HANDS OFF MY CHEST!
I DIDN'T MEAN TO! YOU WERE ABOUT TO HIT ME SO I JUST...
SMACK
WELL, YOU DIDN'T HAFTA SQUEEZE THEM! WHAT A PERV!
TWITCH
NNGH... LOSING TEMPER, BAD FOR COMPLEXION... MUST CALM DOWN...

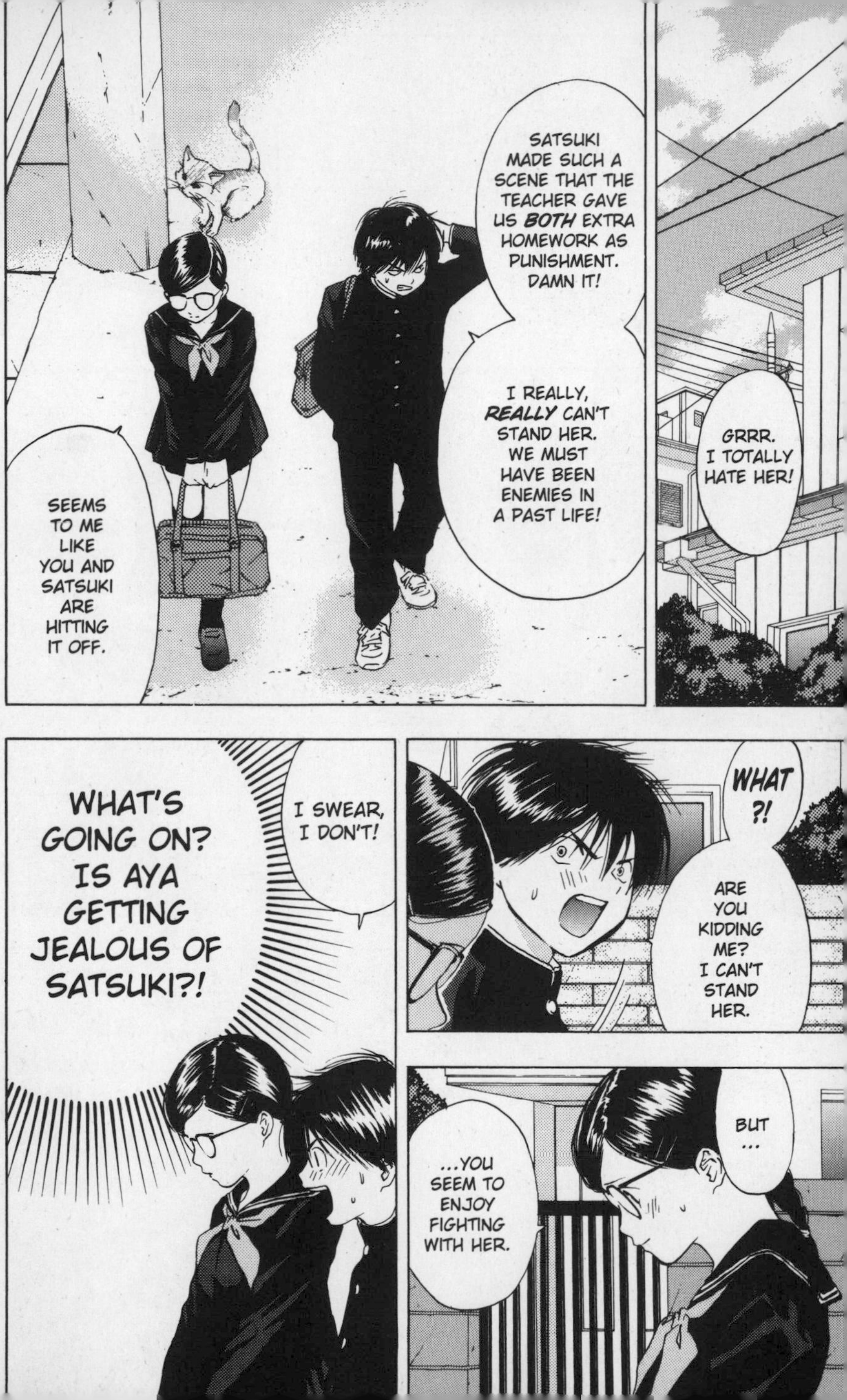
GRRR. I TOTALLY HATE HER!
SATSUKI MADE SUCH A SCENE THAT THE TEACHER GAVE US BOTH EXTRA HOMEWORK AS PUNISHMENT. DAMN IT!
I REALLY, REALLY CAN'T STAND HER. WE MUST HAVE BEEN ENEMIES IN A PAST LIFE!
SEEMS TO ME LIKE YOU AND SATSUKI ARE HITTING IT OFF.
WHAT ?!
ARE YOU KIDDING ME? I CAN'T STAND HER.
BUT ...
...YOU SEEM TO ENJOY FIGHTING WITH HER.
I SWEAR, I DON'T!
WHAT'S GOING ON? IS AYA GETTING JEALOUS OF SATSUKI?!

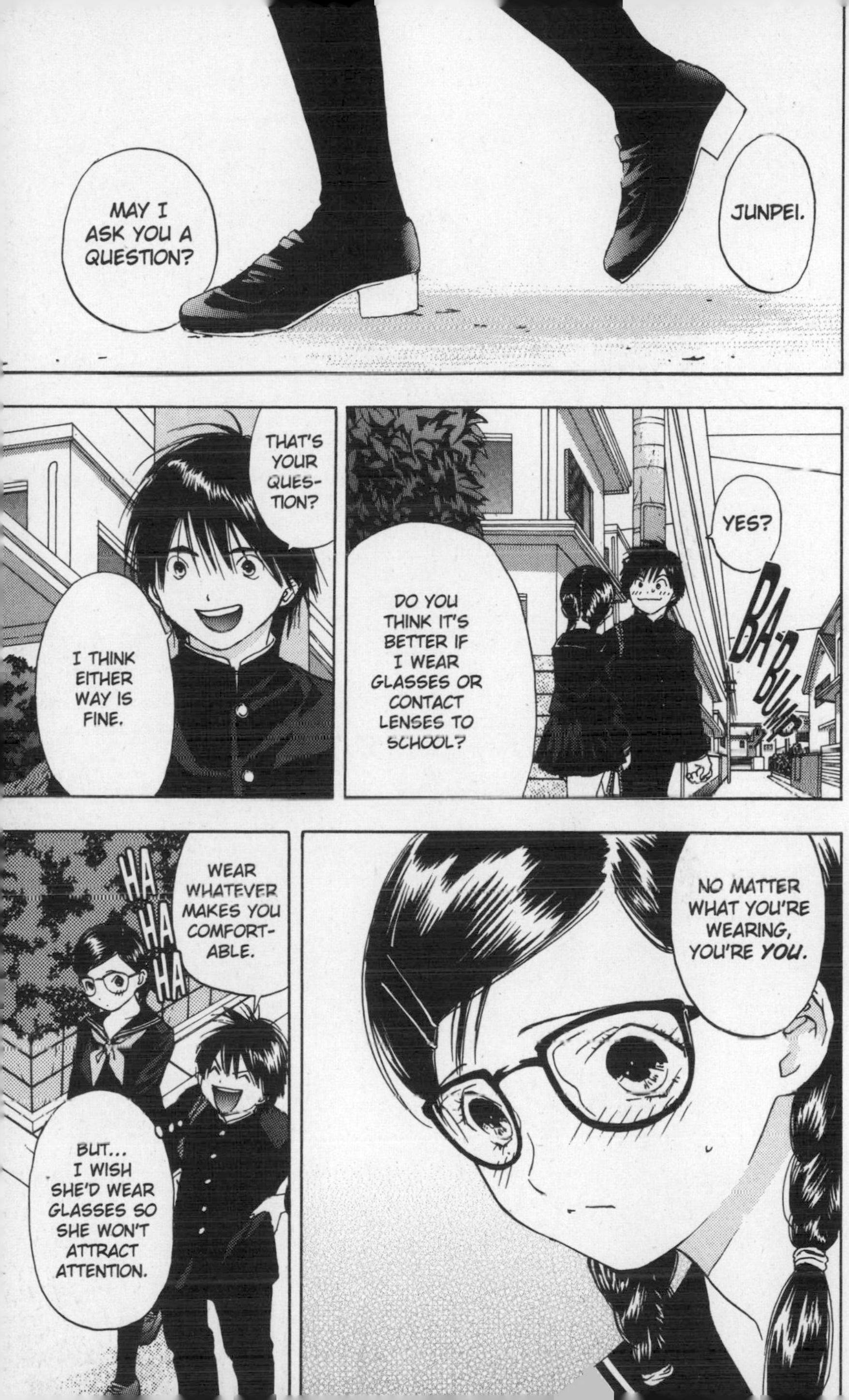
JUNPEI.
MAY I ASK YOU A QUESTION?
YES?
BA-BUMP
DO YOU THINK IT'S BETTER IF I WEAR GLASSES OR CONTACT LENSES TO SCHOOL?
THAT'S YOUR QUES-TION?
I THINK EITHER WAY IS FINE.
NO MATTER WHAT YOU'RE WEARING, YOU'RE *YOU*.
HA HA HA
WEAR WHATEVER MAKES YOU COMFORT-ABLE.
BUT... I WISH SHE'D WEAR GLASSES SO SHE WON'T ATTRACT ATTENTION.

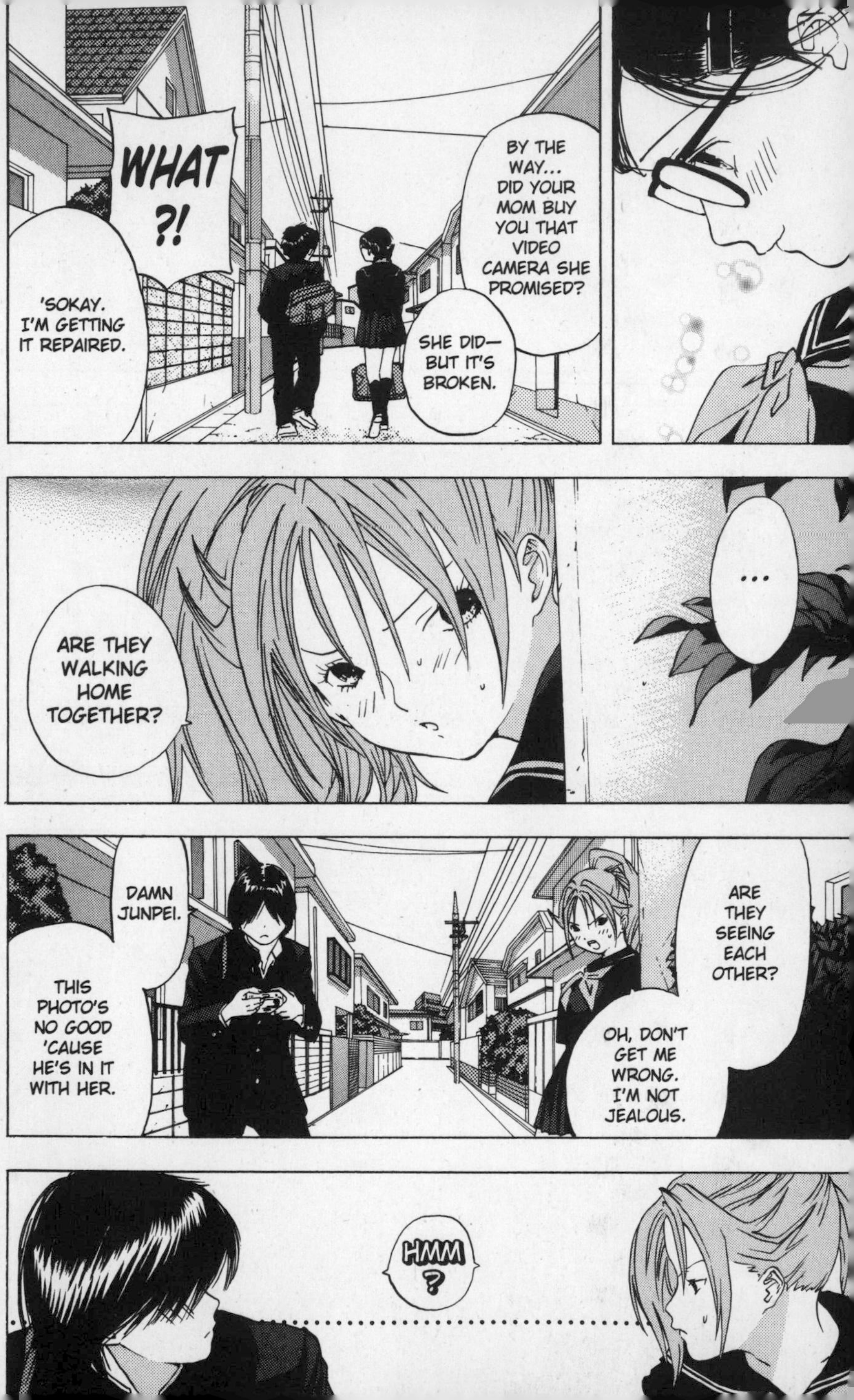
BY THE WAY... DID YOUR MOM BUY YOU THAT VIDEO CAMERA SHE PROMISED?
SHE DID— BUT IT'S BROKEN.
WHAT ?!
'SOKAY. I'M GETTING IT REPAIRED.
...
ARE THEY WALKING HOME TOGETHER?
ARE THEY SEEING EACH OTHER?
OH, DON'T GET ME WRONG. I'M NOT JEALOUS.
DAMN JUNPEI.
THIS PHOTO'S NO GOOD 'CAUSE HE'S IN IT WITH HER.
HMM ?

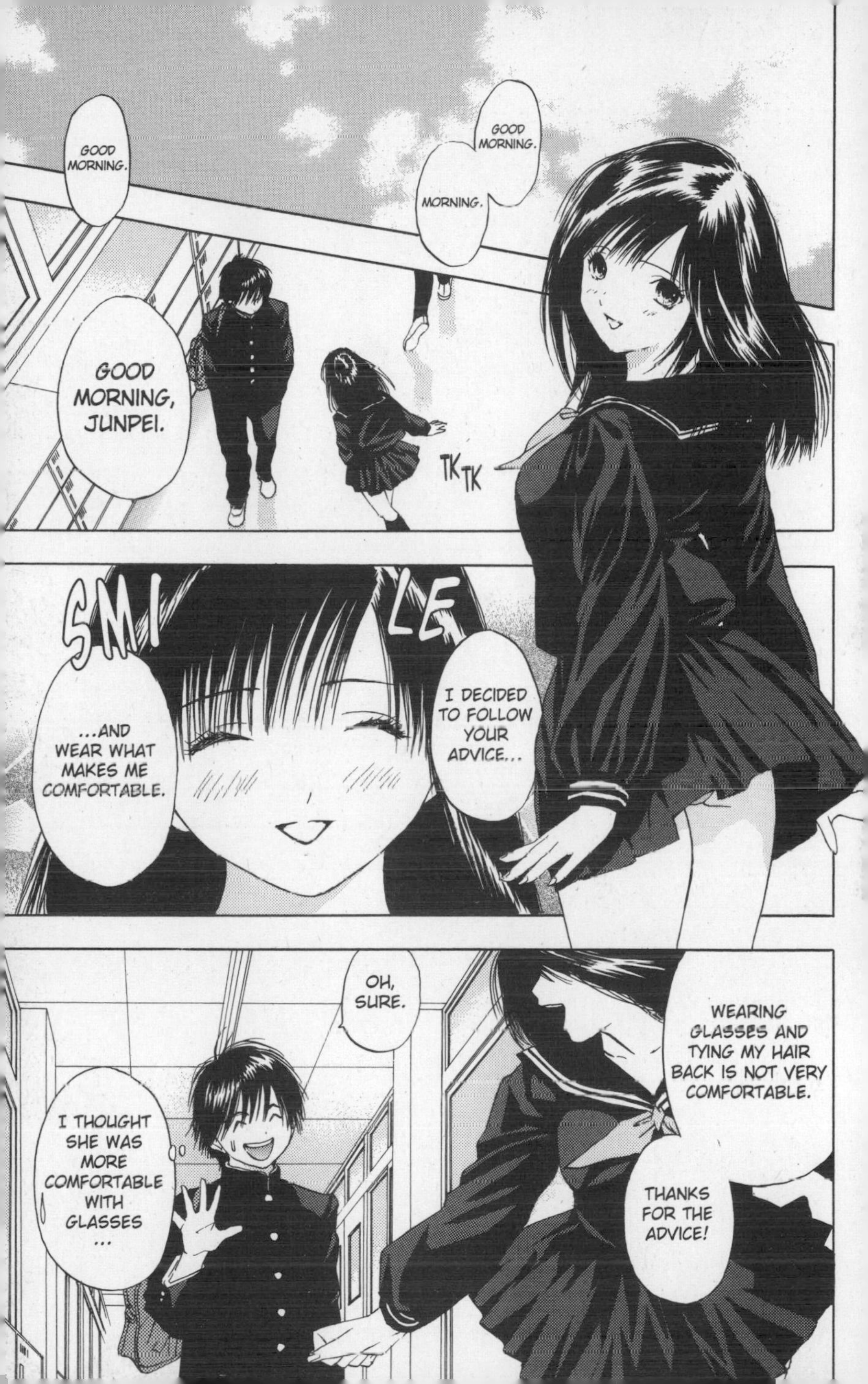
GOOD MORNING.
MORNING.
GOOD MORNING.
TK TK
GOOD MORNING, JUNPEI.
SMILE
I DECIDED TO FOLLOW YOUR ADVICE...
...AND WEAR WHAT MAKES ME COMFORTABLE.
WEARING GLASSES AND TYING MY HAIR BACK IS NOT VERY COMFORTABLE.
OH, SURE.
THANKS FOR THE ADVICE!
I THOUGHT SHE WAS MORE COMFORTABLE WITH GLASSES ...

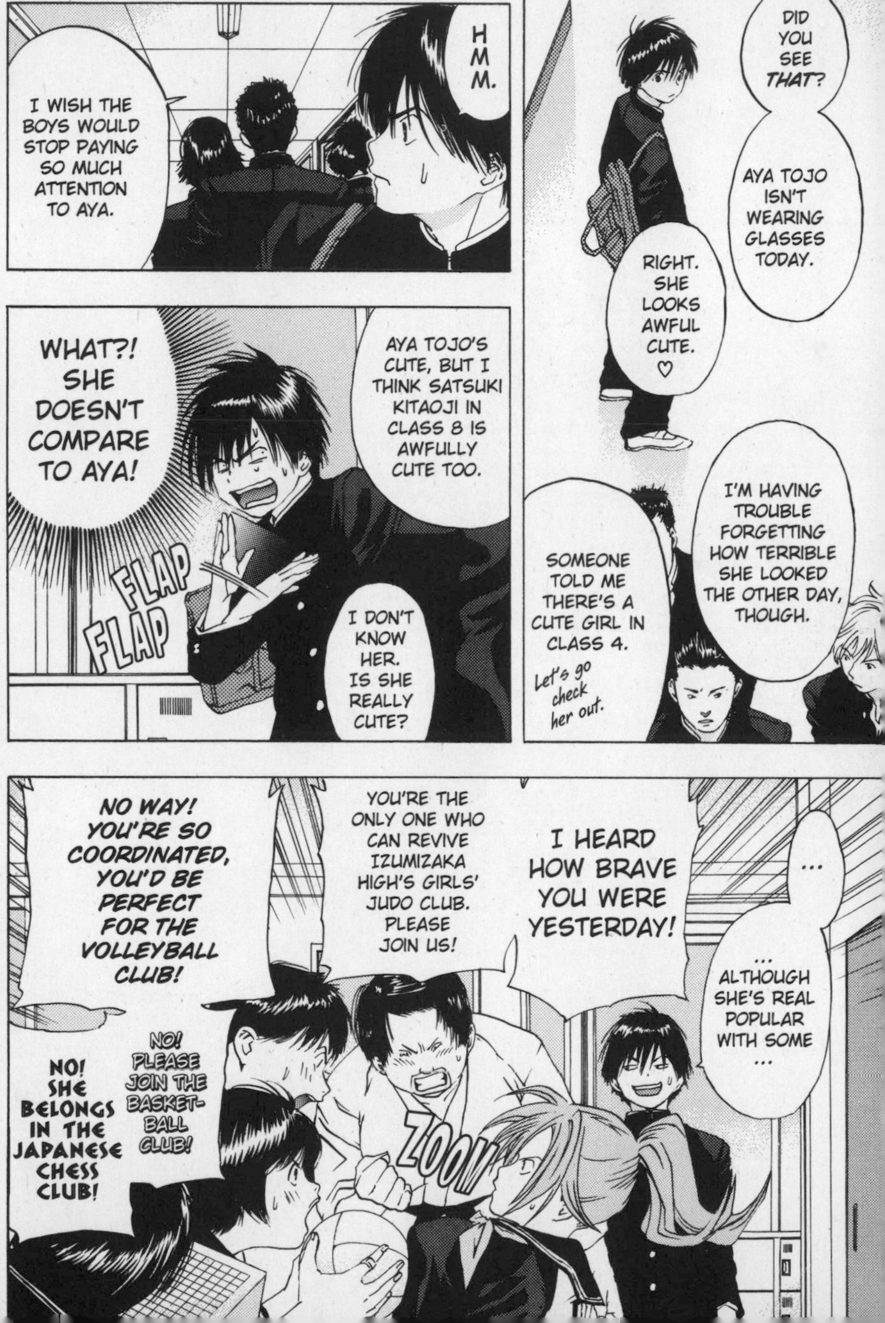
DID YOU SEE THAT?
AYA TOJO ISN'T WEARING GLASSES TODAY.
RIGHT. SHE LOOKS AWFUL CUTE. ♡
I'M HAVING TROUBLE FORGETTING HOW TERRIBLE SHE LOOKED THE OTHER DAY, THOUGH.
SOMEONE TOLD ME THERE'S A CUTE GIRL IN CLASS 4.
Let's go check her out.
HMM.
I WISH THE BOYS WOULD STOP PAYING SO MUCH ATTENTION TO AYA.
AYA TOJO'S CUTE, BUT I THINK SATSUKI KITAOJI IN CLASS 8 IS AWFULLY CUTE TOO.
WHAT?! SHE DOESN'T COMPARE TO AYA!
FLAP FLAP
I DON'T KNOW HER. IS SHE REALLY CUTE?
...
... ALTHOUGH SHE'S REAL POPULAR WITH SOME ...
I HEARD HOW BRAVE YOU WERE YESTERDAY!
YOU'RE THE ONLY ONE WHO CAN REVIVE IZUMIZAKA HIGH'S GIRLS' JUDO CLUB. PLEASE JOIN US!
NO WAY! YOU'RE SO COORDINATED, YOU'D BE PERFECT FOR THE VOLLEYBALL CLUB!
ZOOM
NO! PLEASE JOIN THE BASKET-BALL CLUB!
NO! SHE BELONGS IN THE JAPANESE CHESS CLUB!

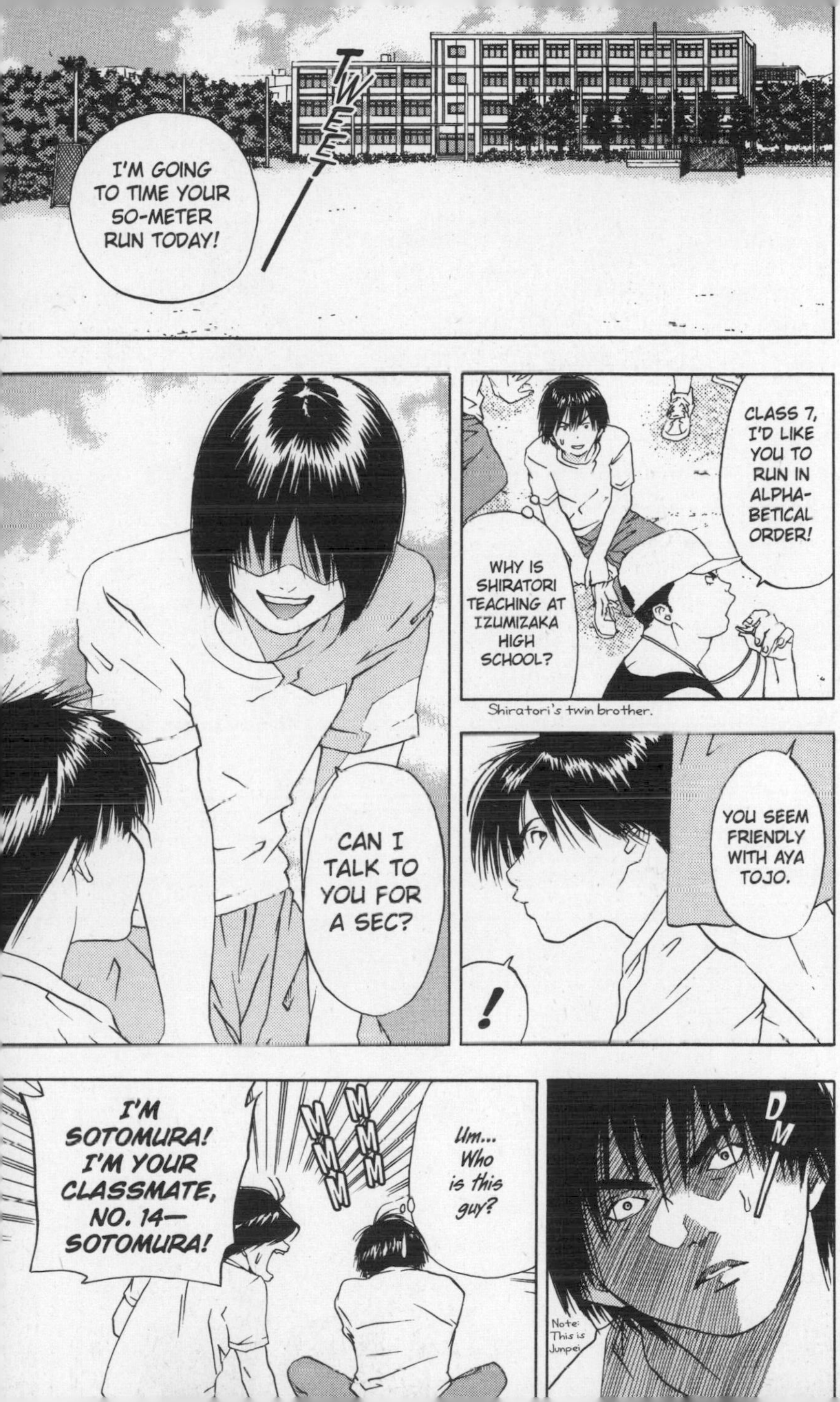
TWEET
I'M GOING TO TIME YOUR 50-METER RUN TODAY!
CLASS 7, I'D LIKE YOU TO RUN IN ALPHA-BETICAL ORDER!
WHY IS SHIRATORI TEACHING AT IZUMIZAKA HIGH SCHOOL?
Shiratori's twin brother.
YOU SEEM FRIENDLY WITH AYA TOJO.
!
CAN I TALK TO YOU FOR A SEC?
DM
Note: This is Junpei
Um... Who is this guy?
MMMM
MMMM
I'M SOTOMURA! I'M YOUR CLASSMATE, NO. 14—SOTOMURA!

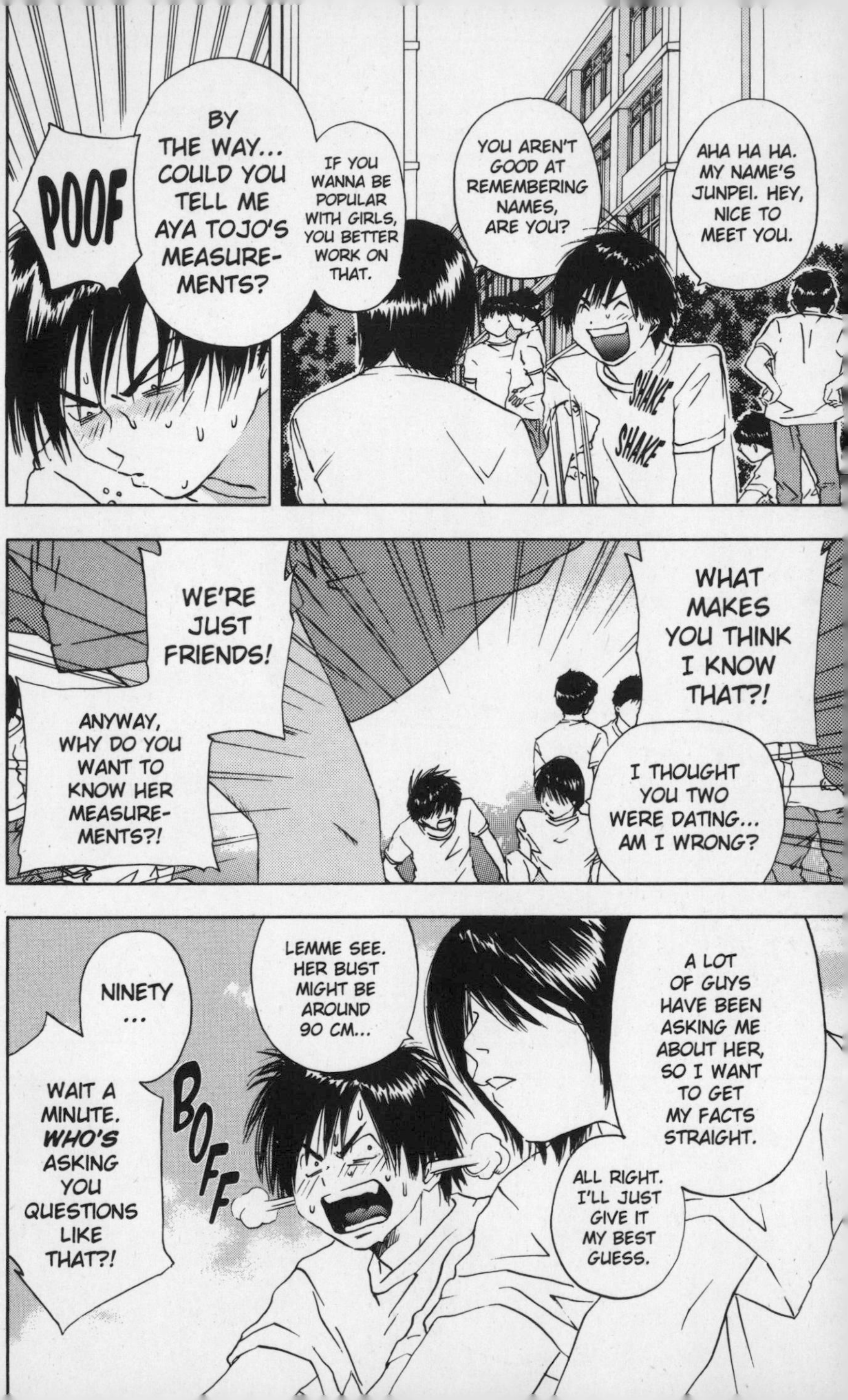
AHA HA HA. MY NAME'S JUNPEI. HEY, NICE TO MEET YOU.
SHAKE
SHAKE
YOU AREN'T GOOD AT REMEMBERING NAMES, ARE YOU?
IF YOU WANNA BE POPULAR WITH GIRLS, YOU BETTER WORK ON THAT.
BY THE WAY... COULD YOU TELL ME AYA TOJO'S MEASUREMENTS?
POOF
WHAT MAKES YOU THINK I KNOW THAT?!
I THOUGHT YOU TWO WERE DATING... AM I WRONG?
WE'RE JUST FRIENDS!
ANYWAY, WHY DO YOU WANT TO KNOW HER MEASUREMENTS?!
A LOT OF GUYS HAVE BEEN ASKING ME ABOUT HER, SO I WANT TO GET MY FACTS STRAIGHT.
ALL RIGHT. I'LL JUST GIVE IT MY BEST GUESS.
LEMME SEE. HER BUST MIGHT BE AROUND 90 CM...
NINETY ...
BOFF
WAIT A MINUTE. ***WHO'S*** ASKING YOU QUESTIONS LIKE THAT?!

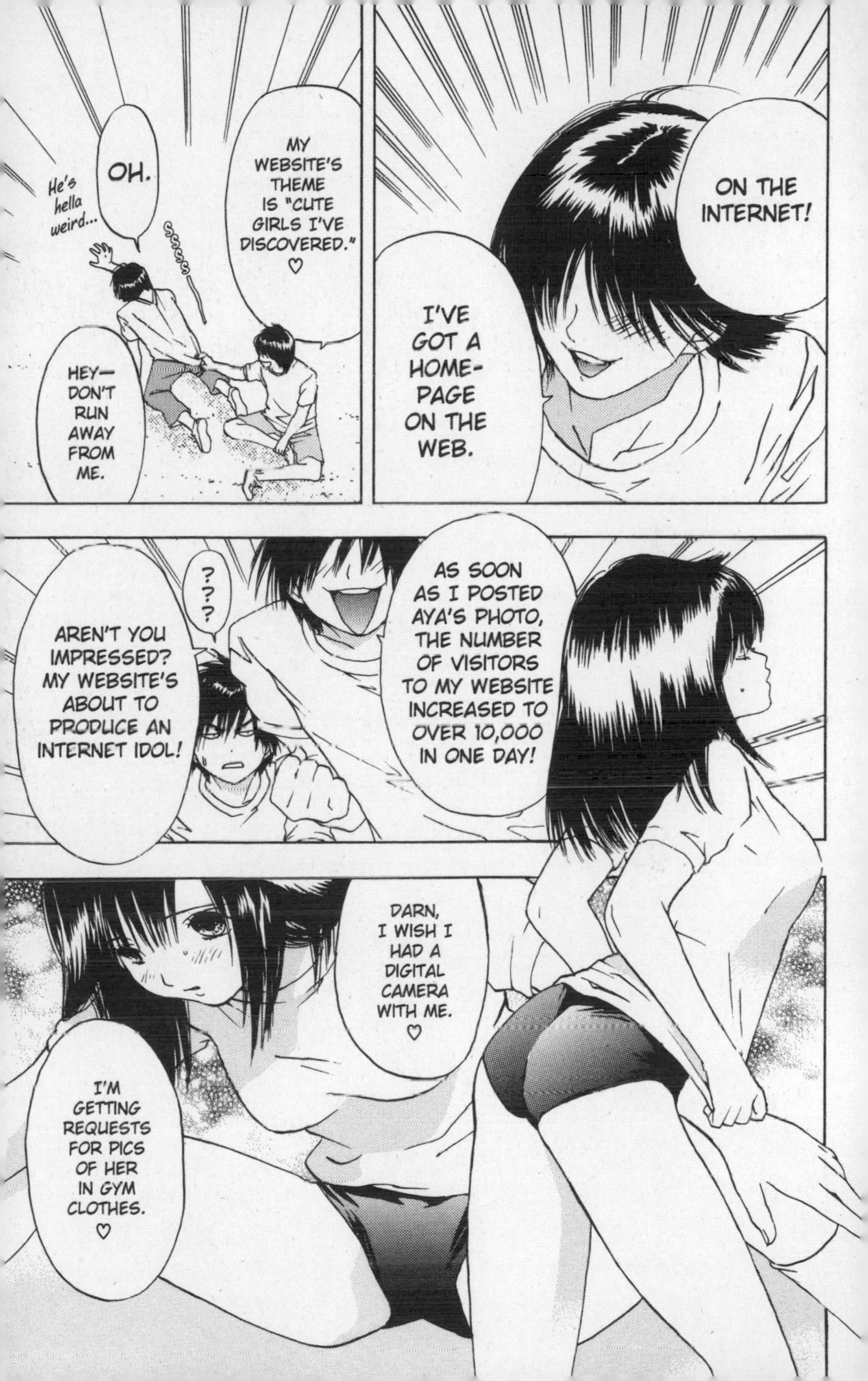
ON THE INTERNET!
I'VE GOT A HOME-PAGE ON THE WEB.
MY WEBSITE'S THEME IS "CUTE GIRLS I'VE DISCOVERED." ♡
OH.
He's hella weird...
SSSS
HEY— DON'T RUN AWAY FROM ME.
AS SOON AS I POSTED AYA'S PHOTO, THE NUMBER OF VISITORS TO MY WEBSITE INCREASED TO OVER 10,000 IN ONE DAY!
?-?-?
AREN'T YOU IMPRESSED? MY WEBSITE'S ABOUT TO PRODUCE AN INTERNET IDOL!
DARN, I WISH I HAD A DIGITAL CAMERA WITH ME. ♡
I'M GETTING REQUESTS FOR PICS OF HER IN GYM CLOTHES. ♡

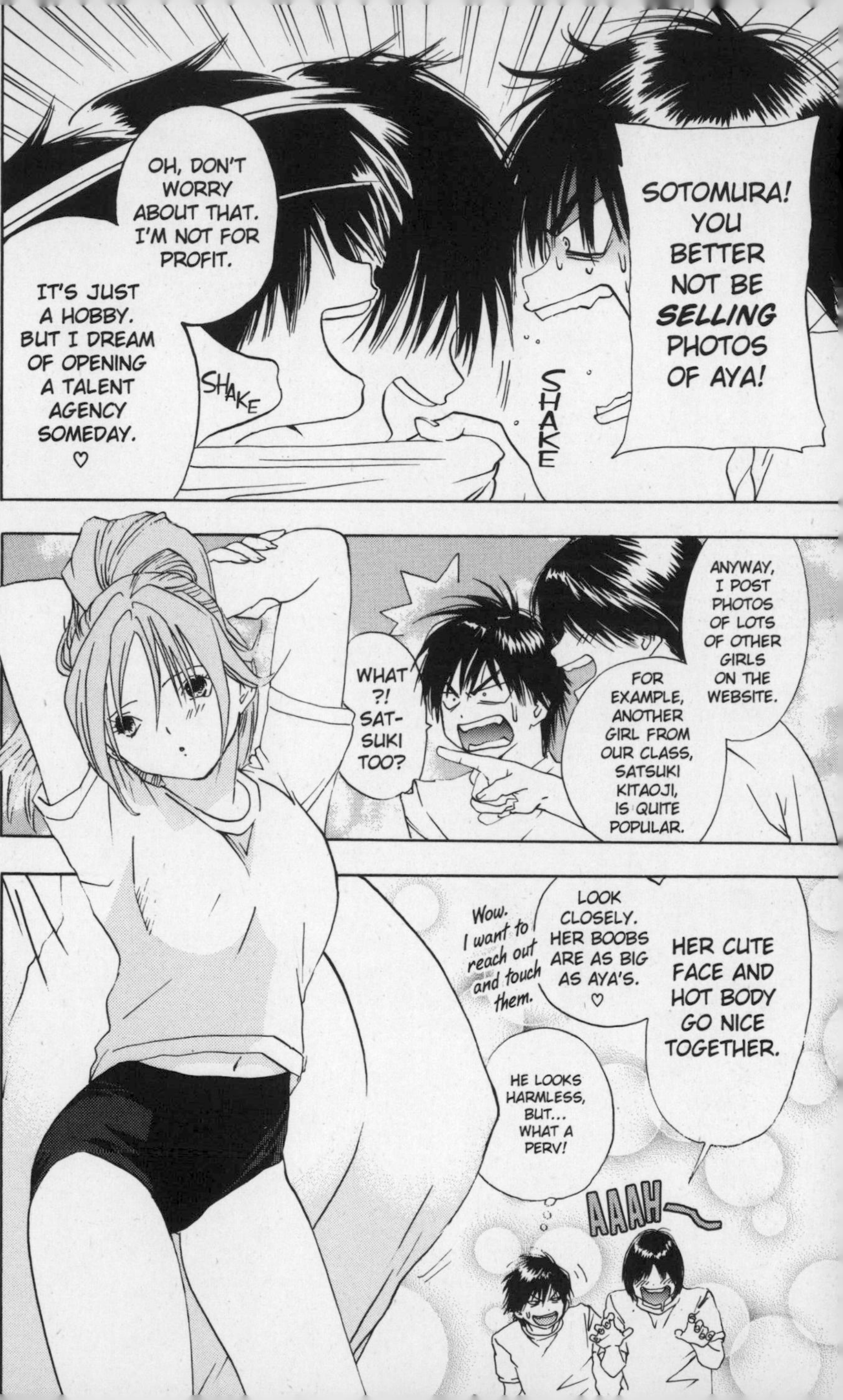
SOTOMURA! YOU BETTER NOT BE SELLING PHOTOS OF AYA!
SHAKE
SHAKE
OH, DON'T WORRY ABOUT THAT. I'M NOT FOR PROFIT.
IT'S JUST A HOBBY. BUT I DREAM OF OPENING A TALENT AGENCY SOMEDAY. ♡
ANYWAY, I POST PHOTOS OF LOTS OF OTHER GIRLS ON THE WEBSITE.
FOR EXAMPLE, ANOTHER GIRL FROM OUR CLASS, SATSUKI KITAOJI, IS QUITE POPULAR.
WHAT?! SATSUKI TOO?
HER CUTE FACE AND HOT BODY GO NICE TOGETHER.
LOOK CLOSELY. HER BOOBS ARE AS BIG AS AYA'S. ♡
Wow. I want to reach out and touch them.
HE LOOKS HARMLESS, BUT... WHAT A PERV!
AAAH~

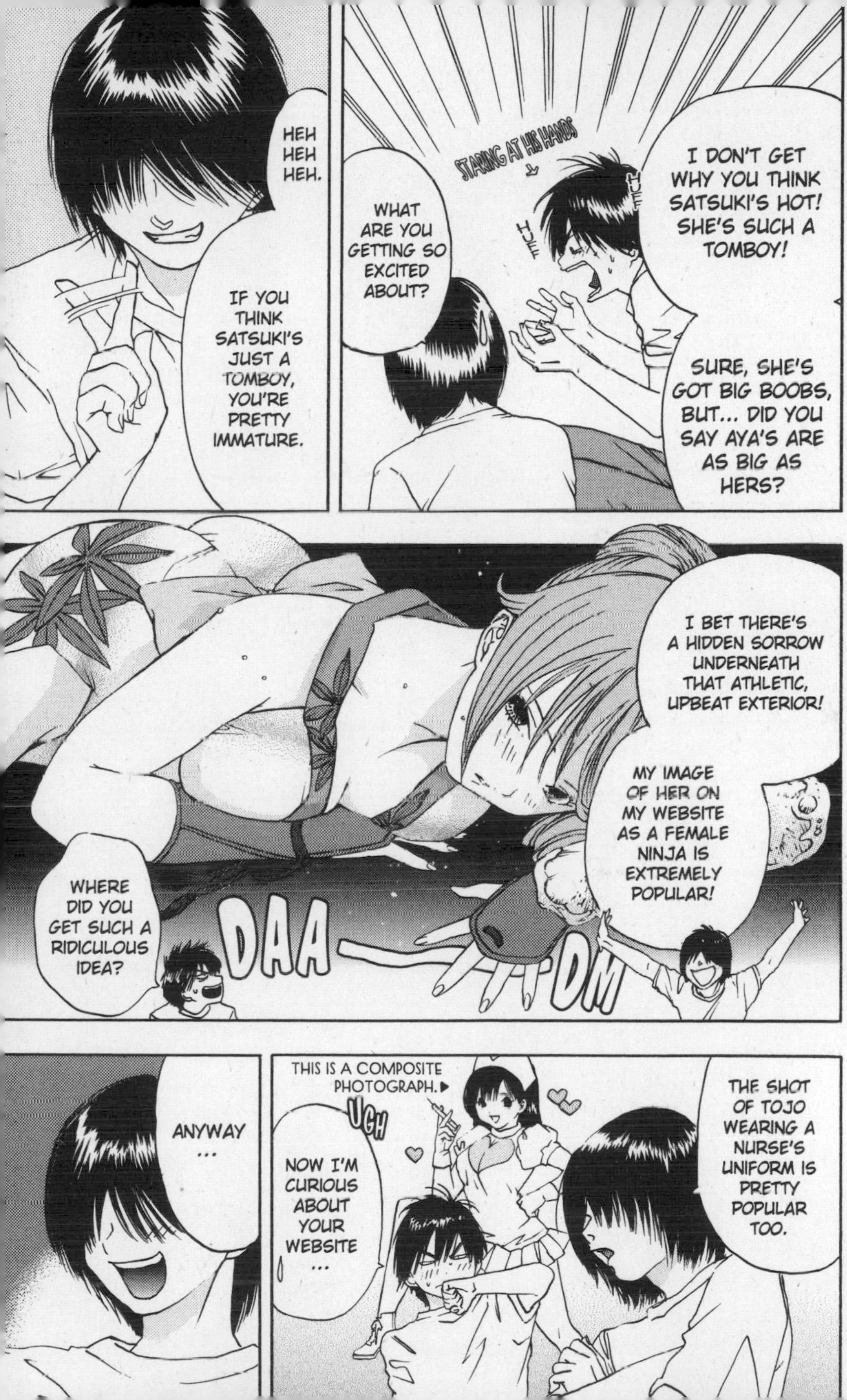
I DON'T GET WHY YOU THINK SATSUKI'S HOT! SHE'S SUCH A TOMBOY!
HUF HUF
STARING AT HIS HANDS
SURE, SHE'S GOT BIG BOOBS, BUT... DID YOU SAY AYA'S ARE AS BIG AS HERS?
WHAT ARE YOU GETTING SO EXCITED ABOUT?
HEH HEH HEH.
IF YOU THINK SATSUKI'S JUST A TOMBOY, YOU'RE PRETTY IMMATURE.
I BET THERE'S A HIDDEN SORROW UNDERNEATH THAT ATHLETIC, UPBEAT EXTERIOR!
MY IMAGE OF HER ON MY WEBSITE AS A FEMALE NINJA IS EXTREMELY POPULAR!
DAA—OM
WHERE DID YOU GET SUCH A RIDICULOUS IDEA?
THE SHOT OF TOJO WEARING A NURSE'S UNIFORM IS PRETTY POPULAR TOO.
THIS IS A COMPOSITE PHOTOGRAPH.
UGH
NOW I'M CURIOUS ABOUT YOUR WEBSITE...
ANYWAY...

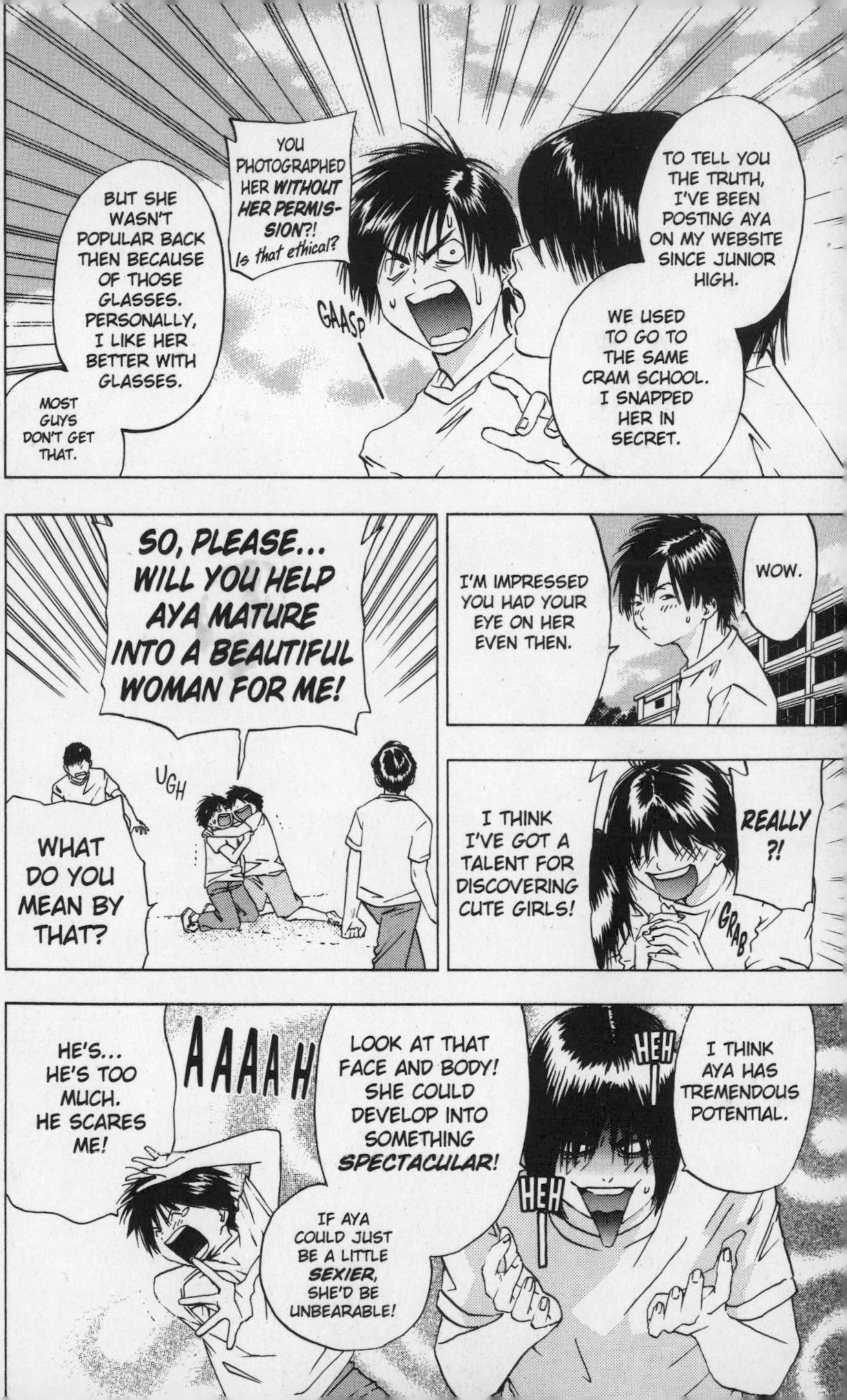
TO TELL YOU THE TRUTH, I'VE BEEN POSTING AYA ON MY WEBSITE SINCE JUNIOR HIGH.
WE USED TO GO TO THE SAME CRAM SCHOOL. I SNAPPED HER IN SECRET.
GAASP
YOU PHOTOGRAPHED HER *WITHOUT HER PERMISSION?!* *Is that ethical?*
BUT SHE WASN'T POPULAR BACK THEN BECAUSE OF THOSE GLASSES. PERSONALLY, I LIKE HER BETTER WITH GLASSES.
MOST GUYS DON'T GET THAT.
WOW.
I'M IMPRESSED YOU HAD YOUR EYE ON HER EVEN THEN.
REALLY?!
GRAB
I THINK I'VE GOT A TALENT FOR DISCOVERING CUTE GIRLS!
SO, PLEASE... WILL YOU HELP AYA MATURE INTO A BEAUTIFUL WOMAN FOR ME!
UGH
WHAT DO YOU MEAN BY THAT?
I THINK AYA HAS TREMENDOUS POTENTIAL.
HEH
HEH
LOOK AT THAT FACE AND BODY! SHE COULD DEVELOP INTO SOMETHING *SPECTACULAR!*
IF AYA COULD JUST BE A LITTLE *SEXIER,* SHE'D BE UNBEARABLE!
AAAAH
HE'S... HE'S TOO MUCH. HE SCARES ME!

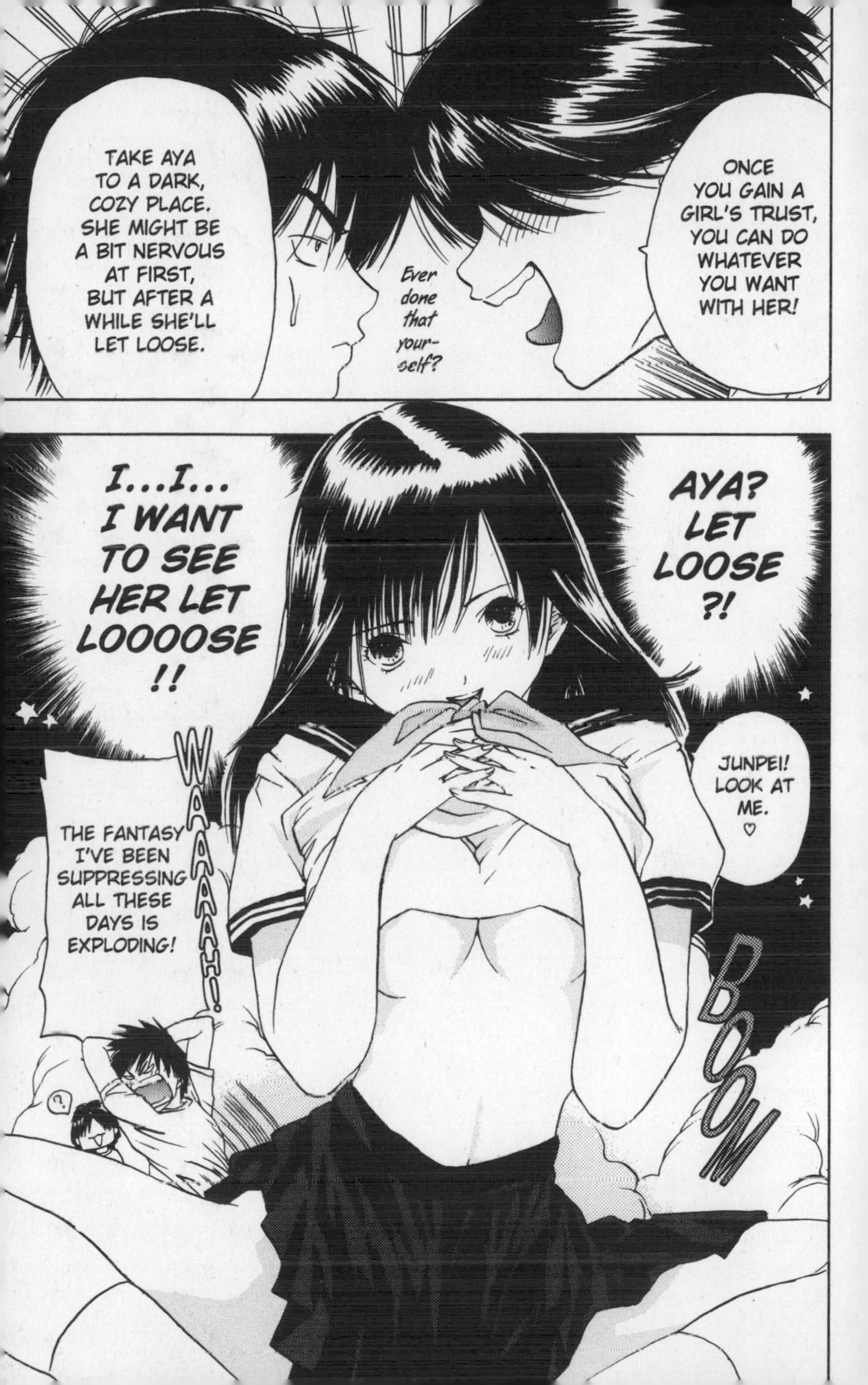
ONCE YOU GAIN A GIRL'S TRUST, YOU CAN DO WHATEVER YOU WANT WITH HER!
Ever done that your-self?
TAKE AYA TO A DARK, COZY PLACE. SHE MIGHT BE A BIT NERVOUS AT FIRST, BUT AFTER A WHILE SHE'LL LET LOOSE.
AYA? LET LOOSE ?!
I...I... I WANT TO SEE HER LET LOOOOSE !!
JUNPEI! LOOK AT ME. ♡
BOOM
WAAAAAH!
THE FANTASY I'VE BEEN SUPPRESSING ALL THESE DAYS IS EXPLODING!

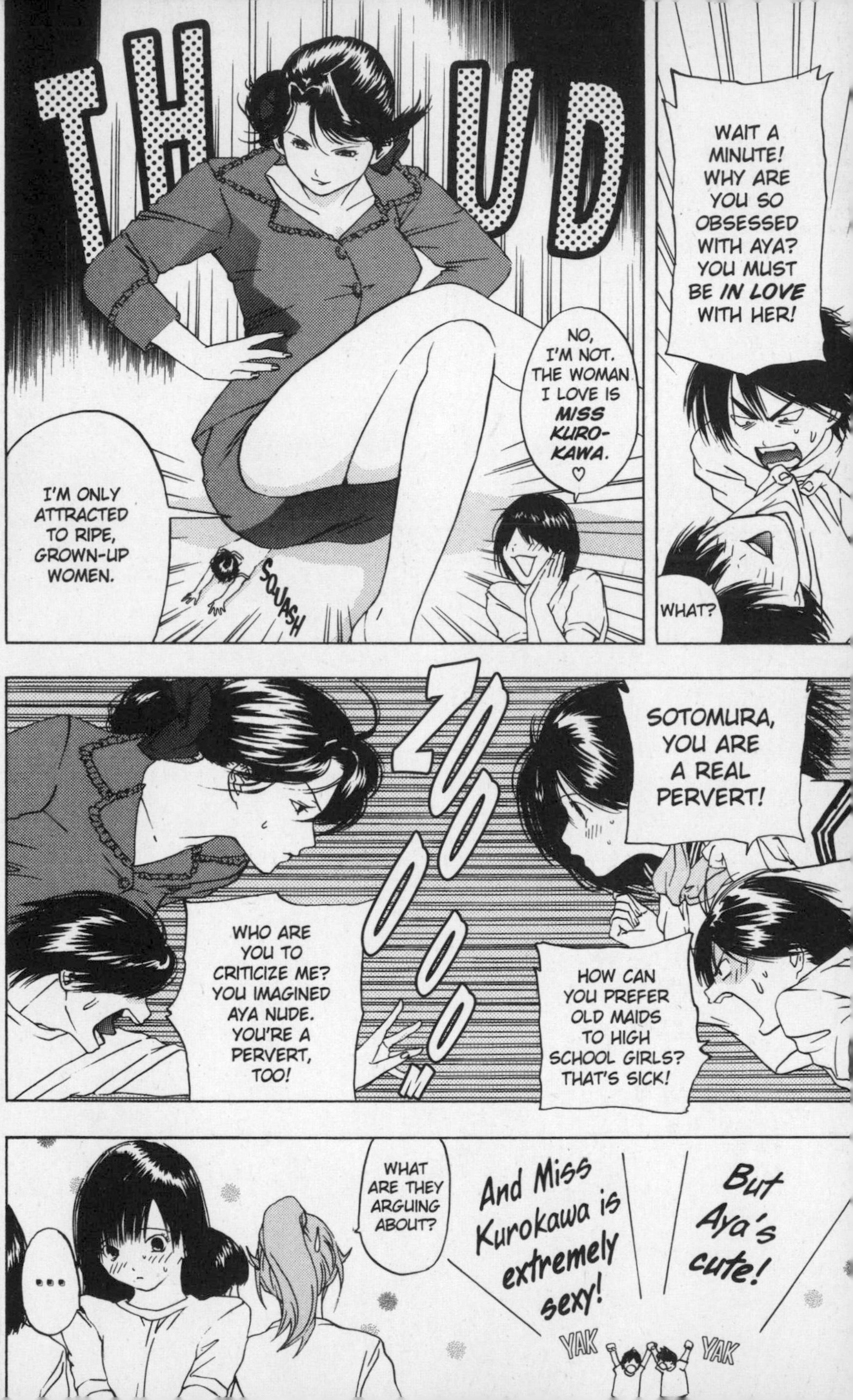
WAIT A MINUTE! WHY ARE YOU SO OBSESSED WITH AYA? YOU MUST BE *IN LOVE* WITH HER!
WHAT?
THUD
NO, I'M NOT. THE WOMAN I LOVE IS *MISS KURO-KAWA*. ♡
I'M ONLY ATTRACTED TO RIPE, GROWN-UP WOMEN.
SQUASH
SOTOMURA, YOU ARE A REAL PERVERT!
ZOOOOOM
HOW CAN YOU PREFER OLD MAIDS TO HIGH SCHOOL GIRLS? THAT'S SICK!
WHO ARE YOU TO CRITICIZE ME? YOU IMAGINED AYA NUDE. YOU'RE A PERVERT, TOO!
But Aya's cute!
And Miss Kurokawa is extremely sexy!
WHAT ARE THEY ARGUING ABOUT?
...
YAK
YAK

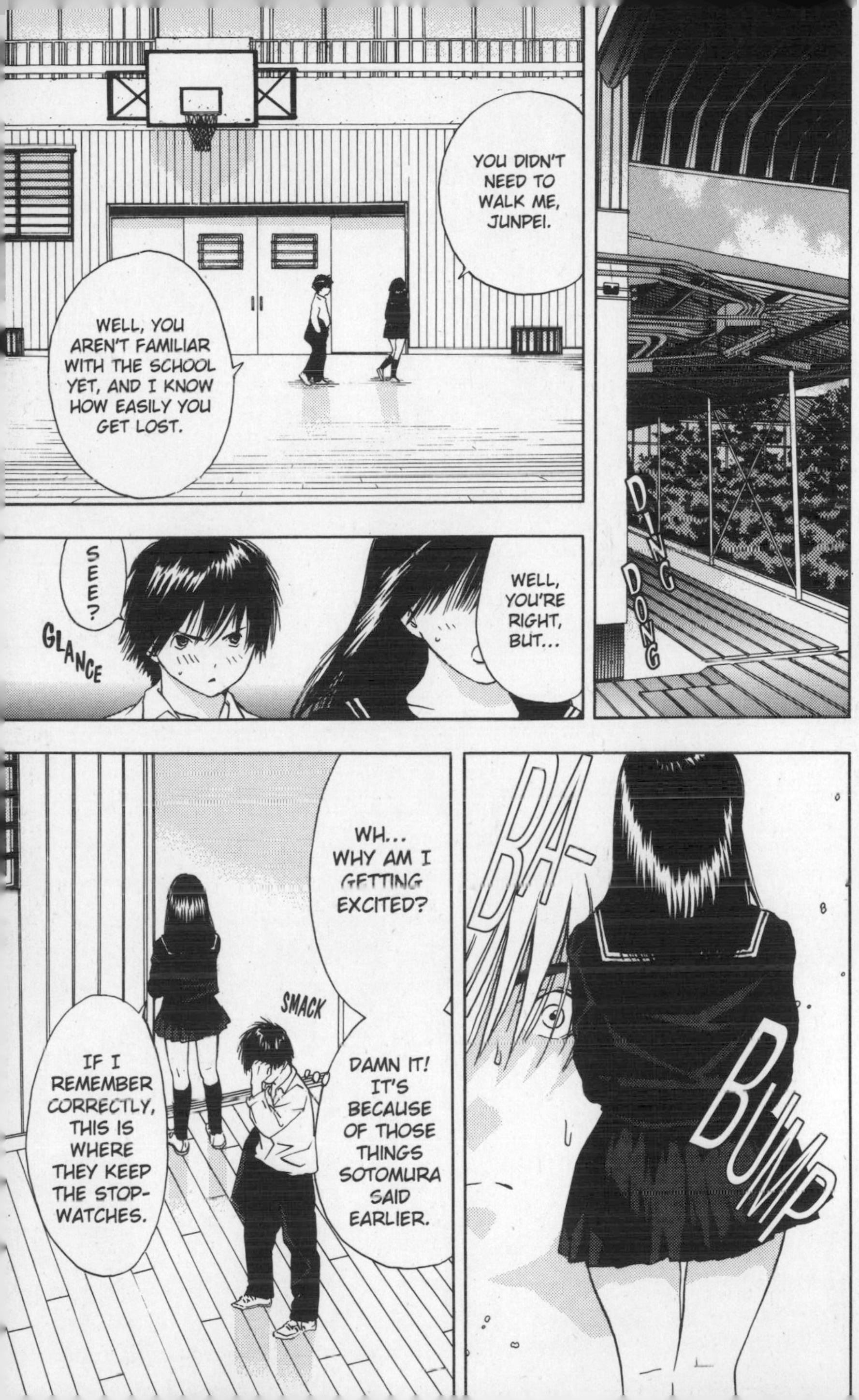
DING DONG
YOU DIDN'T NEED TO WALK ME, JUNPEI.
WELL, YOU AREN'T FAMILIAR WITH THE SCHOOL YET, AND I KNOW HOW EASILY YOU GET LOST.
WELL, YOU'RE RIGHT, BUT...
SEE?
GLANCE
BA-BUMP
WH... WHY AM I GETTING EXCITED?
SMACK
DAMN IT! IT'S BECAUSE OF THOSE THINGS SOTOMURA SAID EARLIER.
IF I REMEMBER CORRECTLY, THIS IS WHERE THEY KEEP THE STOP-WATCHES.

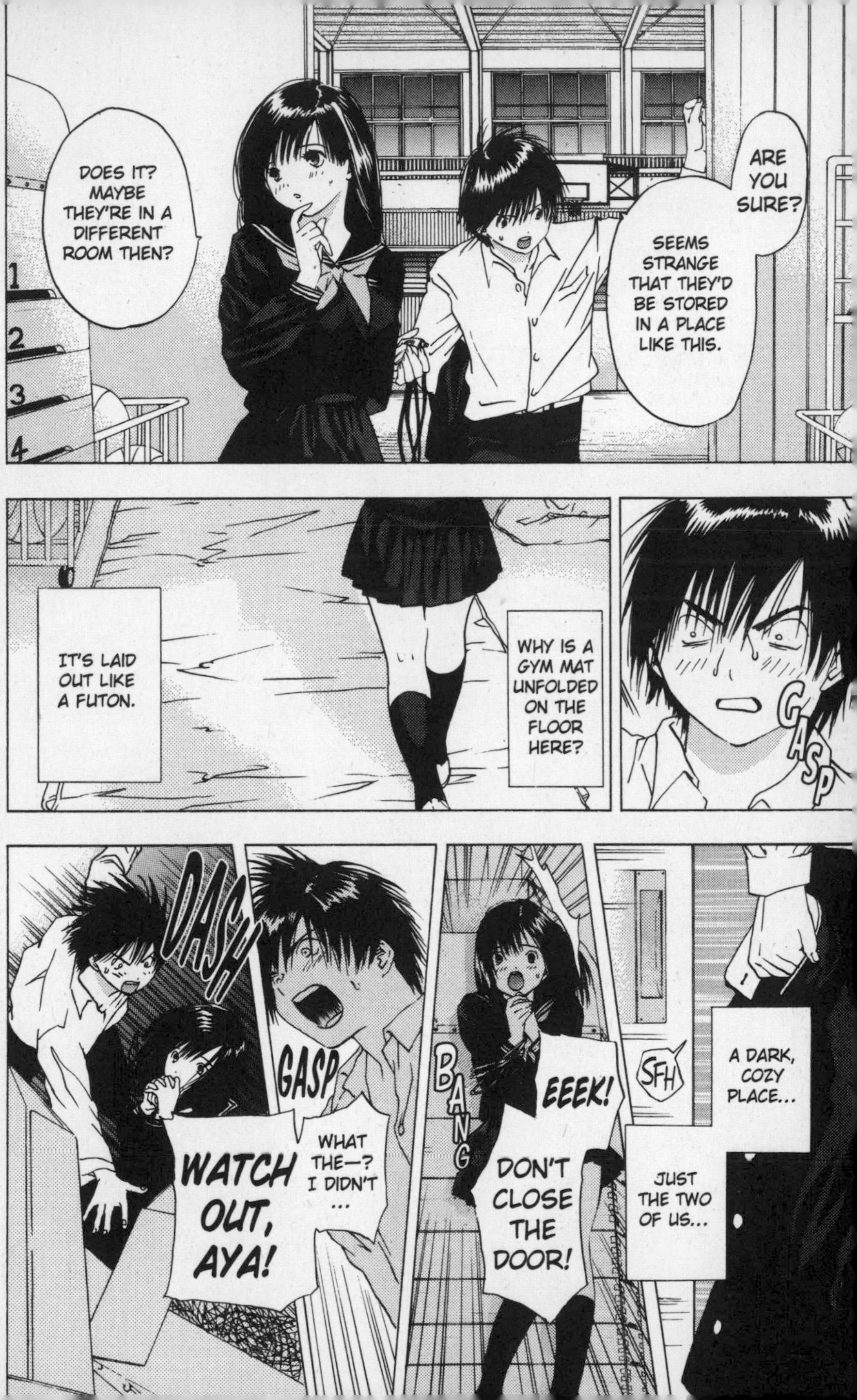
ARE YOU SURE?
SEEMS STRANGE THAT THEY'D BE STORED IN A PLACE LIKE THIS.
DOES IT? MAYBE THEY'RE IN A DIFFERENT ROOM THEN?
GASP
WHY IS A GYM MAT UNFOLDED ON THE FLOOR HERE?
IT'S LAID OUT LIKE A FUTON.
A DARK, COZY PLACE...
JUST THE TWO OF US...
SFH
EEEK!
DON'T CLOSE THE DOOR!
BANG
GASP
WHAT THE—? I DIDN'T ...
DASH
WATCH OUT, AYA!

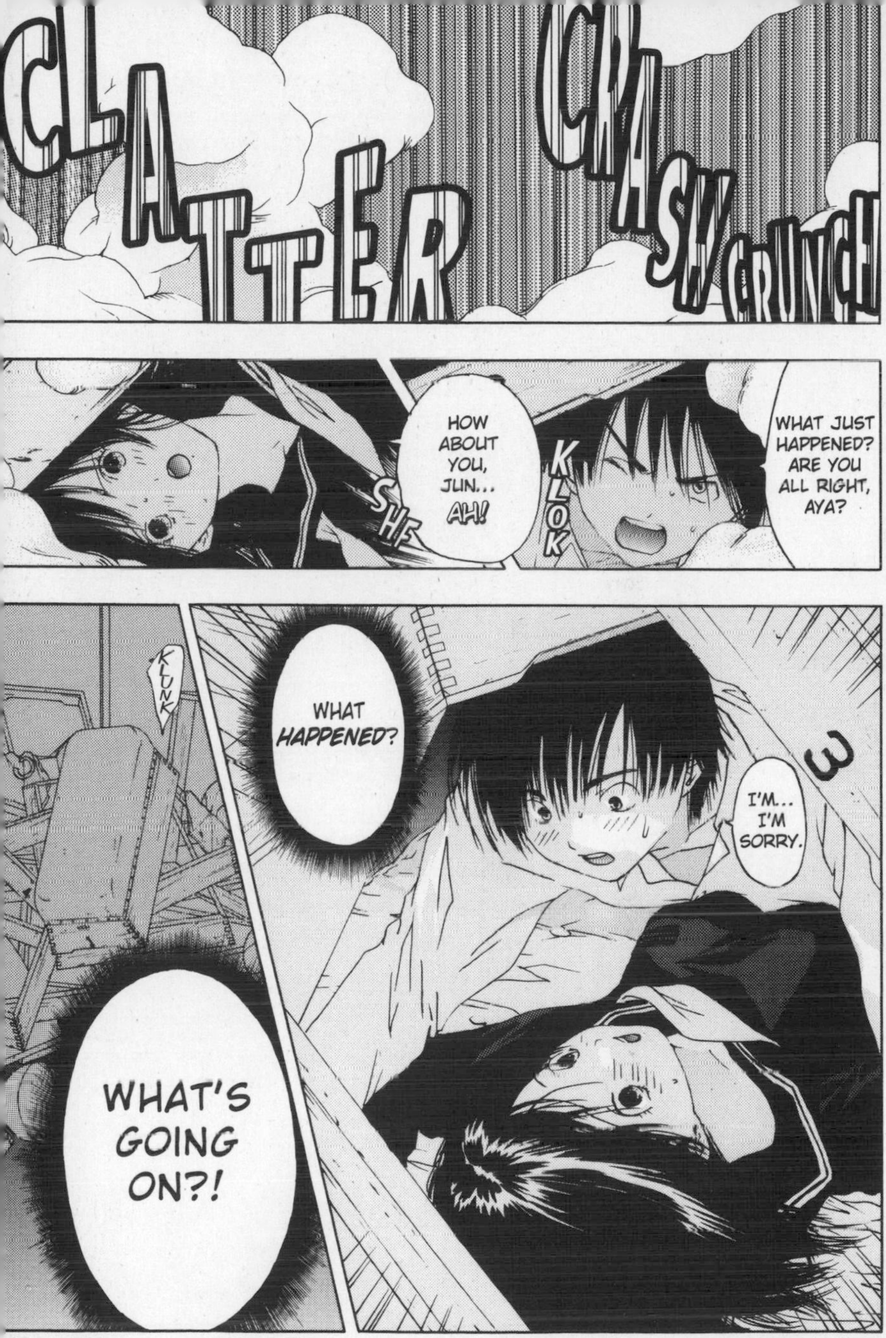
CRASH
CRUNCH
CLATTER
WHAT JUST HAPPENED? ARE YOU ALL RIGHT, AYA?
KLOK
HOW ABOUT YOU, JUN... AH!
SHF
I'M... I'M SORRY.
WHAT HAPPENED?
WHAT'S GOING ON?!
KLUNK

CRUSH 22: MISHAP AT THE GYM

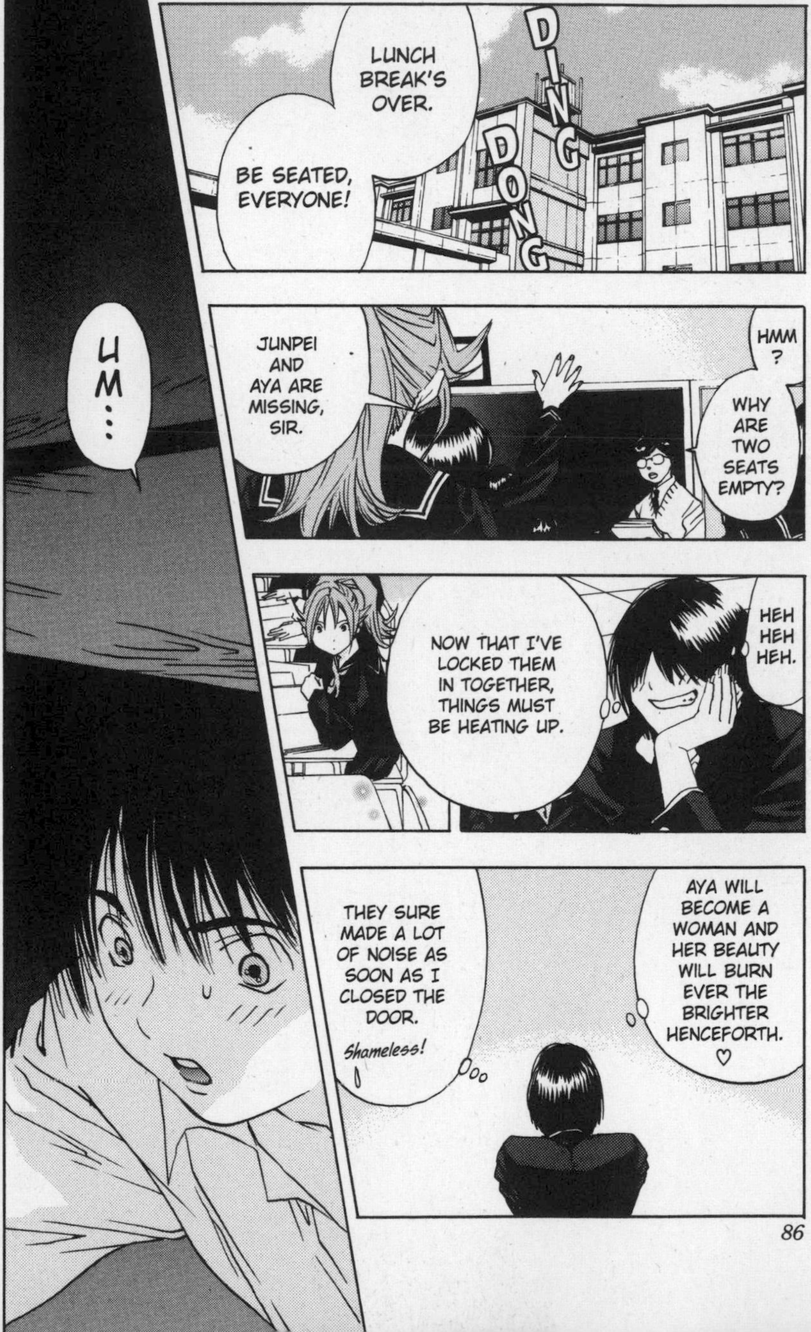
DING DONG
LUNCH BREAK'S OVER.
BE SEATED, EVERYONE!
HMM?
WHY ARE TWO SEATS EMPTY?
JUNPEI AND AYA ARE MISSING, SIR.
HEH HEH HEH.
NOW THAT I'VE LOCKED THEM IN TOGETHER, THINGS MUST BE HEATING UP.
AYA WILL BECOME A WOMAN AND HER BEAUTY WILL BURN EVER THE BRIGHTER HENCEFORTH. ♡
THEY SURE MADE A LOT OF NOISE AS SOON AS I CLOSED THE DOOR.
Shameless!
UM...

CRUSH 22: MISHAP AT THE GYM

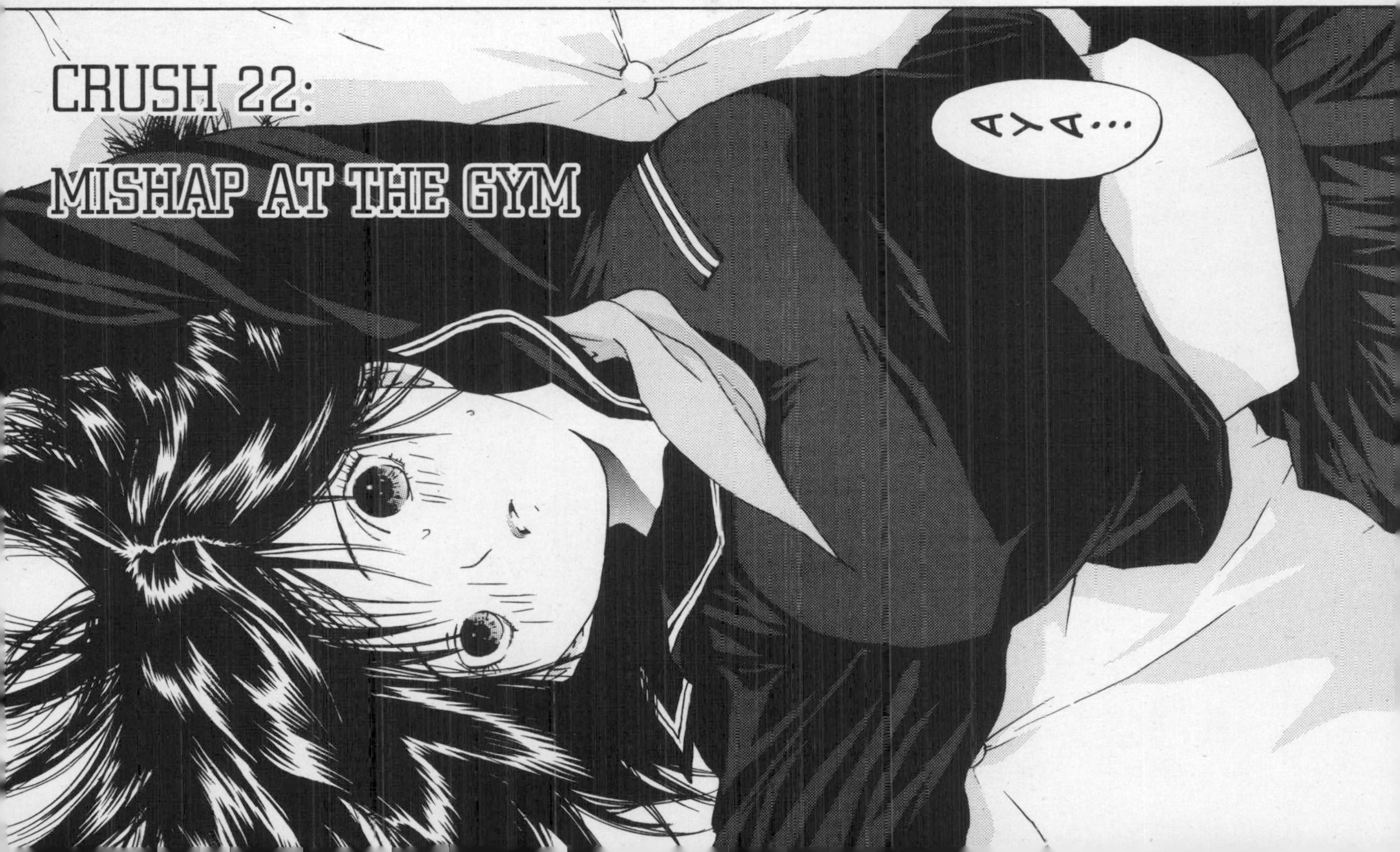
AYA...

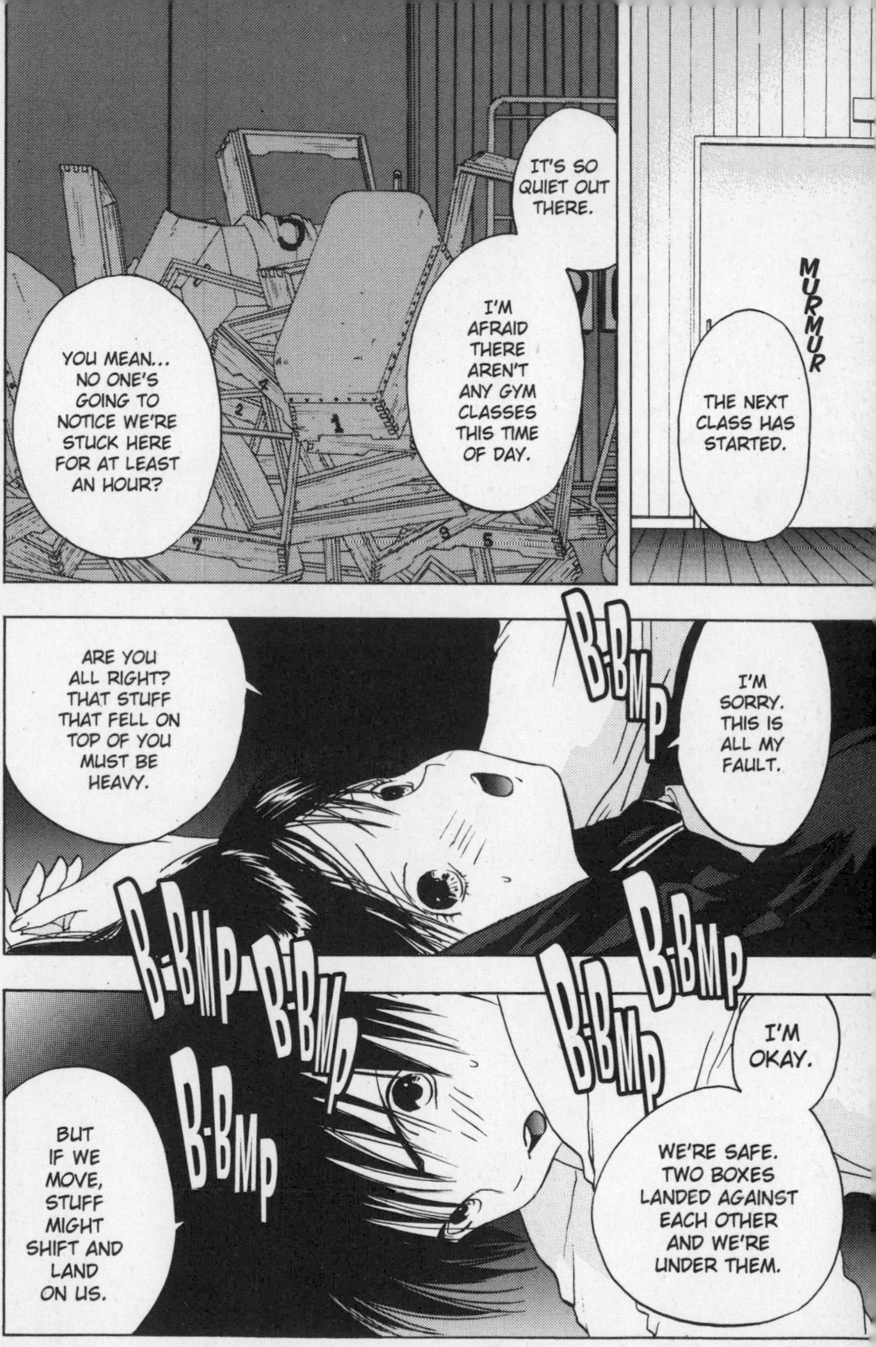
MURMUR
THE NEXT CLASS HAS STARTED.
IT'S SO QUIET OUT THERE.
I'M AFRAID THERE AREN'T ANY GYM CLASSES THIS TIME OF DAY.
YOU MEAN... NO ONE'S GOING TO NOTICE WE'RE STUCK HERE FOR AT LEAST AN HOUR?
B-BMP
I'M SORRY. THIS IS ALL MY FAULT.
ARE YOU ALL RIGHT? THAT STUFF THAT FELL ON TOP OF YOU MUST BE HEAVY.
B-BMP
B-BMP
I'M OKAY.
B-BMP
B-BMP
B-BMP
WE'RE SAFE. TWO BOXES LANDED AGAINST EACH OTHER AND WE'RE UNDER THEM.
BUT IF WE MOVE, STUFF MIGHT SHIFT AND LAND ON US.

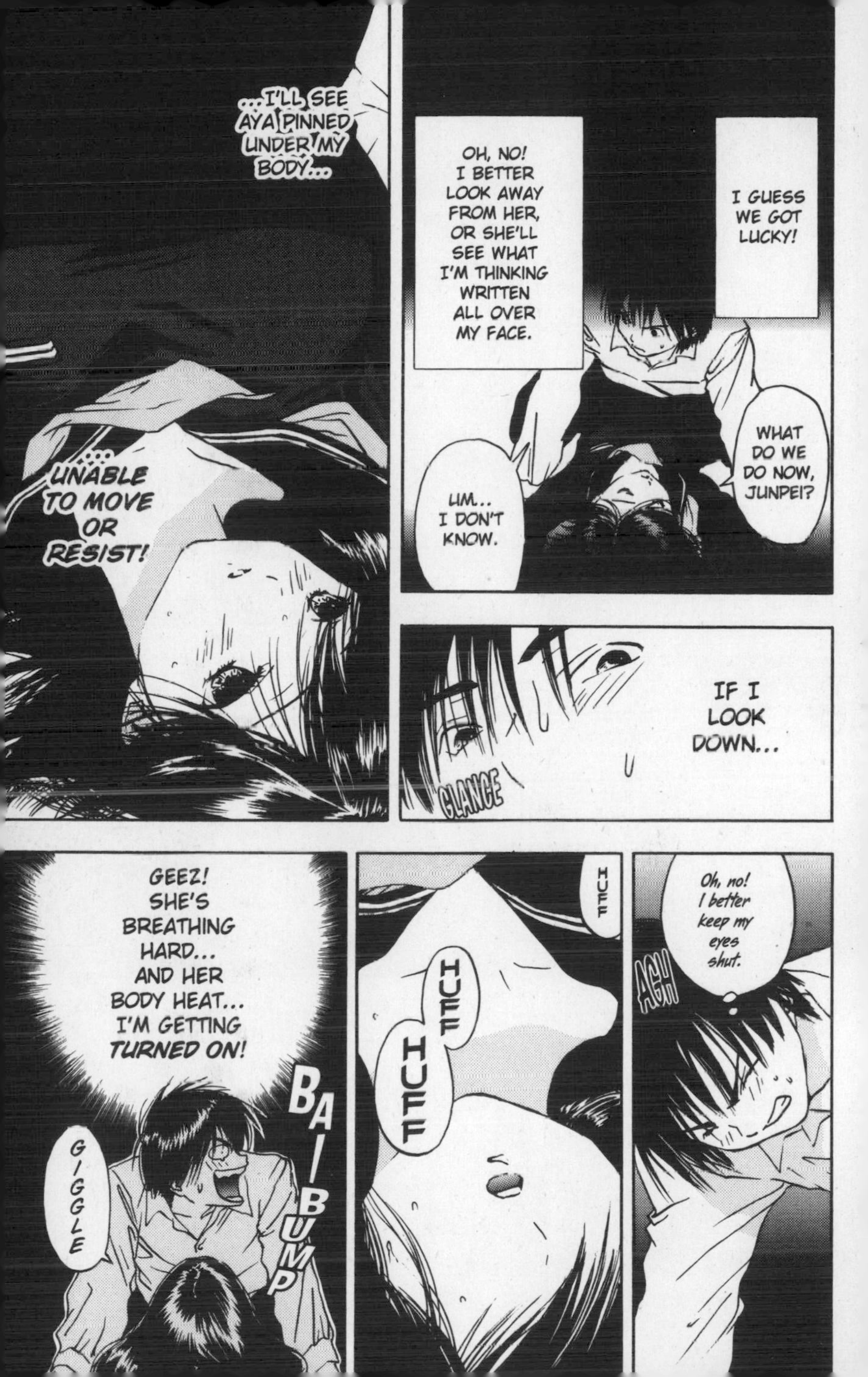
I GUESS WE GOT LUCKY!
OH, NO! I BETTER LOOK AWAY FROM HER, OR SHE'LL SEE WHAT I'M THINKING WRITTEN ALL OVER MY FACE.
WHAT DO WE DO NOW, JUNPEI?
UM... I DON'T KNOW.
IF I LOOK DOWN...
GLANCE
...I'LL SEE AYA PINNED UNDER MY BODY...
...UNABLE TO MOVE OR RESIST!
Oh, no! I better keep my eyes shut.
AGH
HUFF
HUFF HUFF
GEEZ! SHE'S BREATHING HARD... AND HER BODY HEAT... I'M GETTING TURNED ON!
BA-BUMP
GIGGLE

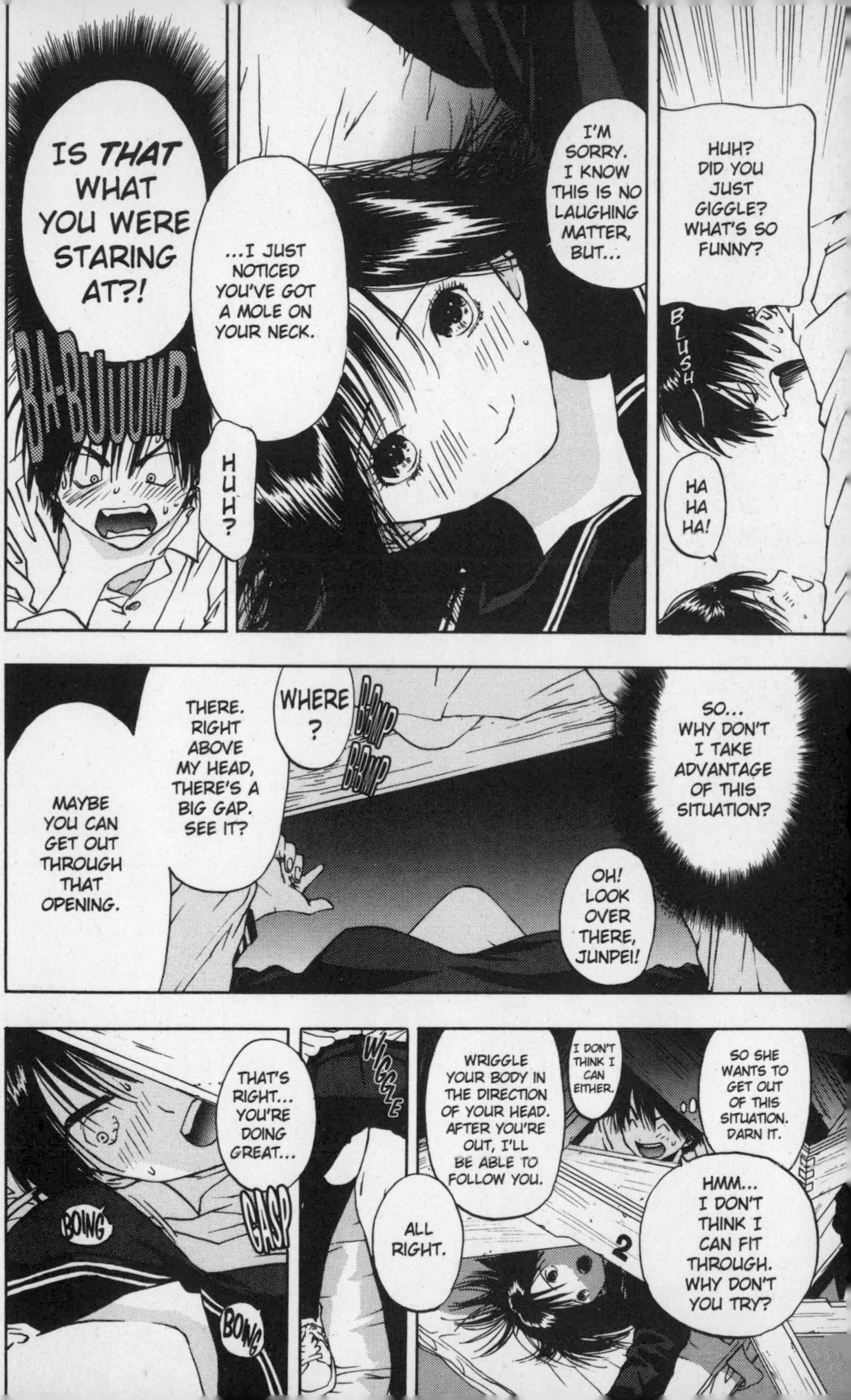
HUH? DID YOU JUST GIGGLE? WHAT'S SO FUNNY?
BLUSH
HA HA HA!
I'M SORRY. I KNOW THIS IS NO LAUGHING MATTER, BUT...
...I JUST NOTICED YOU'VE GOT A MOLE ON YOUR NECK.
HUH?
IS *THAT* WHAT YOU WERE STARING AT?!
BA-BUUUMP
SO... WHY DON'T I TAKE ADVANTAGE OF THIS SITUATION?
OH! LOOK OVER THERE, JUNPEI!
WHERE?
BUMP BUMP
THERE. RIGHT ABOVE MY HEAD, THERE'S A BIG GAP. SEE IT?
MAYBE YOU CAN GET OUT THROUGH THAT OPENING.
SO SHE WANTS TO GET OUT OF THIS SITUATION. DARN IT.
HMM... I DON'T THINK I CAN FIT THROUGH. WHY DON'T YOU TRY?
I DON'T THINK I CAN EITHER.
WRIGGLE YOUR BODY IN THE DIRECTION OF YOUR HEAD. AFTER YOU'RE OUT, I'LL BE ABLE TO FOLLOW YOU.
ALL RIGHT.
WIGGLE
THAT'S RIGHT... YOU'RE DOING GREAT...
GASP
BOING
BOING

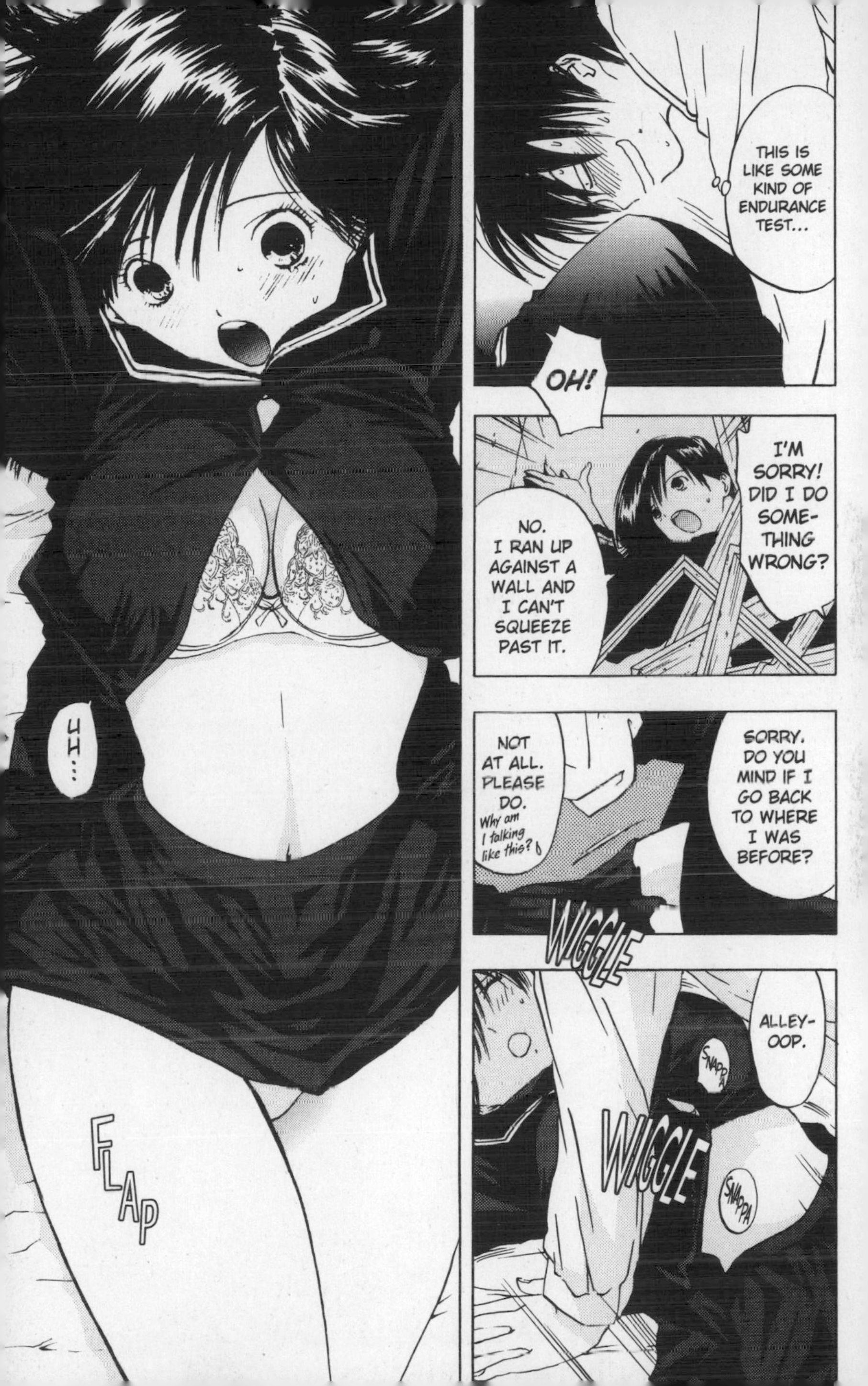

THIS IS LIKE SOME KIND OF ENDURANCE TEST...
OH!
I'M SORRY! DID I DO SOME-THING WRONG?
NO. I RAN UP AGAINST A WALL AND I CAN'T SQUEEZE PAST IT.
SORRY. DO YOU MIND IF I GO BACK TO WHERE I WAS BEFORE?
NOT AT ALL. PLEASE DO.
Why am I talking like this?
WIGGLE
ALLEY-OOP.
SNAPPA
WIGGLE
SNAPPA
UH...
FLAP

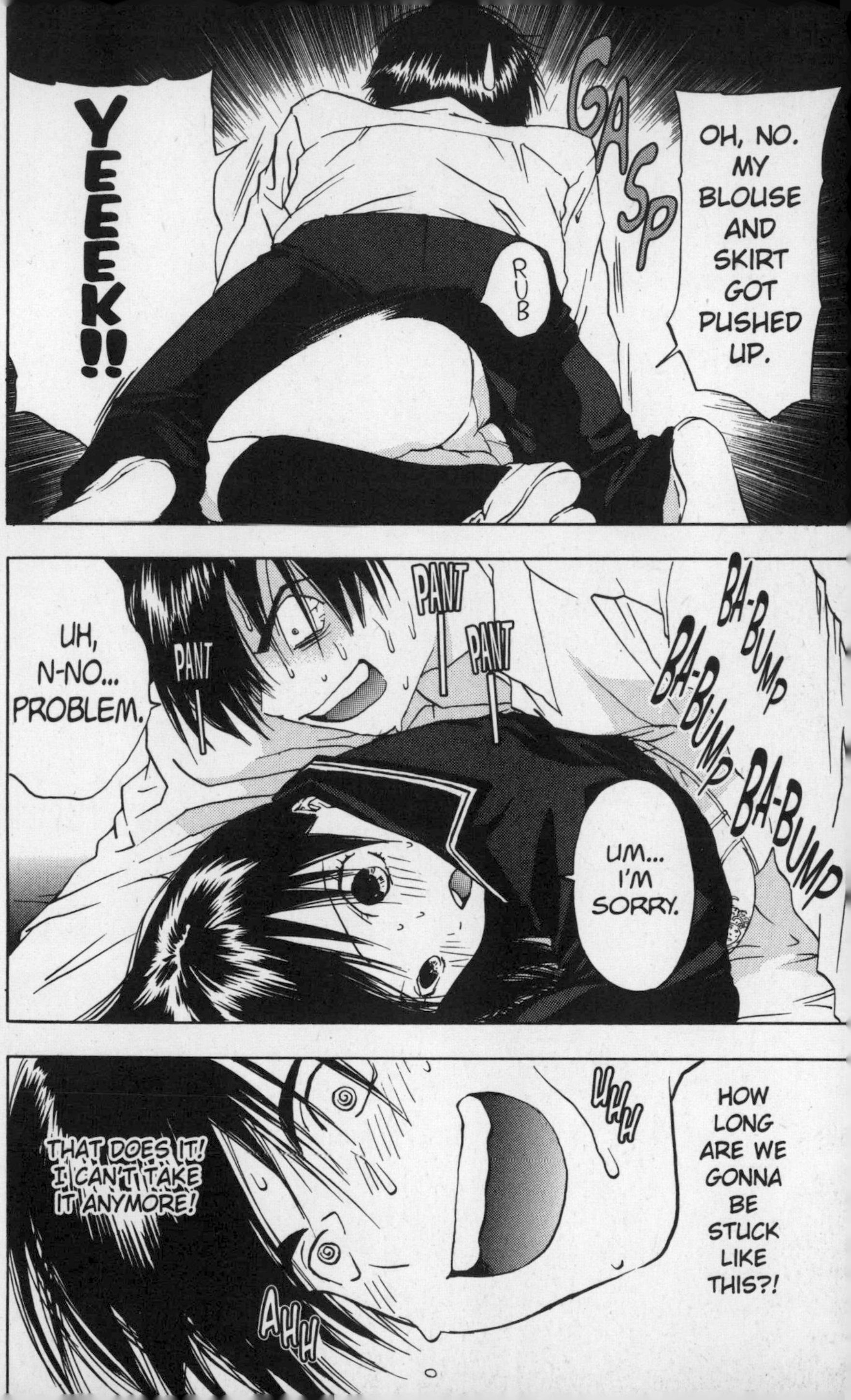
GASP
OH, NO. MY BLOUSE AND SKIRT GOT PUSHED UP.
RUB
YEEEK!!
BA-BUMP
BA-BUMP
BA-BUMP
PANT
PANT
UH, N-NO... PROBLEM.
PANT
UM... I'M SORRY.
HOW LONG ARE WE GONNA BE STUCK LIKE THIS?!
UHHH
THAT DOES IT! I CAN'T TAKE IT ANYMORE!
AHH

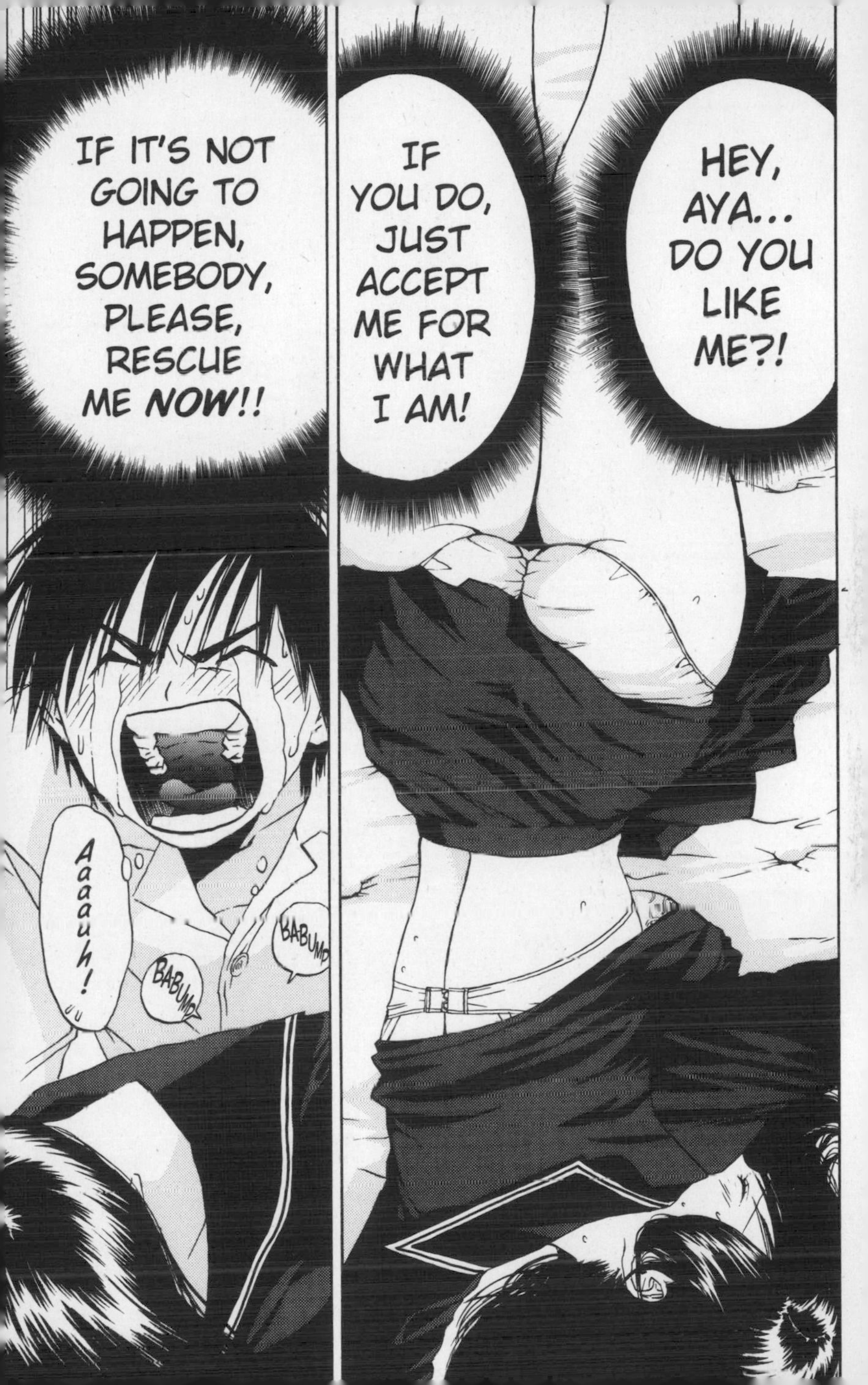
HEY, AYA... DO YOU LIKE ME?!
IF YOU DO, JUST ACCEPT ME FOR WHAT I AM!
IF IT'S NOT GOING TO HAPPEN, SOMEBODY, PLEASE, RESCUE ME *NOW*!!
Aaaauh!
BABUMP
BABUMP

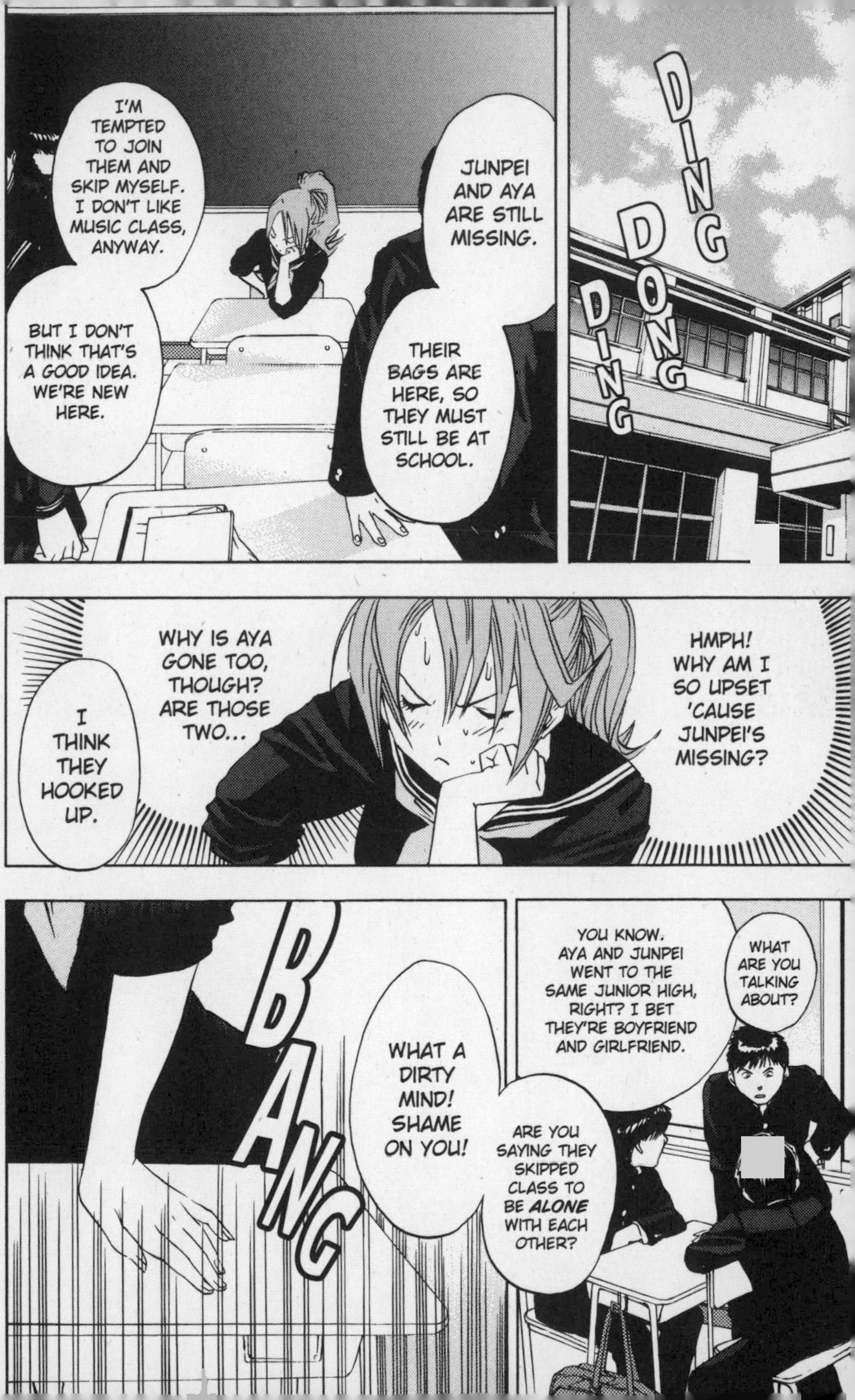
DING DONG DING
JUNPEI AND AYA ARE STILL MISSING.
THEIR BAGS ARE HERE, SO THEY MUST STILL BE AT SCHOOL.
I'M TEMPTED TO JOIN THEM AND SKIP MYSELF. I DON'T LIKE MUSIC CLASS, ANYWAY.
BUT I DON'T THINK THAT'S A GOOD IDEA. WE'RE NEW HERE.
HMPH! WHY AM I SO UPSET 'CAUSE JUNPEI'S MISSING?
WHY IS AYA GONE TOO, THOUGH? ARE THOSE TWO...
I THINK THEY HOOKED UP.
WHAT ARE YOU TALKING ABOUT?
YOU KNOW. AYA AND JUNPEI WENT TO THE SAME JUNIOR HIGH, RIGHT? I BET THEY'RE BOYFRIEND AND GIRLFRIEND.
ARE YOU SAYING THEY SKIPPED CLASS TO BE *ALONE* WITH EACH OTHER?
WHAT A DIRTY MIND! SHAME ON YOU!
BANG

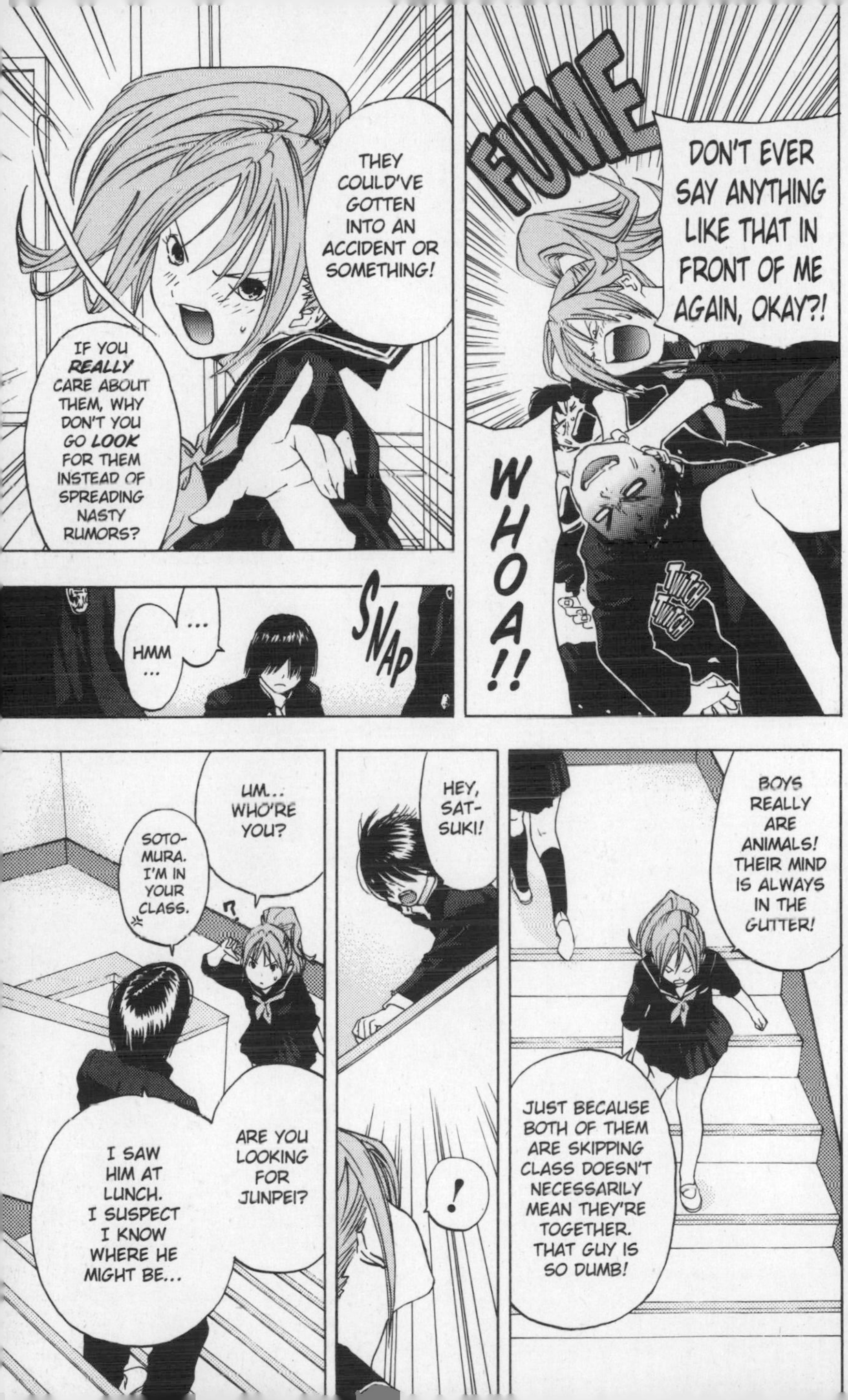
FUME
DON'T EVER SAY ANYTHING LIKE THAT IN FRONT OF ME AGAIN, OKAY?!
WHOA!!
TWITCH TWITCH
THEY COULD'VE GOTTEN INTO AN ACCIDENT OR SOMETHING!
IF YOU **REALLY** CARE ABOUT THEM, WHY DON'T YOU GO **LOOK** FOR THEM INSTEAD OF SPREADING NASTY RUMORS?
...
HMM...
SNAP
BOYS REALLY ARE ANIMALS! THEIR MIND IS ALWAYS IN THE GUTTER!
JUST BECAUSE BOTH OF THEM ARE SKIPPING CLASS DOESN'T NECESSARILY MEAN THEY'RE TOGETHER. THAT GUY IS SO DUMB!
HEY, SAT-SUKI!
!
UM... WHO'RE YOU?
SOTO-MURA. I'M IN YOUR CLASS.
ARE YOU LOOKING FOR JUNPEI?
I SAW HIM AT LUNCH. I SUSPECT I KNOW WHERE HE MIGHT BE...

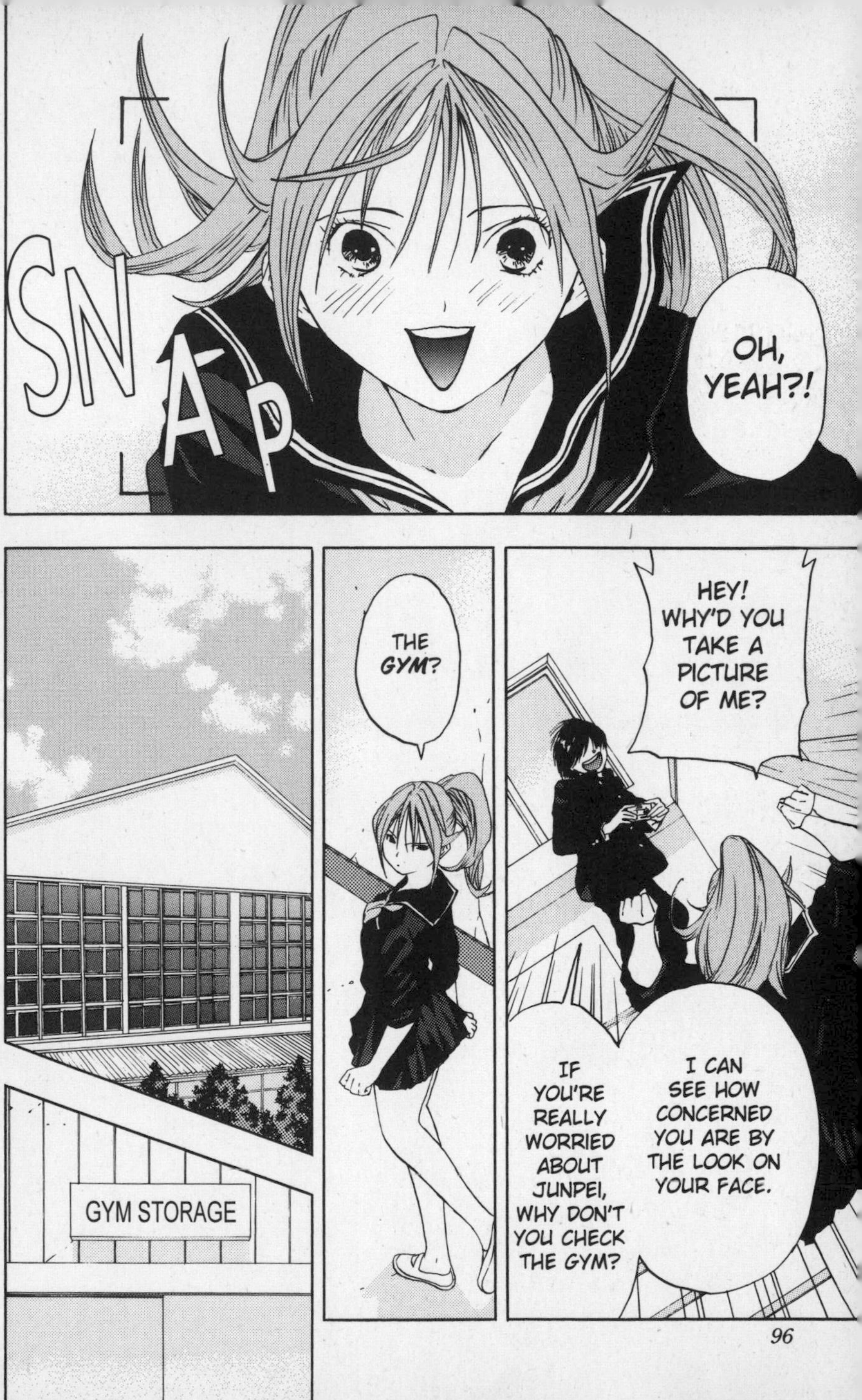
OH, YEAH?!
SNAP
HEY! WHY'D YOU TAKE A PICTURE OF ME?
I CAN SEE HOW CONCERNED YOU ARE BY THE LOOK ON YOUR FACE.
IF YOU'RE REALLY WORRIED ABOUT JUNPEI, WHY DON'T YOU CHECK THE GYM?
THE *GYM*?
GYM STORAGE

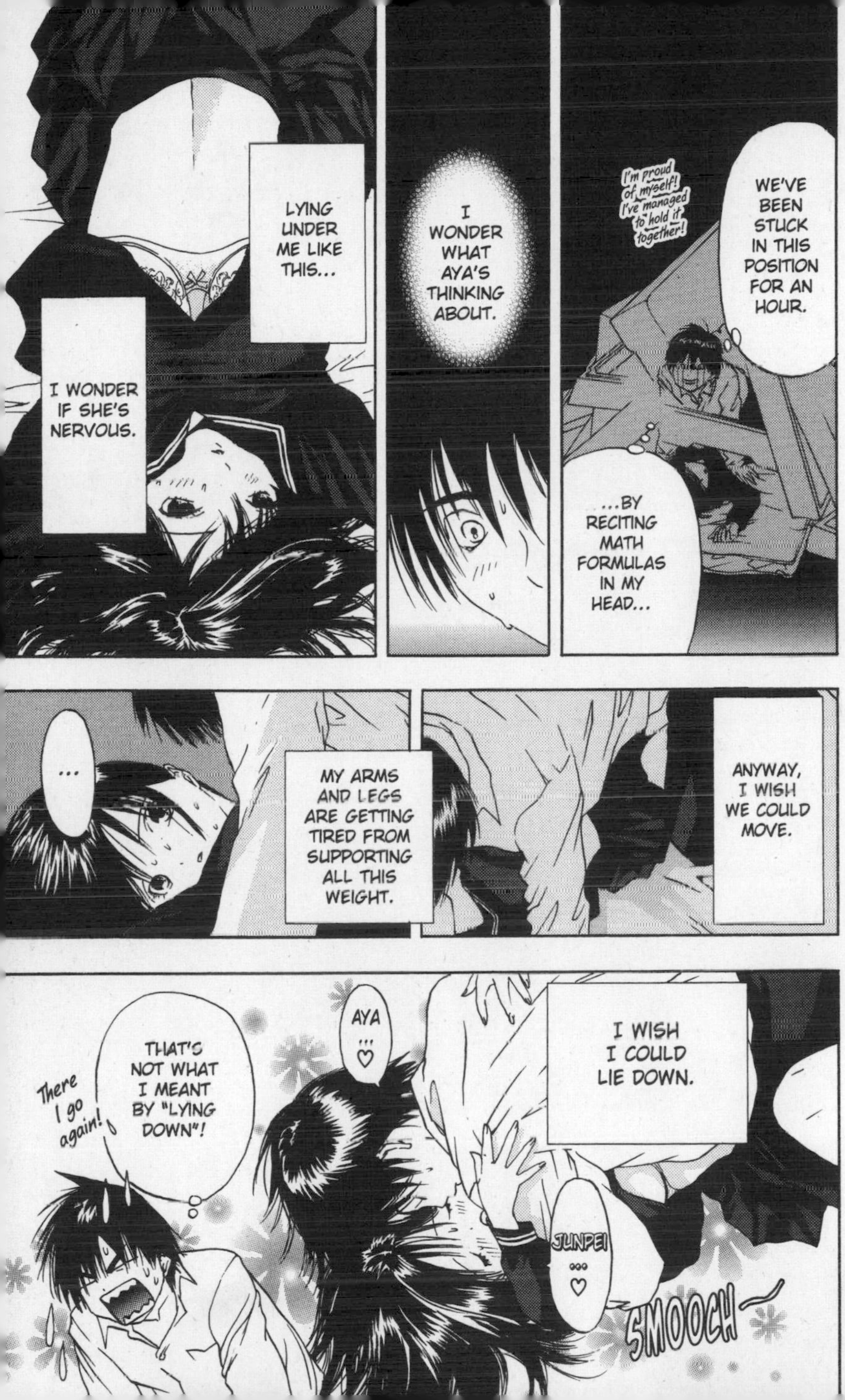
WE'VE BEEN STUCK IN THIS POSITION FOR AN HOUR.
I'm proud of myself! I've managed to hold it together!
...BY RECITING MATH FORMULAS IN MY HEAD...
I WONDER WHAT AYA'S THINKING ABOUT.
LYING UNDER ME LIKE THIS...
I WONDER IF SHE'S NERVOUS.
ANYWAY, I WISH WE COULD MOVE.
MY ARMS AND LEGS ARE GETTING TIRED FROM SUPPORTING ALL THIS WEIGHT.
...
I WISH I COULD LIE DOWN.
AYA... ♡
JUNPEI... ♡
SMOOCH~
THAT'S NOT WHAT I MEANT BY "LYING DOWN"!
There I go again!

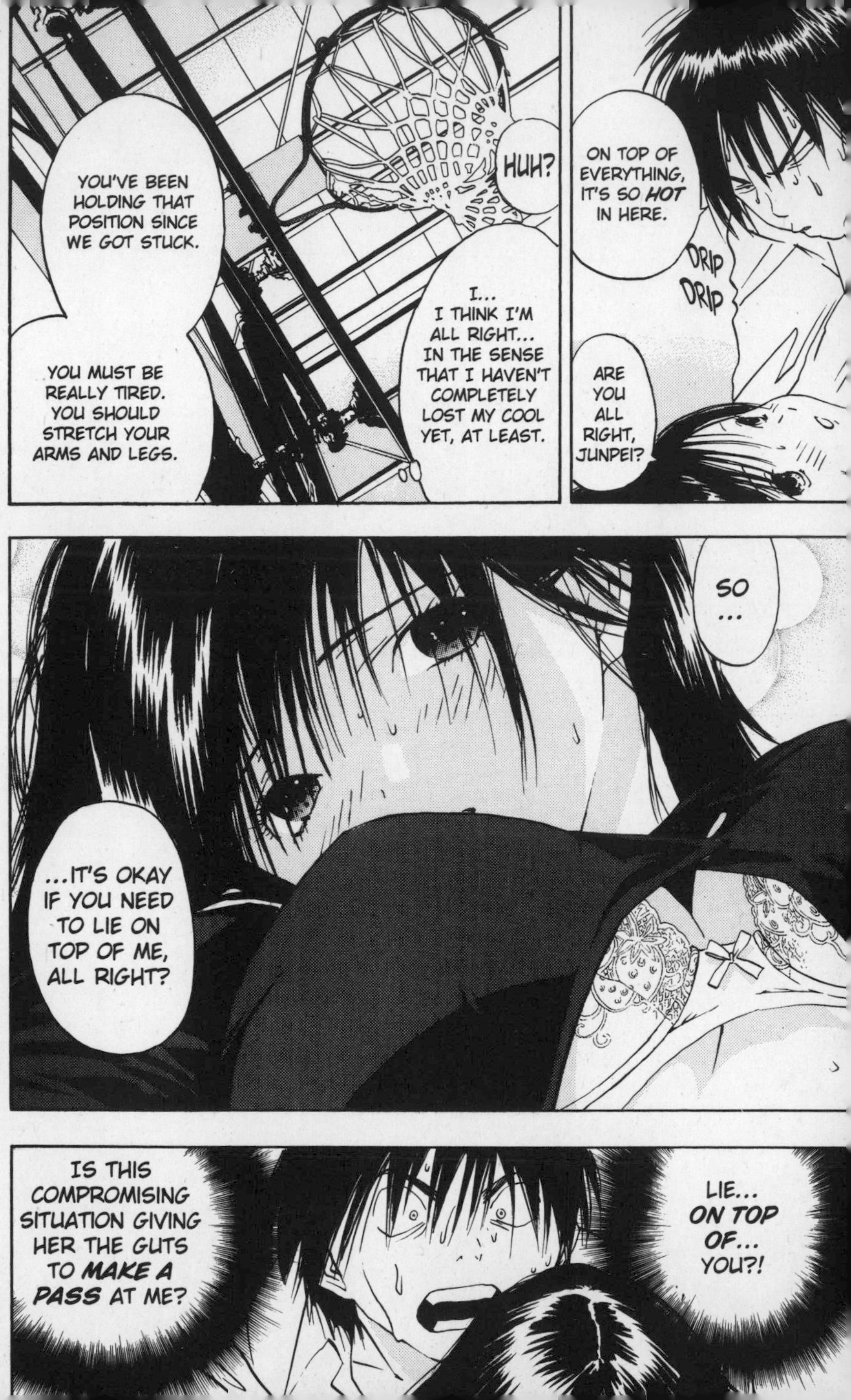
ON TOP OF EVERYTHING, IT'S SO *HOT* IN HERE.
DRIP
DRIP
ARE YOU ALL RIGHT, JUNPEI?
HUH?
I... I THINK I'M ALL RIGHT... IN THE SENSE THAT I HAVEN'T COMPLETELY LOST MY COOL YET, AT LEAST.
YOU'VE BEEN HOLDING THAT POSITION SINCE WE GOT STUCK.
YOU MUST BE REALLY TIRED. YOU SHOULD STRETCH YOUR ARMS AND LEGS.
SO...
...IT'S OKAY IF YOU NEED TO LIE ON TOP OF ME, ALL RIGHT?
LIE... ***ON TOP OF...*** YOU?!
IS THIS COMPROMISING SITUATION GIVING HER THE GUTS TO ***MAKE A PASS*** AT ME?

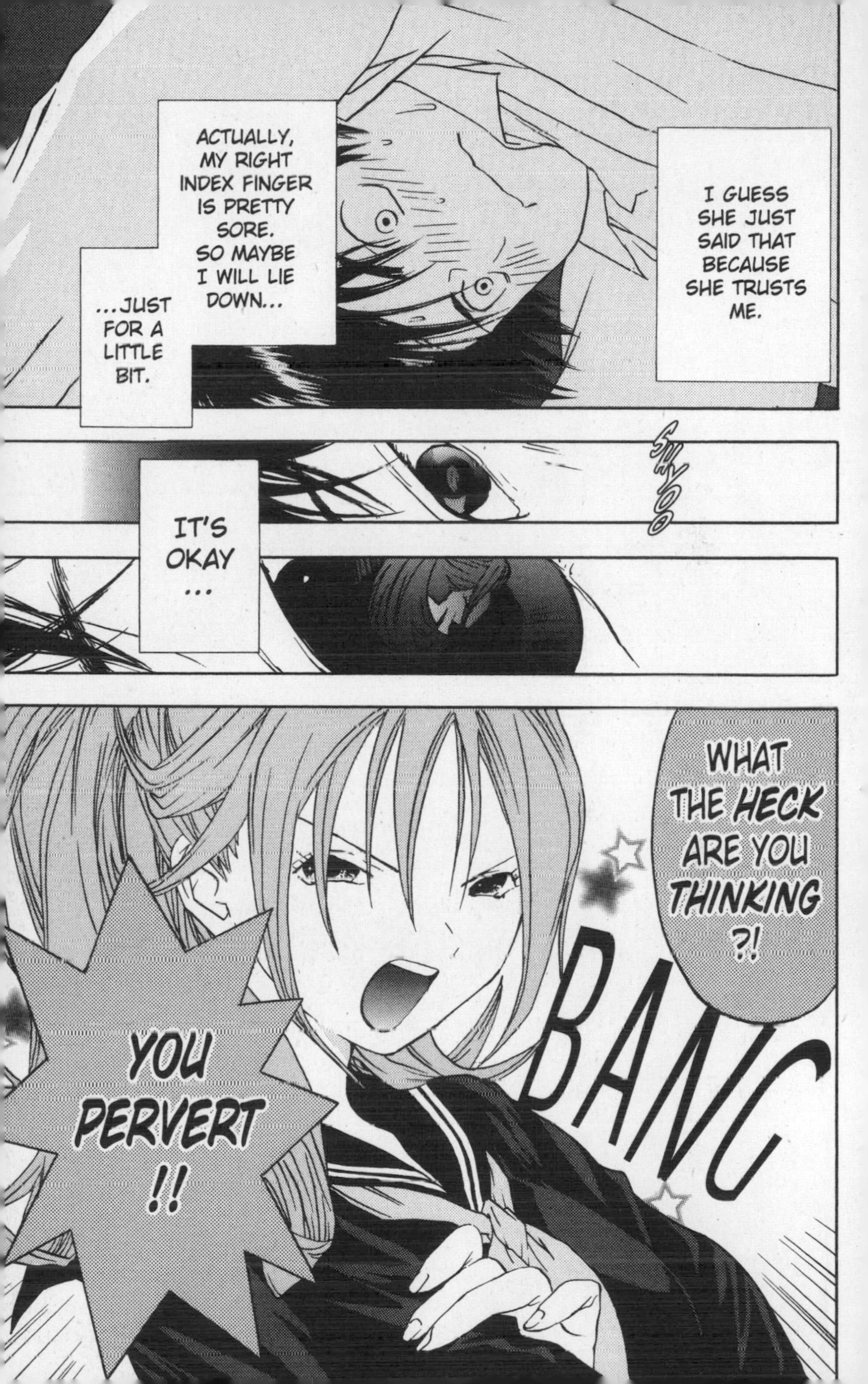
I GUESS SHE JUST SAID THAT BECAUSE SHE TRUSTS ME.
ACTUALLY, MY RIGHT INDEX FINGER IS PRETTY SORE. SO MAYBE I WILL LIE DOWN...
...JUST FOR A LITTLE BIT.
SHOOO
IT'S OKAY ...
WHAT THE HECK ARE YOU THINKING ?!
BANG
YOU PERVERT !!

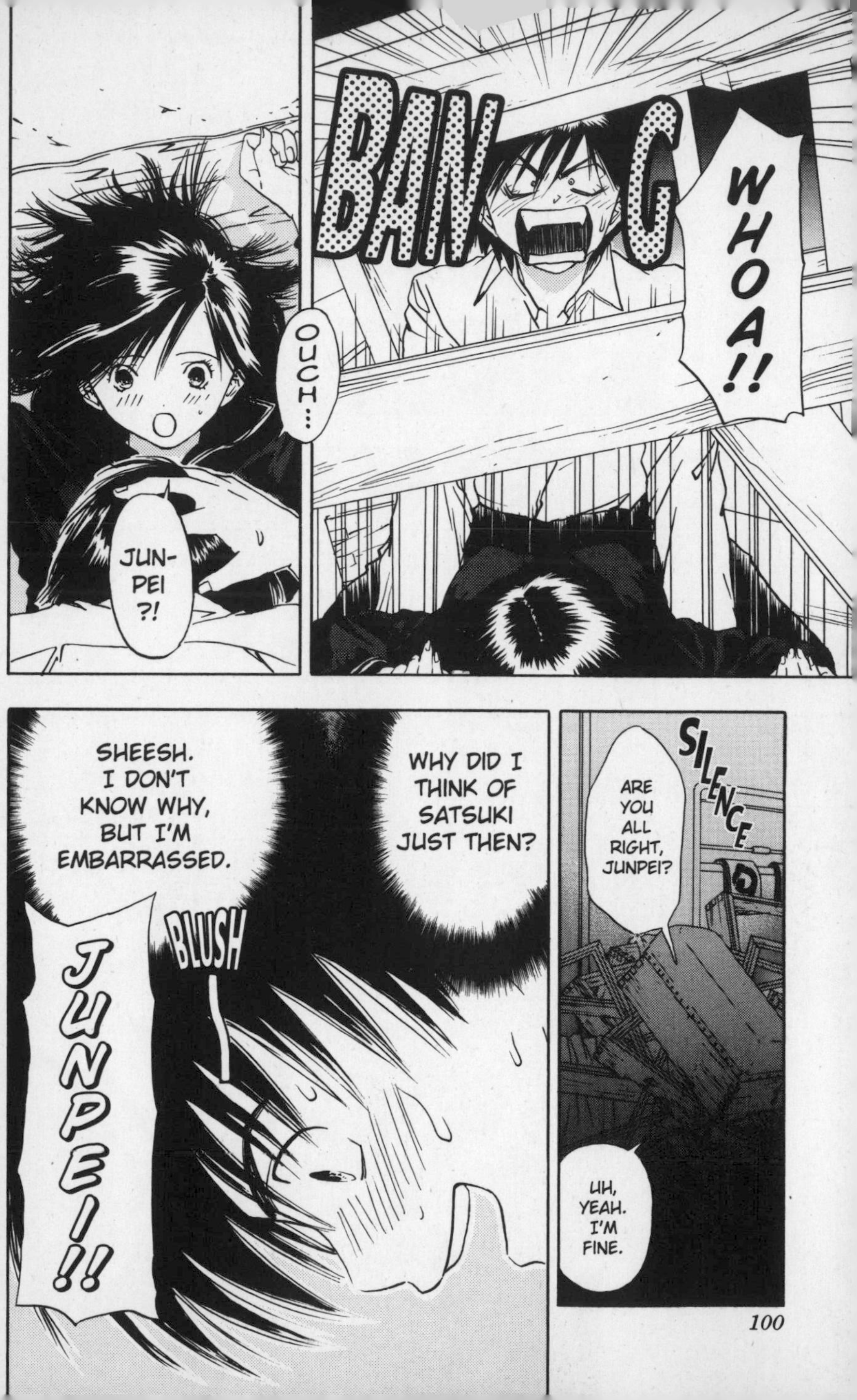
BANG
WHOA!!
OUCH...
JUNPEI?!
SILENCE
ARE YOU ALL RIGHT, JUNPEI?
UH, YEAH. I'M FINE.
WHY DID I THINK OF SATSUKI JUST THEN?
SHEESH. I DON'T KNOW WHY, BUT I'M EMBARRASSED.
BLUSH
JUNPEI!!

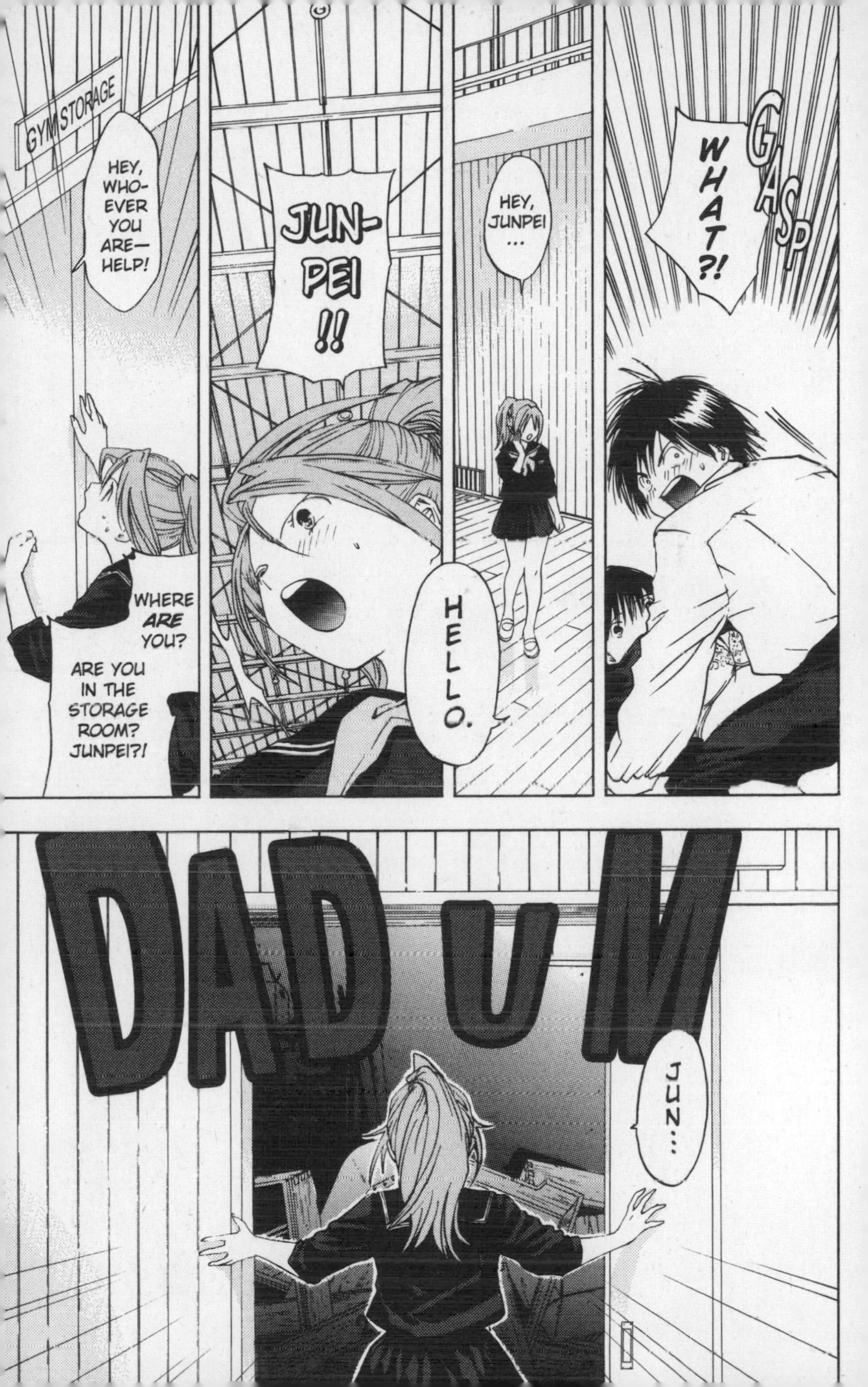
GASP
WHAT?!
HEY, JUNPEI...
HELLO.
JUN-PEI!!
GYM STORAGE
HEY, WHO-EVER YOU ARE—HELP!
WHERE ARE YOU?
ARE YOU IN THE STORAGE ROOM? JUNPEI?!
DADUM
JUN...

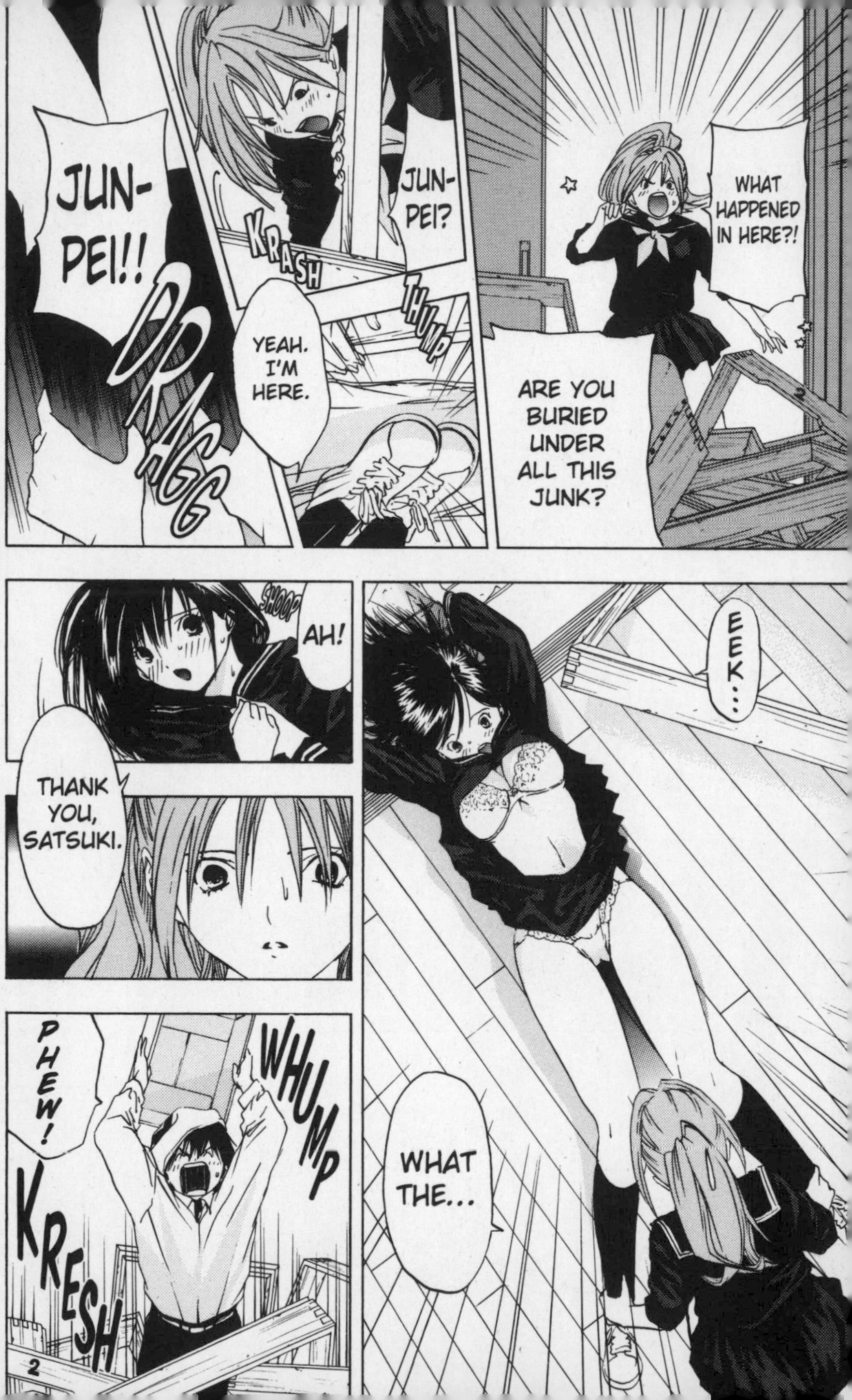
WHAT HAPPENED IN HERE?!
ARE YOU BURIED UNDER ALL THIS JUNK?
JUN-PEI?
KRASH
THUMP
YEAH. I'M HERE.
JUN-PEI!!
DRAGG
EEK...
WHAT THE...
SHOOP
AH!
THANK YOU, SATSUKI.
PHEW!
WHUMP
KRESH

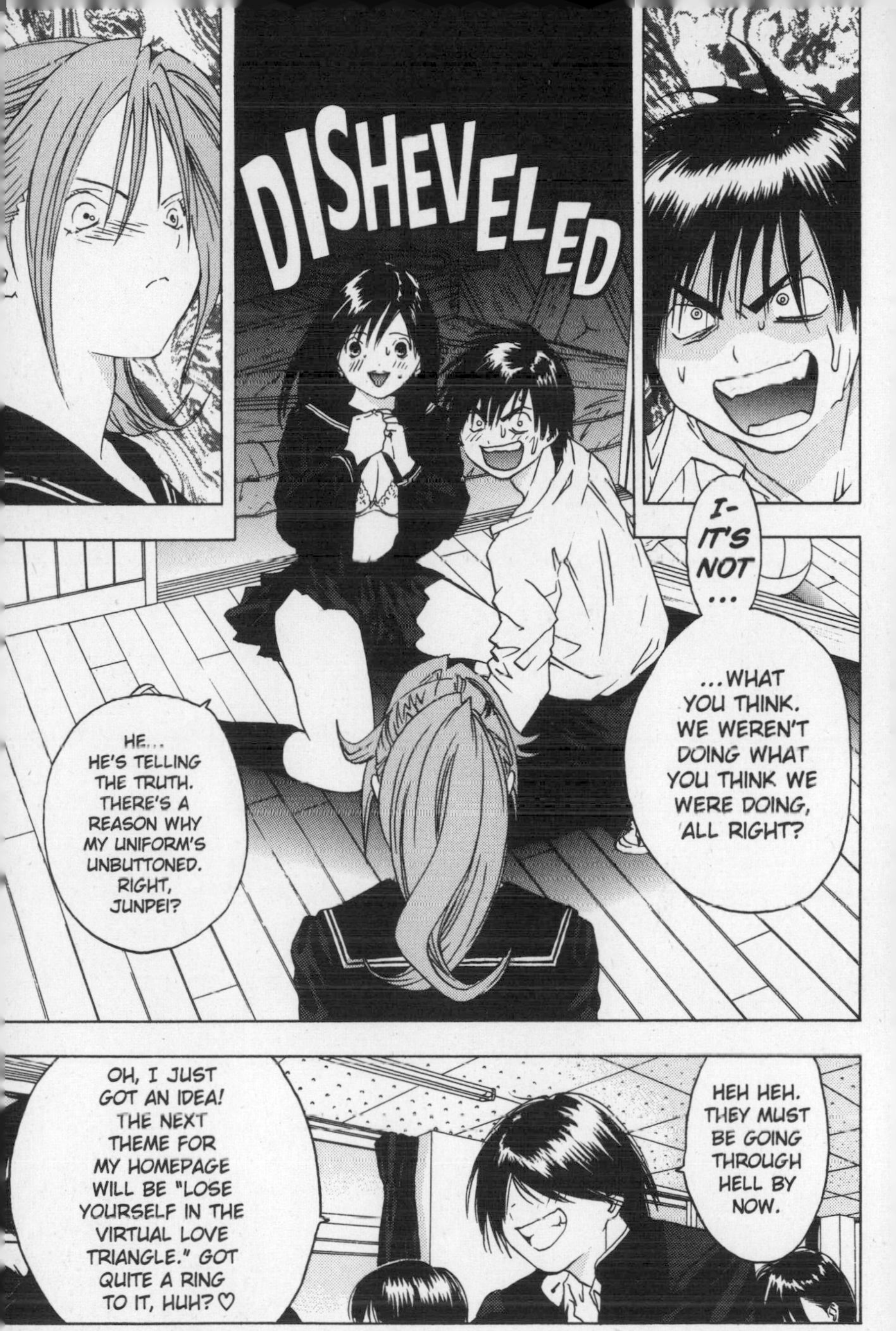
DISHEVELED
I- IT'S NOT...
...WHAT YOU THINK. WE WEREN'T DOING WHAT YOU THINK WE WERE DOING, ALL RIGHT?
HE... HE'S TELLING THE TRUTH. THERE'S A REASON WHY MY UNIFORM'S UNBUTTONED. RIGHT, JUNPEI?
HEH HEH. THEY MUST BE GOING THROUGH HELL BY NOW.
OH, I JUST GOT AN IDEA! THE NEXT THEME FOR MY HOMEPAGE WILL BE "LOSE YOURSELF IN THE VIRTUAL LOVE TRIANGLE." GOT QUITE A RING TO IT, HUH? ♡

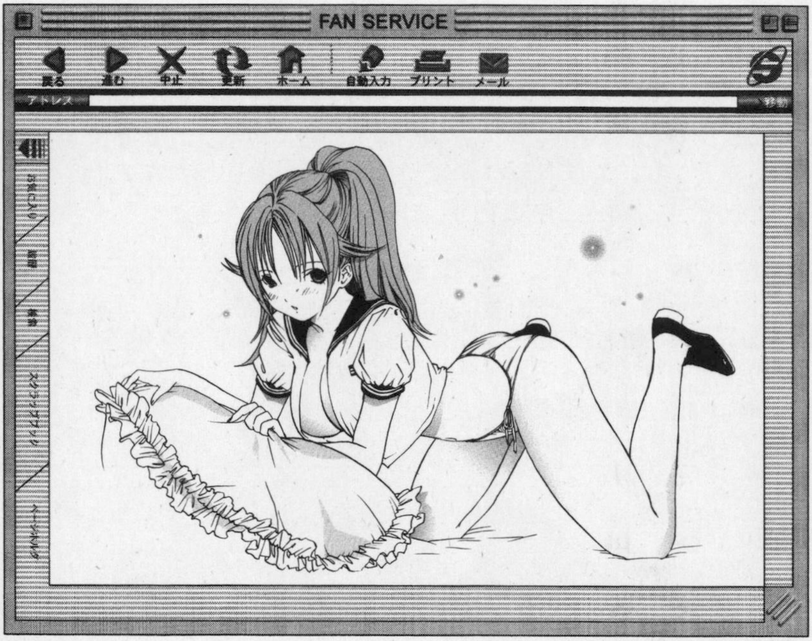
FAN SERVICE
戻る
進む
中止
更新
ホーム
自動入力
プリント
メール
アドレス
移動

NOTE: THIS IS A COMPOSITE PHOTOGRAPH.

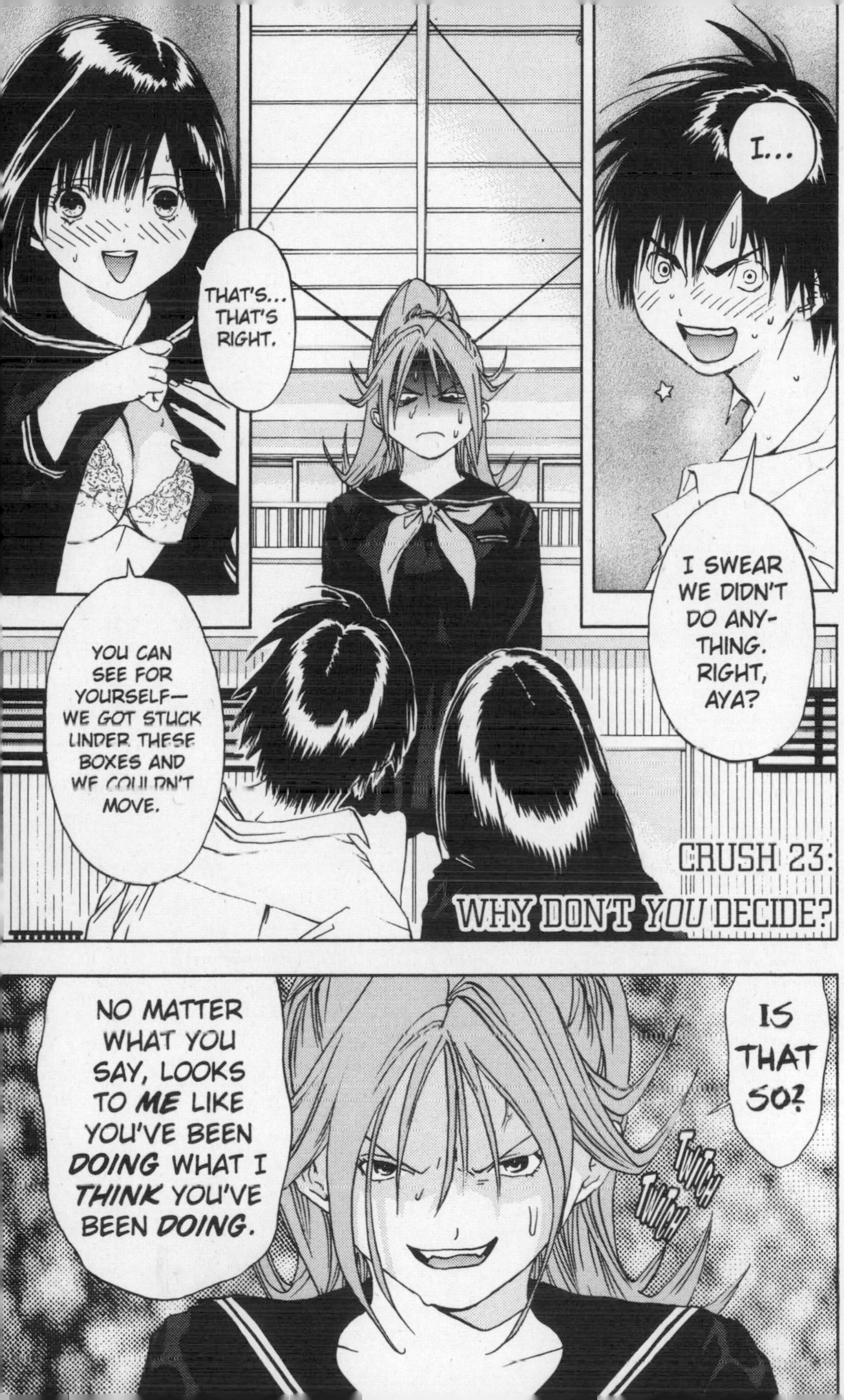
I...
I SWEAR WE DIDN'T DO ANY-THING. RIGHT, AYA?
THAT'S... THAT'S RIGHT.
YOU CAN SEE FOR YOURSELF— WE GOT STUCK UNDER THESE BOXES AND WE COULDN'T MOVE.
CRUSH 23: WHY DON'T YOU DECIDE?
IS THAT SO?
TWITCH TWITCH
NO MATTER WHAT YOU SAY, LOOKS TO ME LIKE YOU'VE BEEN DOING WHAT I THINK YOU'VE BEEN DOING.

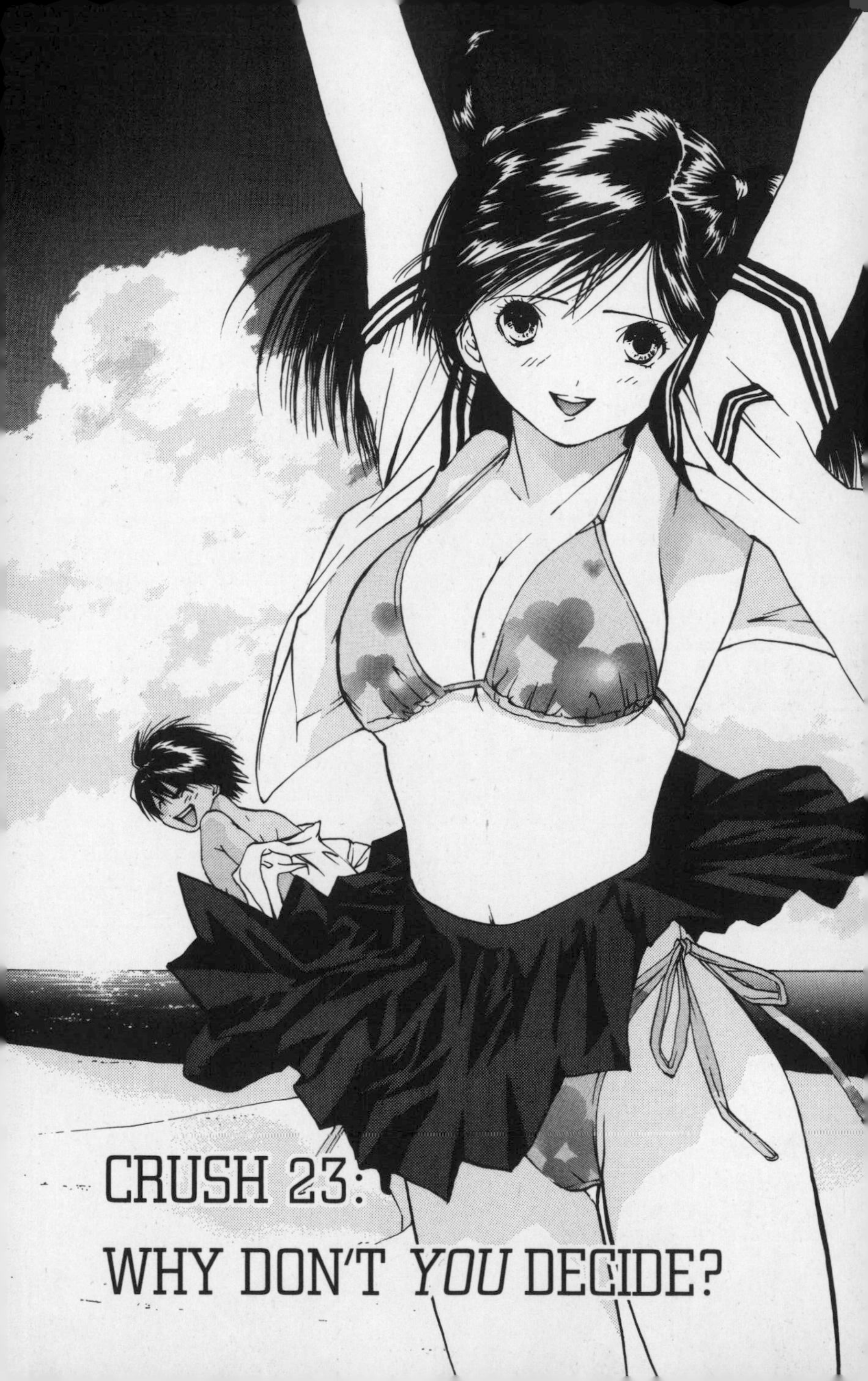
CRUSH 23:
WHY DON'T *YOU* DECIDE?

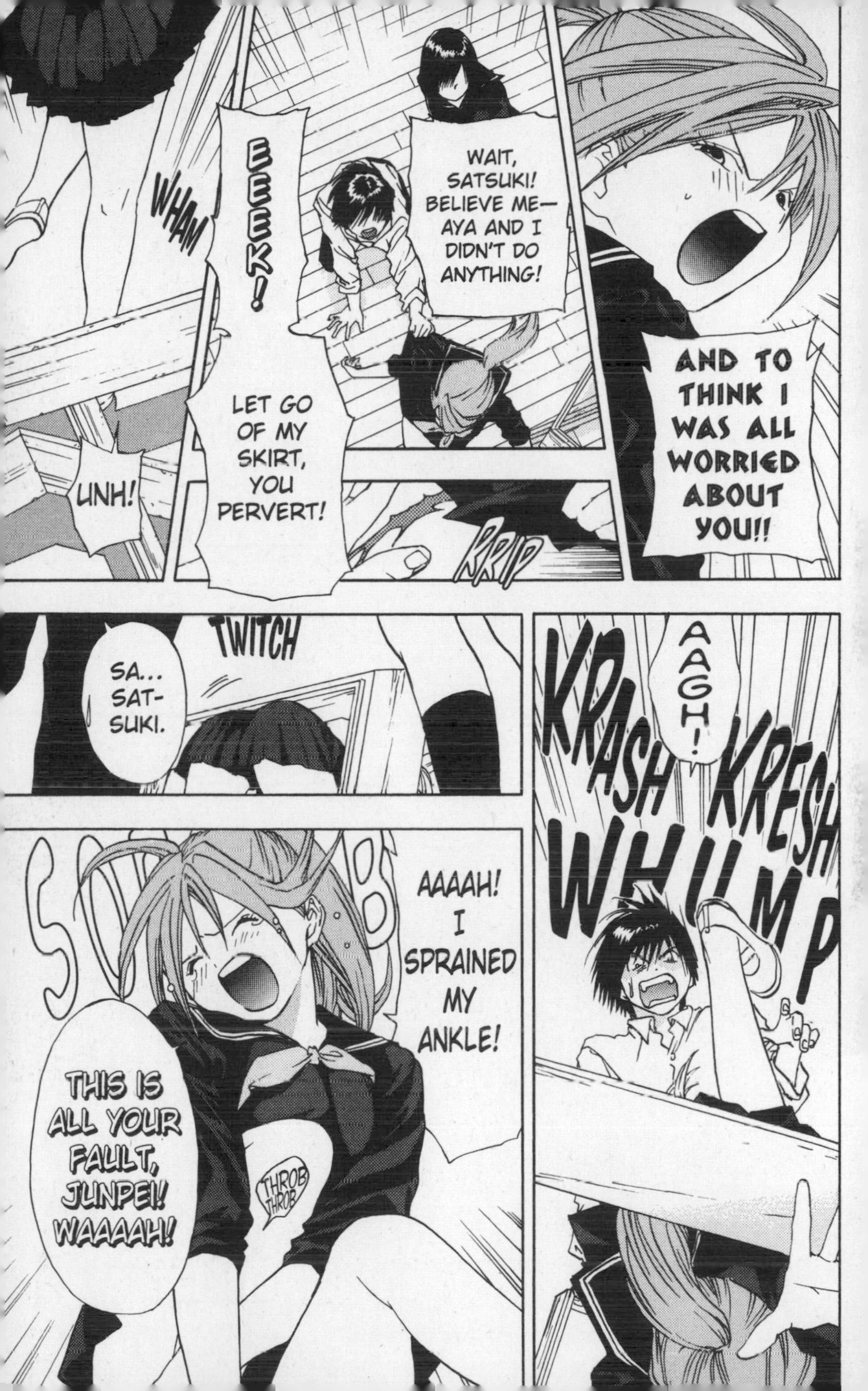
AND TO THINK I WAS ALL WORRIED ABOUT YOU!!
WAIT, SATSUKI! BELIEVE ME—AYA AND I DIDN'T DO ANYTHING!
EEEEK!
RRIP
LET GO OF MY SKIRT, YOU PERVERT!
WHAM
UNH!
KRESH
AAGH!
KRASH
WHUMP
TWITCH
SA... SAT-SUKI.
AAAAH! I SPRAINED MY ANKLE!
THROB THROB
THIS IS ALL YOUR FAULT, JUNPEI! WAAAAH!

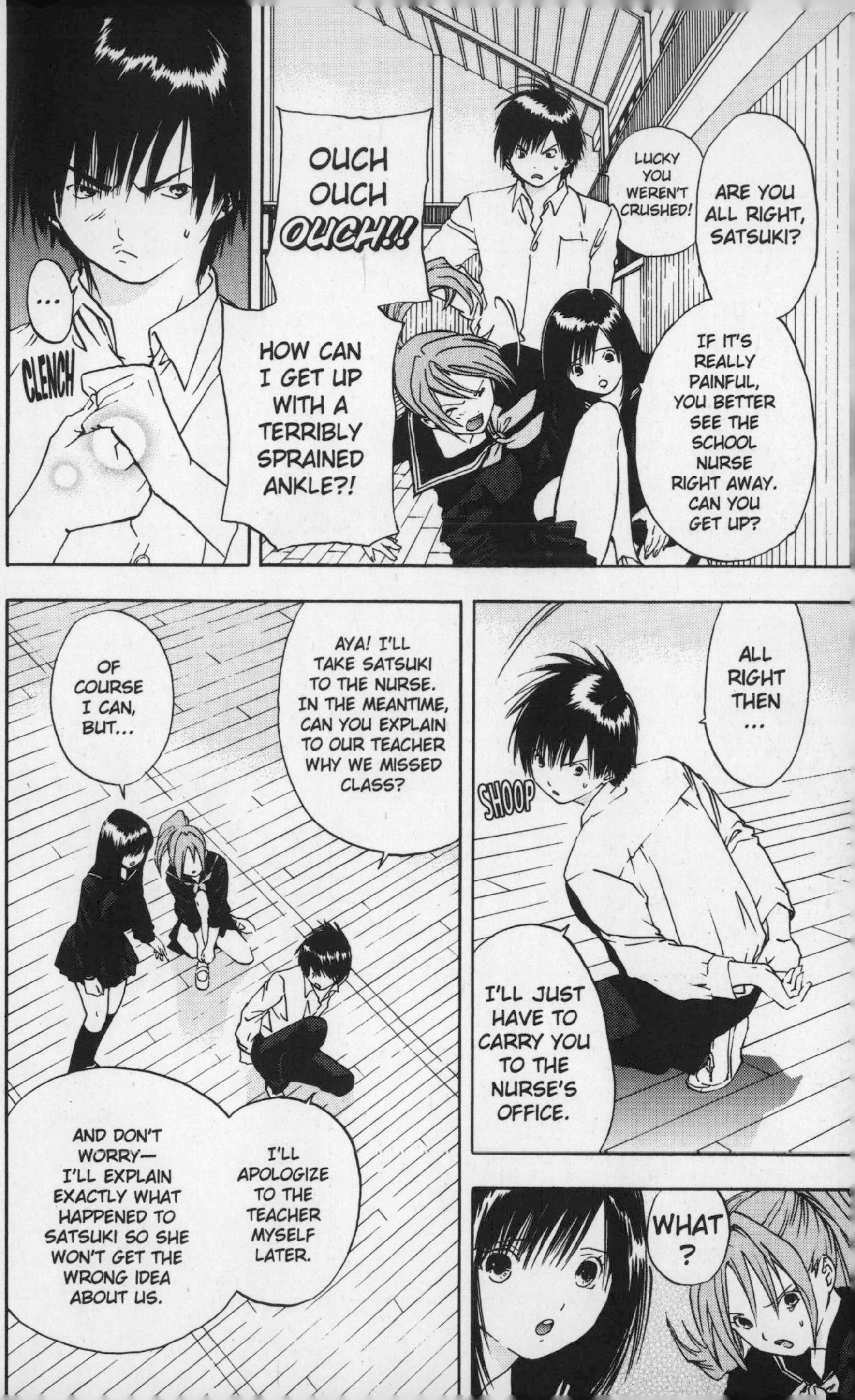
ARE YOU ALL RIGHT, SATSUKI?
LUCKY YOU WEREN'T CRUSHED!
OUCH OUCH OUCH!!
IF IT'S REALLY PAINFUL, YOU BETTER SEE THE SCHOOL NURSE RIGHT AWAY. CAN YOU GET UP?
HOW CAN I GET UP WITH A TERRIBLY SPRAINED ANKLE?!
...
CLENCH
ALL RIGHT THEN...
SHOOP
I'LL JUST HAVE TO CARRY YOU TO THE NURSE'S OFFICE.
WHAT?
AYA! I'LL TAKE SATSUKI TO THE NURSE. IN THE MEANTIME, CAN YOU EXPLAIN TO OUR TEACHER WHY WE MISSED CLASS?
OF COURSE I CAN, BUT...
I'LL APOLOGIZE TO THE TEACHER MYSELF LATER.
AND DON'T WORRY— I'LL EXPLAIN EXACTLY WHAT HAPPENED TO SATSUKI SO SHE WON'T GET THE WRONG IDEA ABOUT US.

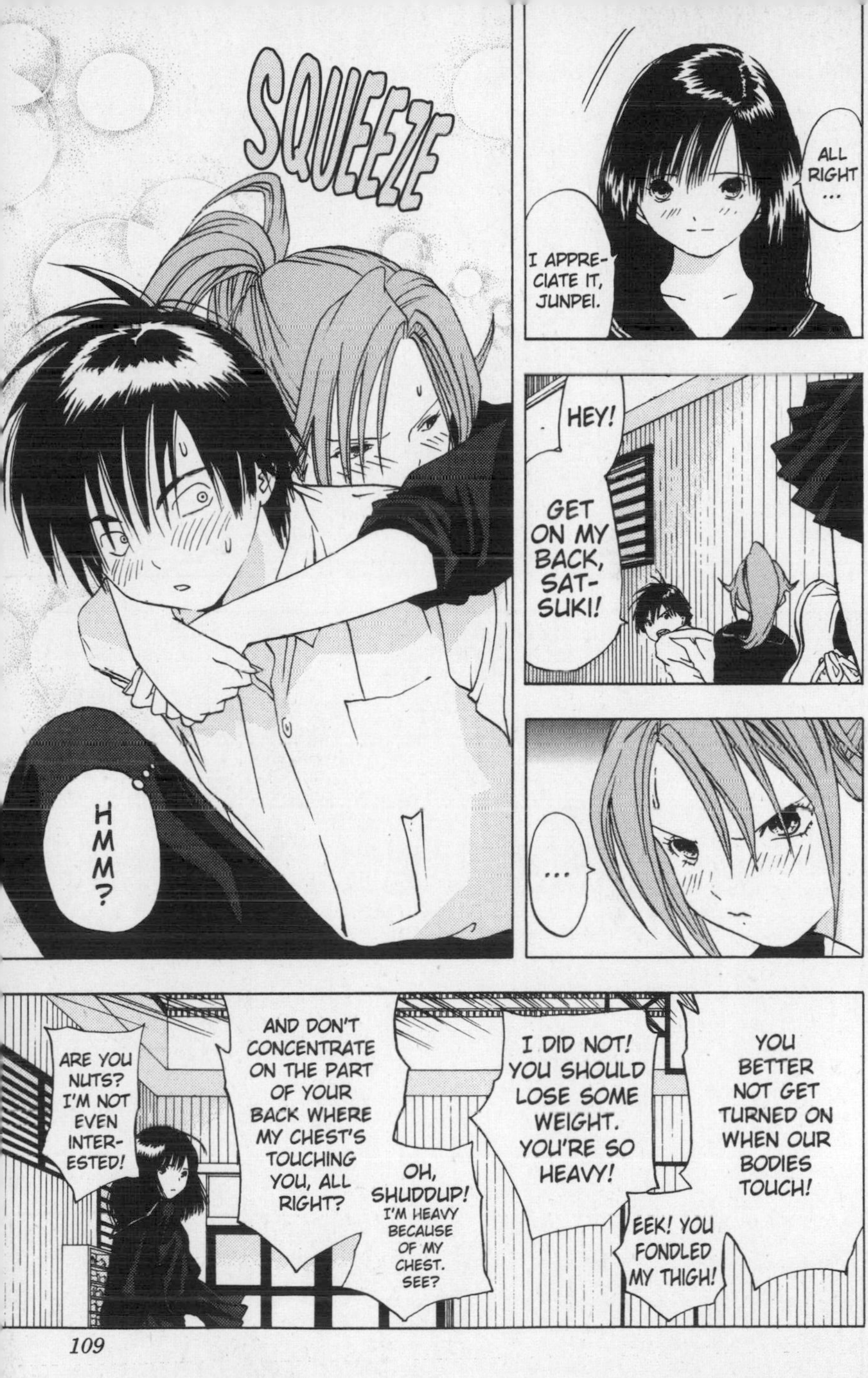
ALL RIGHT ...
I APPRECIATE IT, JUNPEI.
HEY!
GET ON MY BACK, SATSUKI!
...
SQUEEZE
HMM?
YOU BETTER NOT GET TURNED ON WHEN OUR BODIES TOUCH!
EEK! YOU FONDLED MY THIGH!
I DID NOT! YOU SHOULD LOSE SOME WEIGHT. YOU'RE SO HEAVY!
OH, SHUDDUP!
I'M HEAVY BECAUSE OF MY CHEST. SEE?
AND DON'T CONCENTRATE ON THE PART OF YOUR BACK WHERE MY CHEST'S TOUCHING YOU, ALL RIGHT?
ARE YOU NUTS? I'M NOT EVEN INTERESTED!

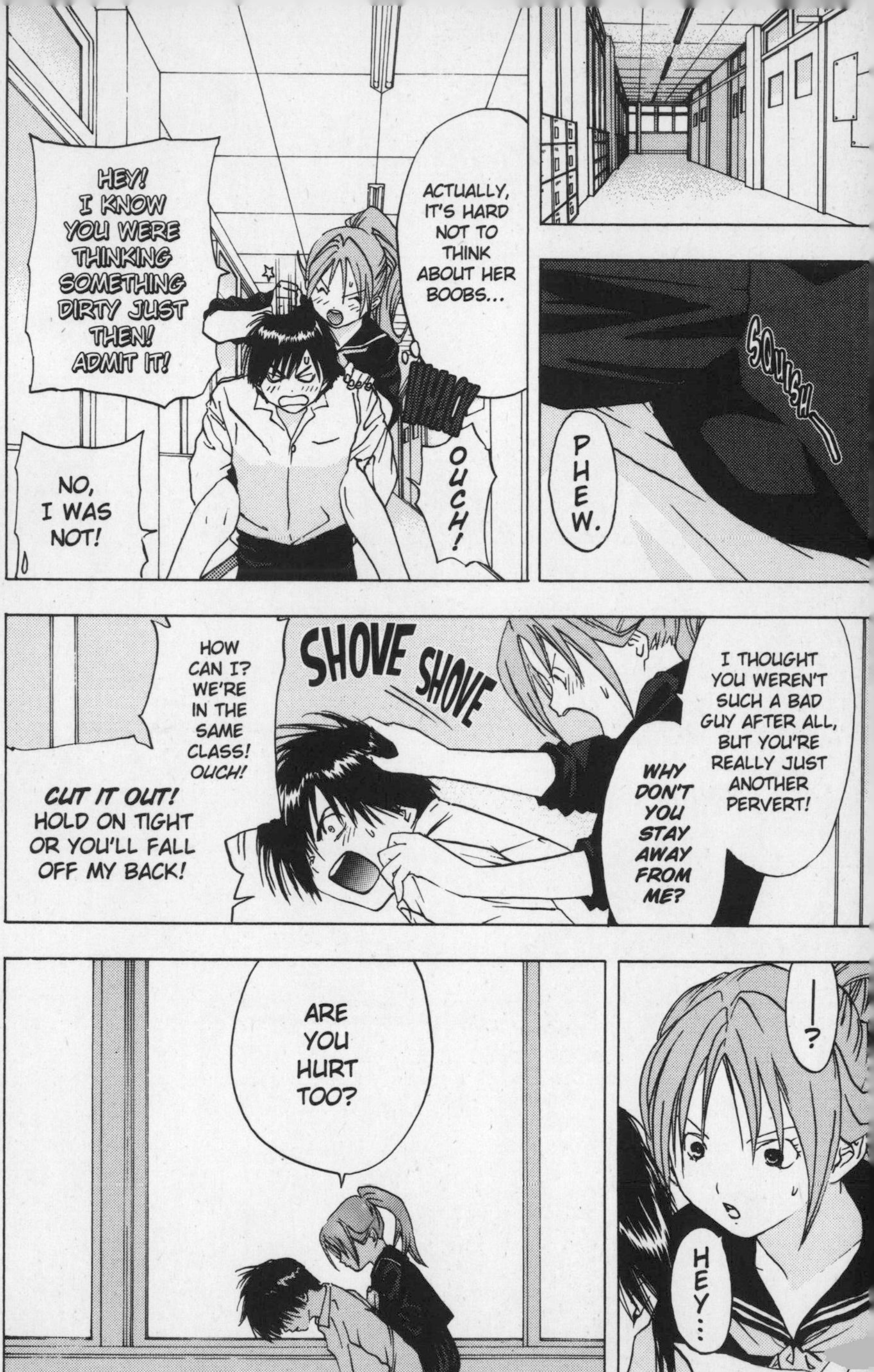
SQUISH—
PHEW.
ACTUALLY, IT'S HARD NOT TO THINK ABOUT HER BOOBS...
HEY! I KNOW YOU WERE THINKING SOMETHING DIRTY JUST THEN! ADMIT IT!
OUCH!
NO, I WAS NOT!
I THOUGHT YOU WEREN'T SUCH A BAD GUY AFTER ALL, BUT YOU'RE REALLY JUST ANOTHER PERVERT!
WHY DON'T YOU STAY AWAY FROM ME?
SHOVE SHOVE
HOW CAN I? WE'RE IN THE SAME CLASS! OUCH!
CUT IT OUT! HOLD ON TIGHT OR YOU'LL FALL OFF MY BACK!
—?
HEY...
ARE YOU HURT TOO?

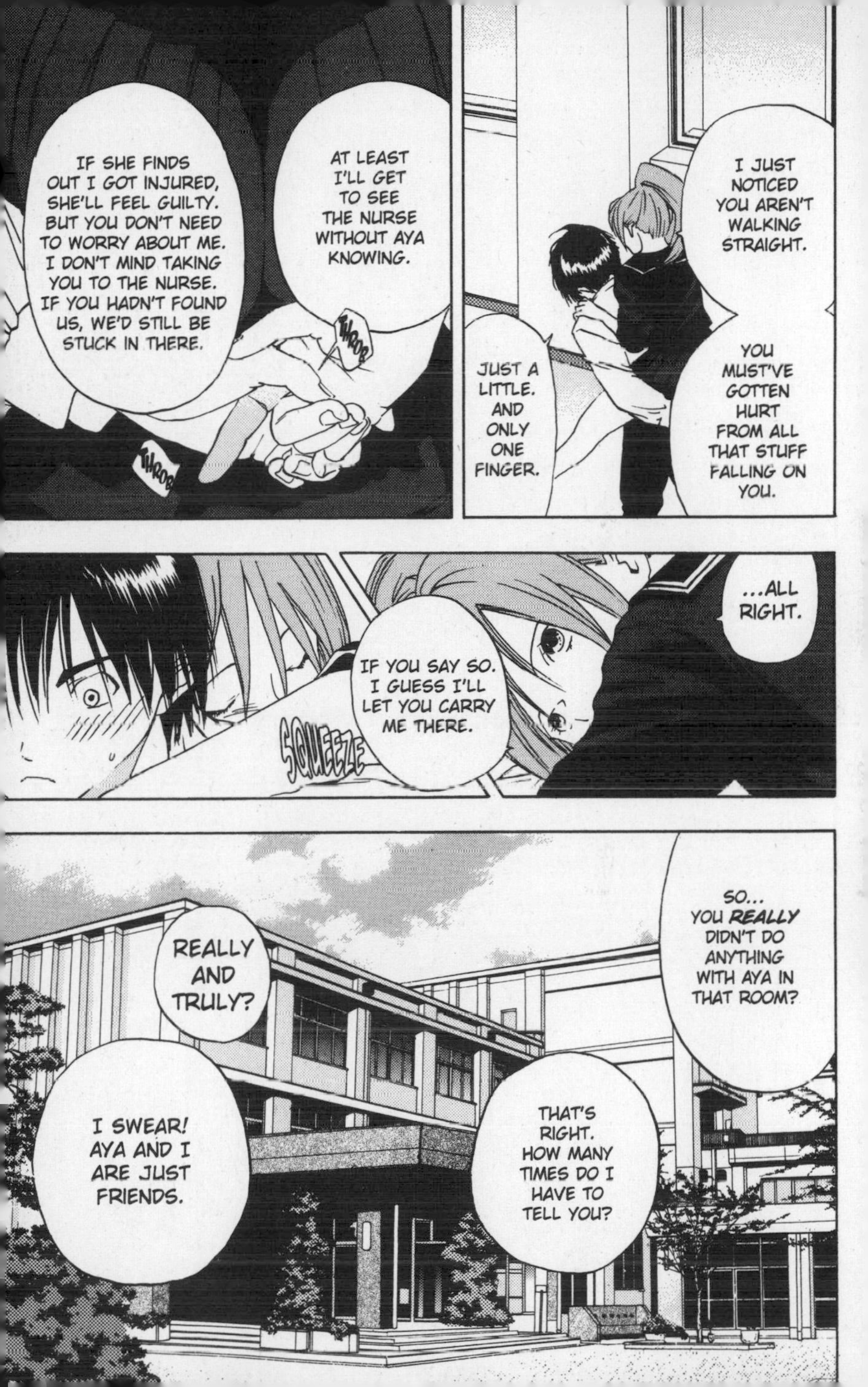
I JUST NOTICED YOU AREN'T WALKING STRAIGHT.
YOU MUST'VE GOTTEN HURT FROM ALL THAT STUFF FALLING ON YOU.
JUST A LITTLE. AND ONLY ONE FINGER.
AT LEAST I'LL GET TO SEE THE NURSE WITHOUT AYA KNOWING.
THROB
IF SHE FINDS OUT I GOT INJURED, SHE'LL FEEL GUILTY. BUT YOU DON'T NEED TO WORRY ABOUT ME. I DON'T MIND TAKING YOU TO THE NURSE. IF YOU HADN'T FOUND US, WE'D STILL BE STUCK IN THERE.
THROB
...ALL RIGHT.
IF YOU SAY SO. I GUESS I'LL LET YOU CARRY ME THERE.
SQUEEZE
SO... YOU *REALLY* DIDN'T DO ANYTHING WITH AYA IN THAT ROOM?
THAT'S RIGHT. HOW MANY TIMES DO I HAVE TO TELL YOU?
REALLY AND TRULY?
I SWEAR! AYA AND I ARE JUST FRIENDS.

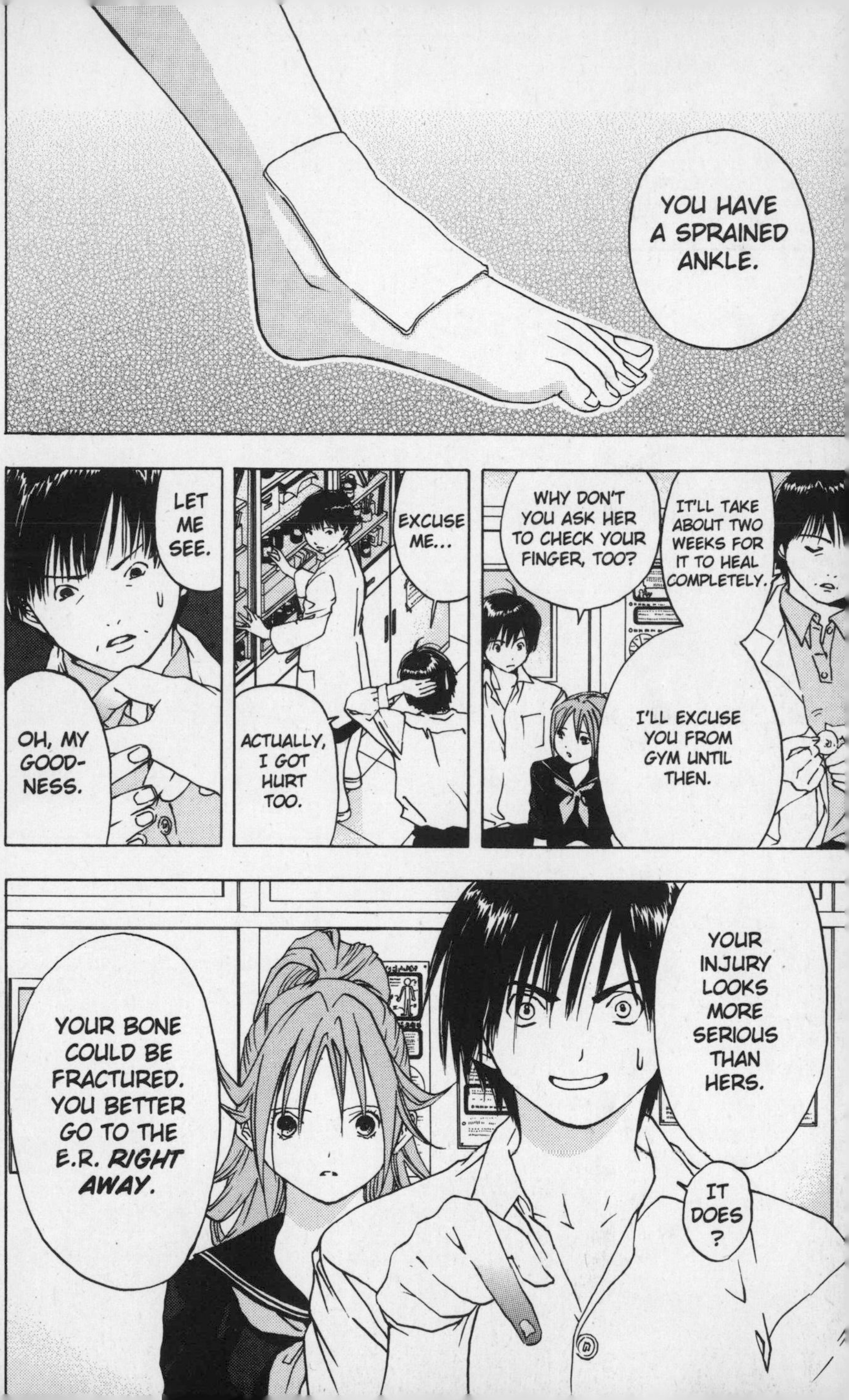
YOU HAVE A SPRAINED ANKLE.
IT'LL TAKE ABOUT TWO WEEKS FOR IT TO HEAL COMPLETELY.
I'LL EXCUSE YOU FROM GYM UNTIL THEN.
WHY DON'T YOU ASK HER TO CHECK YOUR FINGER, TOO?
EXCUSE ME...
ACTUALLY, I GOT HURT TOO.
LET ME SEE.
OH, MY GOODNESS.
YOUR INJURY LOOKS MORE SERIOUS THAN HERS.
IT DOES?
YOUR BONE COULD BE FRACTURED. YOU BETTER GO TO THE E.R. *RIGHT AWAY*.

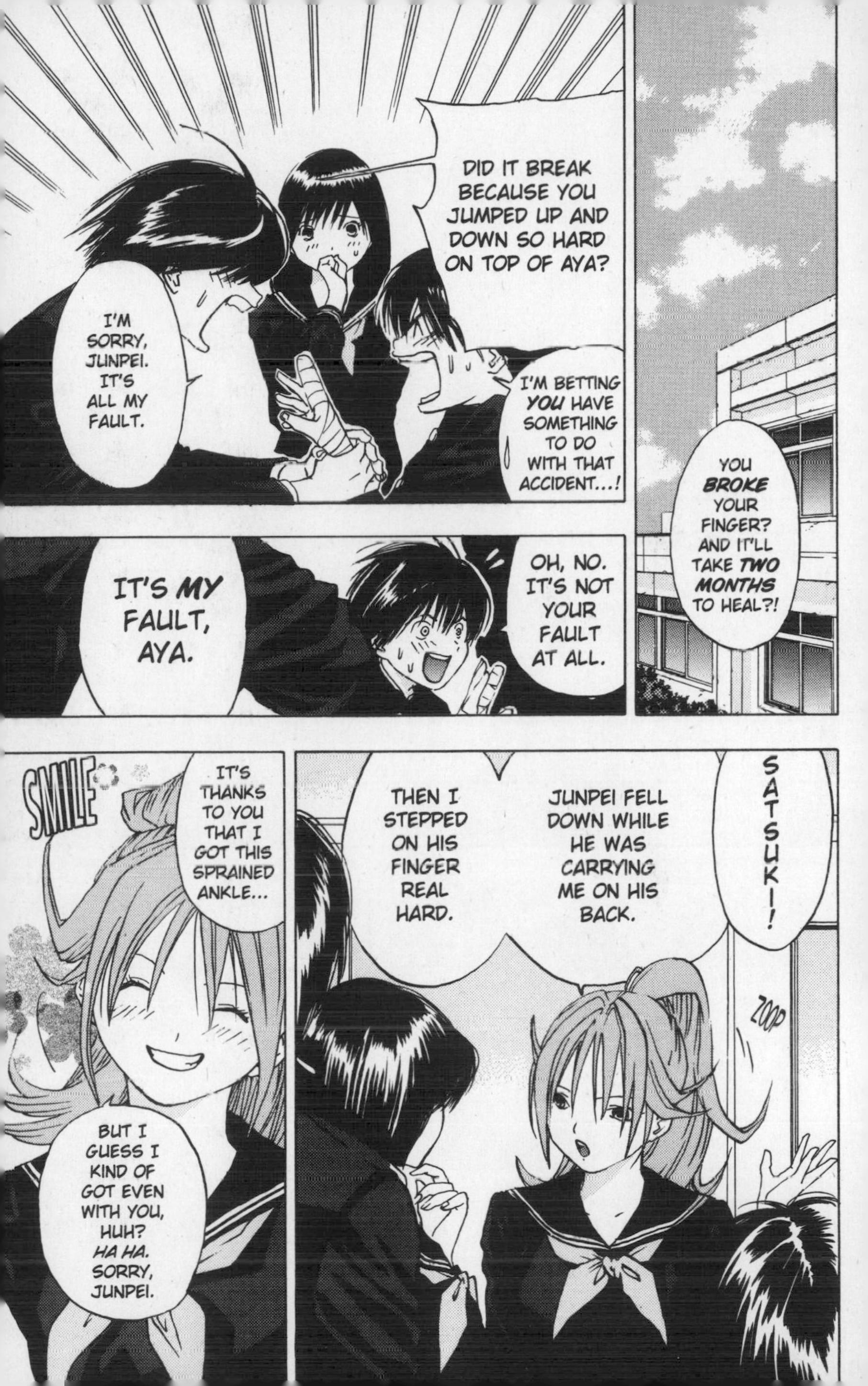
YOU **BROKE** YOUR FINGER? AND IT'LL TAKE **TWO MONTHS** TO HEAL?!
DID IT BREAK BECAUSE YOU JUMPED UP AND DOWN SO HARD ON TOP OF AYA?
I'M BETTING *YOU* HAVE SOMETHING TO DO WITH THAT ACCIDENT...!
I'M SORRY, JUNPEI. IT'S ALL MY FAULT.
OH, NO. IT'S NOT YOUR FAULT AT ALL.
IT'S *MY* FAULT, AYA.
SATSUKI!
ZOOP
JUNPEI FELL DOWN WHILE HE WAS CARRYING ME ON HIS BACK.
THEN I STEPPED ON HIS FINGER REAL HARD.
SMILE
IT'S THANKS TO YOU THAT I GOT THIS SPRAINED ANKLE...
BUT I GUESS I KIND OF GOT EVEN WITH YOU, HUH? *HA HA.* SORRY, JUNPEI.

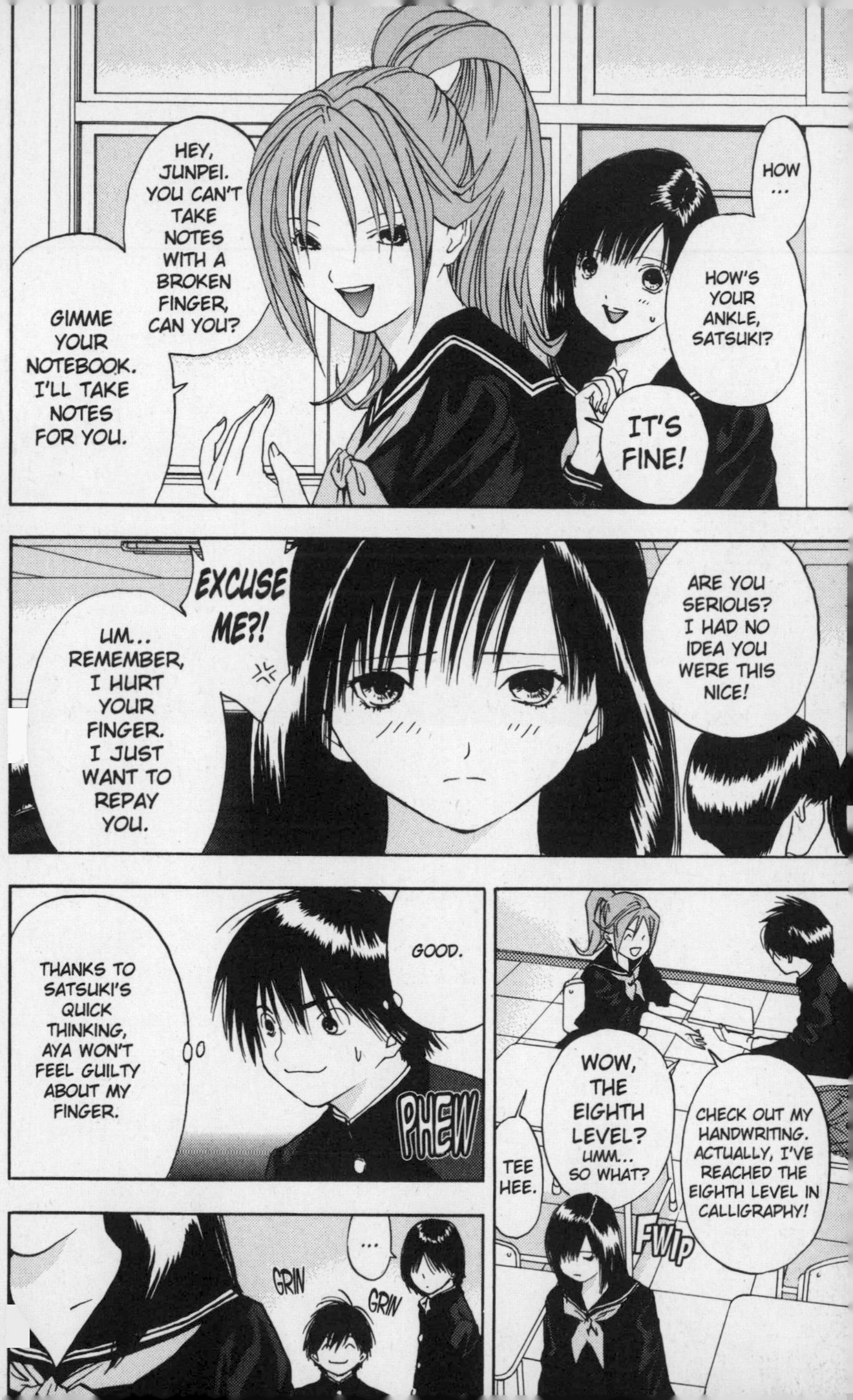
HOW ...
HOW'S YOUR ANKLE, SATSUKI?
IT'S FINE!
HEY, JUNPEI. YOU CAN'T TAKE NOTES WITH A BROKEN FINGER, CAN YOU?
GIMME YOUR NOTEBOOK. I'LL TAKE NOTES FOR YOU.
ARE YOU SERIOUS? I HAD NO IDEA YOU WERE THIS NICE!
EXCUSE ME?!
UM... REMEMBER, I HURT YOUR FINGER. I JUST WANT TO REPAY YOU.
CHECK OUT MY HANDWRITING. ACTUALLY, I'VE REACHED THE EIGHTH LEVEL IN CALLIGRAPHY!
WOW, THE EIGHTH LEVEL? UMM... SO WHAT?
TEE HEE.
FWIP
GOOD.
PHEW
THANKS TO SATSUKI'S QUICK THINKING, AYA WON'T FEEL GUILTY ABOUT MY FINGER.
...
GRIN
GRIN

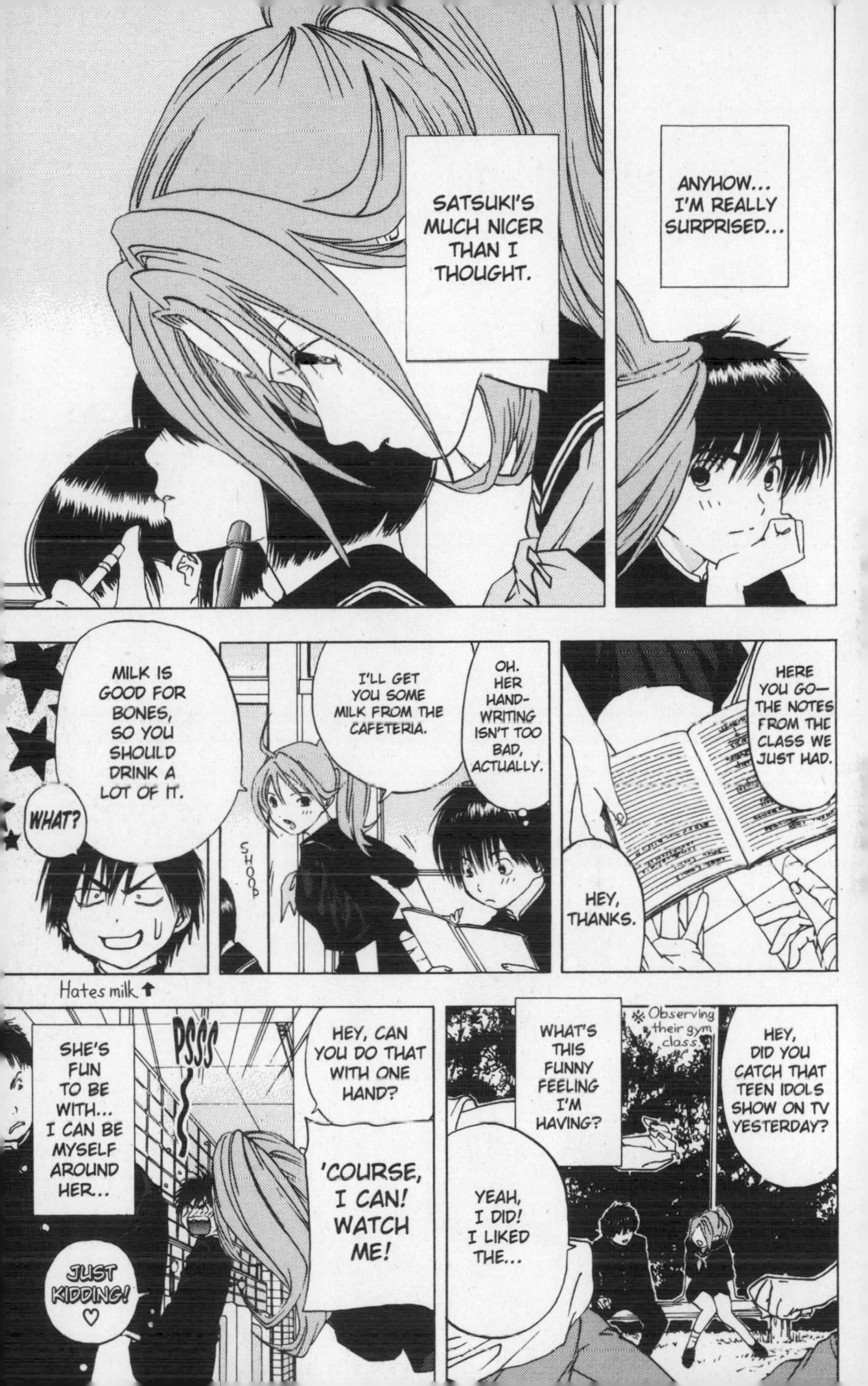
ANYHOW... I'M REALLY SURPRISED...
SATSUKI'S MUCH NICER THAN I THOUGHT.
HERE YOU GO— THE NOTES FROM THE CLASS WE JUST HAD.
HEY, THANKS.
OH. HER HAND-WRITING ISN'T TOO BAD, ACTUALLY.
I'LL GET YOU SOME MILK FROM THE CAFETERIA.
SHOOP
MILK IS GOOD FOR BONES, SO YOU SHOULD DRINK A LOT OF IT.
WHAT?
Hates milk.
※Observing their gym class.
HEY, DID YOU CATCH THAT TEEN IDOLS SHOW ON TV YESTERDAY?
WHAT'S THIS FUNNY FEELING I'M HAVING?
YEAH, I DID! I LIKED THE...
HEY, CAN YOU DO THAT WITH ONE HAND?
'COURSE, I CAN! WATCH ME!
PSSS
SHE'S FUN TO BE WITH... I CAN BE MYSELF AROUND HER..
JUST KIDDING! ♡

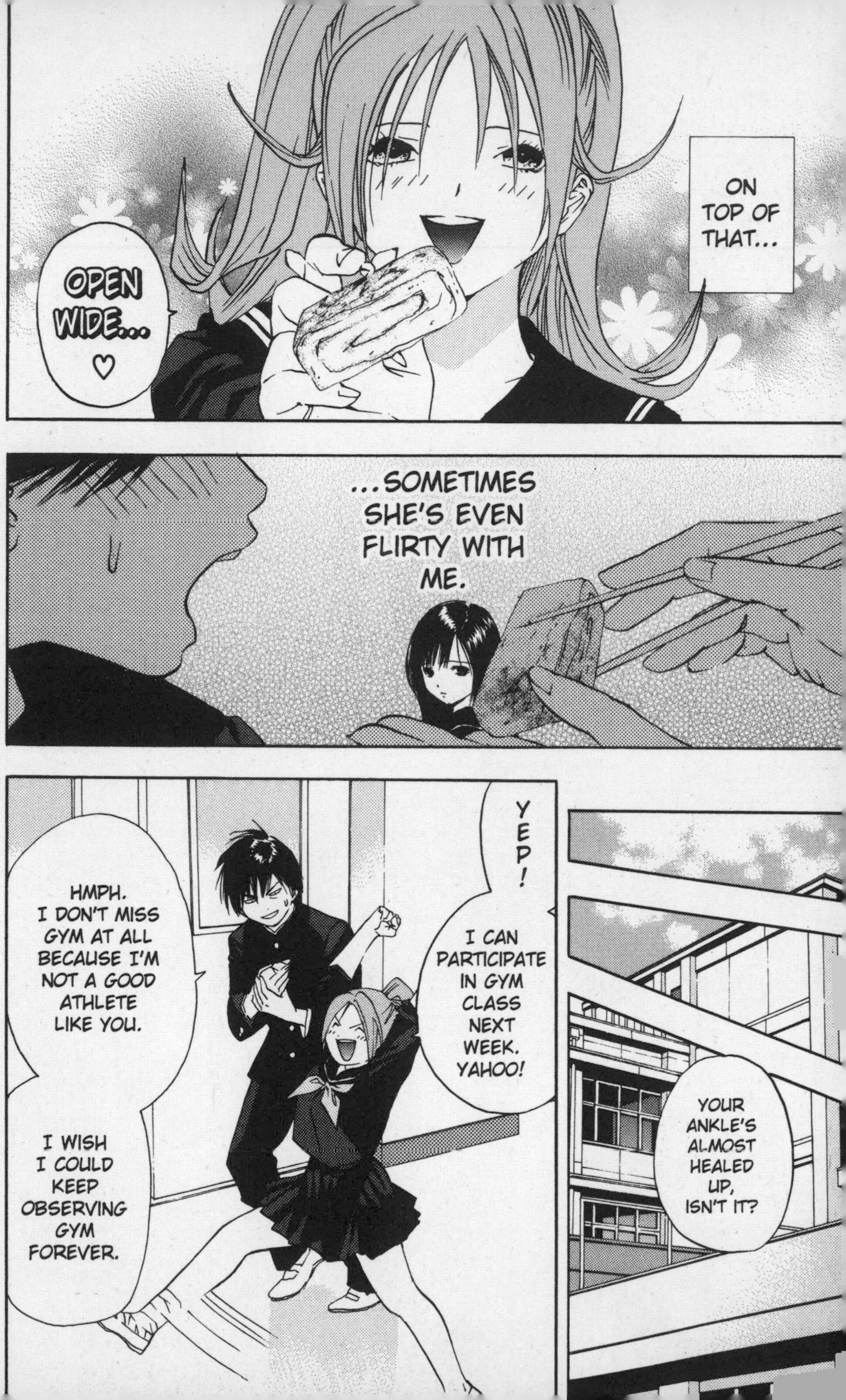
ON TOP OF THAT...
OPEN WIDE... ♡
...SOMETIMES SHE'S EVEN FLIRTY WITH ME.
YOUR ANKLE'S ALMOST HEALED UP, ISN'T IT?
YEP!
I CAN PARTICIPATE IN GYM CLASS NEXT WEEK. YAHOO!
HMPH. I DON'T MISS GYM AT ALL BECAUSE I'M NOT A GOOD ATHLETE LIKE YOU.
I WISH I COULD KEEP OBSERVING GYM FOREVER.

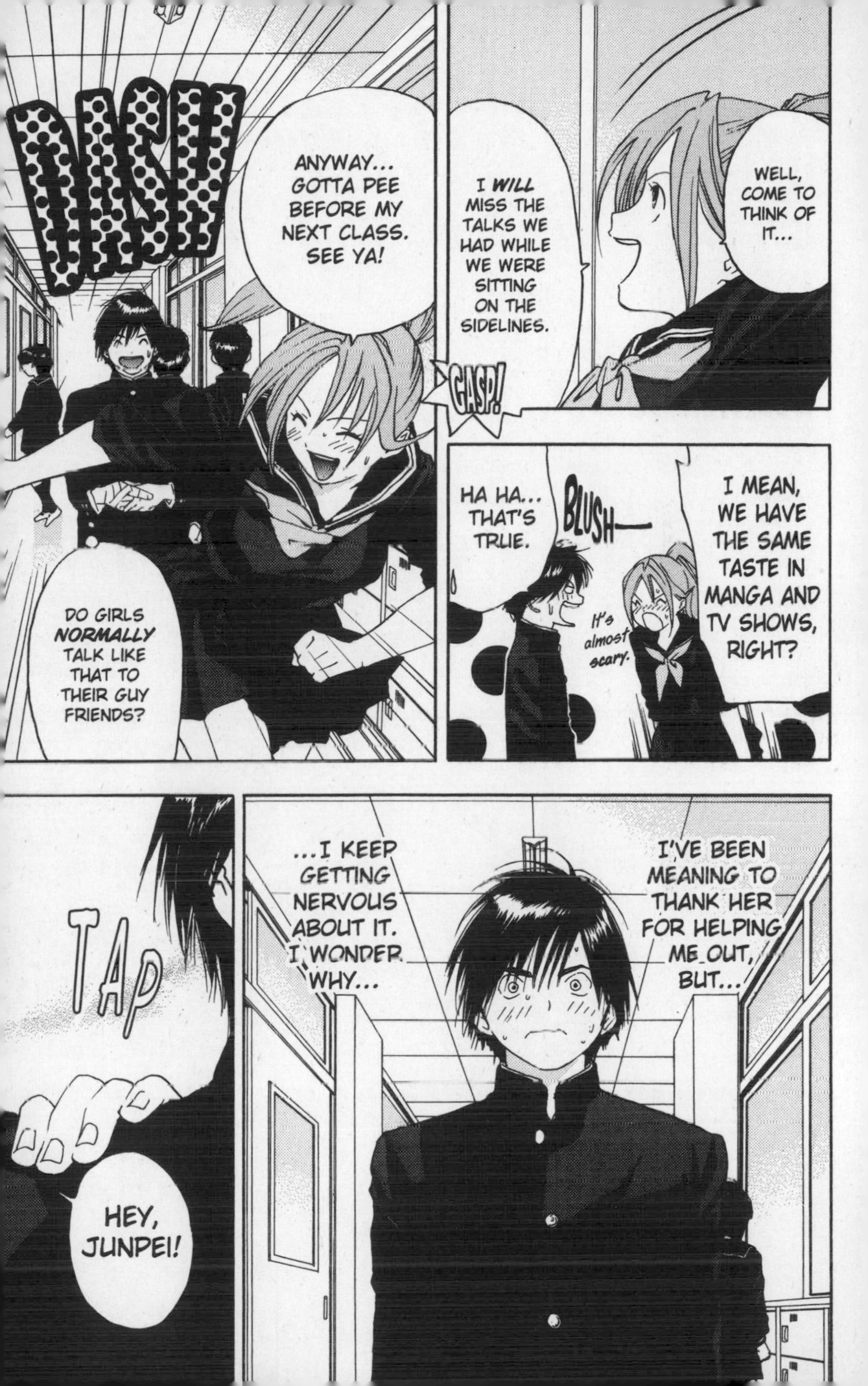
WELL, COME TO THINK OF IT...
I WILL MISS THE TALKS WE HAD WHILE WE WERE SITTING ON THE SIDELINES.
I MEAN, WE HAVE THE SAME TASTE IN MANGA AND TV SHOWS, RIGHT?
BLUSH—
It's almost scary.
HA HA... THAT'S TRUE.
DASH!
ANYWAY... GOTTA PEE BEFORE MY NEXT CLASS. SEE YA!
GASP!
DO GIRLS NORMALLY TALK LIKE THAT TO THEIR GUY FRIENDS?
I'VE BEEN MEANING TO THANK HER FOR HELPING ME OUT, BUT...
...I KEEP GETTING NERVOUS ABOUT IT. I WONDER WHY...
TAP
HEY, JUNPEI!

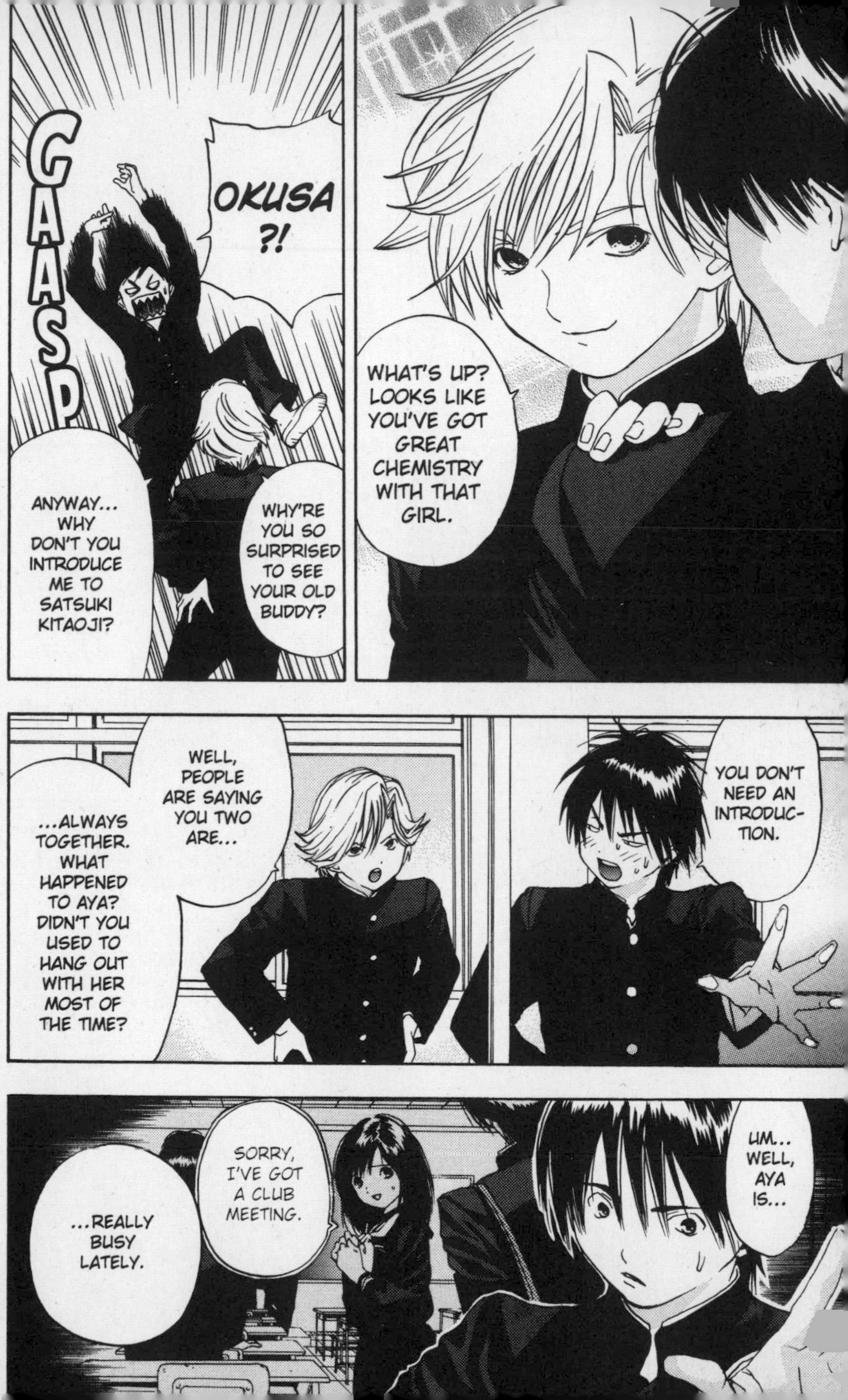

WHAT'S UP? LOOKS LIKE YOU'VE GOT GREAT CHEMISTRY WITH THAT GIRL.
OKUSA ?!
GAASP
WHY'RE YOU SO SURPRISED TO SEE YOUR OLD BUDDY?
ANYWAY... WHY DON'T YOU INTRODUCE ME TO SATSUKI KITAOJI?
YOU DON'T NEED AN INTRODUC-TION.
WELL, PEOPLE ARE SAYING YOU TWO ARE...
...ALWAYS TOGETHER. WHAT HAPPENED TO AYA? DIDN'T YOU USED TO HANG OUT WITH HER MOST OF THE TIME?
UM... WELL, AYA IS...
SORRY, I'VE GOT A CLUB MEETING.
...REALLY BUSY LATELY.

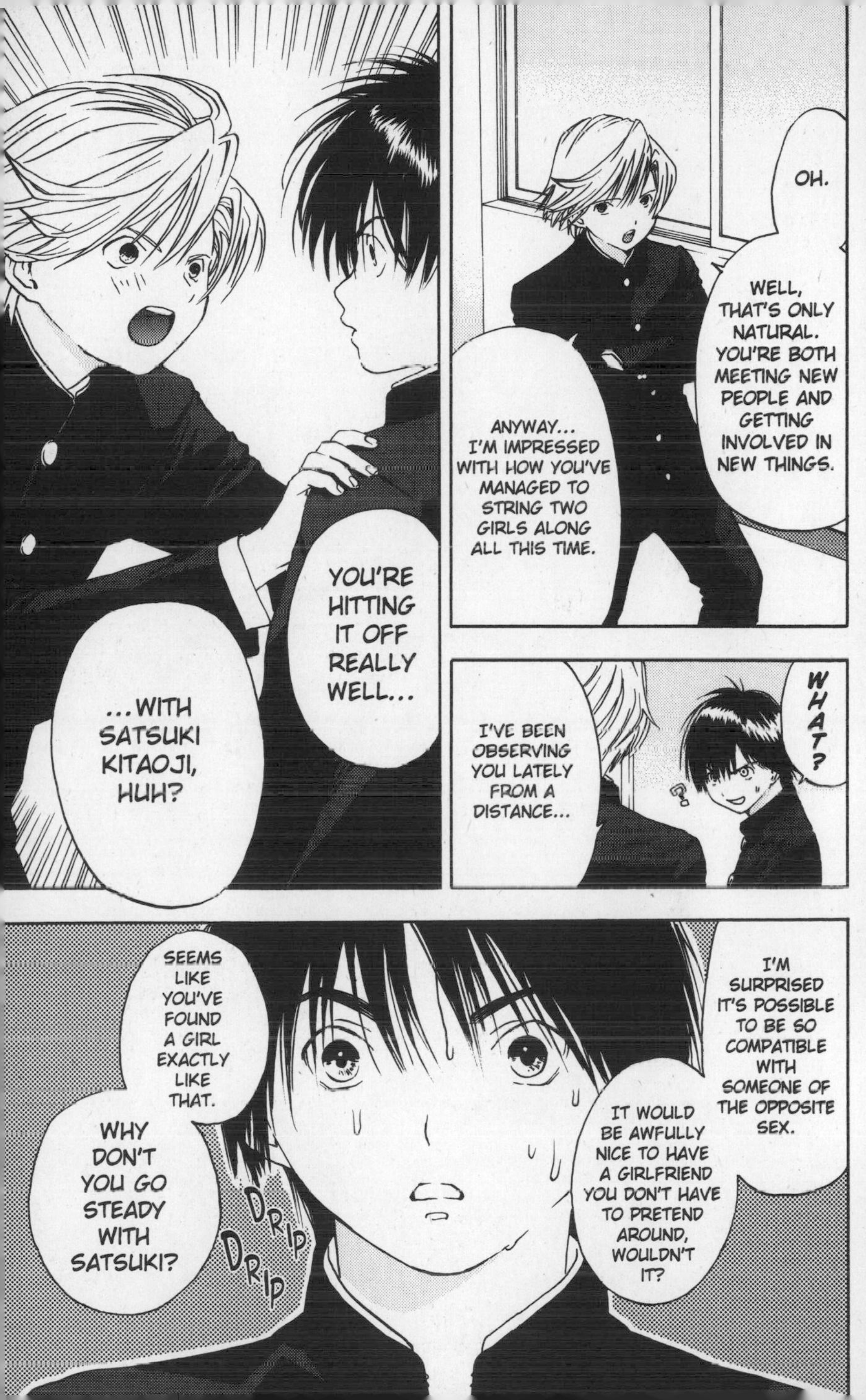
OH.
WELL, THAT'S ONLY NATURAL. YOU'RE BOTH MEETING NEW PEOPLE AND GETTING INVOLVED IN NEW THINGS.
ANYWAY... I'M IMPRESSED WITH HOW YOU'VE MANAGED TO STRING TWO GIRLS ALONG ALL THIS TIME.
WHAT?
I'VE BEEN OBSERVING YOU LATELY FROM A DISTANCE...
YOU'RE HITTING IT OFF REALLY WELL...
...WITH SATSUKI KITAOJI, HUH?
I'M SURPRISED IT'S POSSIBLE TO BE SO COMPATIBLE WITH SOMEONE OF THE OPPOSITE SEX.
IT WOULD BE AWFULLY NICE TO HAVE A GIRLFRIEND YOU DON'T HAVE TO PRETEND AROUND, WOULDN'T IT?
SEEMS LIKE YOU'VE FOUND A GIRL EXACTLY LIKE THAT.
WHY DON'T YOU GO STEADY WITH SATSUKI?
DRIP
DRIP

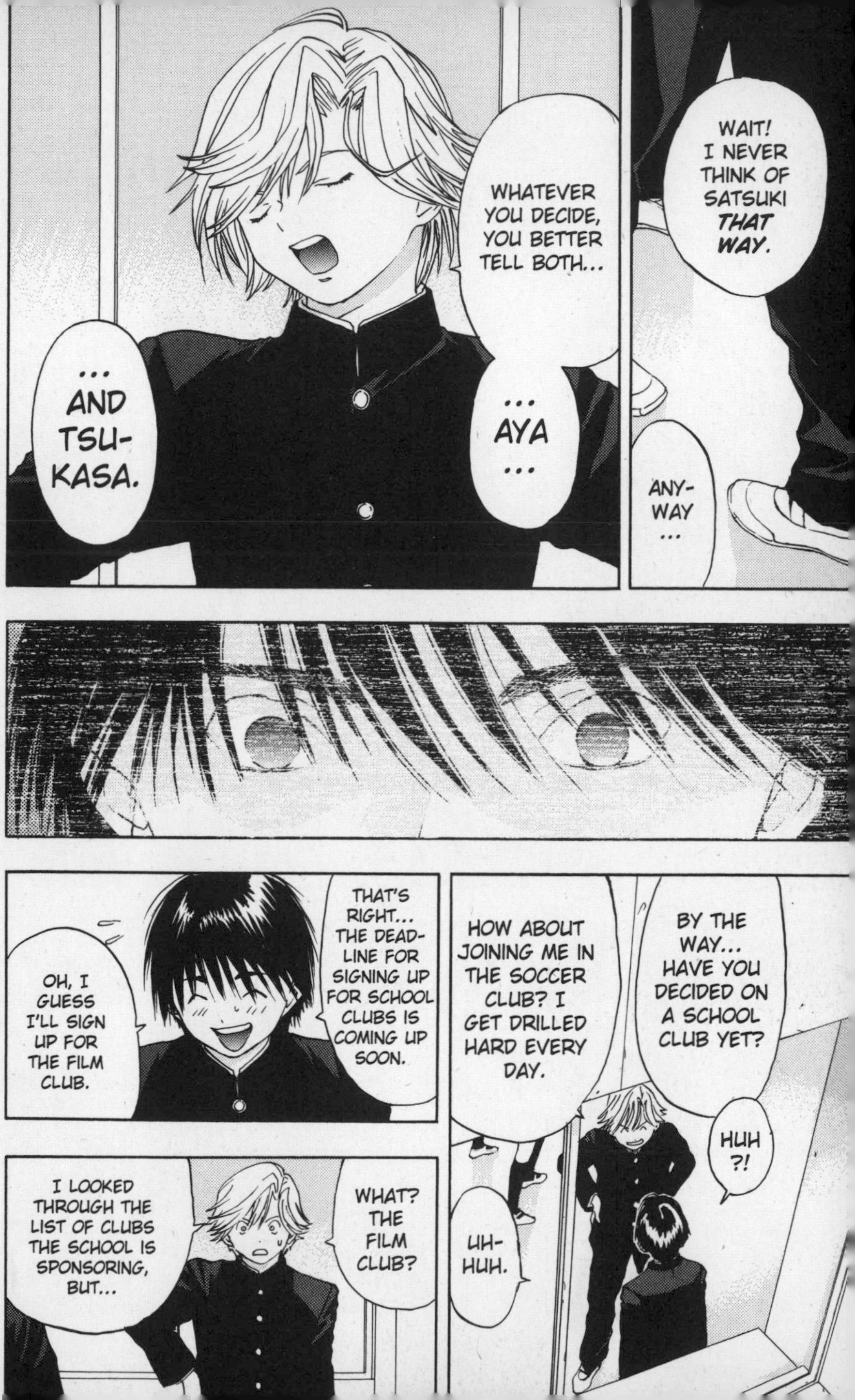
WAIT! I NEVER THINK OF SATSUKI *THAT WAY.*
ANY-WAY...
WHATEVER YOU DECIDE, YOU BETTER TELL BOTH...
...AYA...
...AND TSU-KASA.
BY THE WAY... HAVE YOU DECIDED ON A SCHOOL CLUB YET?
HOW ABOUT JOINING ME IN THE SOCCER CLUB? I GET DRILLED HARD EVERY DAY.
HUH?!
UH-HUH.
THAT'S RIGHT... THE DEAD-LINE FOR SIGNING UP FOR SCHOOL CLUBS IS COMING UP SOON.
OH, I GUESS I'LL SIGN UP FOR THE FILM CLUB.
WHAT? THE FILM CLUB?
I LOOKED THROUGH THE LIST OF CLUBS THE SCHOOL IS SPONSORING, BUT...

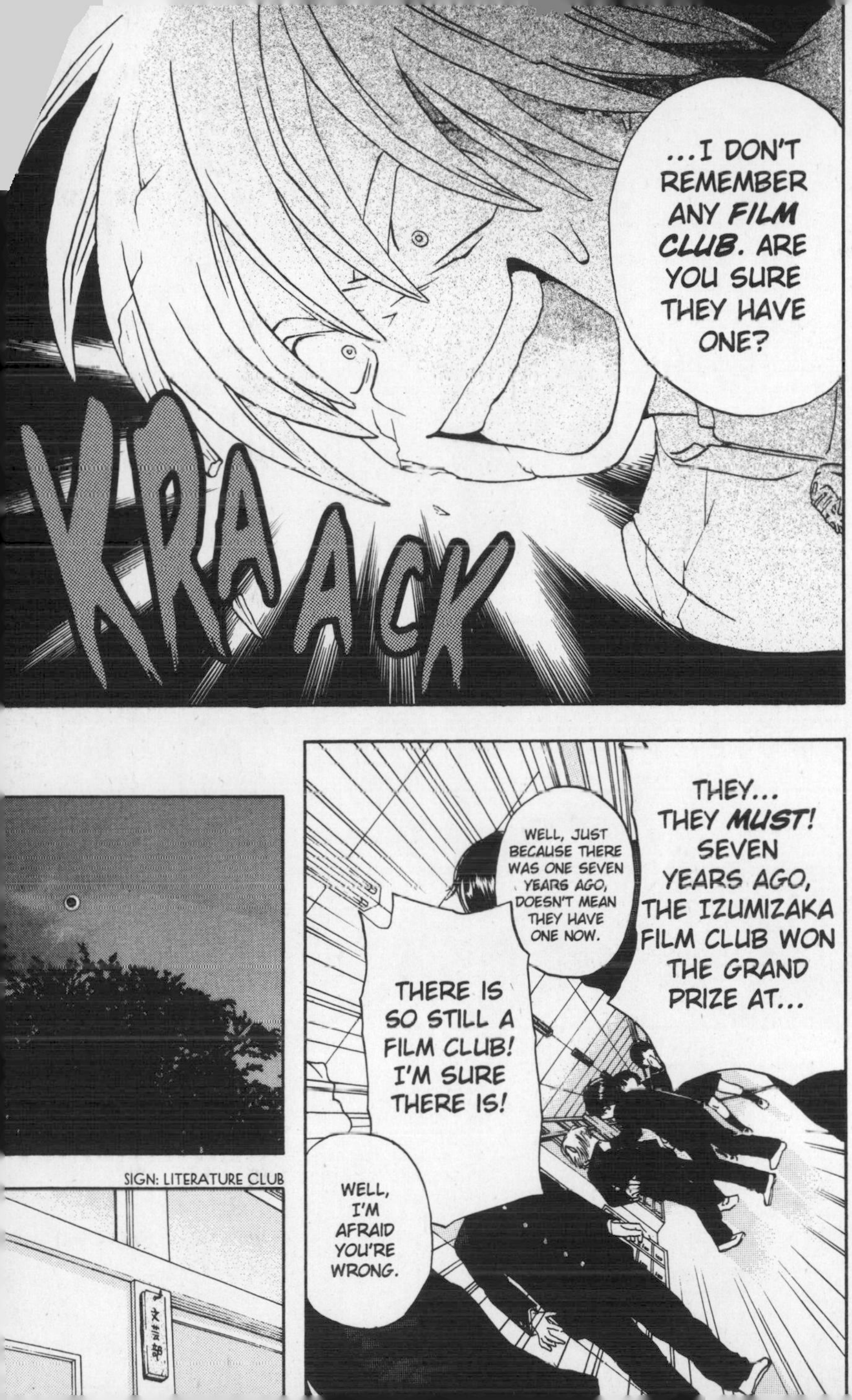
...I DON'T REMEMBER ANY *FILM CLUB*. ARE YOU SURE THEY HAVE ONE?
KRAACK
THEY... THEY *MUST*! SEVEN YEARS AGO, THE IZUMIZAKA FILM CLUB WON THE GRAND PRIZE AT...
WELL, JUST BECAUSE THERE WAS ONE SEVEN YEARS AGO, DOESN'T MEAN THEY HAVE ONE NOW.
THERE IS SO STILL A FILM CLUB! I'M SURE THERE IS!
WELL, I'M AFRAID YOU'RE WRONG.
SIGN: LITERATURE CLUB

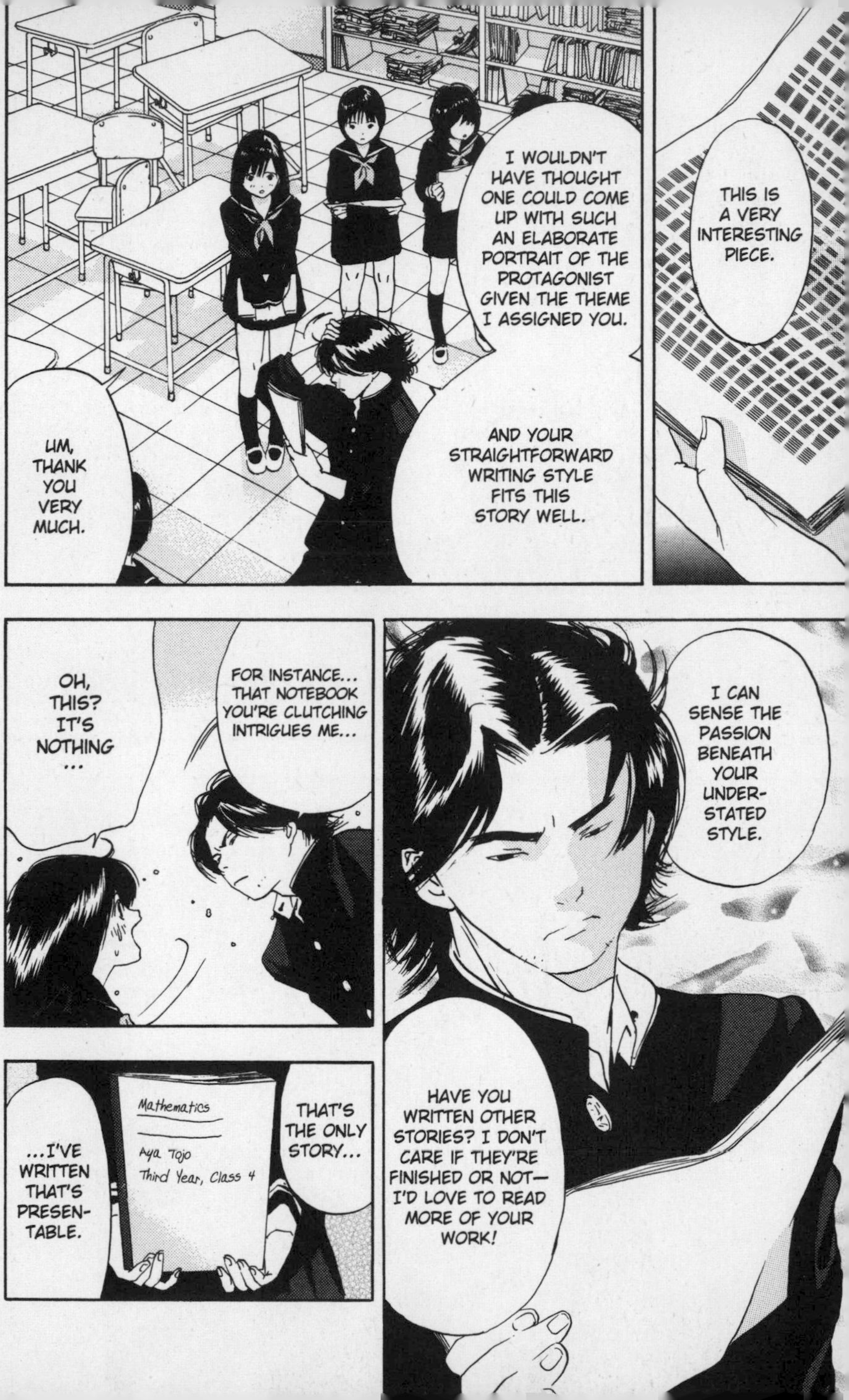
THIS IS A VERY INTERESTING PIECE.
I WOULDN'T HAVE THOUGHT ONE COULD COME UP WITH SUCH AN ELABORATE PORTRAIT OF THE PROTAGONIST GIVEN THE THEME I ASSIGNED YOU.
AND YOUR STRAIGHTFORWARD WRITING STYLE FITS THIS STORY WELL.
UM, THANK YOU VERY MUCH.
I CAN SENSE THE PASSION BENEATH YOUR UNDER-STATED STYLE.
HAVE YOU WRITTEN OTHER STORIES? I DON'T CARE IF THEY'RE FINISHED OR NOT— I'D LOVE TO READ MORE OF YOUR WORK!
FOR INSTANCE... THAT NOTEBOOK YOU'RE CLUTCHING INTRIGUES ME...
OH, THIS? IT'S NOTHING ...
Mathematics
Aya Tojo
Third Year, Class 4
THAT'S THE ONLY STORY...
...I'VE WRITTEN THAT'S PRESEN-TABLE.

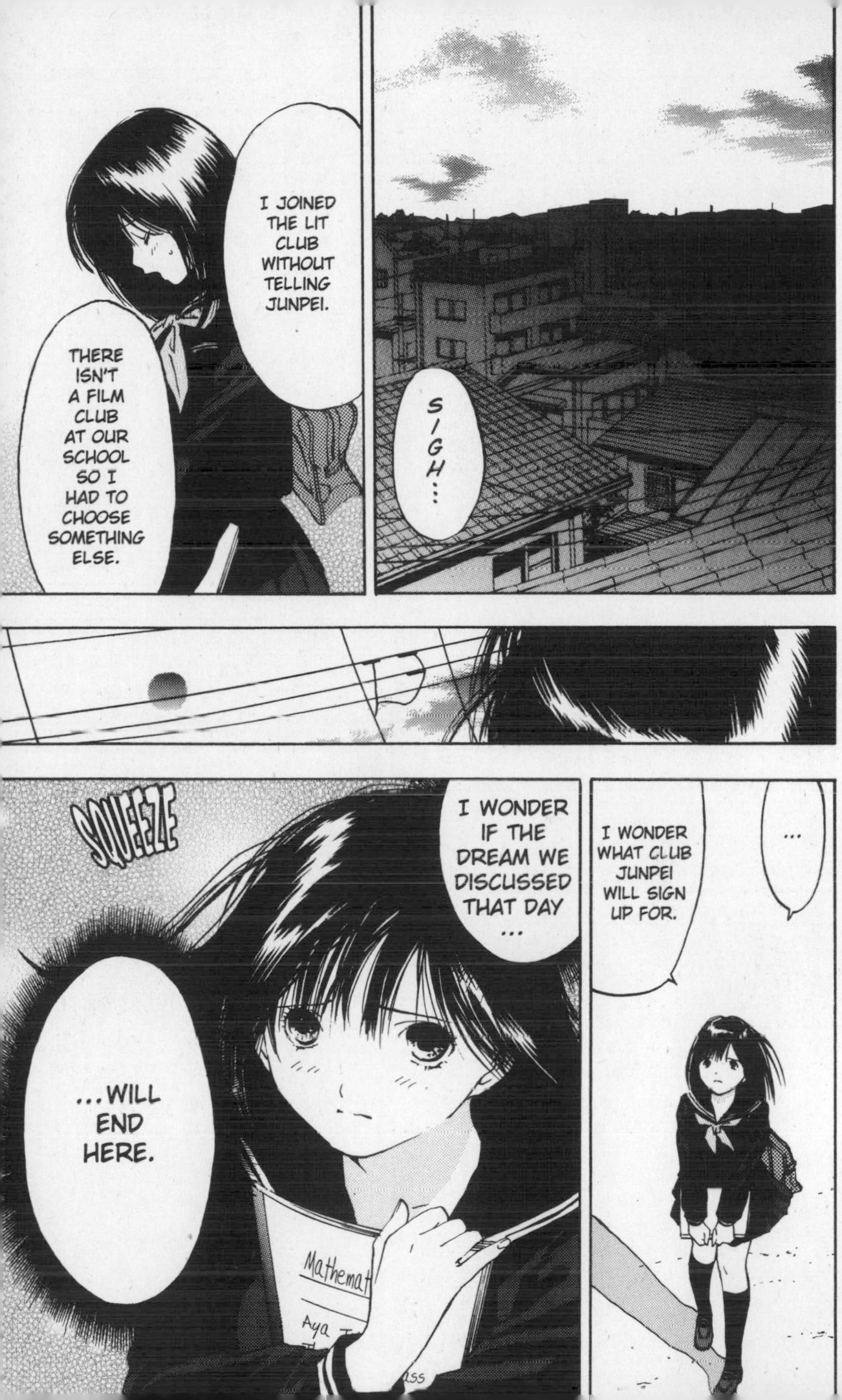
S/GH...
I JOINED THE LIT CLUB WITHOUT TELLING JUNPEI.
THERE ISN'T A FILM CLUB AT OUR SCHOOL SO I HAD TO CHOOSE SOMETHING ELSE.
...
I WONDER WHAT CLUB JUNPEI WILL SIGN UP FOR.
I WONDER IF THE DREAM WE DISCUSSED THAT DAY ...
SQUEEZE
...WILL END HERE.
Mathemat
Aya

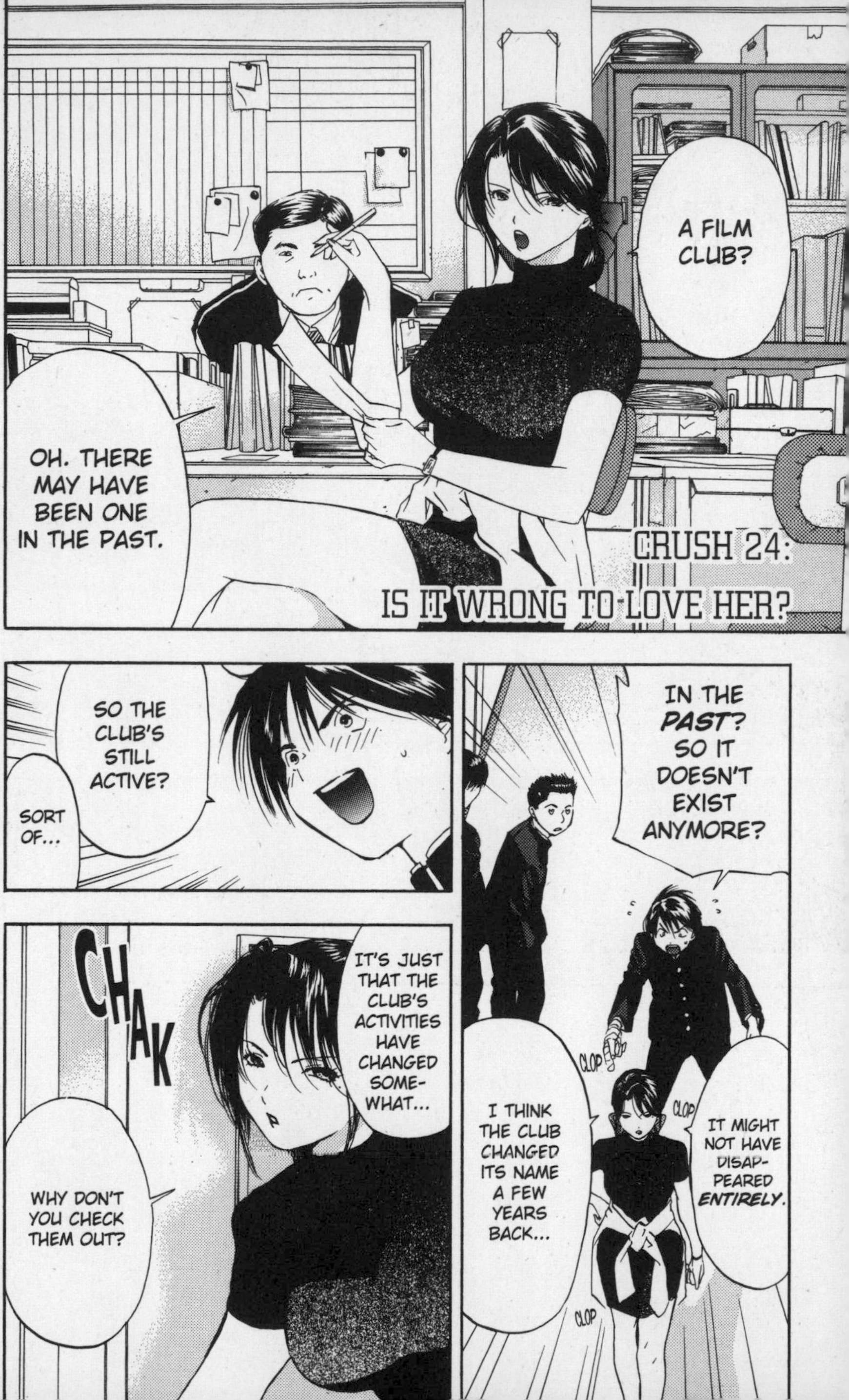
A FILM CLUB?
OH. THERE MAY HAVE BEEN ONE IN THE PAST.
CRUSH 24: IS IT WRONG TO LOVE HER?
IN THE *PAST*? SO IT DOESN'T EXIST ANYMORE?
CLOP
CLOP
IT MIGHT NOT HAVE DISAPPEARED *ENTIRELY*.
I THINK THE CLUB CHANGED ITS NAME A FEW YEARS BACK...
CLOP
SO THE CLUB'S STILL ACTIVE?
SORT OF...
CHAK
IT'S JUST THAT THE CLUB'S ACTIVITIES HAVE CHANGED SOMEWHAT...
WHY DON'T YOU CHECK THEM OUT?

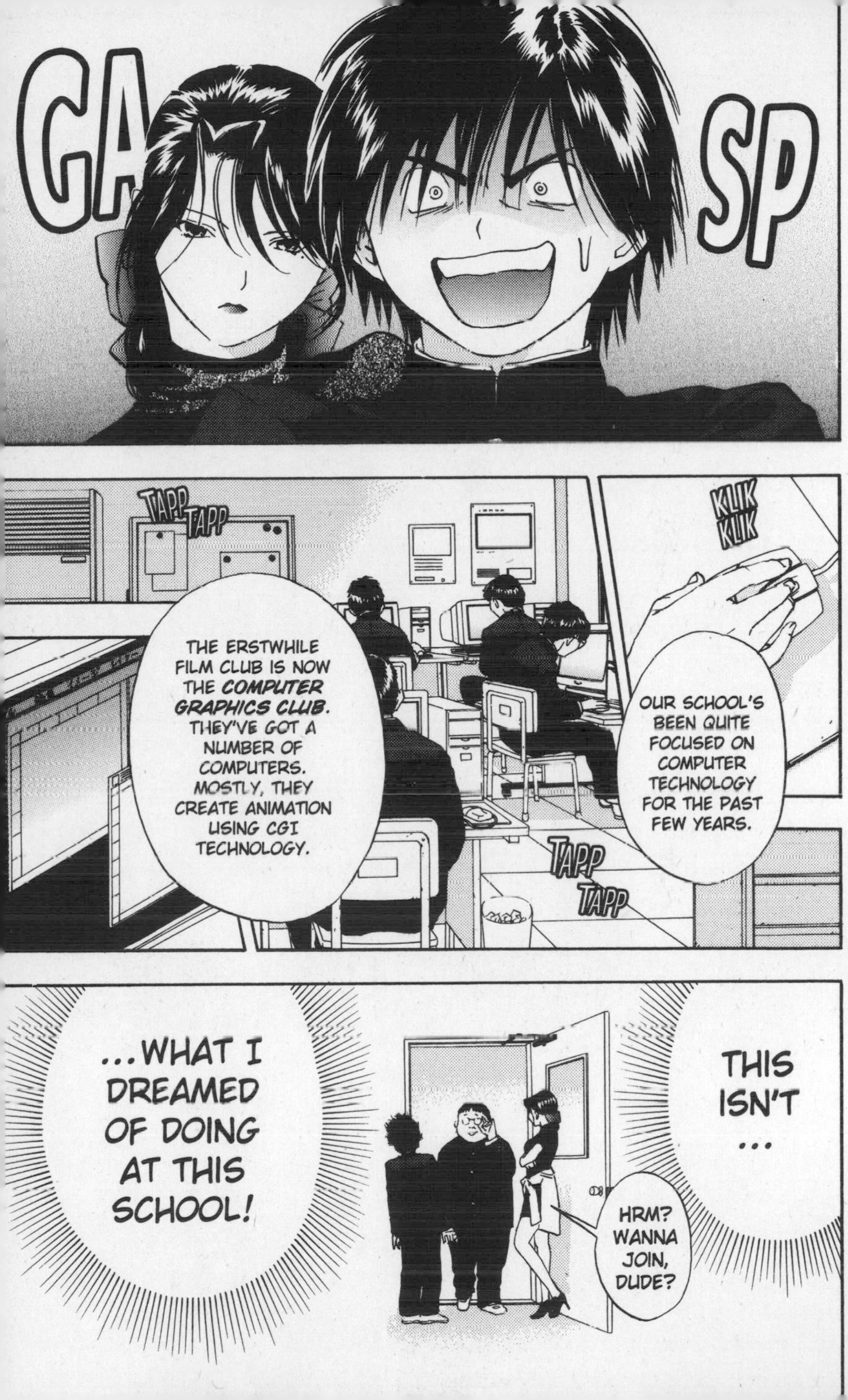
GA SP
KLIK KLIK
OUR SCHOOL'S BEEN QUITE FOCUSED ON COMPUTER TECHNOLOGY FOR THE PAST FEW YEARS.
TAPP TAPP
THE ERSTWHILE FILM CLUB IS NOW THE ***COMPUTER GRAPHICS CLUB***. THEY'VE GOT A NUMBER OF COMPUTERS. MOSTLY, THEY CREATE ANIMATION USING CGI TECHNOLOGY.
TAPP TAPP
THIS ISN'T ...
HRM? WANNA JOIN, DUDE?
...WHAT I DREAMED OF DOING AT THIS SCHOOL!

CRUSH 24: IS IT WRONG TO LOVE HER?

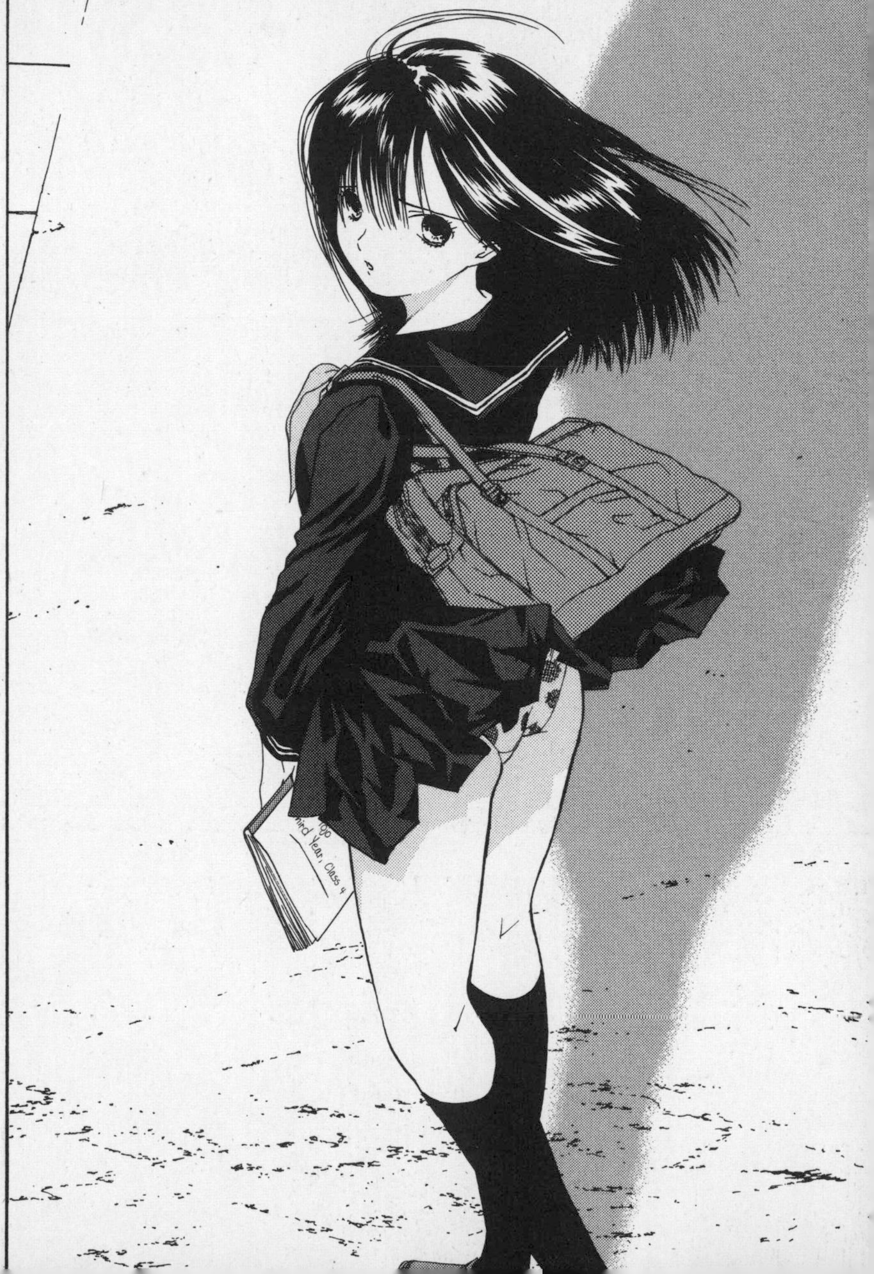

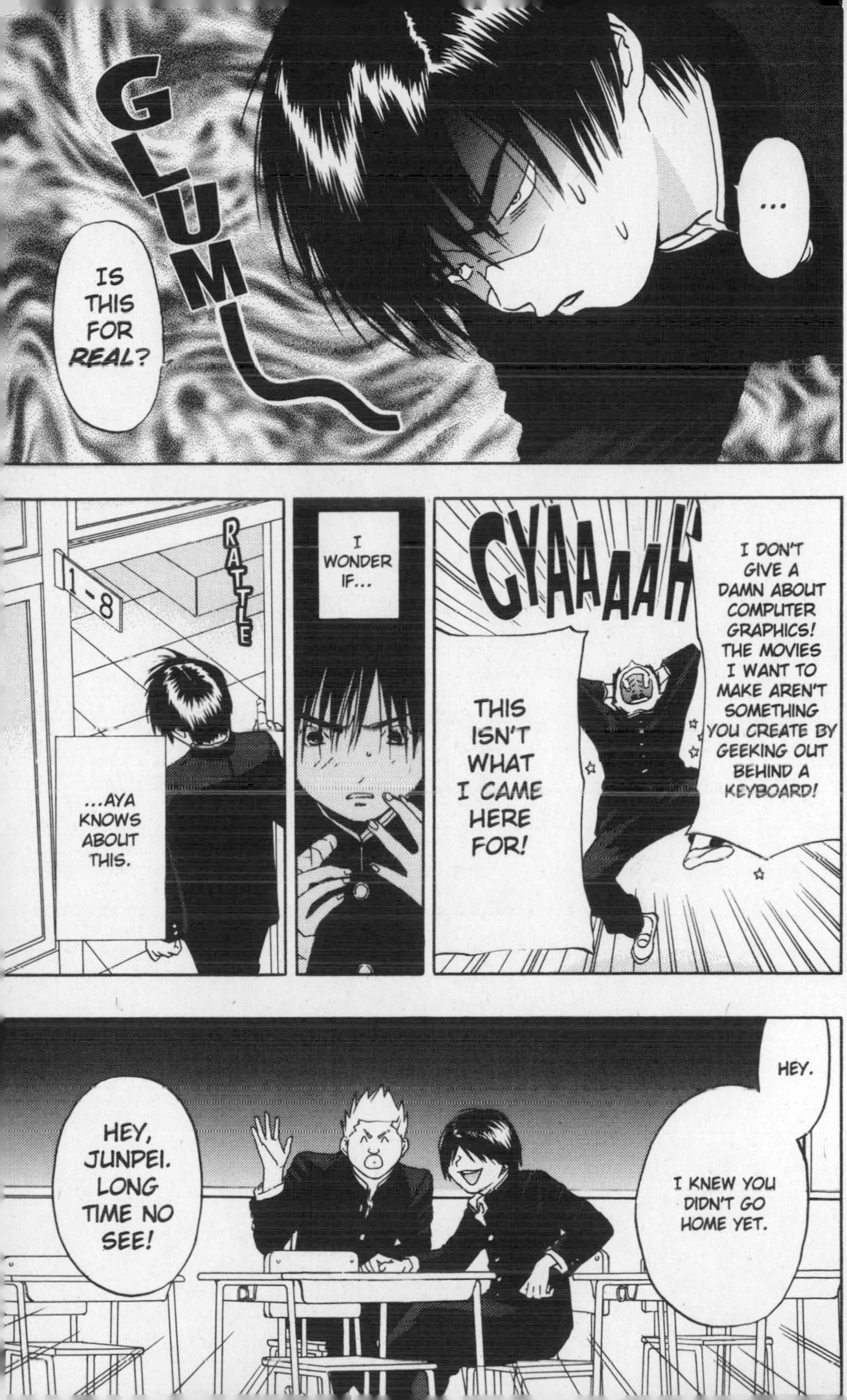
...
GLUM
IS THIS FOR *REAL*?
CYAAAAH
I DON'T GIVE A DAMN ABOUT COMPUTER GRAPHICS! THE MOVIES I WANT TO MAKE AREN'T SOMETHING YOU CREATE BY GEEKING OUT BEHIND A KEYBOARD!
THIS ISN'T WHAT I CAME HERE FOR!
I WONDER IF...
RATTLE
1-8
...AYA KNOWS ABOUT THIS.
HEY.
I KNEW YOU DIDN'T GO HOME YET.
HEY, JUNPEI. LONG TIME NO SEE!

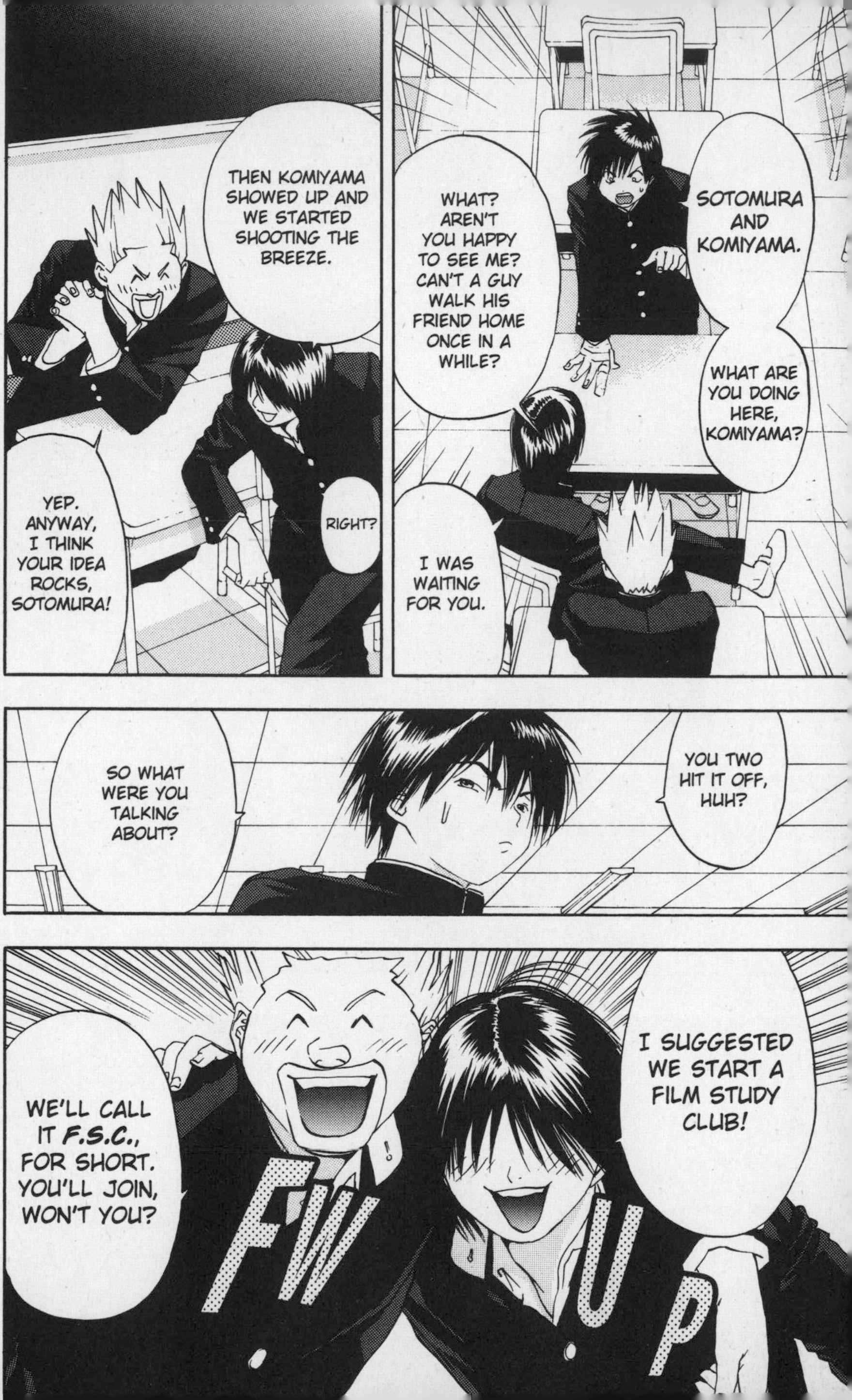
SOTOMURA AND KOMIYAMA.
WHAT ARE YOU DOING HERE, KOMIYAMA?
WHAT? AREN'T YOU HAPPY TO SEE ME? CAN'T A GUY WALK HIS FRIEND HOME ONCE IN A WHILE?
I WAS WAITING FOR YOU.
THEN KOMIYAMA SHOWED UP AND WE STARTED SHOOTING THE BREEZE.
RIGHT?
YEP. ANYWAY, I THINK YOUR IDEA ROCKS, SOTOMURA!
YOU TWO HIT IT OFF, HUH?
SO WHAT WERE YOU TALKING ABOUT?
I SUGGESTED WE START A FILM STUDY CLUB!
WE'LL CALL IT ***F.S.C.***, FOR SHORT. YOU'LL JOIN, WON'T YOU?
FWUP

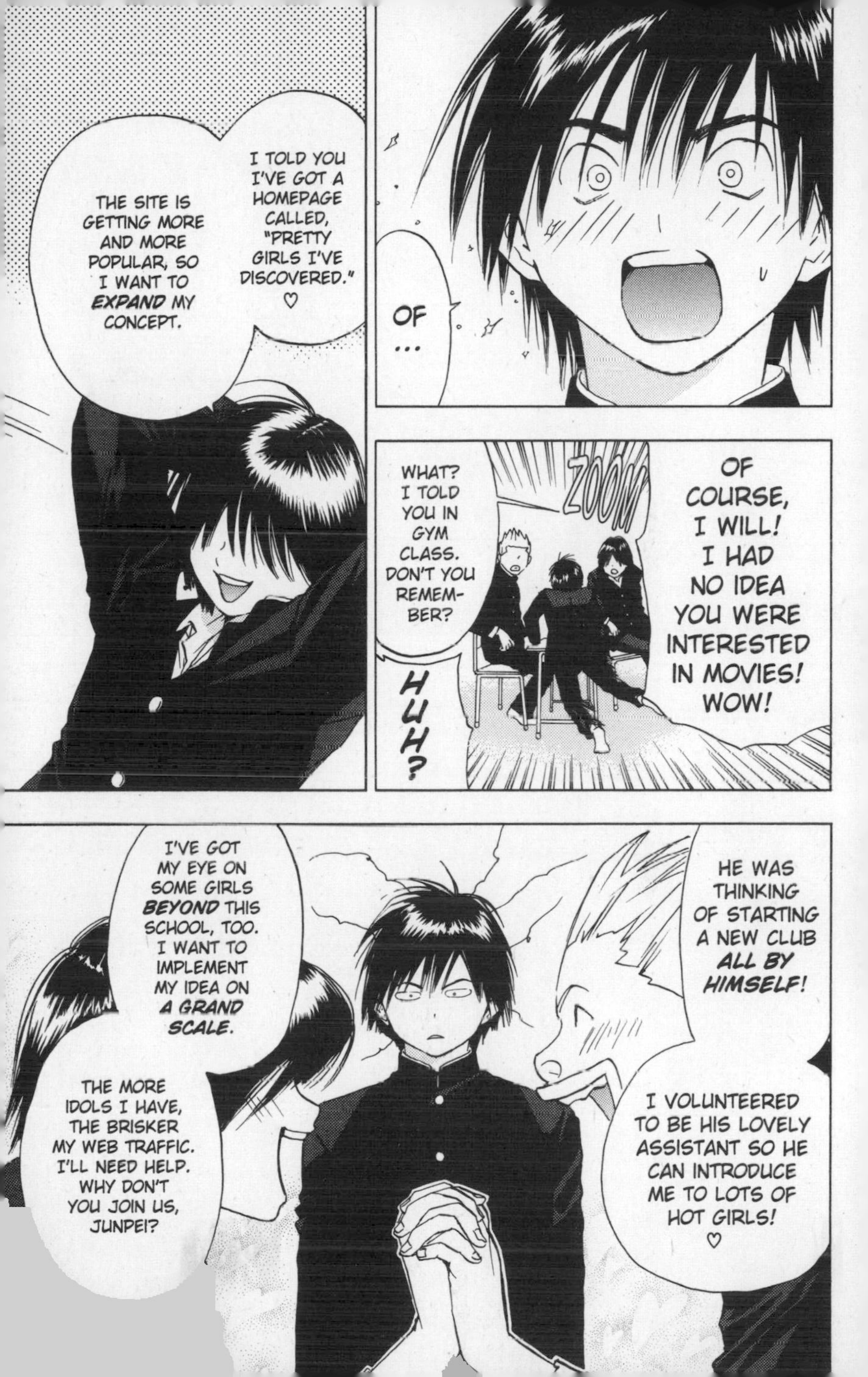
OF ...
OF COURSE, I WILL! I HAD NO IDEA YOU WERE INTERESTED IN MOVIES! WOW!
ZOOM
WHAT? I TOLD YOU IN GYM CLASS. DON'T YOU REMEMBER?
HUH?
I TOLD YOU I'VE GOT A HOMEPAGE CALLED, "PRETTY GIRLS I'VE DISCOVERED." ♡
THE SITE IS GETTING MORE AND MORE POPULAR, SO I WANT TO ***EXPAND*** MY CONCEPT.
HE WAS THINKING OF STARTING A NEW CLUB ***ALL BY HIMSELF***!
I VOLUNTEERED TO BE HIS LOVELY ASSISTANT SO HE CAN INTRODUCE ME TO LOTS OF HOT GIRLS! ♡
I'VE GOT MY EYE ON SOME GIRLS ***BEYOND*** THIS SCHOOL, TOO. I WANT TO IMPLEMENT MY IDEA ON ***A GRAND SCALE***.
THE MORE IDOLS I HAVE, THE BRISKER MY WEB TRAFFIC. I'LL NEED HELP. WHY DON'T YOU JOIN US, JUNPEI?

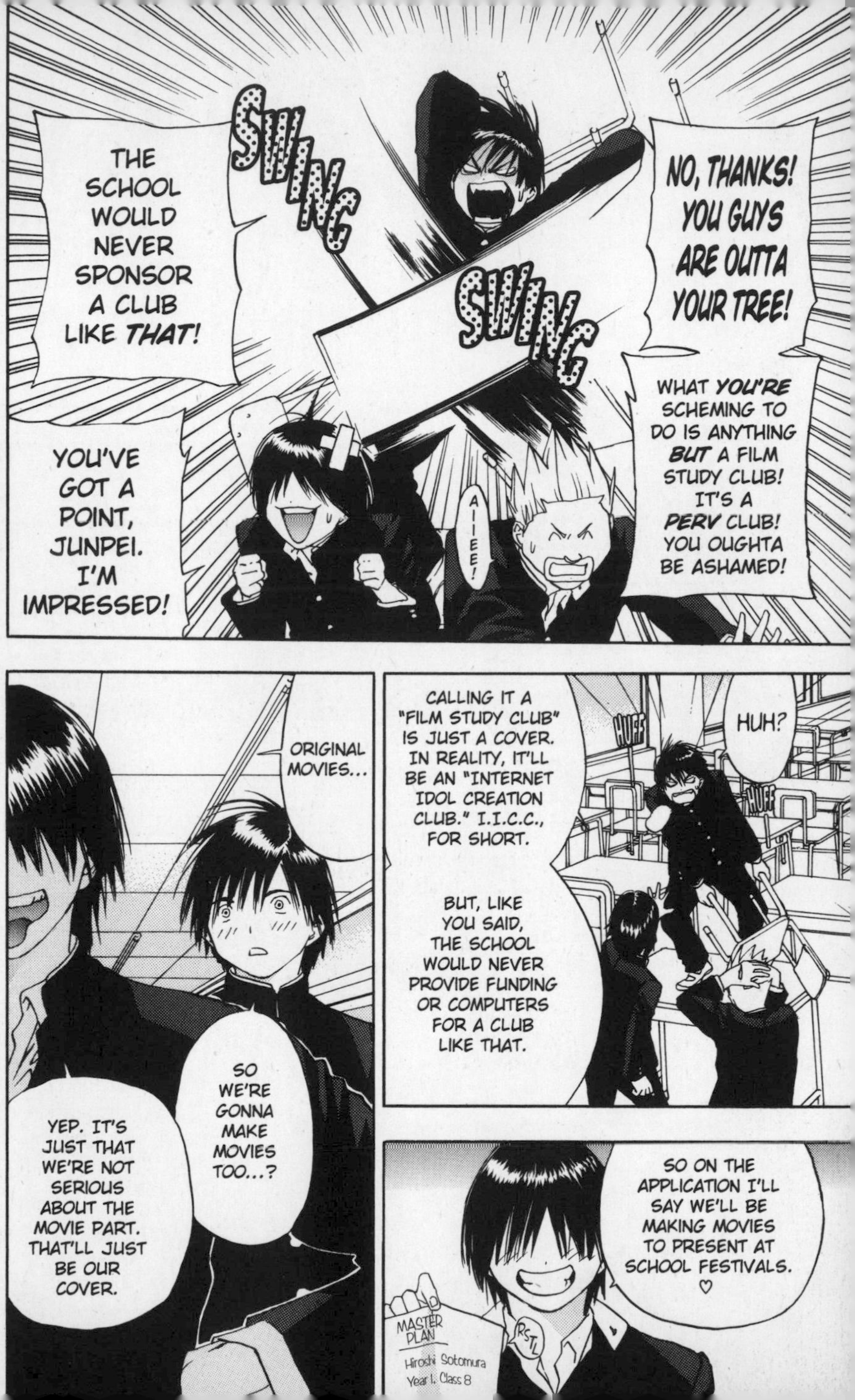
NO, THANKS! YOU GUYS ARE OUTTA YOUR TREE!
SWING
SWING
THE SCHOOL WOULD NEVER SPONSOR A CLUB LIKE *THAT*!
WHAT *YOU'RE* SCHEMING TO DO IS ANYTHING *BUT* A FILM STUDY CLUB! IT'S A *PERV* CLUB! YOU OUGHTA BE ASHAMED!
AIIEE!
YOU'VE GOT A POINT, JUNPEI. I'M IMPRESSED!
HUH?
HUFF
HUFF
CALLING IT A "FILM STUDY CLUB" IS JUST A COVER. IN REALITY, IT'LL BE AN "INTERNET IDOL CREATION CLUB." I.I.C.C., FOR SHORT.
BUT, LIKE YOU SAID, THE SCHOOL WOULD NEVER PROVIDE FUNDING OR COMPUTERS FOR A CLUB LIKE THAT.
SO ON THE APPLICATION I'LL SAY WE'LL BE MAKING MOVIES TO PRESENT AT SCHOOL FESTIVALS. ♡
MASTER PLAN
RSTL
Hiroshi Sotomura
Year 1, Class 8
ORIGINAL MOVIES...
SO WE'RE GONNA MAKE MOVIES TOO...?
YEP. IT'S JUST THAT WE'RE NOT SERIOUS ABOUT THE MOVIE PART. THAT'LL JUST BE OUR COVER.

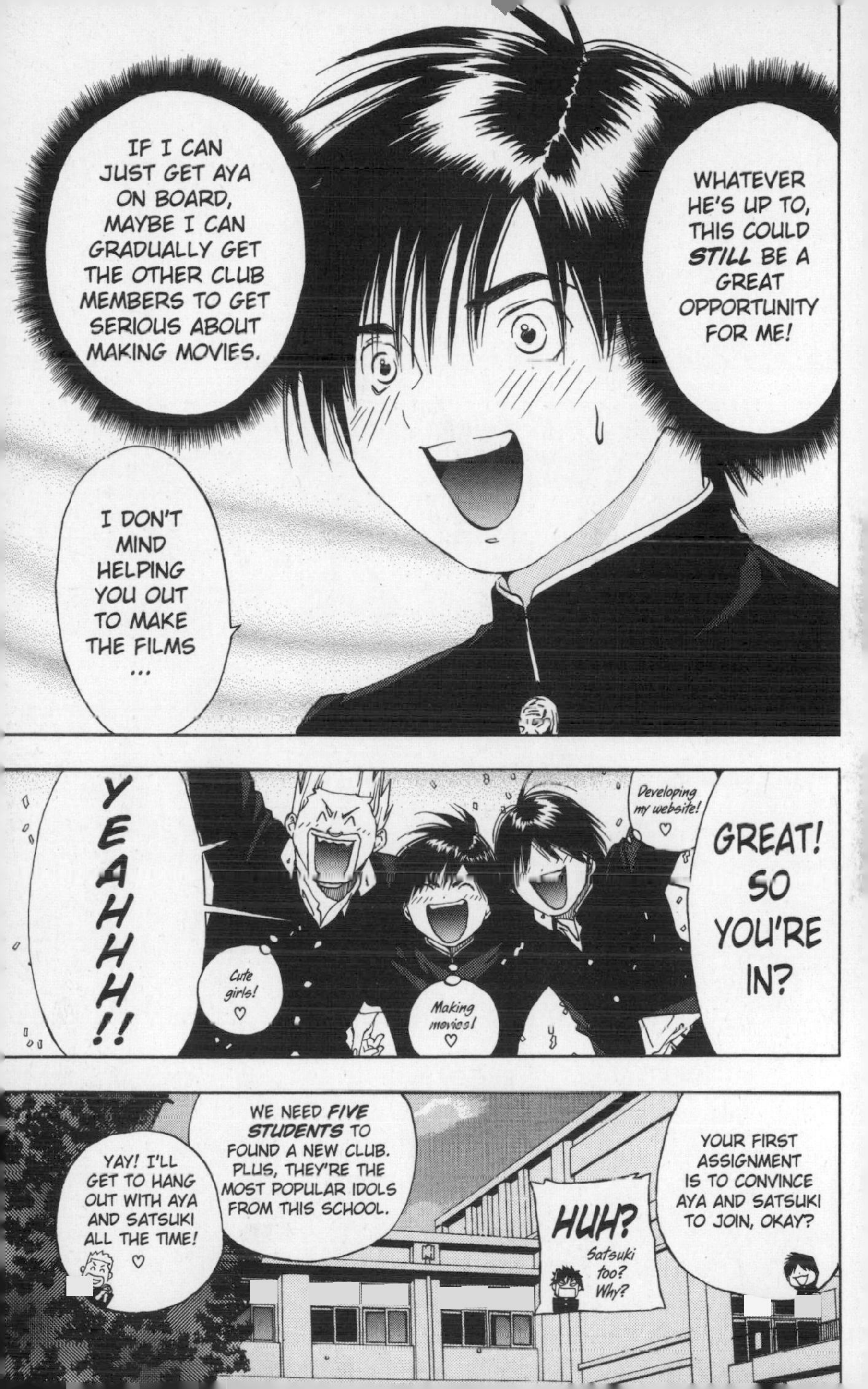
WHATEVER HE'S UP TO, THIS COULD ***STILL*** BE A GREAT OPPORTUNITY FOR ME!
IF I CAN JUST GET AYA ON BOARD, MAYBE I CAN GRADUALLY GET THE OTHER CLUB MEMBERS TO GET SERIOUS ABOUT MAKING MOVIES.
I DON'T MIND HELPING YOU OUT TO MAKE THE FILMS ...
GREAT! SO YOU'RE IN?
Developing my website! ♡
Making movies! ♡
Cute girls! ♡
YEAHHHH!!
YOUR FIRST ASSIGNMENT IS TO CONVINCE AYA AND SATSUKI TO JOIN, OKAY?
HUH?
Satsuki too? Why?
WE NEED ***FIVE STUDENTS*** TO FOUND A NEW CLUB. PLUS, THEY'RE THE MOST POPULAR IDOLS FROM THIS SCHOOL.
YAY! I'LL GET TO HANG OUT WITH AYA AND SATSUKI ALL THE TIME! ♡

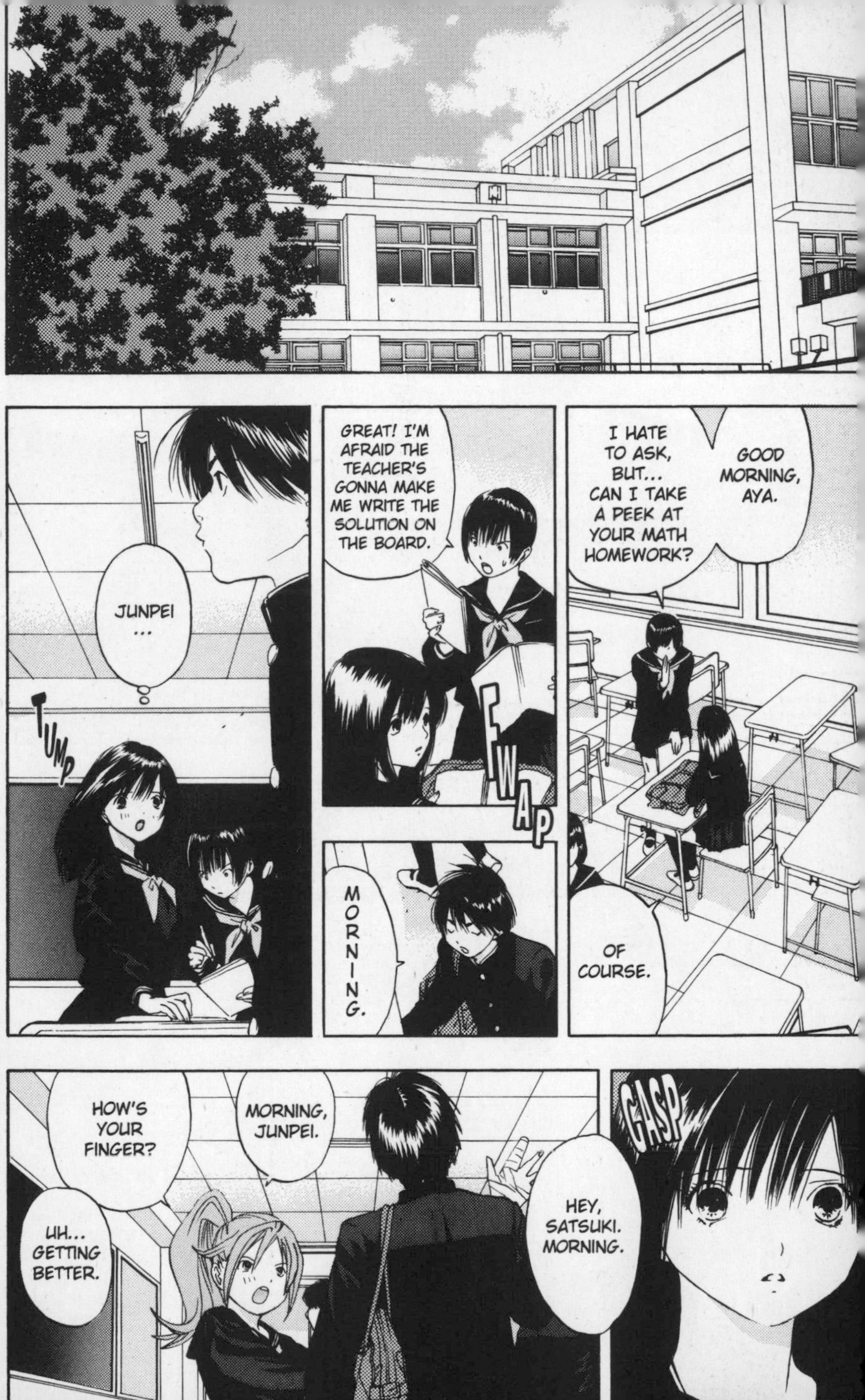
GOOD MORNING, AYA.
I HATE TO ASK, BUT... CAN I TAKE A PEEK AT YOUR MATH HOMEWORK?
OF COURSE.
GREAT! I'M AFRAID THE TEACHER'S GONNA MAKE ME WRITE THE SOLUTION ON THE BOARD.
FWAP
MORNING.
JUNPEI ...
TUMP
GASP
HEY, SATSUKI. MORNING.
MORNING, JUNPEI.
HOW'S YOUR FINGER?
UH... GETTING BETTER.

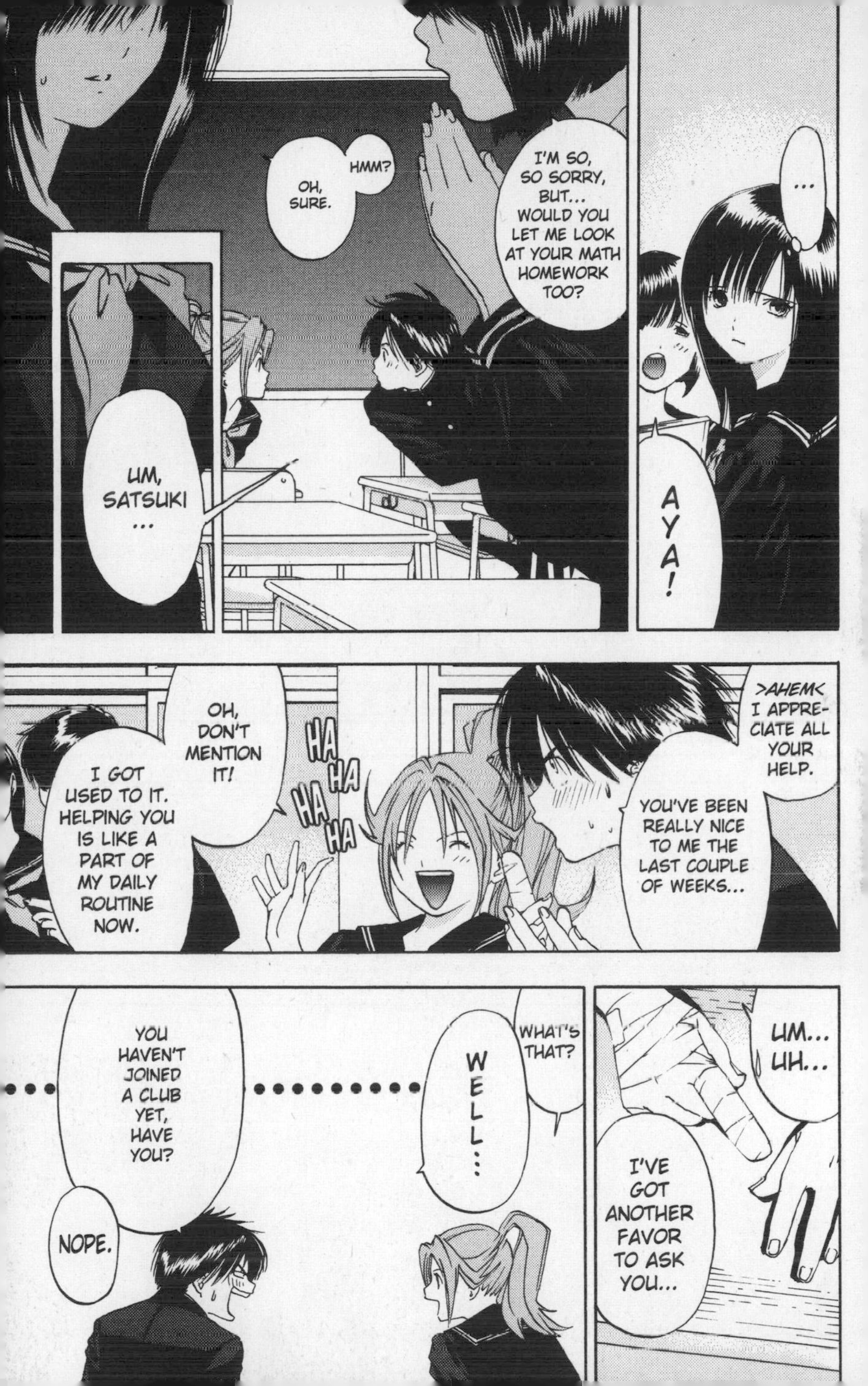
...
AYA!
I'M SO, SO SORRY, BUT... WOULD YOU LET ME LOOK AT YOUR MATH HOMEWORK TOO?
HMM?
OH, SURE.
UM, SATSUKI ...
>AHEM< I APPRECIATE ALL YOUR HELP.
YOU'VE BEEN REALLY NICE TO ME THE LAST COUPLE OF WEEKS...
HA HA HA HA
OH, DON'T MENTION IT!
I GOT USED TO IT. HELPING YOU IS LIKE A PART OF MY DAILY ROUTINE NOW.
UM... UH...
I'VE GOT ANOTHER FAVOR TO ASK YOU...
WHAT'S THAT?
WELL...
....
YOU HAVEN'T JOINED A CLUB YET, HAVE YOU?
NOPE.

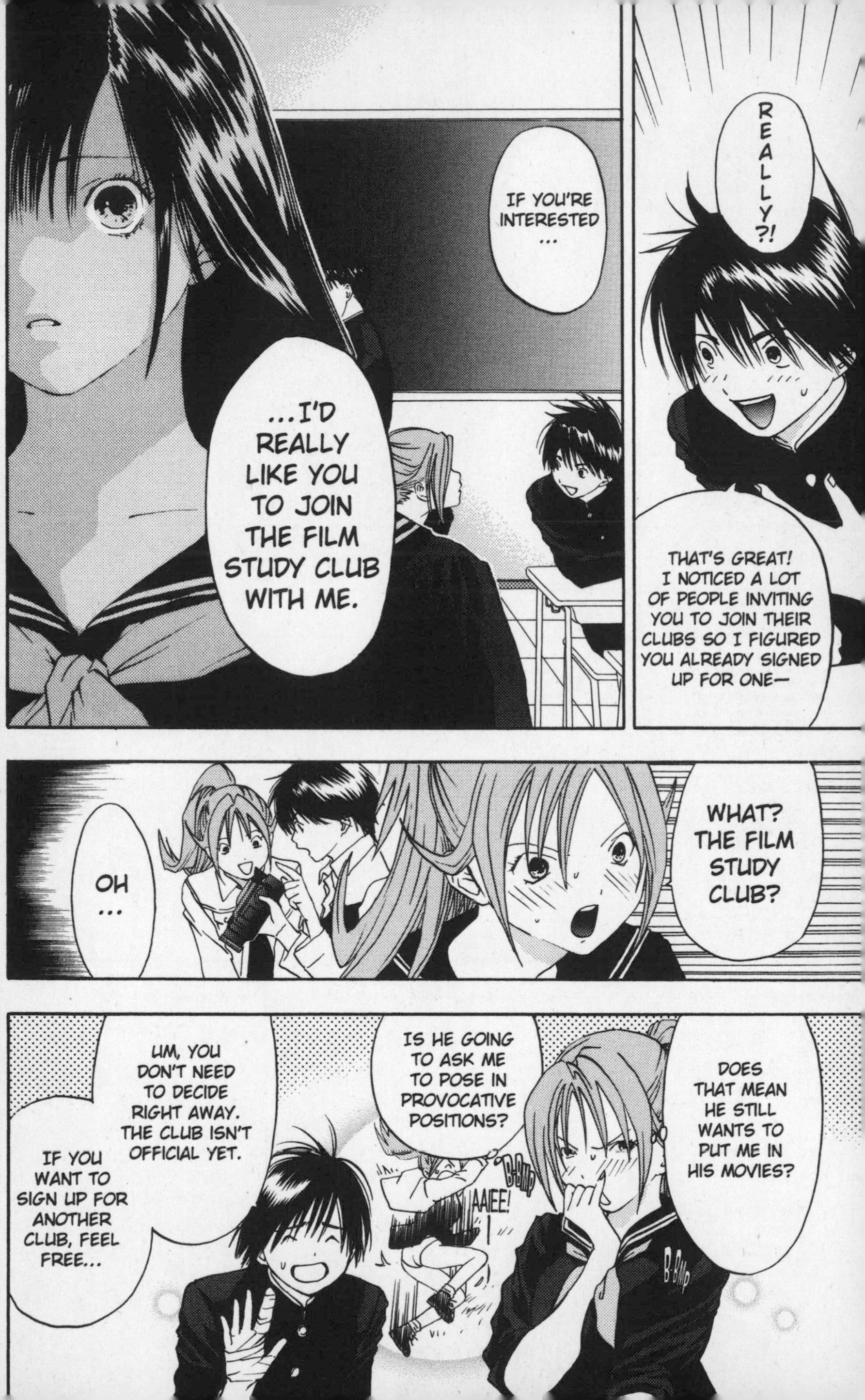
REALLY?!
THAT'S GREAT! I NOTICED A LOT OF PEOPLE INVITING YOU TO JOIN THEIR CLUBS SO I FIGURED YOU ALREADY SIGNED UP FOR ONE—
IF YOU'RE INTERESTED ...
...I'D REALLY LIKE YOU TO JOIN THE FILM STUDY CLUB WITH ME.
WHAT? THE FILM STUDY CLUB?
OH ...
DOES THAT MEAN HE STILL WANTS TO PUT ME IN HIS MOVIES?
B-BMP
B-BMP
IS HE GOING TO ASK ME TO POSE IN PROVOCATIVE POSITIONS?
AAIEE!
UM, YOU DON'T NEED TO DECIDE RIGHT AWAY. THE CLUB ISN'T OFFICIAL YET.
IF YOU WANT TO SIGN UP FOR ANOTHER CLUB, FEEL FREE...

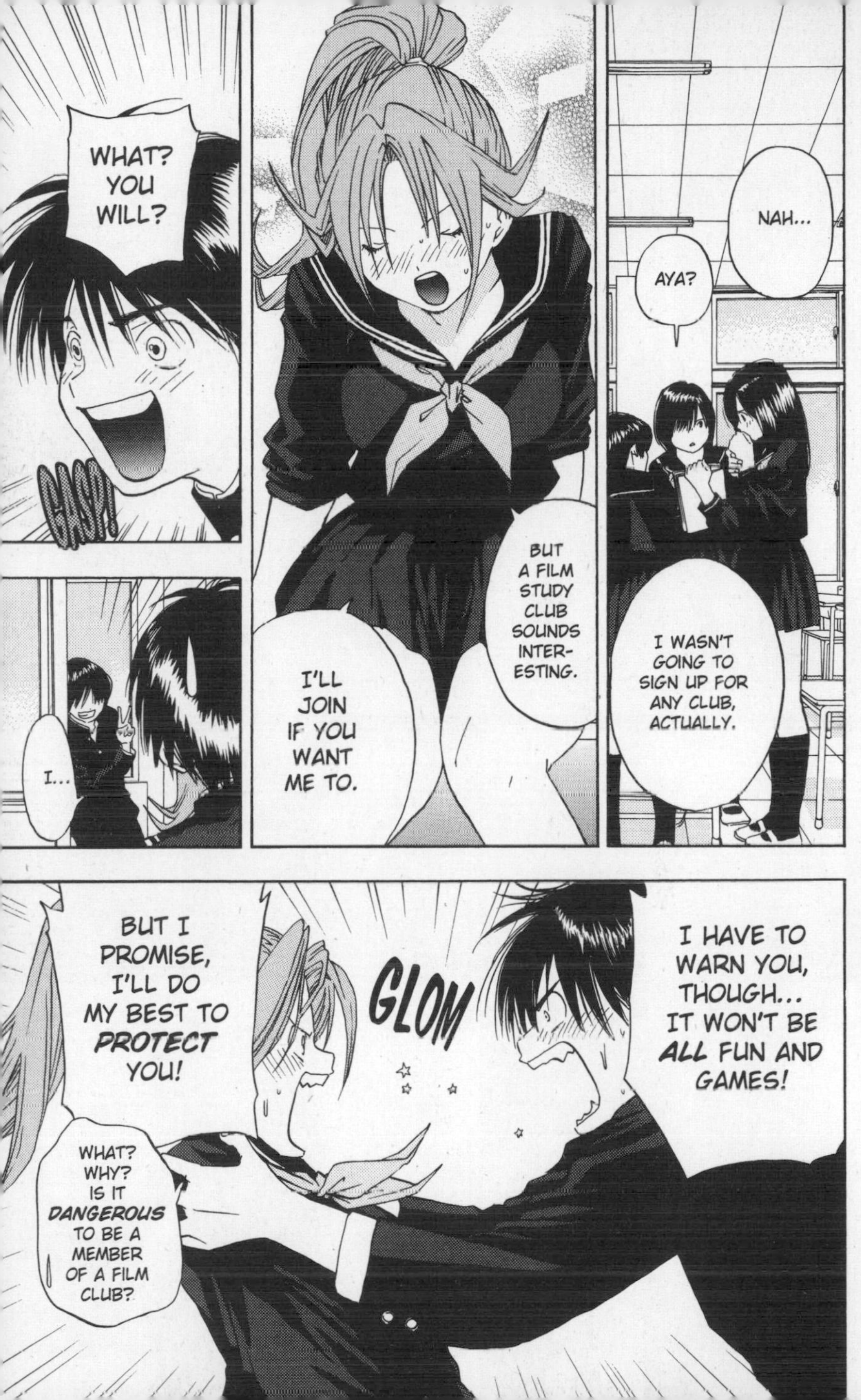
NAH...
AYA?
I WASN'T GOING TO SIGN UP FOR ANY CLUB, ACTUALLY.
BUT A FILM STUDY CLUB SOUNDS INTER-ESTING.
I'LL JOIN IF YOU WANT ME TO.
WHAT? YOU WILL?
GASP!
I...
I HAVE TO WARN YOU, THOUGH... IT WON'T BE **ALL** FUN AND GAMES!
GLOM
BUT I PROMISE, I'LL DO MY BEST TO **PROTECT** YOU!
WHAT? WHY? IS IT **DANGEROUS** TO BE A MEMBER OF A FILM CLUB?

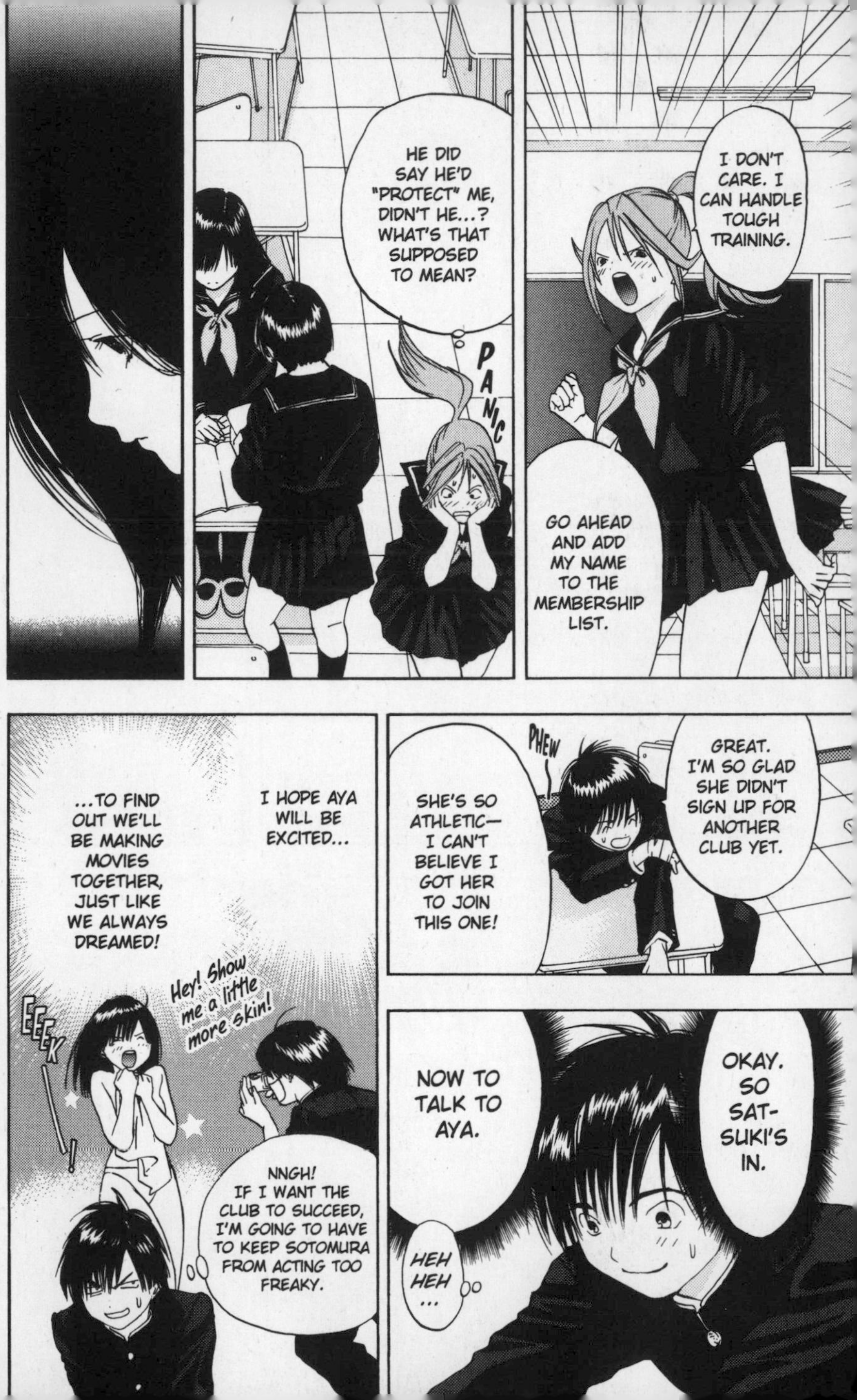
I DON'T CARE. I CAN HANDLE TOUGH TRAINING.
GO AHEAD AND ADD MY NAME TO THE MEMBERSHIP LIST.
HE DID SAY HE'D "PROTECT" ME, DIDN'T HE...? WHAT'S THAT SUPPOSED TO MEAN?
PANIC
PHEW
GREAT. I'M SO GLAD SHE DIDN'T SIGN UP FOR ANOTHER CLUB YET.
SHE'S SO ATHLETIC— I CAN'T BELIEVE I GOT HER TO JOIN THIS ONE!
OKAY. SO SAT-SUKI'S IN.
NOW TO TALK TO AYA.
HEH HEH ...
I HOPE AYA WILL BE EXCITED...
...TO FIND OUT WE'LL BE MAKING MOVIES TOGETHER, JUST LIKE WE ALWAYS DREAMED!
Hey! Show me a little more skin!
EEEK!
NNGH! IF I WANT THE CLUB TO SUCCEED, I'M GOING TO HAVE TO KEEP SOTOMURA FROM ACTING TOO FREAKY.

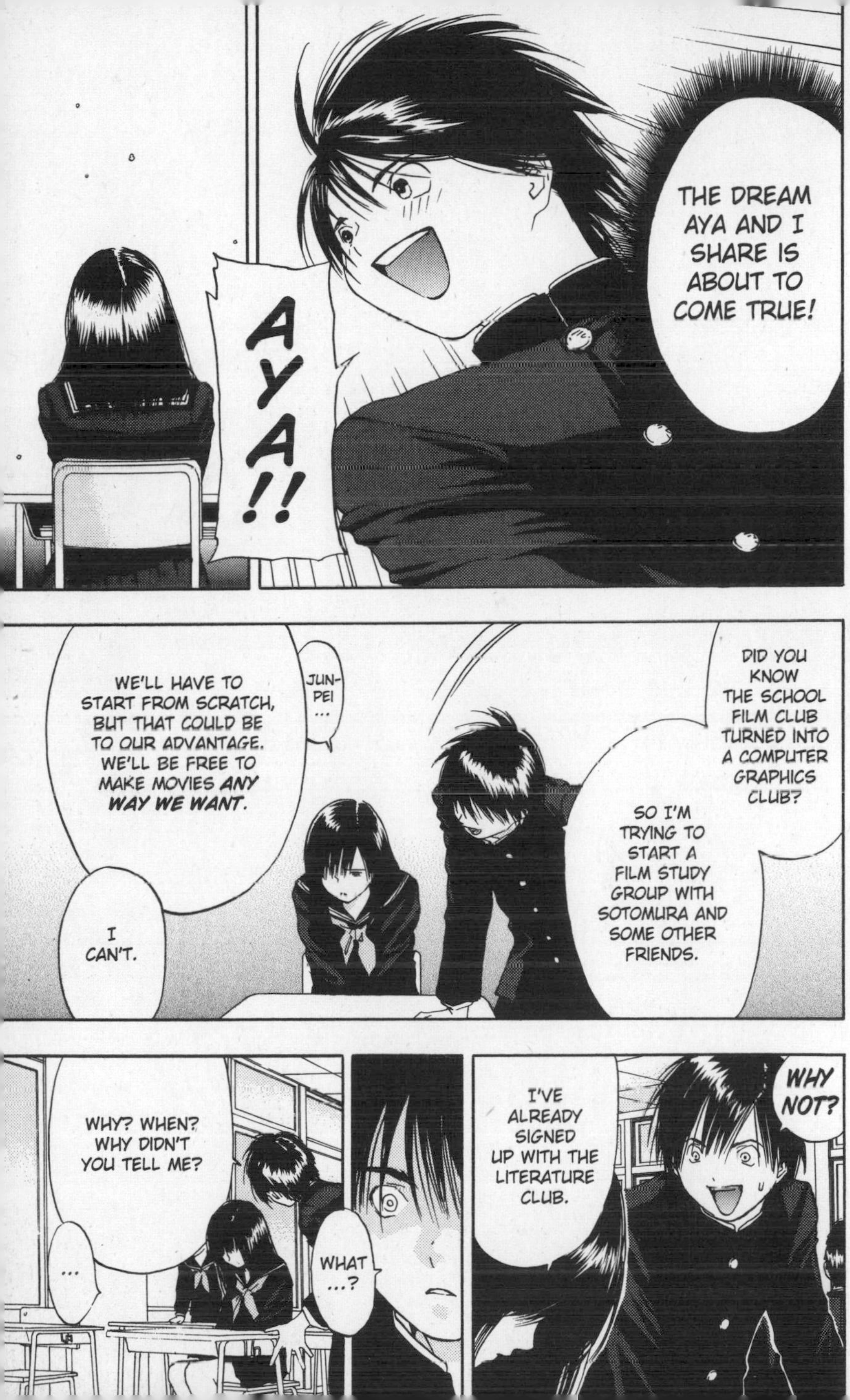
THE DREAM AYA AND I SHARE IS ABOUT TO COME TRUE!
AYA!!
DID YOU KNOW THE SCHOOL FILM CLUB TURNED INTO A COMPUTER GRAPHICS CLUB?
SO I'M TRYING TO START A FILM STUDY GROUP WITH SOTOMURA AND SOME OTHER FRIENDS.
JUN-PEI ...
WE'LL HAVE TO START FROM SCRATCH, BUT THAT COULD BE TO OUR ADVANTAGE. WE'LL BE FREE TO MAKE MOVIES *ANY WAY WE WANT*.
I CAN'T.
WHY NOT?
I'VE ALREADY SIGNED UP WITH THE LITERATURE CLUB.
WHAT ...?
WHY? WHEN? WHY DIDN'T YOU TELL ME?
...

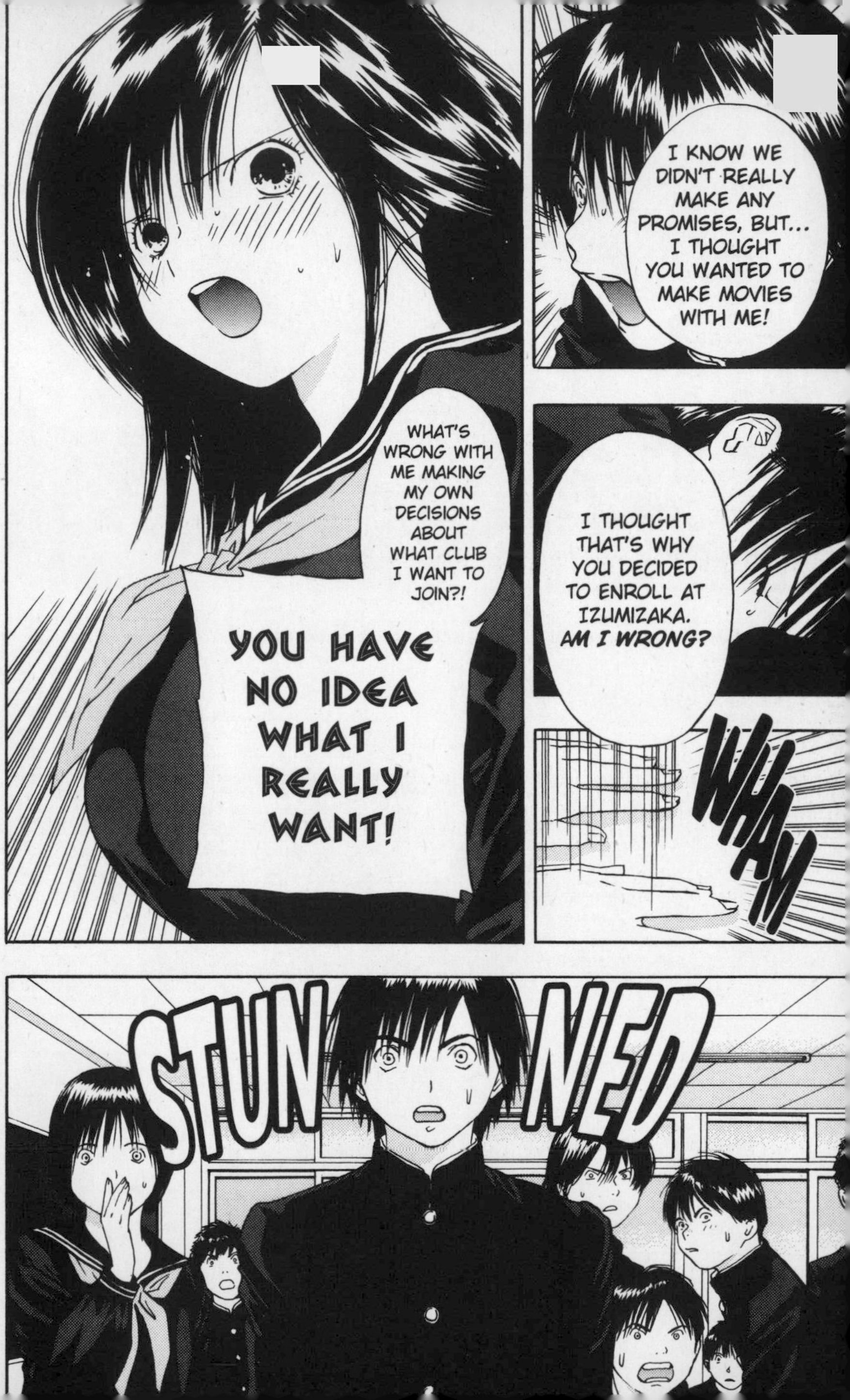
I KNOW WE DIDN'T REALLY MAKE ANY PROMISES, BUT... I THOUGHT YOU WANTED TO MAKE MOVIES WITH ME!
I THOUGHT THAT'S WHY YOU DECIDED TO ENROLL AT IZUMIZAKA. AM I WRONG?
WHAM
WHAT'S WRONG WITH ME MAKING MY OWN DECISIONS ABOUT WHAT CLUB I WANT TO JOIN?!
YOU HAVE NO IDEA WHAT I REALLY WANT!
STUNNED

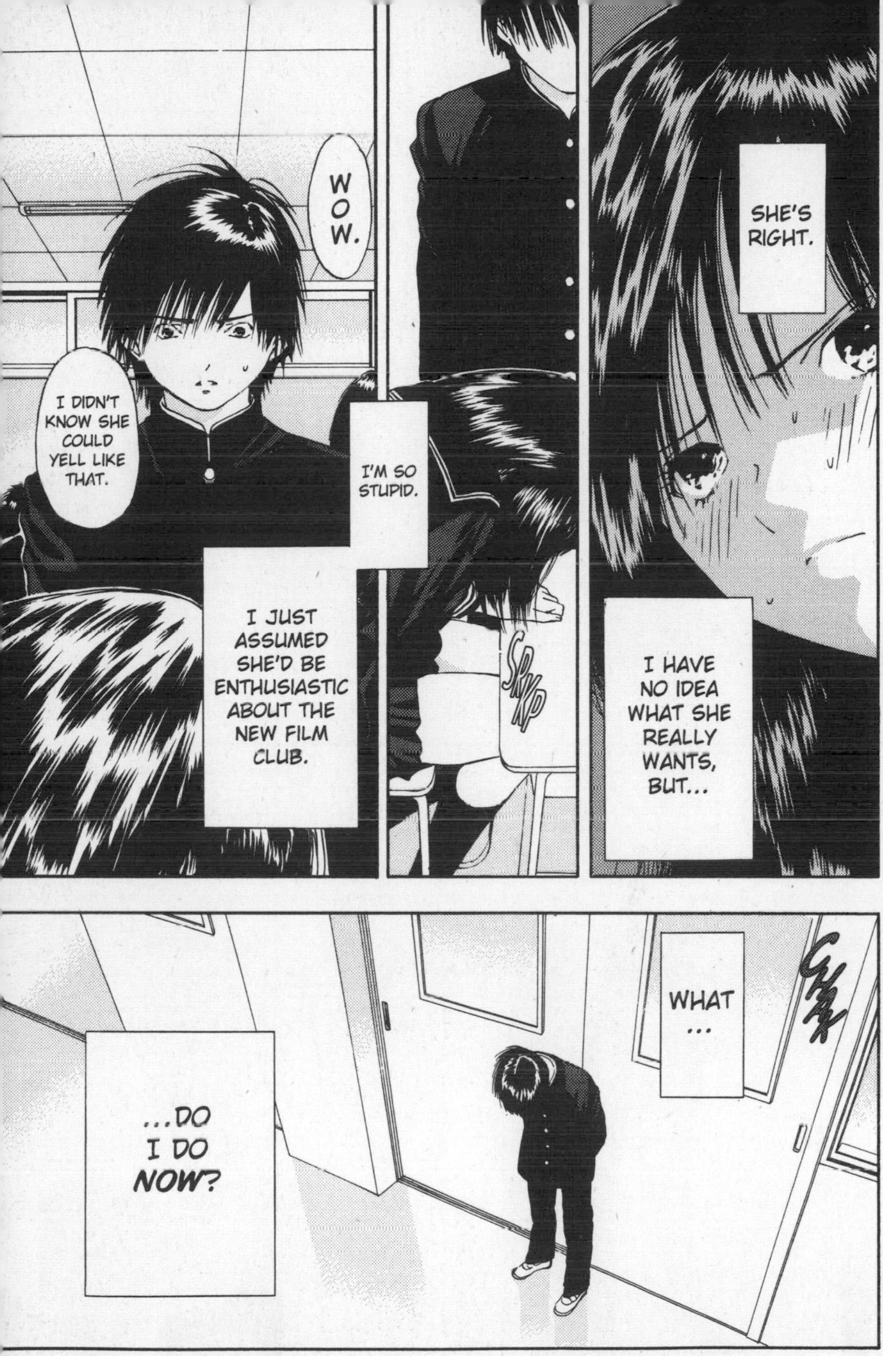
SHE'S RIGHT.
I HAVE NO IDEA WHAT SHE REALLY WANTS, BUT...
I'M SO STUPID.
SRKP
WOW.
I DIDN'T KNOW SHE COULD YELL LIKE THAT.
I JUST ASSUMED SHE'D BE ENTHUSIASTIC ABOUT THE NEW FILM CLUB.
CHAK
WHAT ...
...DO I DO *NOW?*

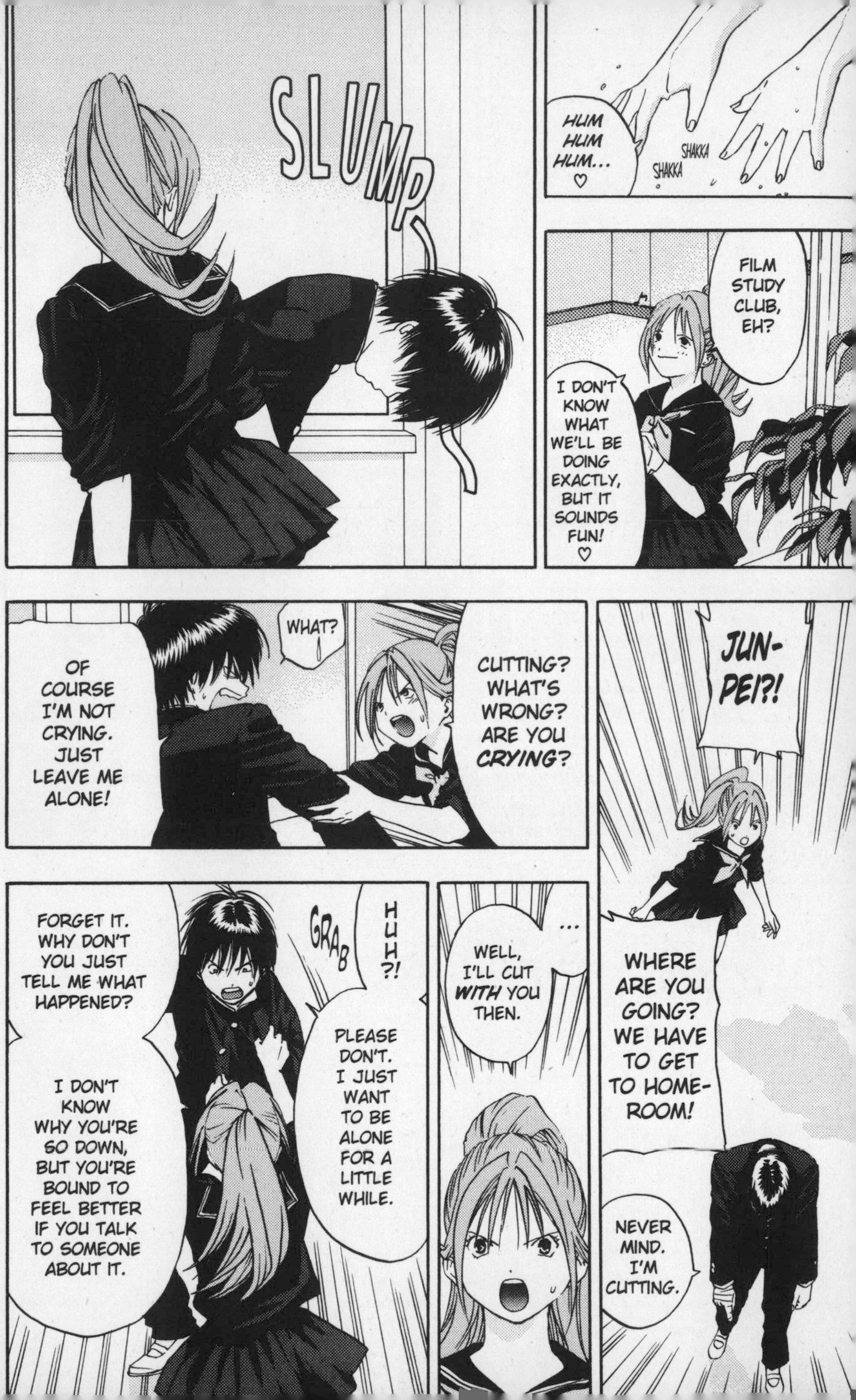
HUM HUM HUM... ♡
SHAKKA
SHAKKA
FILM STUDY CLUB, EH?
I DON'T KNOW WHAT WE'LL BE DOING EXACTLY, BUT IT SOUNDS FUN! ♡
SLUMP
JUN-PEI?!
WHERE ARE YOU GOING? WE HAVE TO GET TO HOME-ROOM!
NEVER MIND. I'M CUTTING.
CUTTING? WHAT'S WRONG? ARE YOU *CRYING*?
WHAT?
OF COURSE I'M NOT CRYING. JUST LEAVE ME ALONE!
...
WELL, I'LL CUT *WITH* YOU THEN.
HUH?!
GRAB
PLEASE DON'T. I JUST WANT TO BE ALONE FOR A LITTLE WHILE.
FORGET IT. WHY DON'T YOU JUST TELL ME WHAT HAPPENED?
I DON'T KNOW WHY YOU'RE SO DOWN, BUT YOU'RE BOUND TO FEEL BETTER IF YOU TALK TO SOMEONE ABOUT IT.

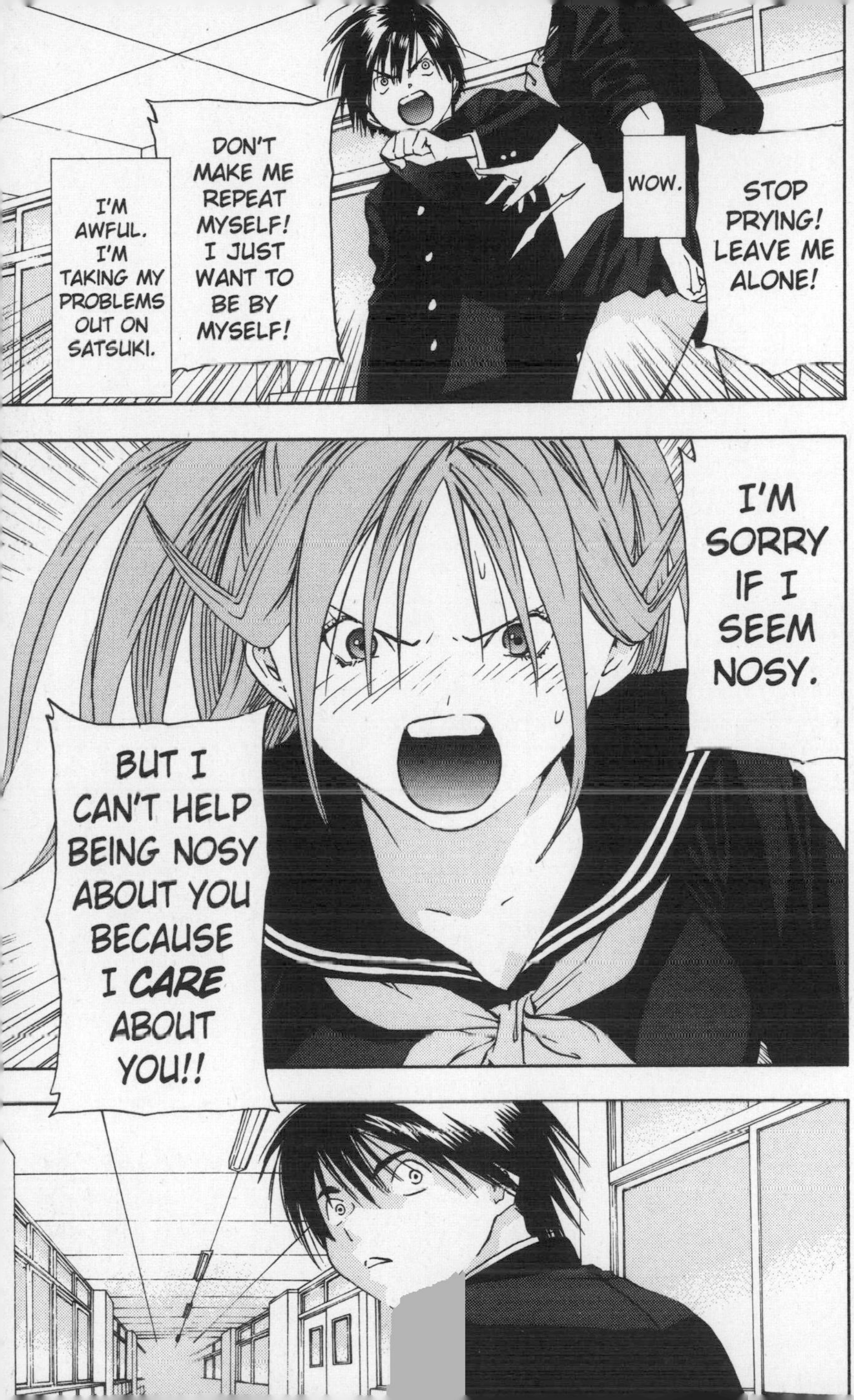
STOP PRYING! LEAVE ME ALONE!
WOW.
DON'T MAKE ME REPEAT MYSELF! I JUST WANT TO BE BY MYSELF!
I'M AWFUL. I'M TAKING MY PROBLEMS OUT ON SATSUKI.
I'M SORRY IF I SEEM NOSY.
BUT I CAN'T HELP BEING NOSY ABOUT YOU BECAUSE I *CARE* ABOUT YOU!!

FAN SERVICE
戻る
進む
中止
更新
ホーム
自動入力
プリント
メール

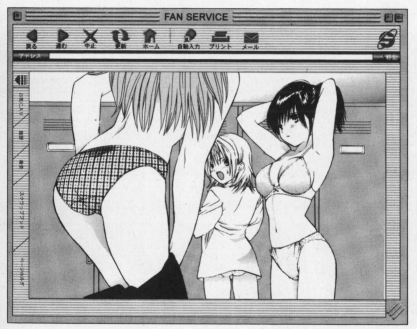

NOTE: THIS IS A COMPOSITE PHOTOGRAPH.

CRUSH 25: DETERMINED GIRL, INDECISIVE BOY

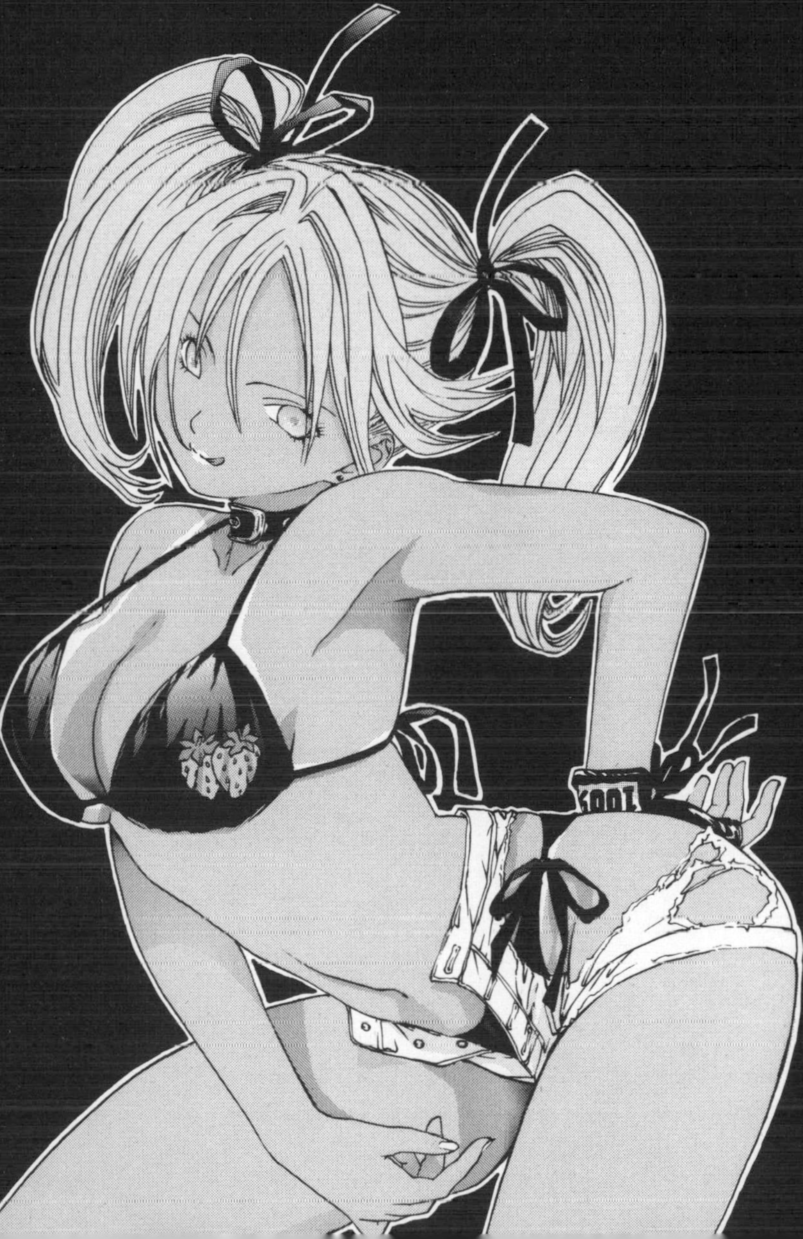

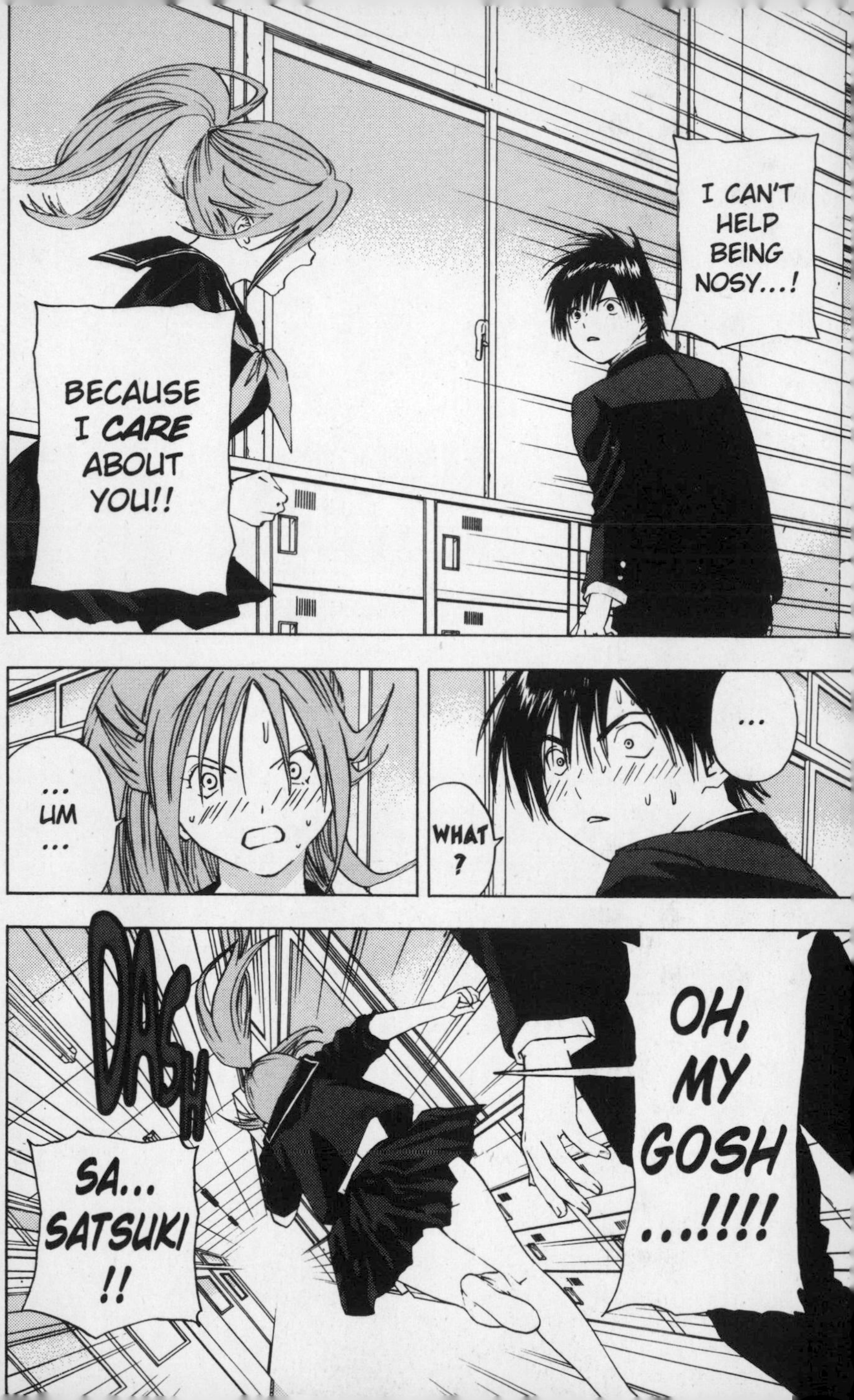
I CAN'T HELP BEING NOSY...!
BECAUSE I CARE ABOUT YOU!!
...
WHAT?
... UM ...
OH, MY GOSH ....!!!!
DASH
SA... SATSUKI!!

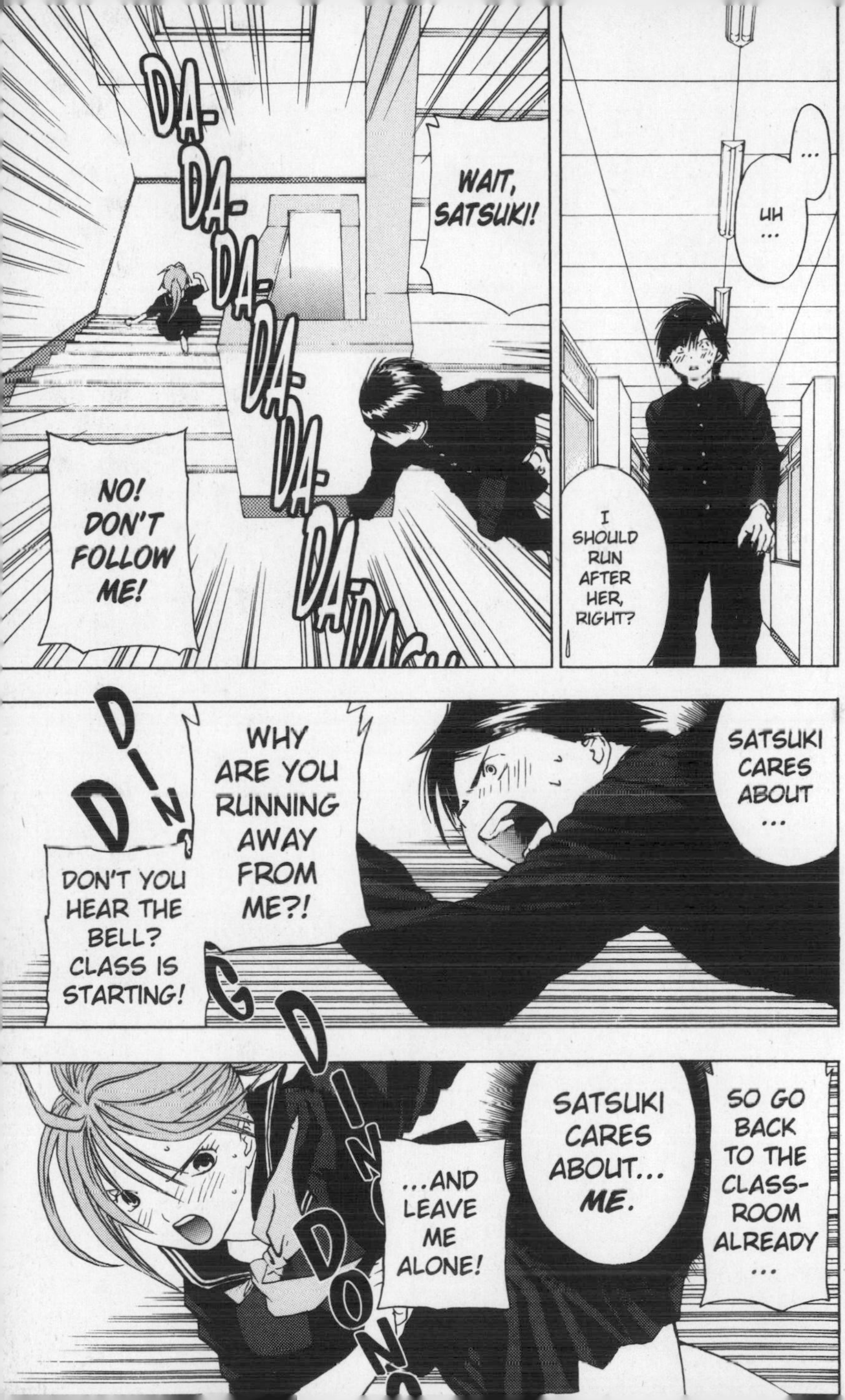
...
UH ...
I SHOULD RUN AFTER HER, RIGHT?
WAIT, SATSUKI!
DA-DA-DA-DA-DA-DA-DA-
NO! DON'T FOLLOW ME!
SATSUKI CARES ABOUT ...
WHY ARE YOU RUNNING AWAY FROM ME?!
DIN D
DON'T YOU HEAR THE BELL? CLASS IS STARTING!
SO GO BACK TO THE CLASS-ROOM ALREADY ...
SATSUKI CARES ABOUT... *ME*.
...AND LEAVE ME ALONE!
G DIN DON

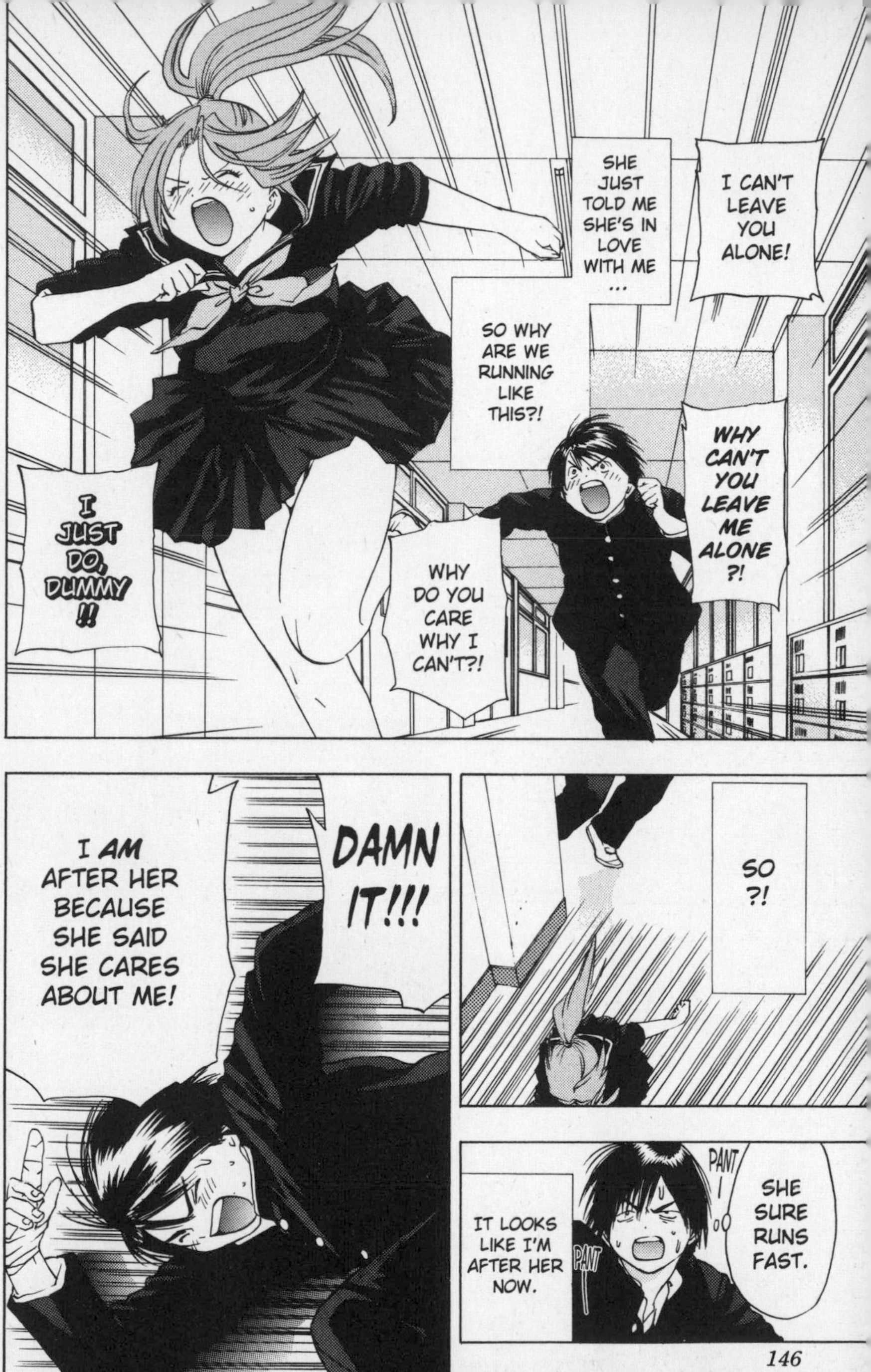
I CAN'T LEAVE YOU ALONE!
SHE JUST TOLD ME SHE'S IN LOVE WITH ME ...
SO WHY ARE WE RUNNING LIKE THIS?!
WHY CAN'T YOU LEAVE ME ALONE ?!
WHY DO YOU CARE WHY I CAN'T?!
I JUST DO, DUMMY !!
SO ?!
SHE SURE RUNS FAST.
PANT
PANT
IT LOOKS LIKE I'M AFTER HER NOW.
DAMN IT!!!
I AM AFTER HER BECAUSE SHE SAID SHE CARES ABOUT ME!

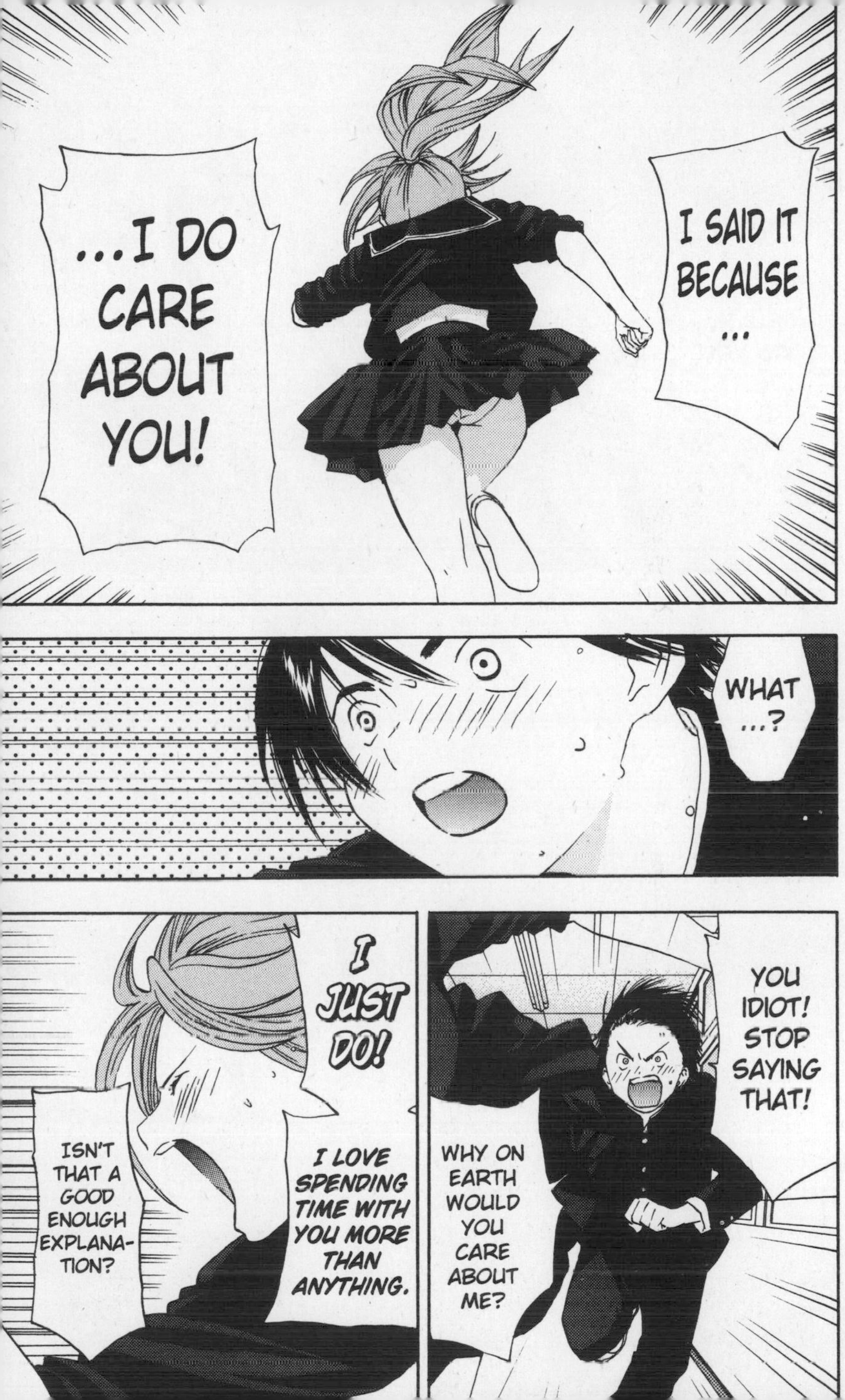
I SAID IT BECAUSE ...
...I DO CARE ABOUT YOU!
WHAT ...?
YOU IDIOT! STOP SAYING THAT!
WHY ON EARTH WOULD YOU CARE ABOUT ME?
I JUST DO!
I LOVE SPENDING TIME WITH YOU MORE THAN ANYTHING.
ISN'T THAT A GOOD ENOUGH EXPLANATION?

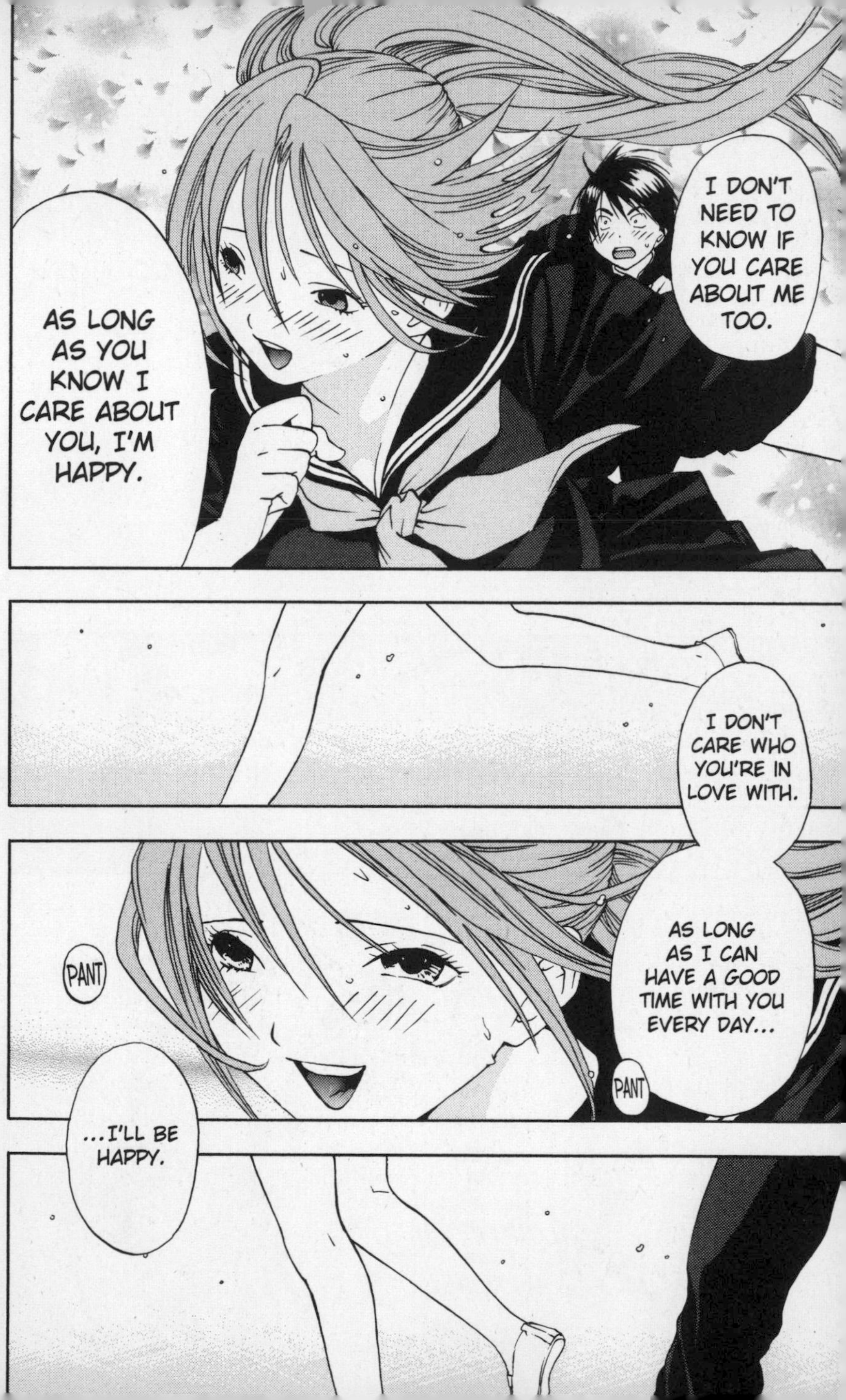
I DON'T NEED TO KNOW IF YOU CARE ABOUT ME TOO.
AS LONG AS YOU KNOW I CARE ABOUT YOU, I'M HAPPY.
I DON'T CARE WHO YOU'RE IN LOVE WITH.
AS LONG AS I CAN HAVE A GOOD TIME WITH YOU EVERY DAY...
PANT
PANT
...I'LL BE HAPPY.

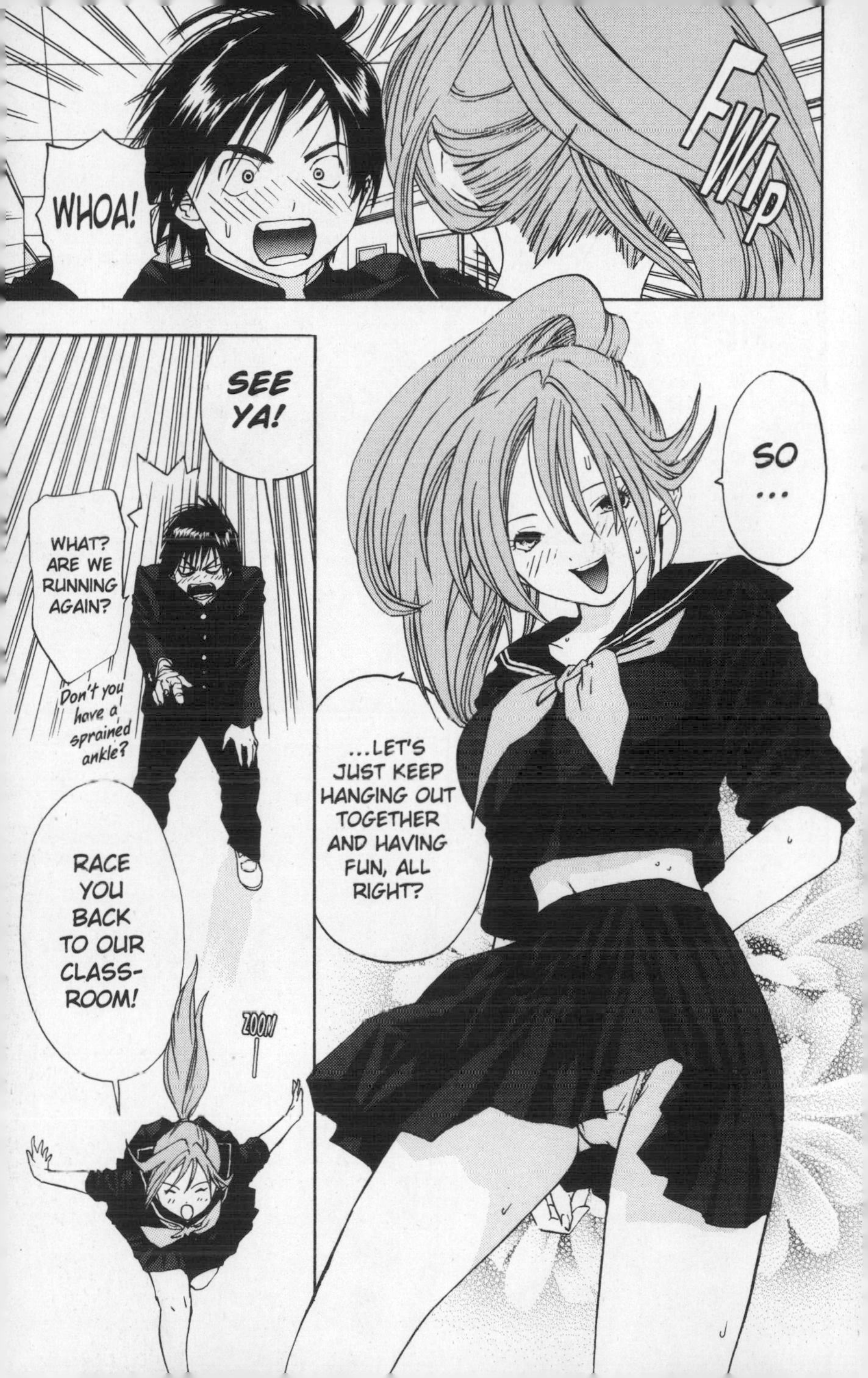
FWIP
WHOA!
SO ...
...LET'S JUST KEEP HANGING OUT TOGETHER AND HAVING FUN, ALL RIGHT?
SEE YA!
WHAT? ARE WE RUNNING AGAIN?
Don't you have a sprained ankle?
RACE YOU BACK TO OUR CLASS-ROOM!
ZOOM

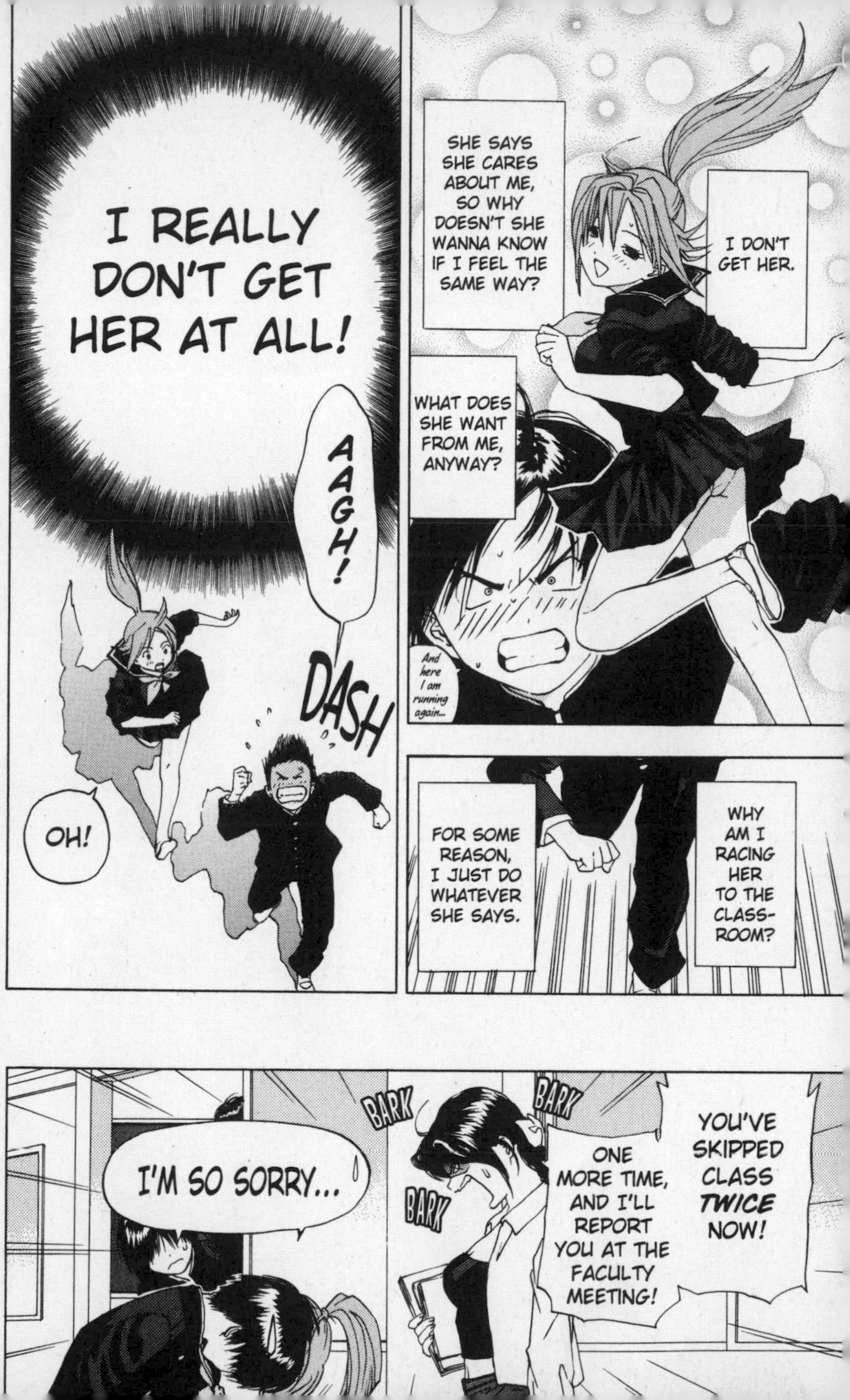
I DON'T GET HER.
SHE SAYS SHE CARES ABOUT ME, SO WHY DOESN'T SHE WANNA KNOW IF I FEEL THE SAME WAY?
WHAT DOES SHE WANT FROM ME, ANYWAY?
And here I am running again...
WHY AM I RACING HER TO THE CLASS-ROOM?
FOR SOME REASON, I JUST DO WHATEVER SHE SAYS.
I REALLY DON'T GET HER AT ALL!
AAGH!
DASH
OH!
YOU'VE SKIPPED CLASS *TWICE* NOW!
BARK
ONE MORE TIME, AND I'LL REPORT YOU AT THE FACULTY MEETING!
BARK
BARK
I'M SO SORRY...

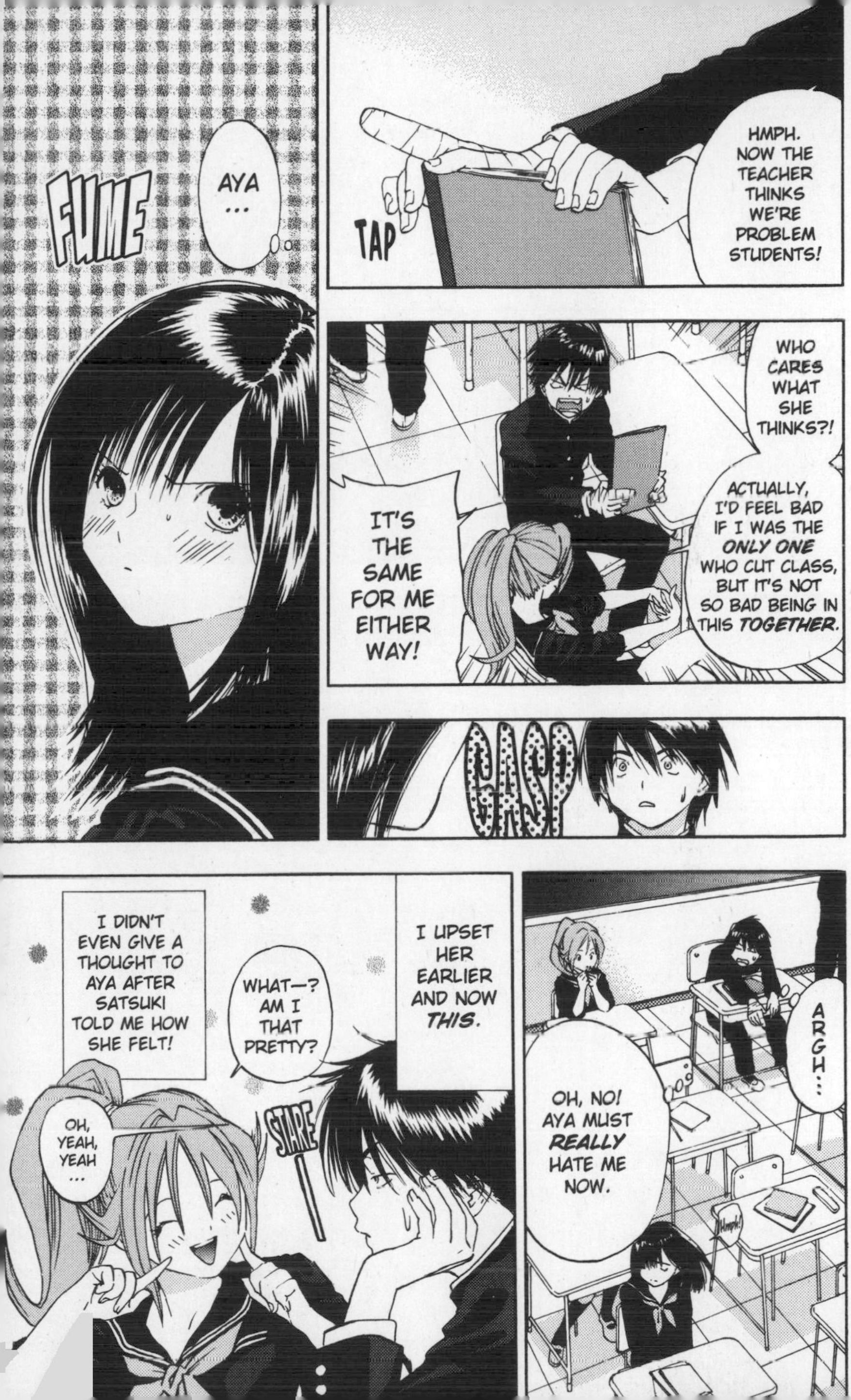
HMPH. NOW THE TEACHER THINKS WE'RE PROBLEM STUDENTS!
TAP
WHO CARES WHAT SHE THINKS?!
ACTUALLY, I'D FEEL BAD IF I WAS THE *ONLY ONE* WHO CUT CLASS, BUT IT'S NOT SO BAD BEING IN THIS *TOGETHER*.
IT'S THE SAME FOR ME EITHER WAY!
GASP
AYA ...
FUME
ARGH...
OH, NO! AYA MUST *REALLY* HATE ME NOW.
Hmph!
I UPSET HER EARLIER AND NOW *THIS*.
I DIDN'T EVEN GIVE A THOUGHT TO AYA AFTER SATSUKI TOLD ME HOW SHE FELT!
WHAT—? AM I THAT PRETTY?
STARE
OH, YEAH, YEAH ...

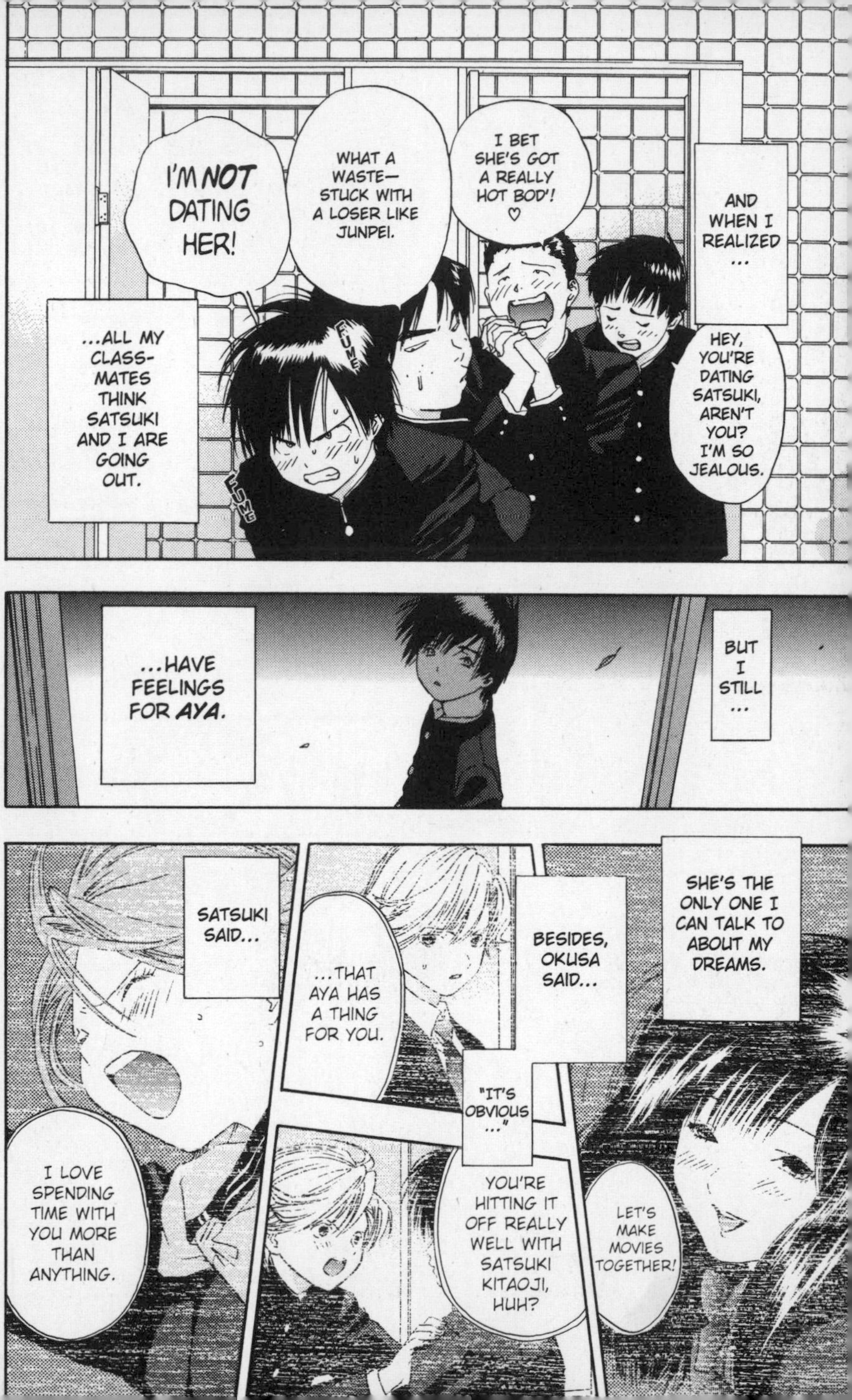
AND WHEN I REALIZED ...
HEY, YOU'RE DATING SATSUKI, AREN'T YOU? I'M SO JEALOUS.
I BET SHE'S GOT A REALLY HOT BOD'! ♡
WHAT A WASTE— STUCK WITH A LOSER LIKE JUNPEI.
I'M **NOT** DATING HER!
...ALL MY CLASS-MATES THINK SATSUKI AND I ARE GOING OUT.
FUME
FUME
BUT I STILL ...
...HAVE FEELINGS FOR ***AYA***.
SHE'S THE ONLY ONE I CAN TALK TO ABOUT MY DREAMS.
LET'S MAKE MOVIES TOGETHER!
BESIDES, OKUSA SAID...
...THAT AYA HAS A THING FOR YOU.
"IT'S OBVIOUS ..."
YOU'RE HITTING IT OFF REALLY WELL WITH SATSUKI KITAOJI, HUH?
SATSUKI SAID...
I LOVE SPENDING TIME WITH YOU MORE THAN ANYTHING.

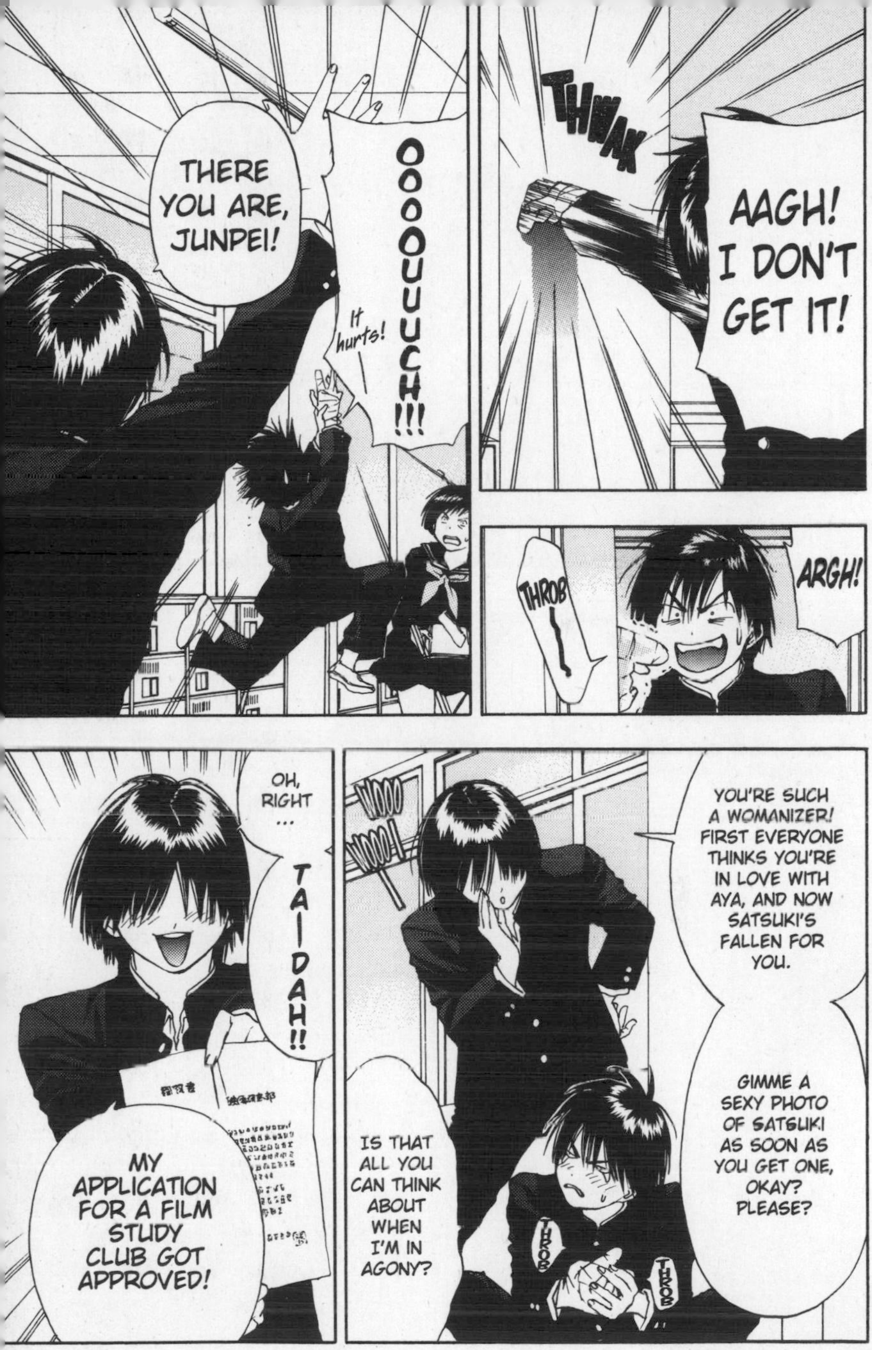
THWAK
AAGH! I DON'T GET IT!
ARGH!
THROB
OOOOUUUCH!!!
It hurts!
THERE YOU ARE, JUNPEI!
YOU'RE SUCH A WOMANIZER! FIRST EVERYONE THINKS YOU'RE IN LOVE WITH AYA, AND NOW SATSUKI'S FALLEN FOR YOU.
GIMME A SEXY PHOTO OF SATSUKI AS SOON AS YOU GET ONE, OKAY? PLEASE?
THROB
THROB
IS THAT ALL YOU CAN THINK ABOUT WHEN I'M IN AGONY?
OH, RIGHT...
TAIDAH!!
MY APPLICATION FOR A FILM STUDY CLUB GOT APPROVED!

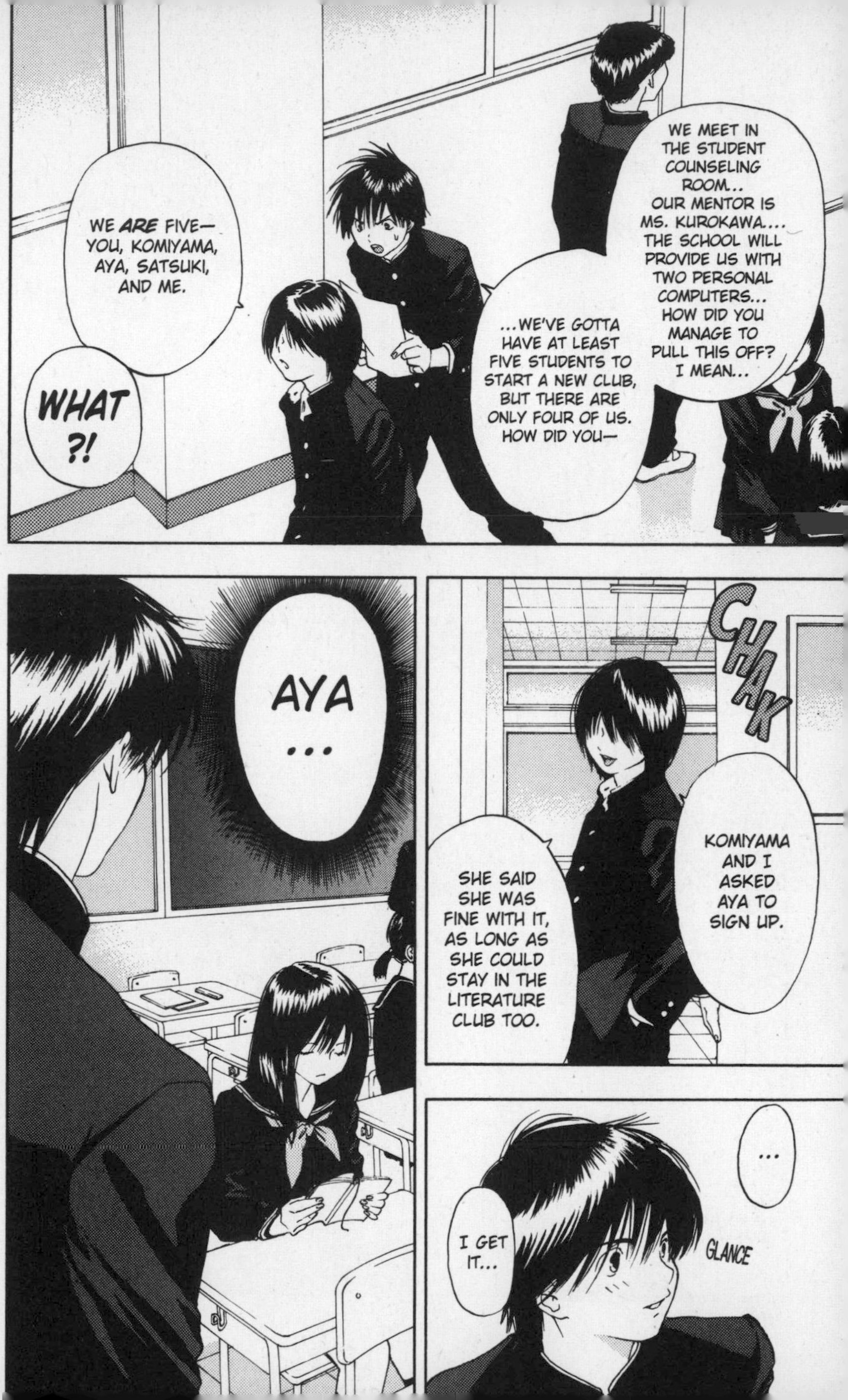
WE MEET IN THE STUDENT COUNSELING ROOM... OUR MENTOR IS MS. KUROKAWA.... THE SCHOOL WILL PROVIDE US WITH TWO PERSONAL COMPUTERS... HOW DID YOU MANAGE TO PULL THIS OFF? I MEAN...
...WE'VE GOTTA HAVE AT LEAST FIVE STUDENTS TO START A NEW CLUB, BUT THERE ARE ONLY FOUR OF US. HOW DID YOU—
WE *ARE* FIVE— YOU, KOMIYAMA, AYA, SATSUKI, AND ME.
WHAT ?!
CHAK
KOMIYAMA AND I ASKED AYA TO SIGN UP.
SHE SAID SHE WAS FINE WITH IT, AS LONG AS SHE COULD STAY IN THE LITERATURE CLUB TOO.
...
I GET IT...
GLANCE
AYA ...

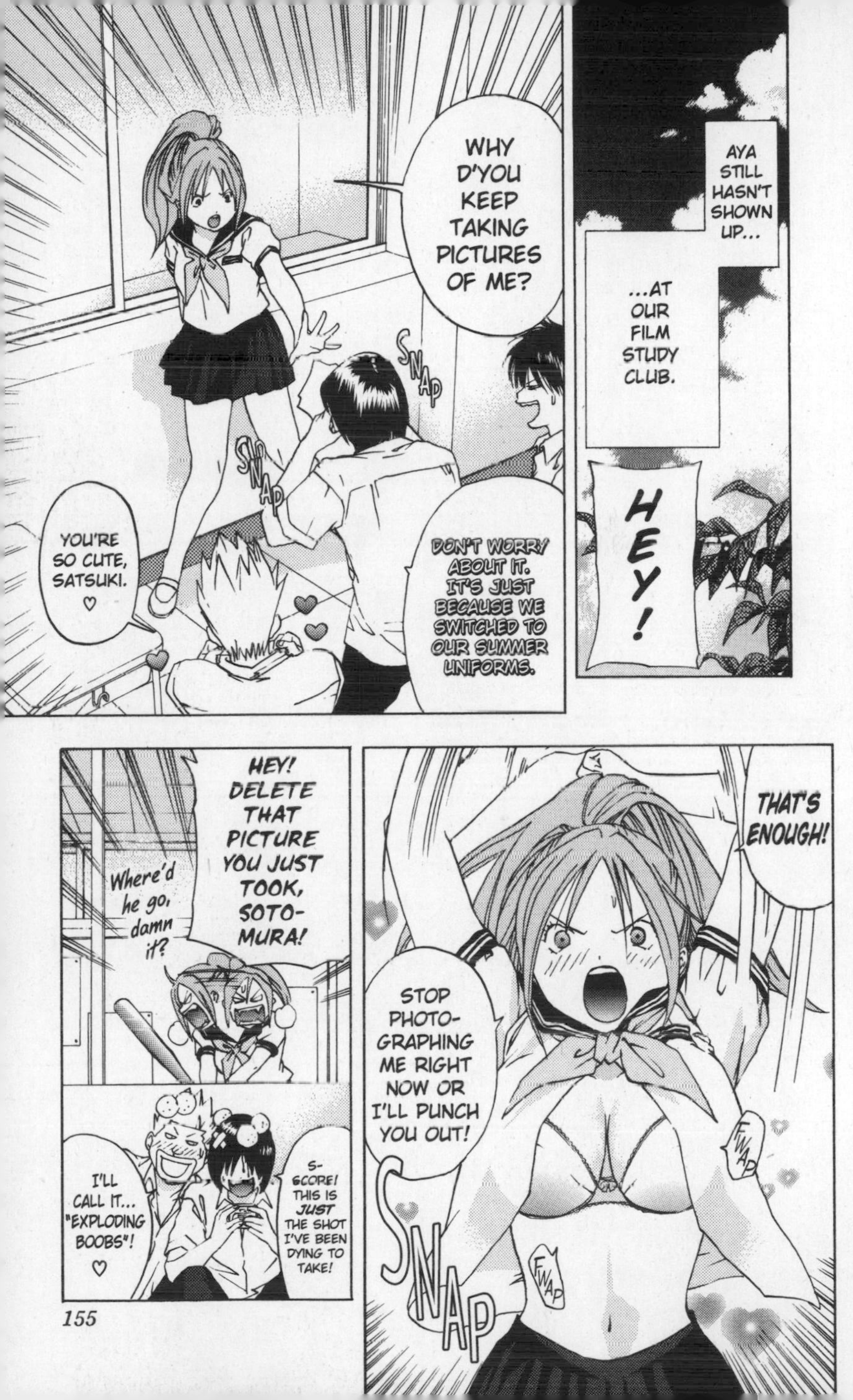
AYA STILL HASN'T SHOWN UP...
...AT OUR FILM STUDY CLUB.
HEY!
WHY D'YOU KEEP TAKING PICTURES OF ME?
SNAP
SNAP
DON'T WORRY ABOUT IT. IT'S JUST BECAUSE WE SWITCHED TO OUR SUMMER UNIFORMS.
YOU'RE SO CUTE, SATSUKI. ♡
THAT'S ENOUGH!
STOP PHOTOGRAPHING ME RIGHT NOW OR I'LL PUNCH YOU OUT!
FWAP
FWAP
SNAP
HEY! DELETE THAT PICTURE YOU JUST TOOK, SOTOMURA!
Where'd he go, damn it?
S-SCORE! THIS IS JUST THE SHOT I'VE BEEN DYING TO TAKE!
I'LL CALL IT... "EXPLODING BOOBS"! ♡

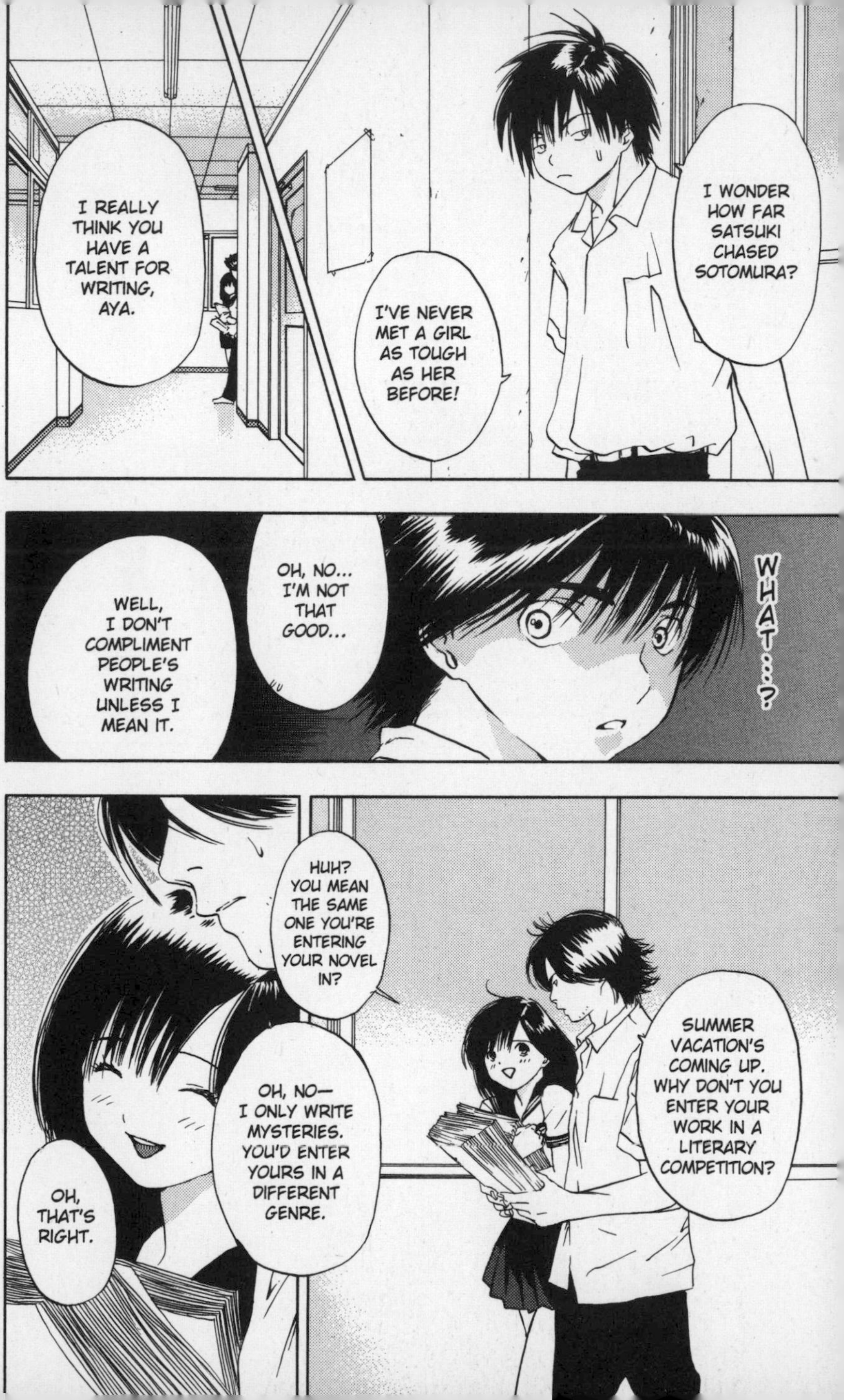
I WONDER HOW FAR SATSUKI CHASED SOTOMURA?
I'VE NEVER MET A GIRL AS TOUGH AS HER BEFORE!
I REALLY THINK YOU HAVE A TALENT FOR WRITING, AYA.
WHAT...?
OH, NO... I'M NOT THAT GOOD...
WELL, I DON'T COMPLIMENT PEOPLE'S WRITING UNLESS I MEAN IT.
SUMMER VACATION'S COMING UP. WHY DON'T YOU ENTER YOUR WORK IN A LITERARY COMPETITION?
HUH? YOU MEAN THE SAME ONE YOU'RE ENTERING YOUR NOVEL IN?
OH, NO— I ONLY WRITE MYSTERIES. YOU'D ENTER YOURS IN A DIFFERENT GENRE.
OH, THAT'S RIGHT.

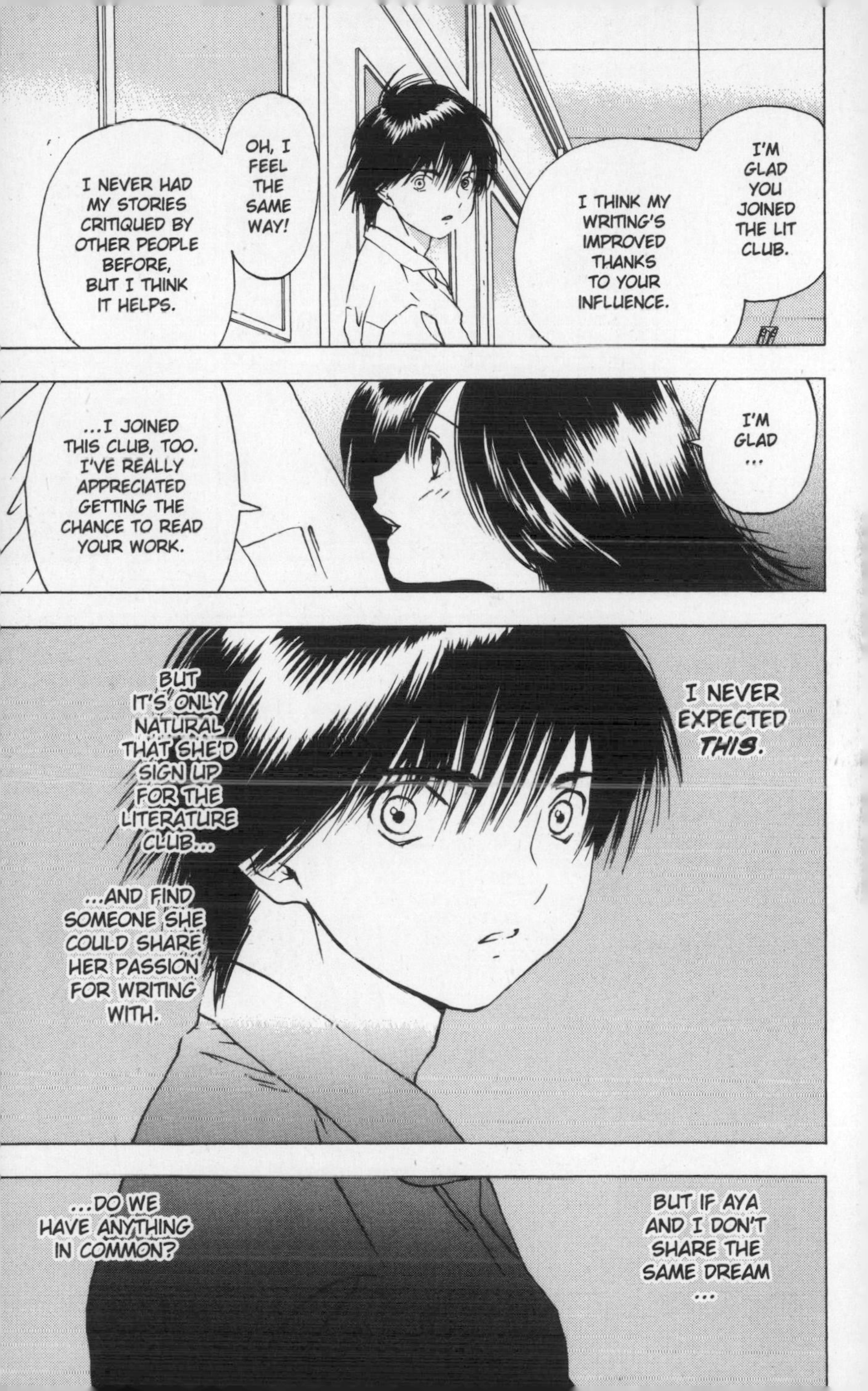
I'M GLAD YOU JOINED THE LIT CLUB.
I THINK MY WRITING'S IMPROVED THANKS TO YOUR INFLUENCE.
OH, I FEEL THE SAME WAY!
I NEVER HAD MY STORIES CRITIQUED BY OTHER PEOPLE BEFORE, BUT I THINK IT HELPS.
I'M GLAD ...
...I JOINED THIS CLUB, TOO. I'VE REALLY APPRECIATED GETTING THE CHANCE TO READ YOUR WORK.
I NEVER EXPECTED *THIS*.
BUT IT'S ONLY NATURAL THAT SHE'D SIGN UP FOR THE LITERATURE CLUB...
...AND FIND SOMEONE SHE COULD SHARE HER PASSION FOR WRITING WITH.
BUT IF AYA AND I DON'T SHARE THE SAME DREAM ...
...DO WE HAVE ANYTHING IN COMMON?

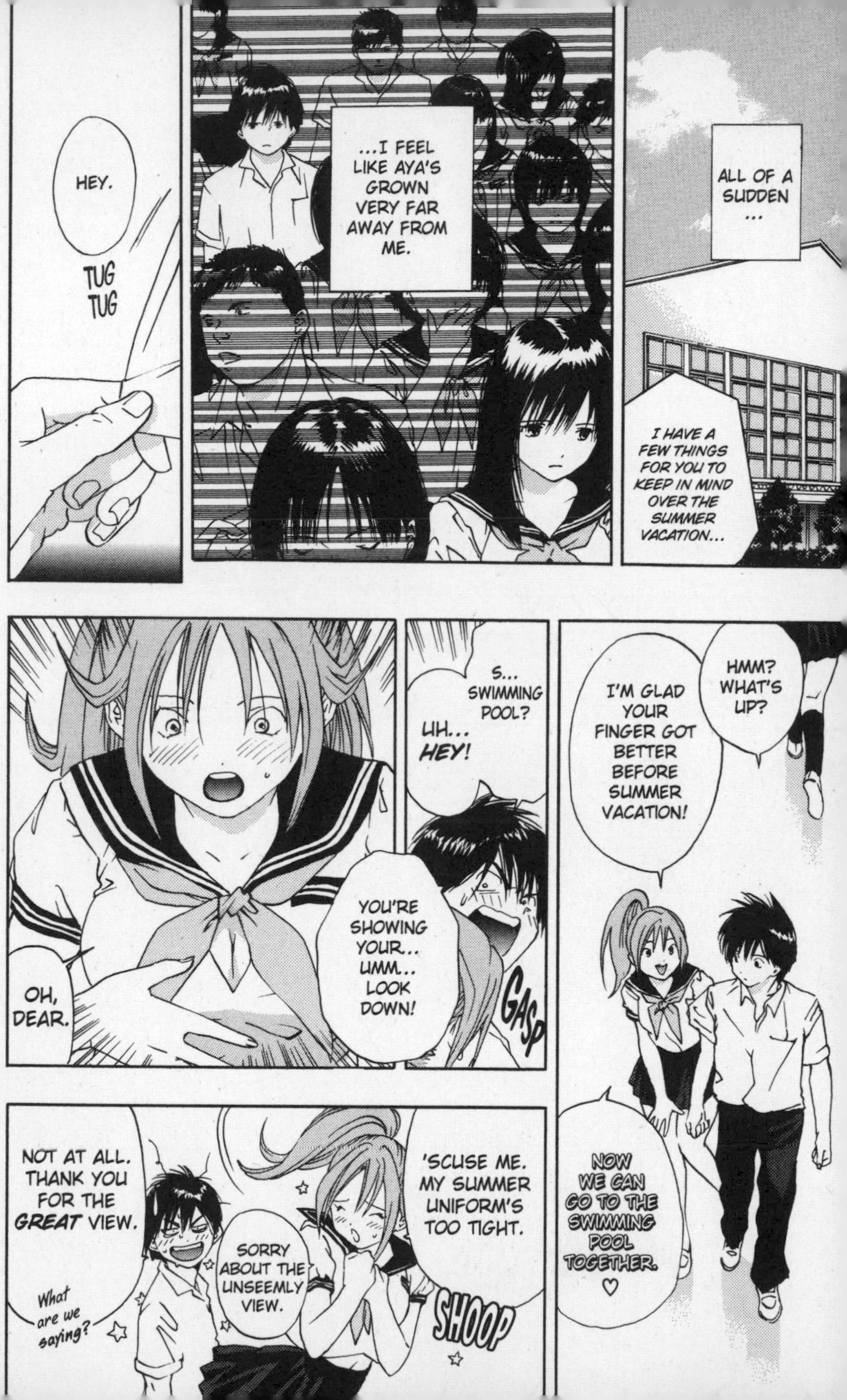
ALL OF A SUDDEN ...
I HAVE A FEW THINGS FOR YOU TO KEEP IN MIND OVER THE SUMMER VACATION...
...I FEEL LIKE AYA'S GROWN VERY FAR AWAY FROM ME.
HEY.
TUG TUG
HMM? WHAT'S UP?
I'M GLAD YOUR FINGER GOT BETTER BEFORE SUMMER VACATION!
NOW WE CAN GO TO THE SWIMMING POOL TOGETHER. ♡
S... SWIMMING POOL?
UH... HEY!
YOU'RE SHOWING YOUR... UMM... LOOK DOWN!
GASP
OH, DEAR.
'SCUSE ME. MY SUMMER UNIFORM'S TOO TIGHT.
SHOOP
SORRY ABOUT THE UNSEEMLY VIEW.
NOT AT ALL. THANK YOU FOR THE GREAT VIEW.
What are we saying?

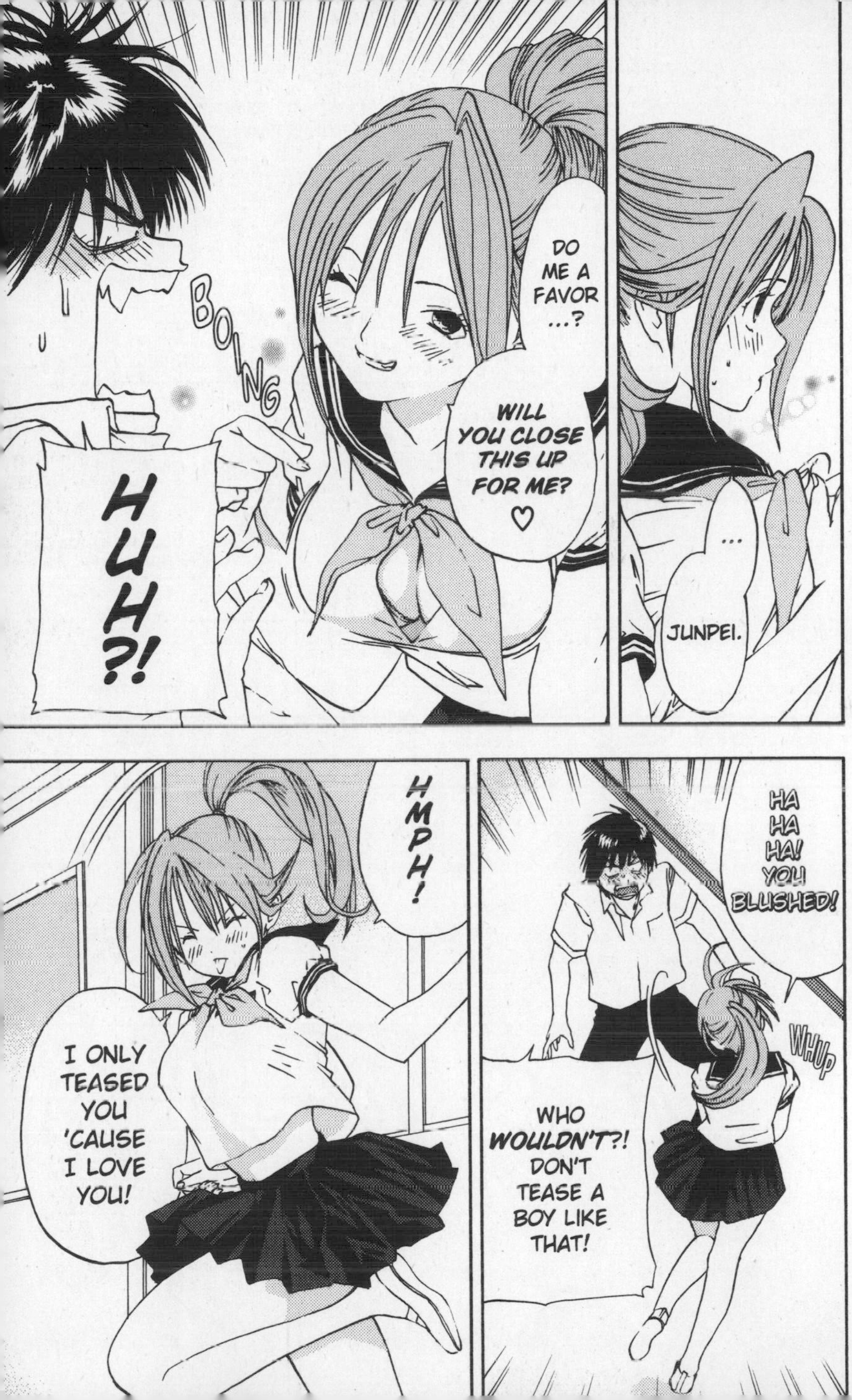
...
JUNPEI.
DO ME A FAVOR ...?
WILL YOU CLOSE THIS UP FOR ME? ♡
BOING
HUH?!
HA HA HA! YOU BLUSHED!
WHUP
WHO WOULDN'T?! DON'T TEASE A BOY LIKE THAT!
HMPH!
I ONLY TEASED YOU 'CAUSE I LOVE YOU!

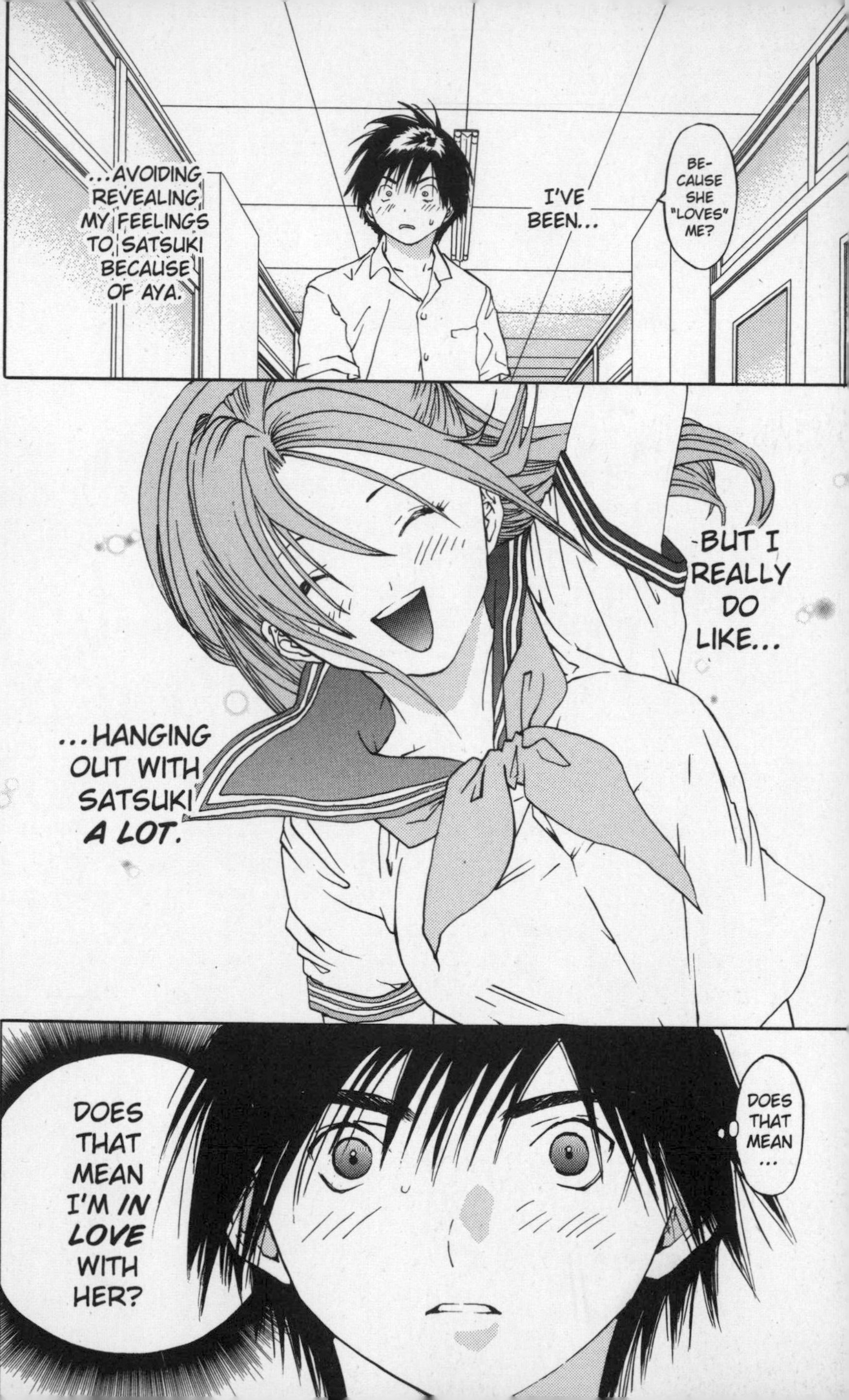
BE-CAUSE SHE "LOVES" ME?
I'VE BEEN...
...AVOIDING REVEALING MY FEELINGS TO SATSUKI BECAUSE OF AYA.
BUT I REALLY DO LIKE...
...HANGING OUT WITH SATSUKI *A LOT*.
DOES THAT MEAN...
DOES THAT MEAN I'M *IN LOVE* WITH HER?

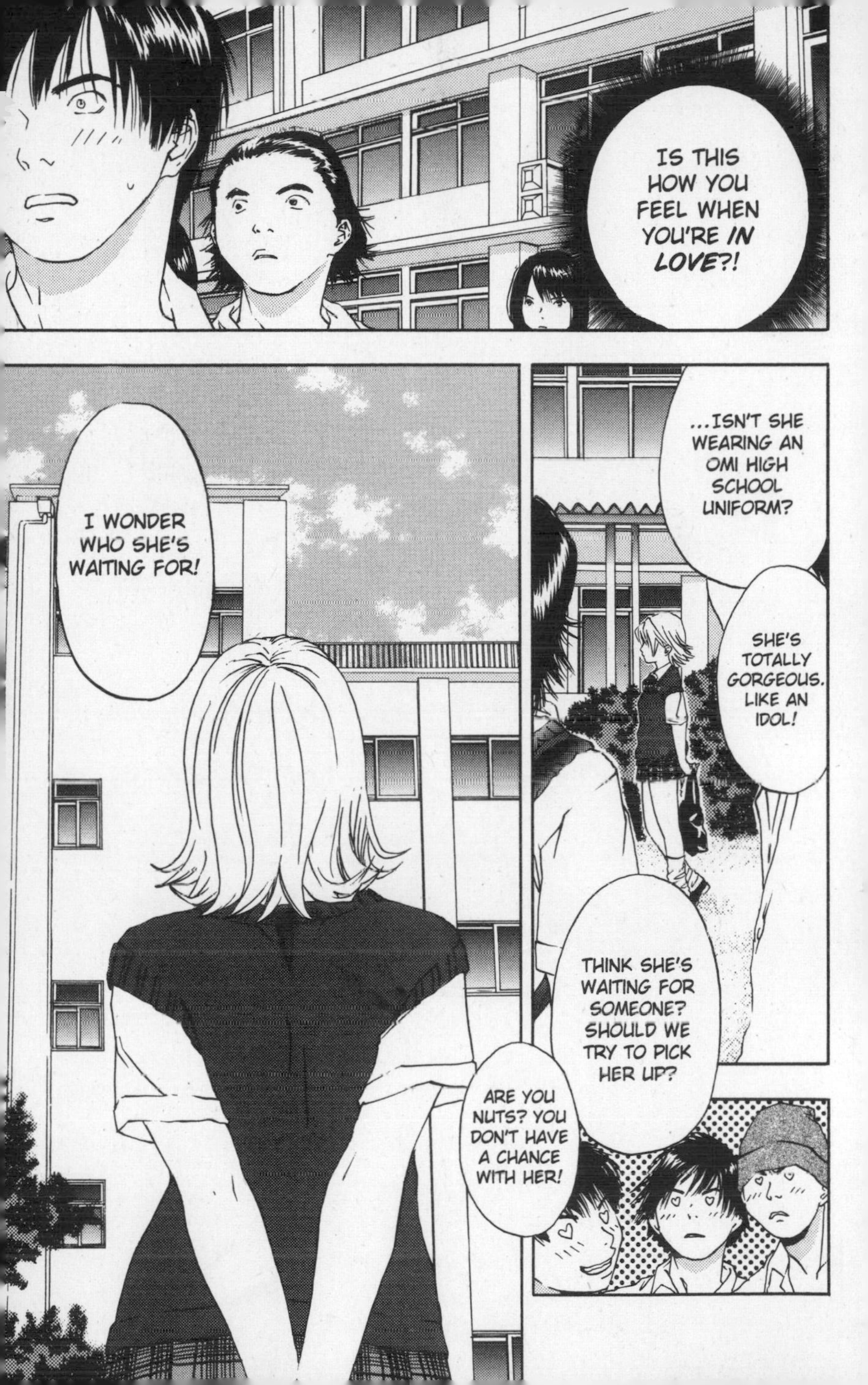
IS THIS HOW YOU FEEL WHEN YOU'RE *IN LOVE*?!
...ISN'T SHE WEARING AN OMI HIGH SCHOOL UNIFORM?
SHE'S TOTALLY GORGEOUS. LIKE AN IDOL!
THINK SHE'S WAITING FOR SOMEONE? SHOULD WE TRY TO PICK HER UP?
ARE YOU NUTS? YOU DON'T HAVE A CHANCE WITH HER!
I WONDER WHO SHE'S WAITING FOR!

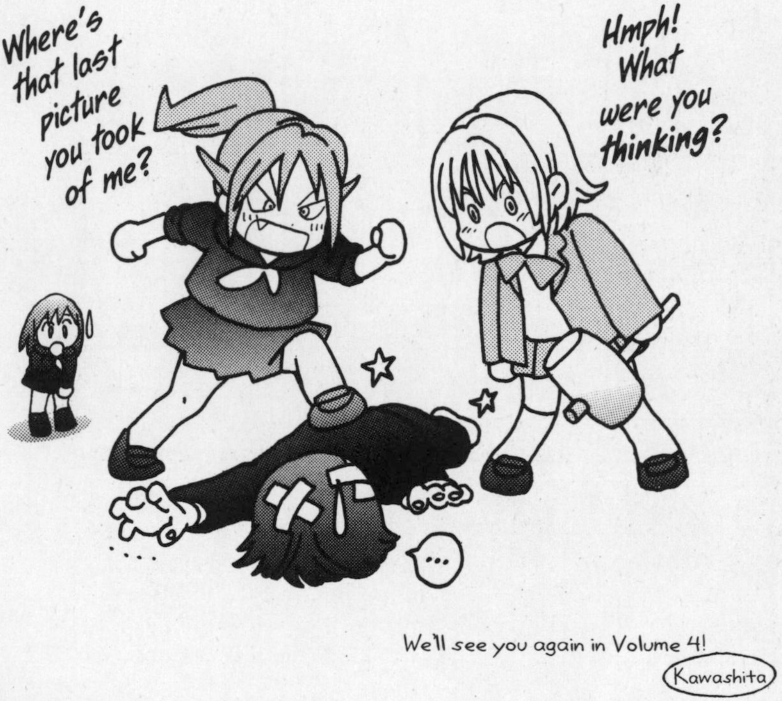
Hmph! What were you thinking?
Where's that last picture you took of me?
...
....
We'll see you again in Volume 4!
Kawashita

CRUSH 26: REUNION

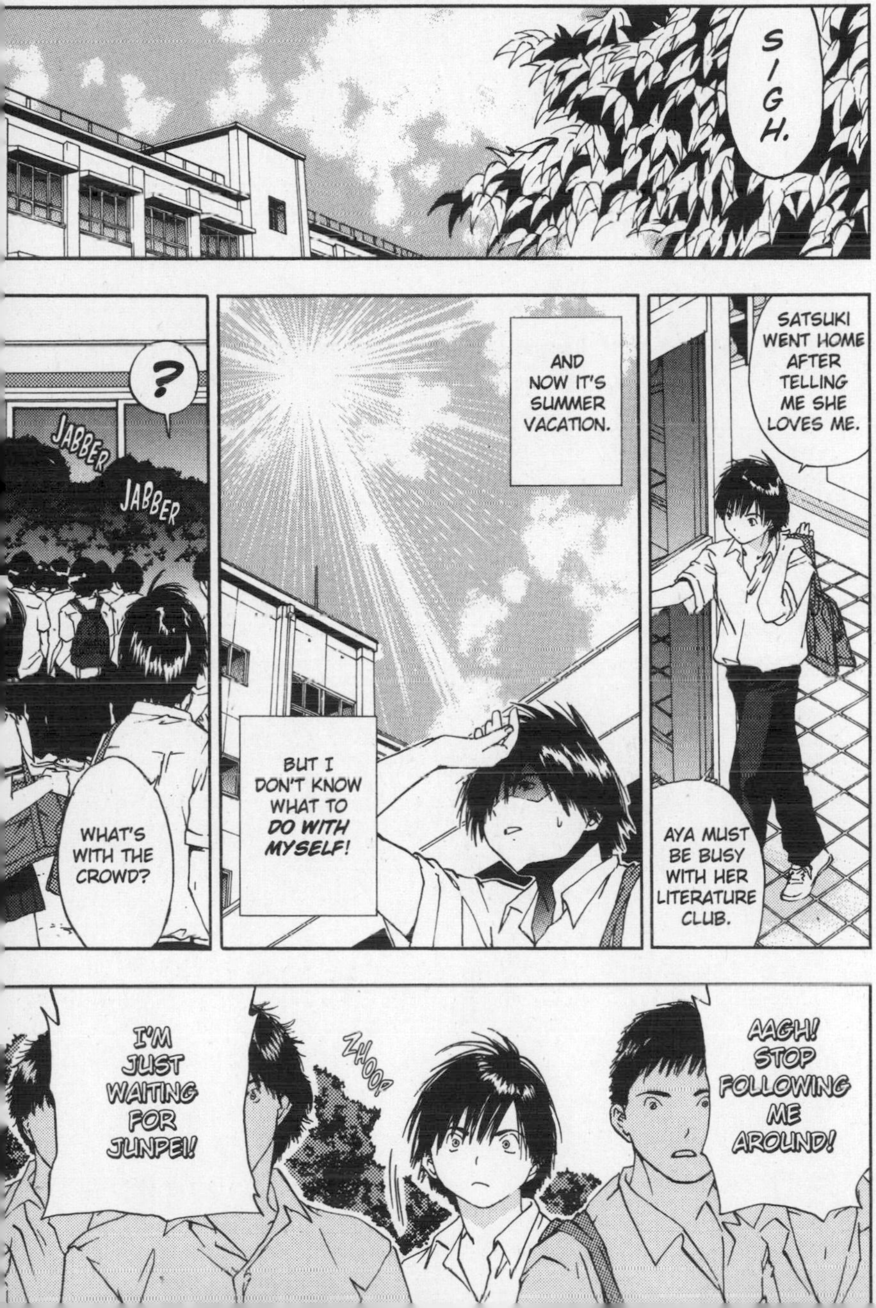
SIGH.
SATSUKI WENT HOME AFTER TELLING ME SHE LOVES ME.
AYA MUST BE BUSY WITH HER LITERATURE CLUB.
AND NOW IT'S SUMMER VACATION.
BUT I DON'T KNOW WHAT TO DO WITH MYSELF!
?
JABBER
JABBER
WHAT'S WITH THE CROWD?
AAGH! STOP FOLLOWING ME AROUND!
ZHOOP
I'M JUST WAITING FOR JUNPEI!

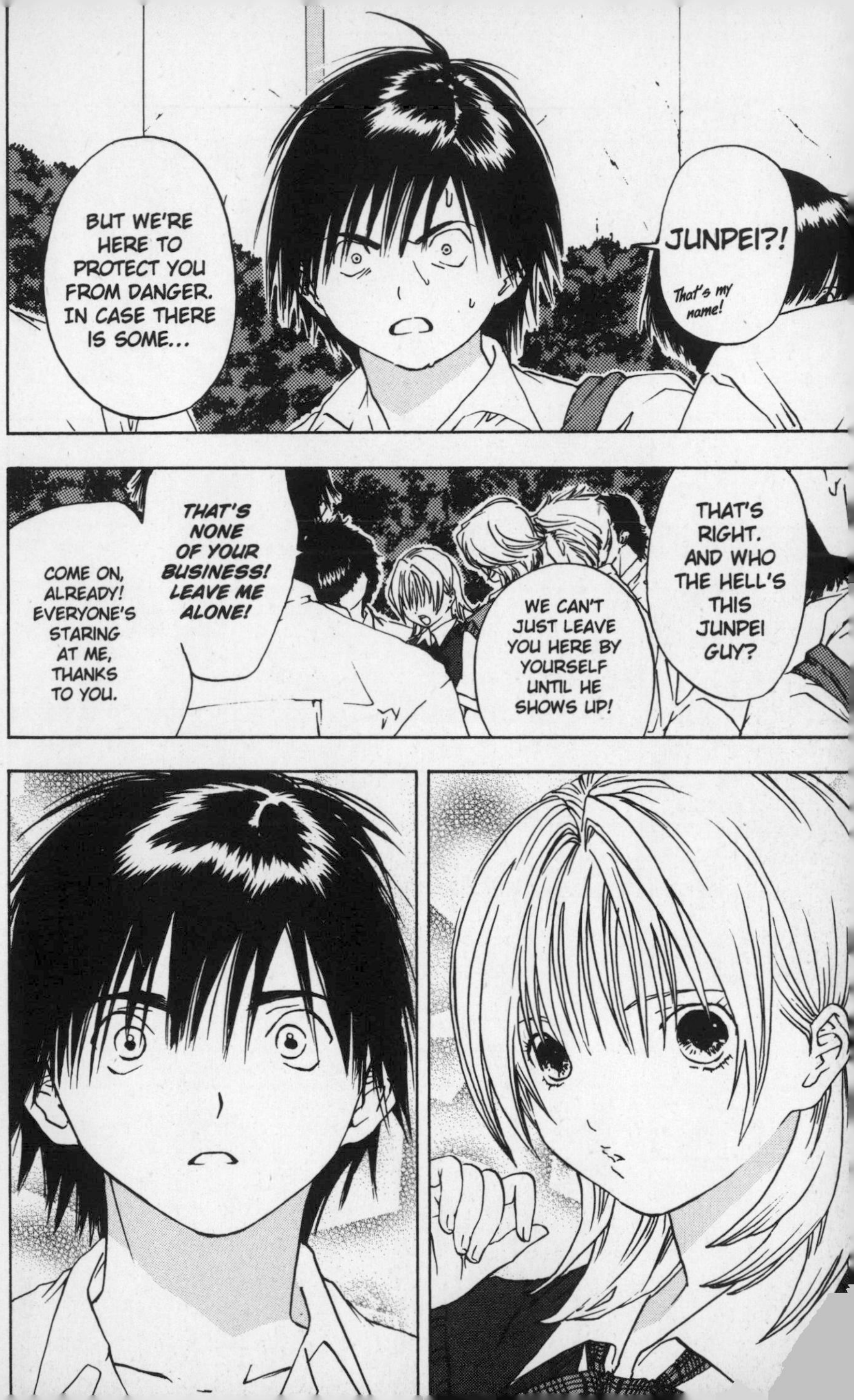
JUNPEI?!
That's my name!
BUT WE'RE HERE TO PROTECT YOU FROM DANGER. IN CASE THERE IS SOME...
THAT'S RIGHT. AND WHO THE HELL'S THIS JUNPEI GUY?
WE CAN'T JUST LEAVE YOU HERE BY YOURSELF UNTIL HE SHOWS UP!
THAT'S NONE OF YOUR BUSINESS! LEAVE ME ALONE!
COME ON, ALREADY! EVERYONE'S STARING AT ME, THANKS TO YOU.

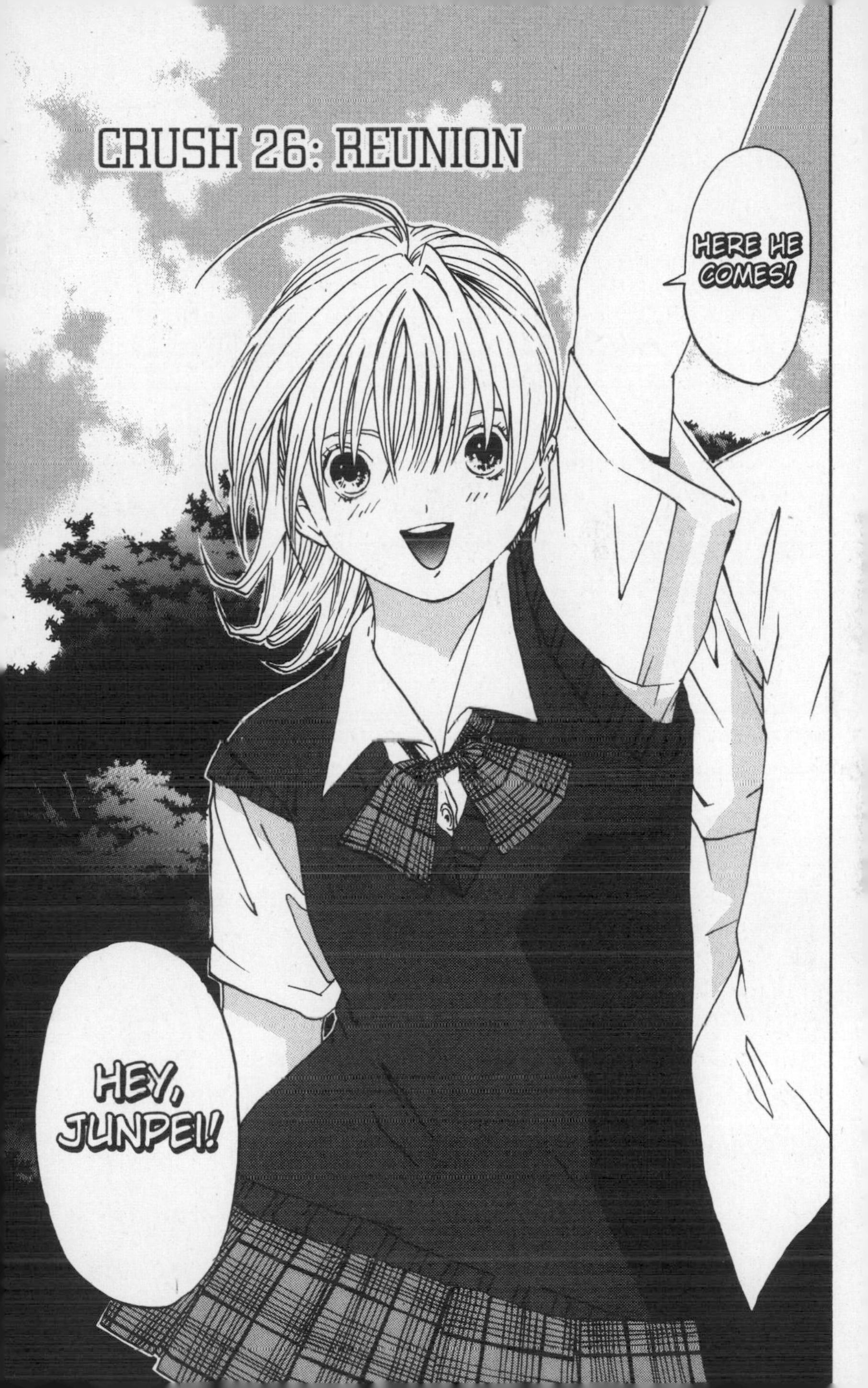
CRUSH 26: REUNION
HERE HE COMES!
HEY, JUNPEI!

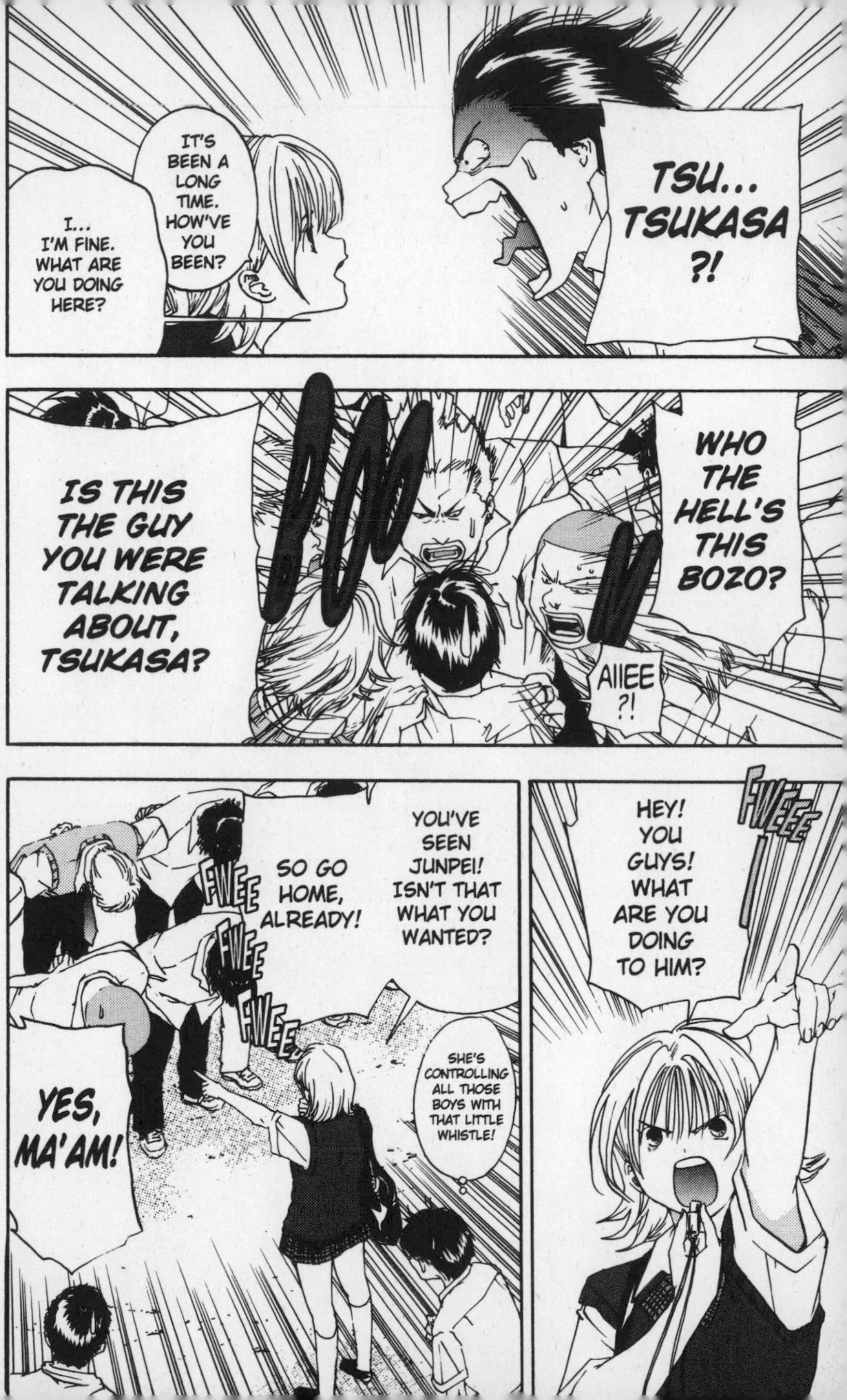
TSU... TSUKASA ?!
IT'S BEEN A LONG TIME. HOW'VE YOU BEEN?
I... I'M FINE. WHAT ARE YOU DOING HERE?
WHO THE HELL'S THIS BOZO?
AIIEE ?!
IS THIS THE GUY YOU WERE TALKING ABOUT, TSUKASA?
FWEEEE
HEY! YOU GUYS! WHAT ARE YOU DOING TO HIM?
YOU'VE SEEN JUNPEI! ISN'T THAT WHAT YOU WANTED?
SO GO HOME, ALREADY!
FWEE
FWEE
FWEE
SHE'S CONTROLLING ALL THOSE BOYS WITH THAT LITTLE WHISTLE!
YES, MA'AM!

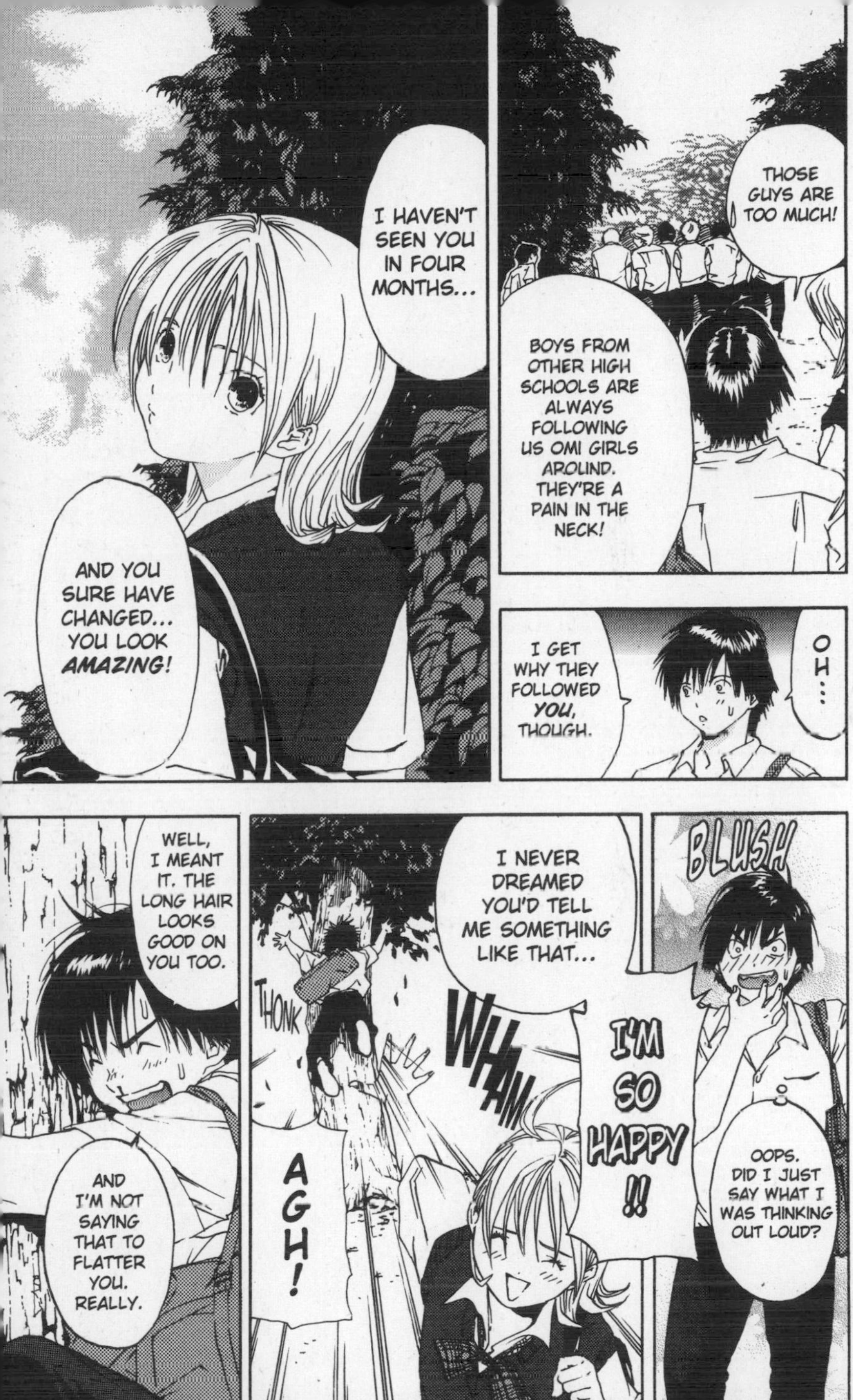

THOSE GUYS ARE TOO MUCH!
BOYS FROM OTHER HIGH SCHOOLS ARE ALWAYS FOLLOWING US OMI GIRLS AROUND. THEY'RE A PAIN IN THE NECK!
OH...
I GET WHY THEY FOLLOWED *YOU*, THOUGH.
I HAVEN'T SEEN YOU IN FOUR MONTHS...
AND YOU SURE HAVE CHANGED... YOU LOOK ***AMAZING***!
BLUSH
OOPS. DID I JUST SAY WHAT I WAS THINKING OUT LOUD?
I NEVER DREAMED YOU'D TELL ME SOMETHING LIKE THAT...
I'M SO HAPPY!!
WHAM
THONK
AGH!
WELL, I MEANT IT. THE LONG HAIR LOOKS GOOD ON YOU TOO.
AND I'M NOT SAYING THAT TO FLATTER YOU. REALLY.

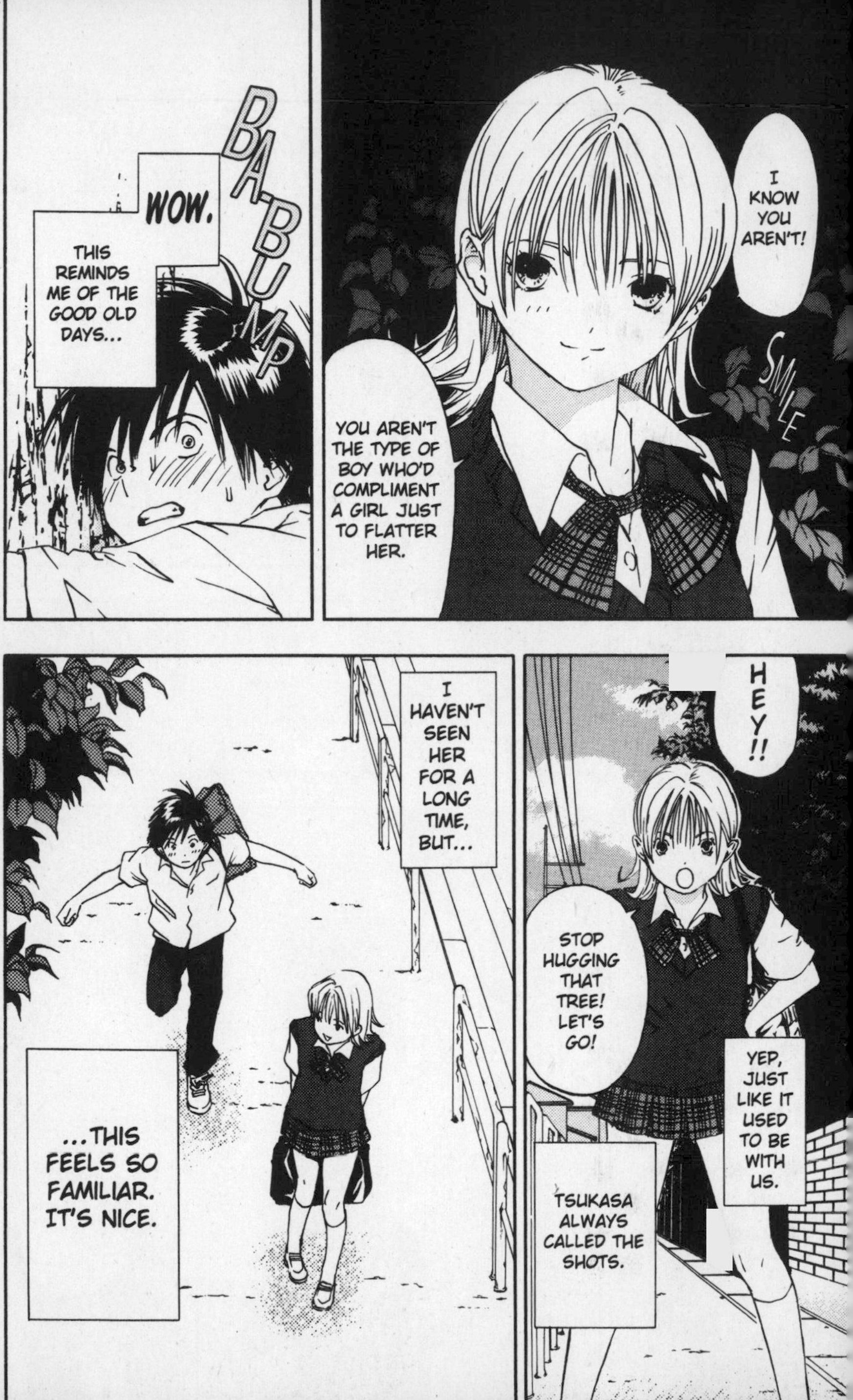
I KNOW YOU AREN'T!
YOU AREN'T THE TYPE OF BOY WHO'D COMPLIMENT A GIRL JUST TO FLATTER HER.
SMILE
BA-BUMP
WOW.
THIS REMINDS ME OF THE GOOD OLD DAYS...
HEY!!
STOP HUGGING THAT TREE! LET'S GO!
YEP, JUST LIKE IT USED TO BE WITH US.
TSUKASA ALWAYS CALLED THE SHOTS.
I HAVEN'T SEEN HER FOR A LONG TIME, BUT...
...THIS FEELS SO FAMILIAR. IT'S NICE.

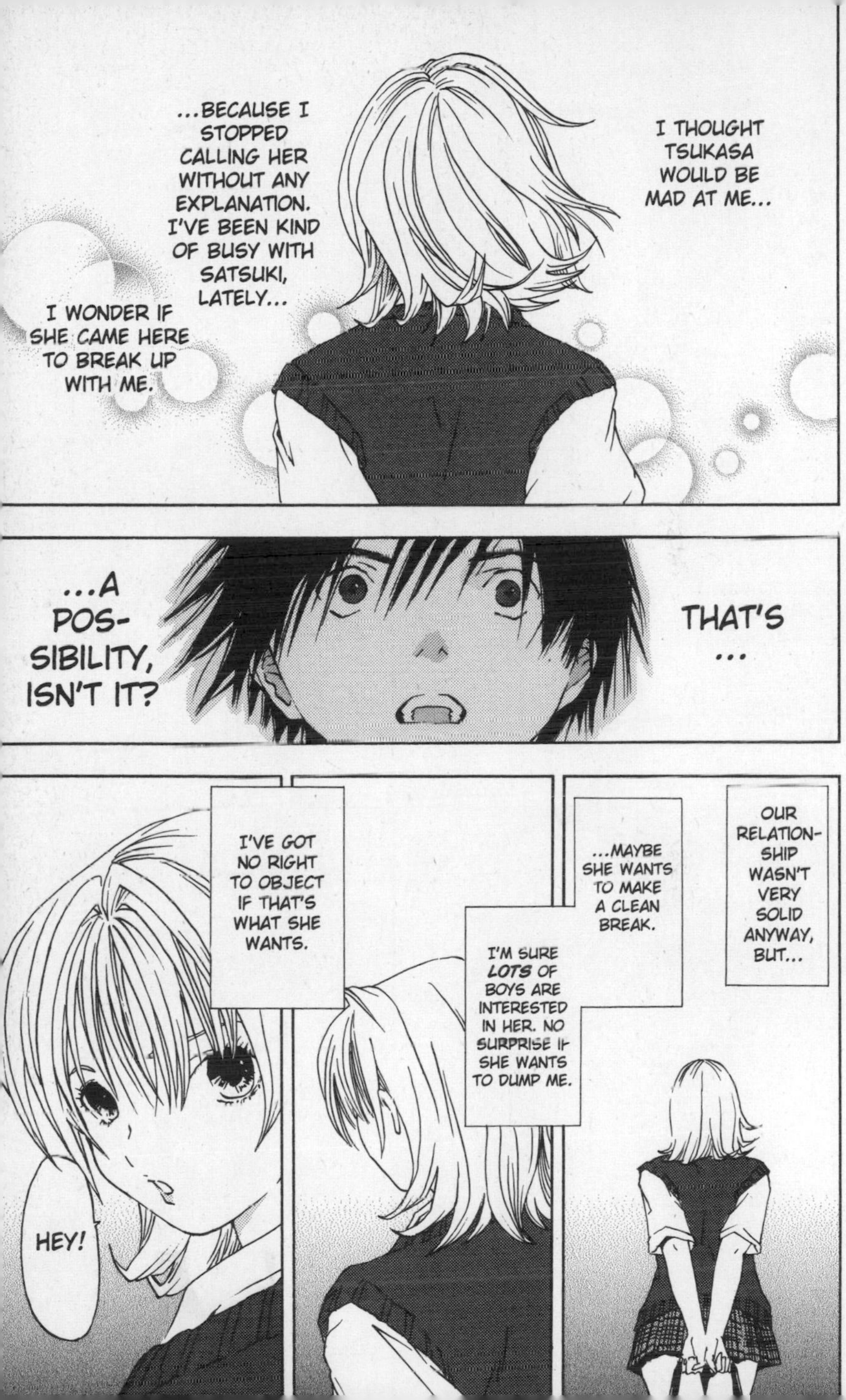
I THOUGHT TSUKASA WOULD BE MAD AT ME...
...BECAUSE I STOPPED CALLING HER WITHOUT ANY EXPLANATION.
I'VE BEEN KIND OF BUSY WITH SATSUKI, LATELY...
I WONDER IF SHE CAME HERE TO BREAK UP WITH ME.
THAT'S ...
...A POS-SIBILITY, ISN'T IT?
OUR RELATION-SHIP WASN'T VERY SOLID ANYWAY, BUT...
...MAYBE SHE WANTS TO MAKE A CLEAN BREAK.
I'M SURE *LOTS* OF BOYS ARE INTERESTED IN HER.
NO SURPRISE IF SHE WANTS TO DUMP ME.
I'VE GOT NO RIGHT TO OBJECT IF THAT'S WHAT SHE WANTS.
HEY!

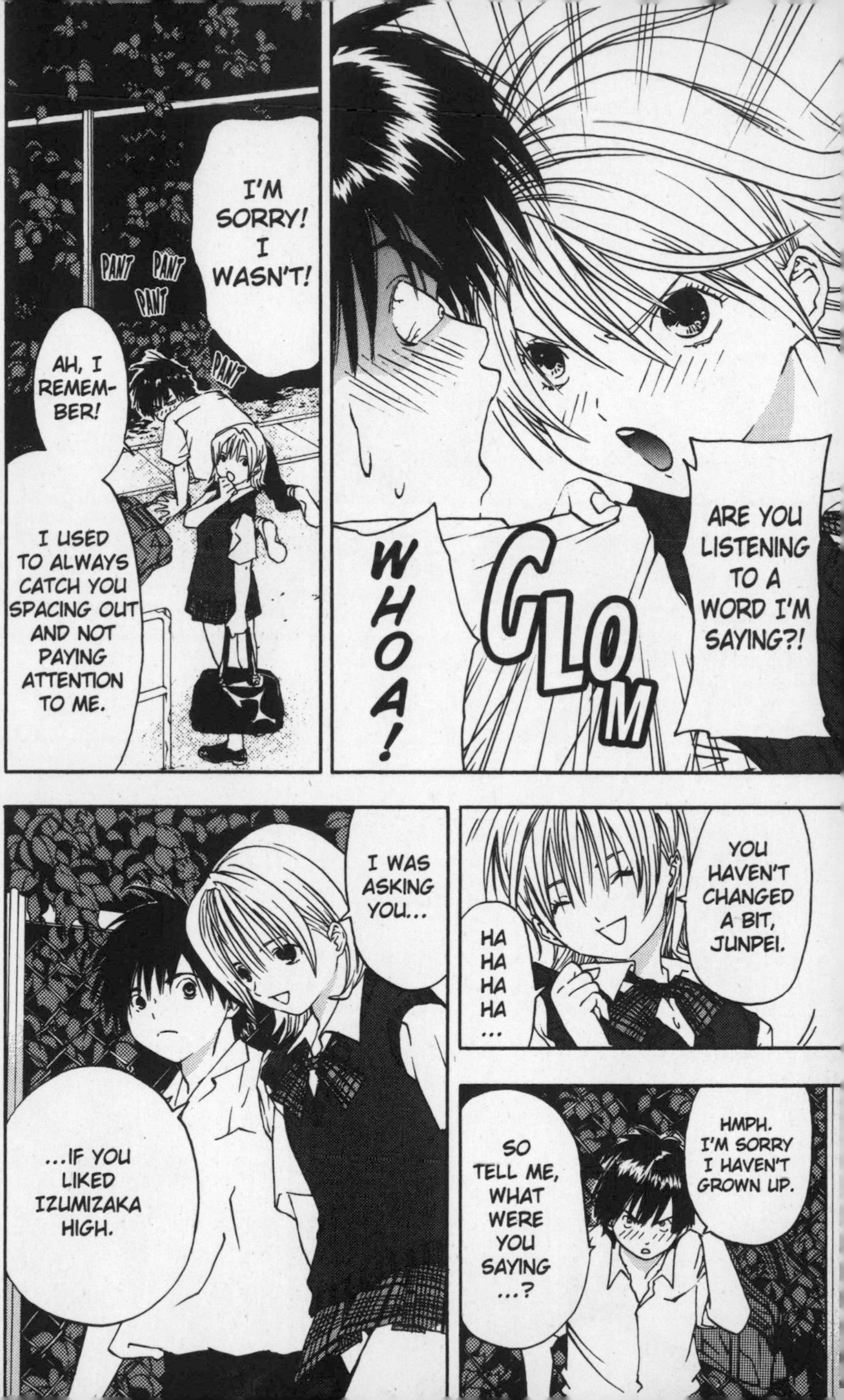
ARE YOU LISTENING TO A WORD I'M SAYING?!
GLOM
WHOA!
I'M SORRY! I WASN'T!
PANT PANT PANT PANT
AH, I REMEMBER!
I USED TO ALWAYS CATCH YOU SPACING OUT AND NOT PAYING ATTENTION TO ME.
YOU HAVEN'T CHANGED A BIT, JUNPEI.
HA HA HA HA ...
HMPH. I'M SORRY I HAVEN'T GROWN UP.
SO TELL ME, WHAT WERE YOU SAYING ...?
I WAS ASKING YOU...
...IF YOU LIKED IZUMIZAKA HIGH.

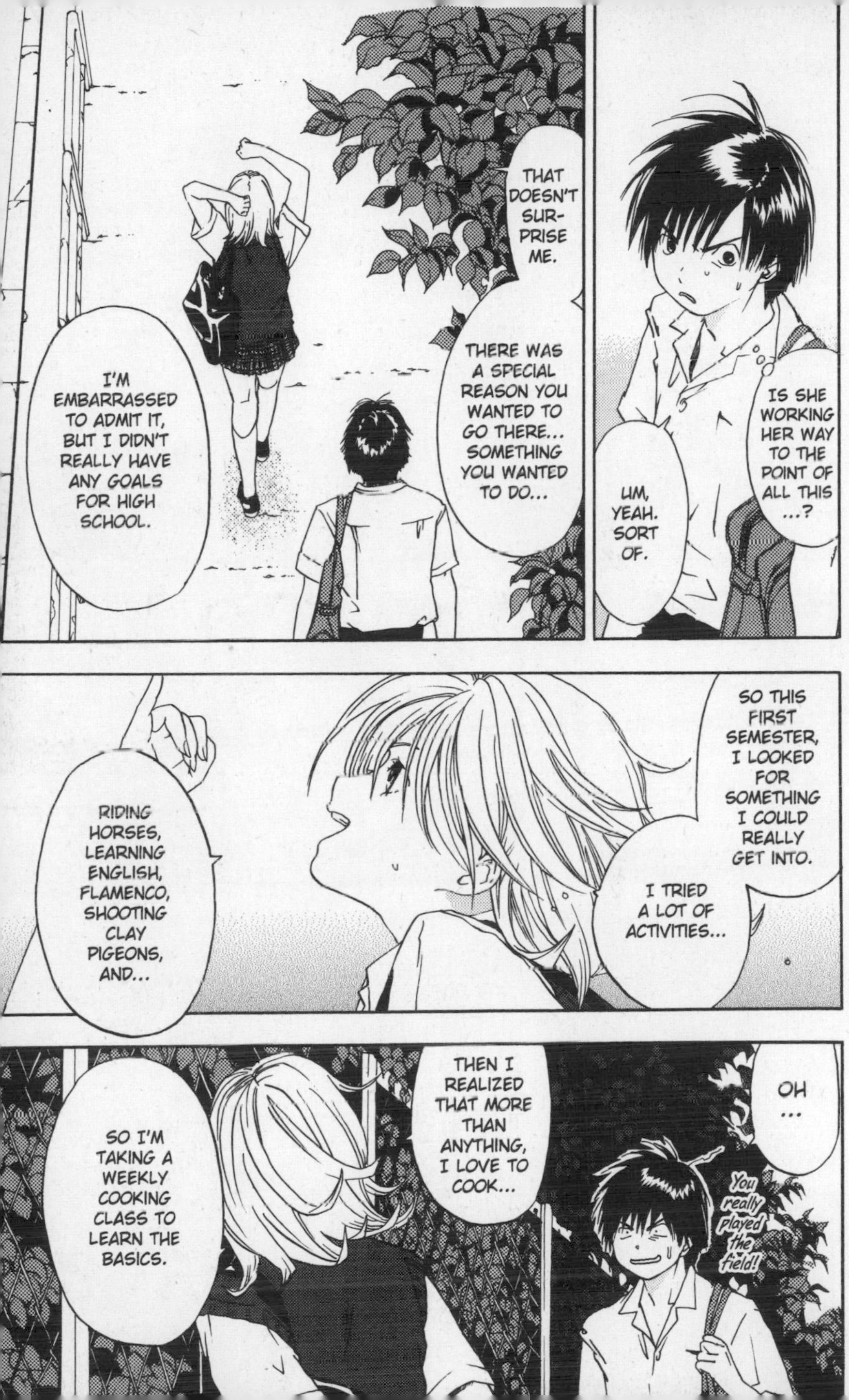
IS SHE WORKING HER WAY TO THE POINT OF ALL THIS ...?
UM, YEAH. SORT OF.
THAT DOESN'T SURPRISE ME.
THERE WAS A SPECIAL REASON YOU WANTED TO GO THERE... SOMETHING YOU WANTED TO DO...
I'M EMBARRASSED TO ADMIT IT, BUT I DIDN'T REALLY HAVE ANY GOALS FOR HIGH SCHOOL.
SO THIS FIRST SEMESTER, I LOOKED FOR SOMETHING I COULD REALLY GET INTO.
I TRIED A LOT OF ACTIVITIES...
RIDING HORSES, LEARNING ENGLISH, FLAMENCO, SHOOTING CLAY PIGEONS, AND...
OH ...
You really played the field!
THEN I REALIZED THAT MORE THAN ANYTHING, I LOVE TO COOK...
SO I'M TAKING A WEEKLY COOKING CLASS TO LEARN THE BASICS.

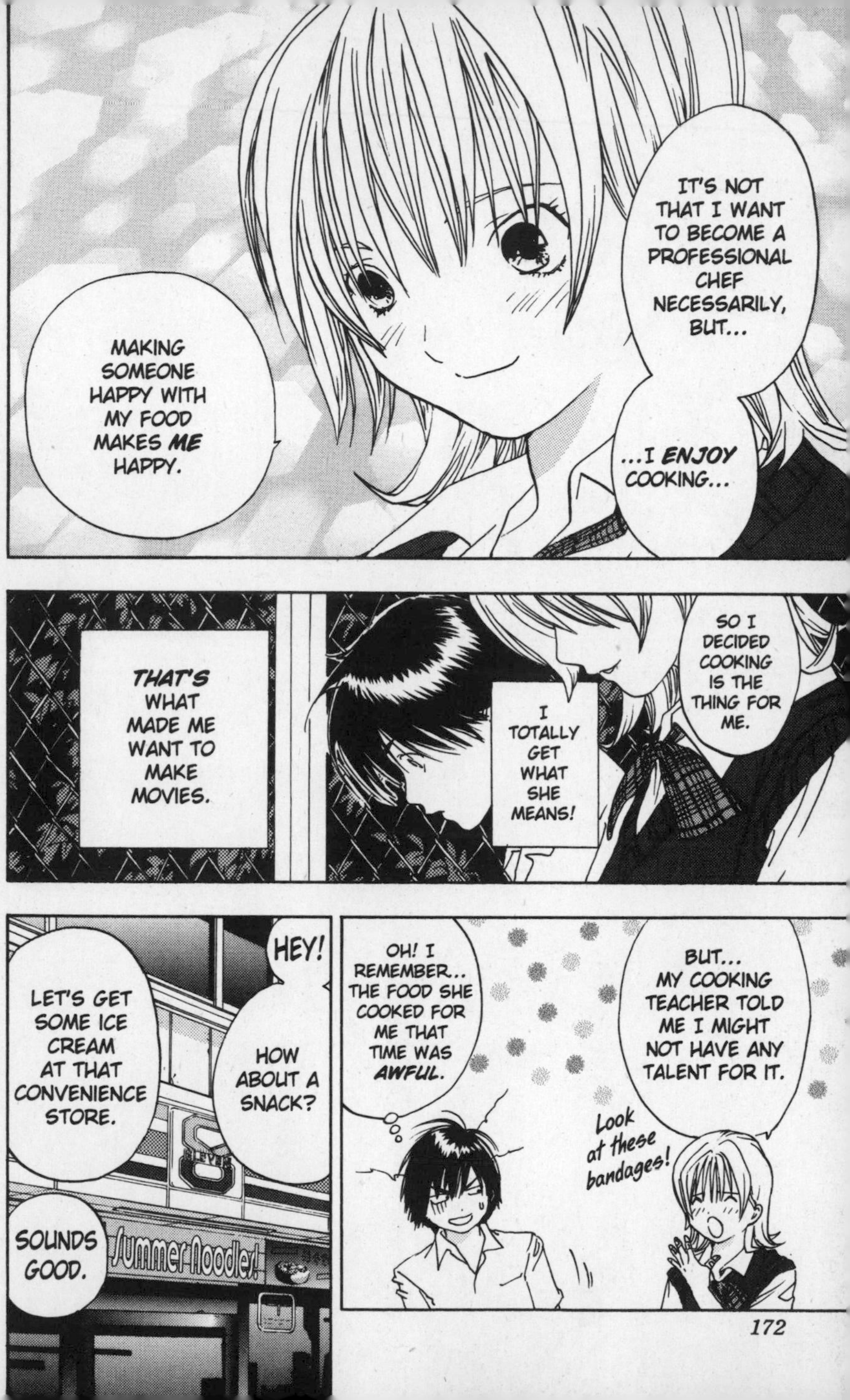
IT'S NOT THAT I WANT TO BECOME A PROFESSIONAL CHEF NECESSARILY, BUT...
...I ENJOY COOKING...
MAKING SOMEONE HAPPY WITH MY FOOD MAKES ME HAPPY.
SO I DECIDED COOKING IS THE THING FOR ME.
I TOTALLY GET WHAT SHE MEANS!
THAT'S WHAT MADE ME WANT TO MAKE MOVIES.
BUT... MY COOKING TEACHER TOLD ME I MIGHT NOT HAVE ANY TALENT FOR IT.
Look at these bandages!
OH! I REMEMBER... THE FOOD SHE COOKED FOR ME THAT TIME WAS AWFUL.
HEY!
HOW ABOUT A SNACK?
LET'S GET SOME ICE CREAM AT THAT CONVENIENCE STORE.
SOUNDS GOOD.
Summer Noodles!

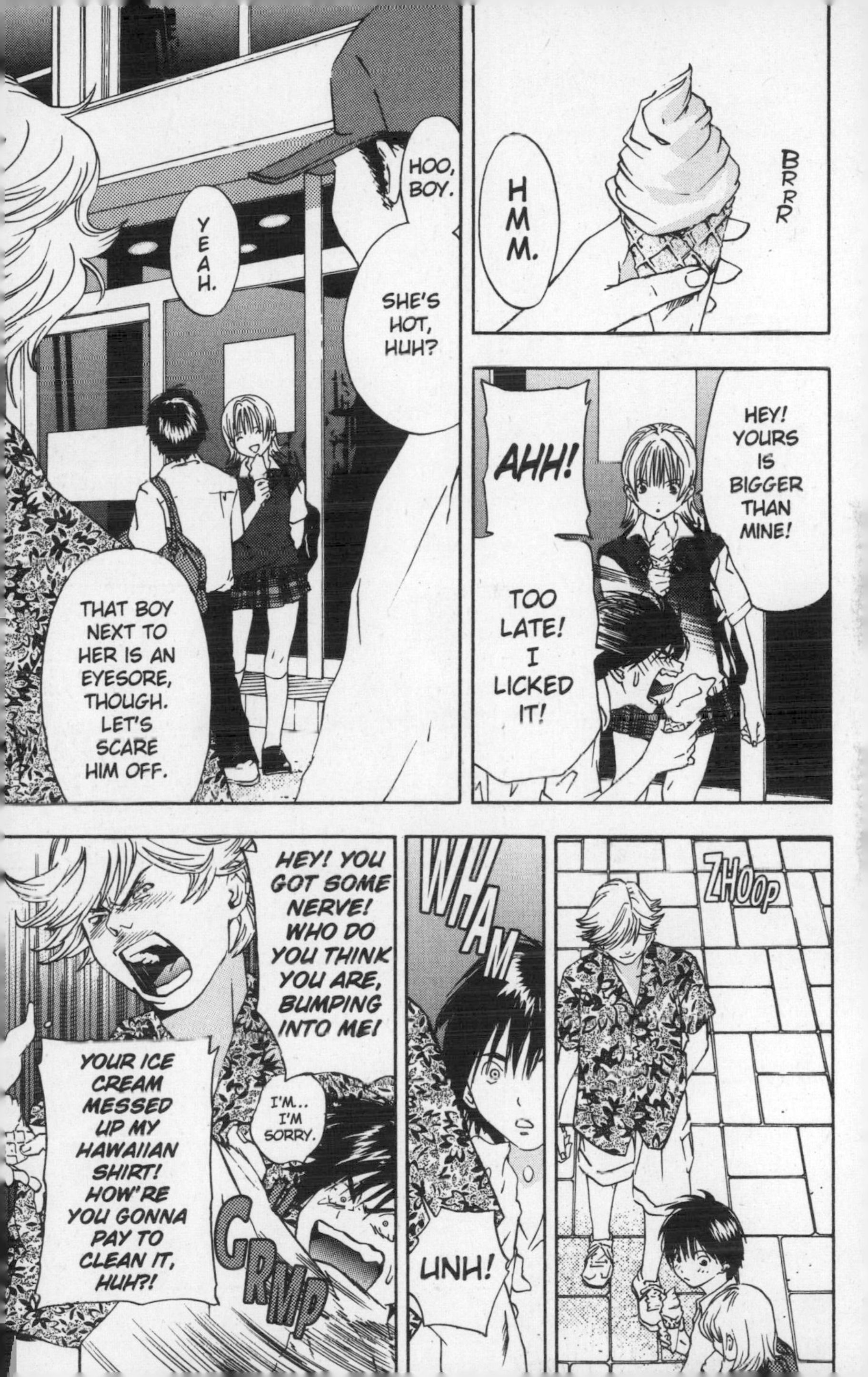
BRRR
HMM.
HEY! YOURS IS BIGGER THAN MINE!
AHH!
TOO LATE! I LICKED IT!
HOO, BOY.
YEAH.
SHE'S HOT, HUH?
THAT BOY NEXT TO HER IS AN EYESORE, THOUGH. LET'S SCARE HIM OFF.
ZHOOP
WHAM
UNH!
HEY! YOU GOT SOME NERVE! WHO DO YOU THINK YOU ARE, BUMPING INTO ME!
YOUR ICE CREAM MESSED UP MY HAWAIIAN SHIRT! HOW'RE YOU GONNA PAY TO CLEAN IT, HUH?!
I'M... I'M SORRY.
GRMP

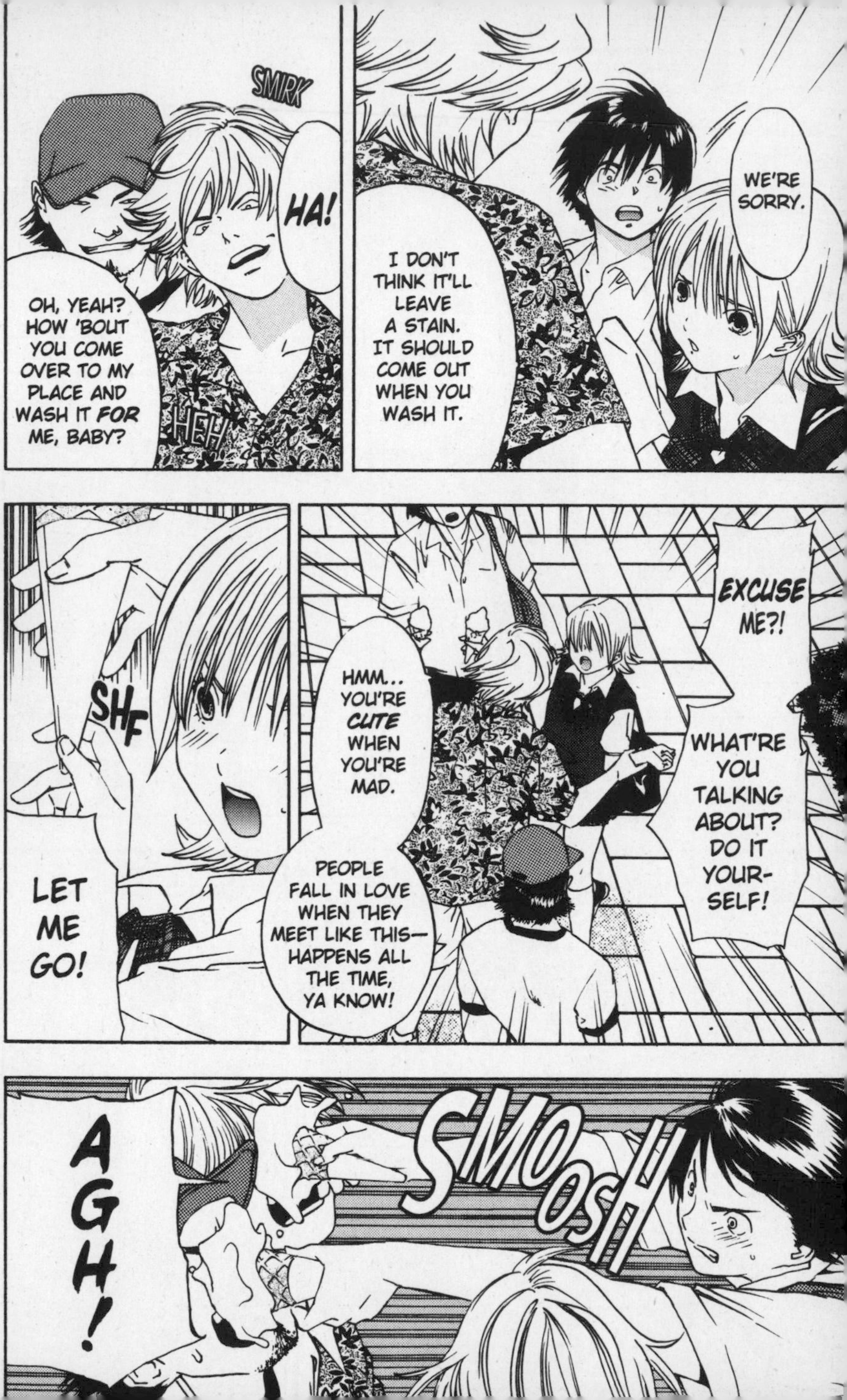
WE'RE SORRY.
I DON'T THINK IT'LL LEAVE A STAIN. IT SHOULD COME OUT WHEN YOU WASH IT.
SMIRK
HA!
OH, YEAH? HOW 'BOUT YOU COME OVER TO MY PLACE AND WASH IT *FOR* ME, BABY?
HEH
EXCUSE ME?!
WHAT'RE YOU TALKING ABOUT? DO IT YOUR-SELF!
HMM... YOU'RE *CUTE* WHEN YOU'RE MAD.
PEOPLE FALL IN LOVE WHEN THEY MEET LIKE THIS—HAPPENS ALL THE TIME, YA KNOW!
SHF
LET ME GO!
SMOOSH
AGH!

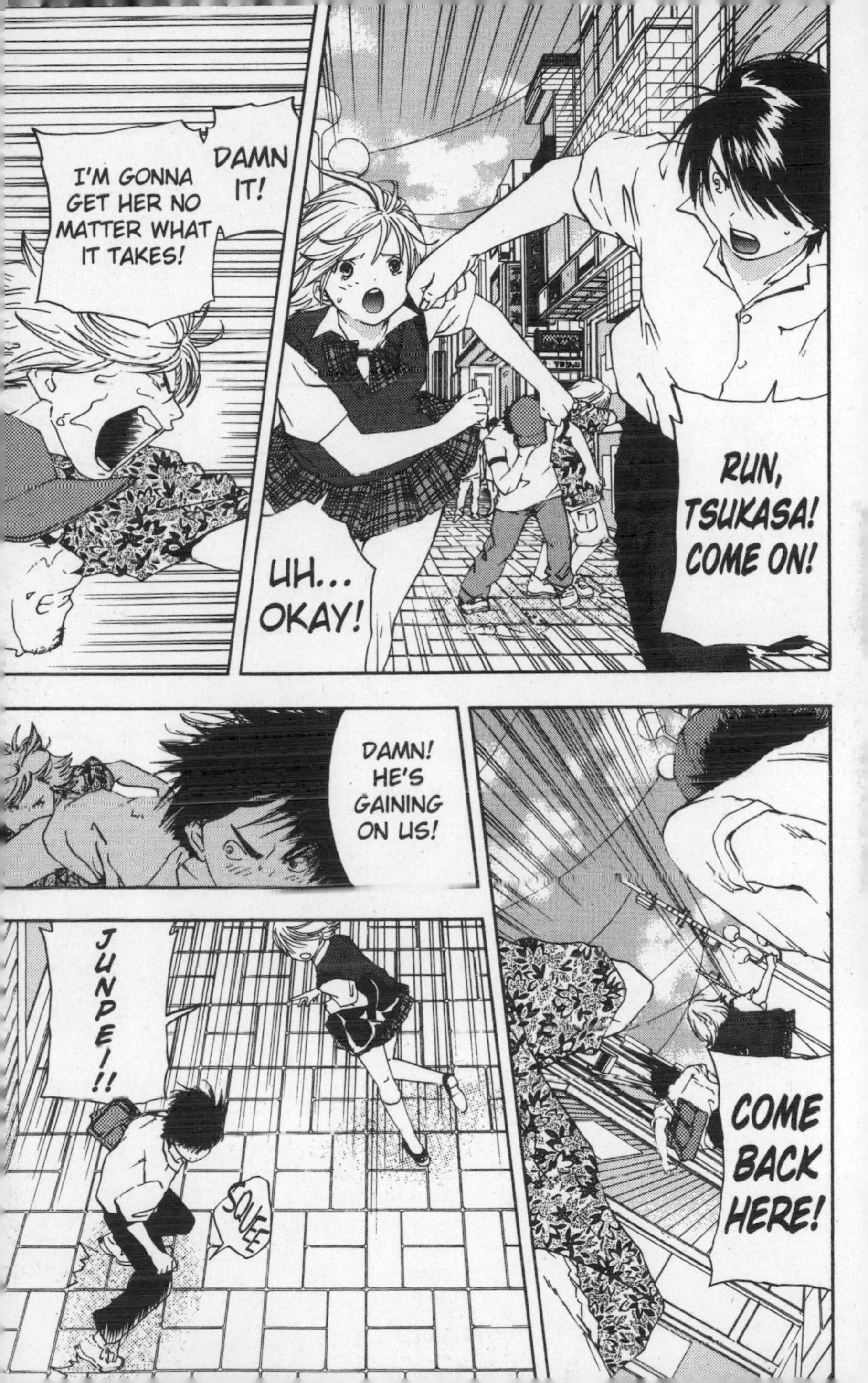
RUN, TSUKASA! COME ON!
UH... OKAY!
DAMN IT!
I'M GONNA GET HER NO MATTER WHAT IT TAKES!
COME BACK HERE!
DAMN! HE'S GAINING ON US!
JUNPEI!!
SQUEE

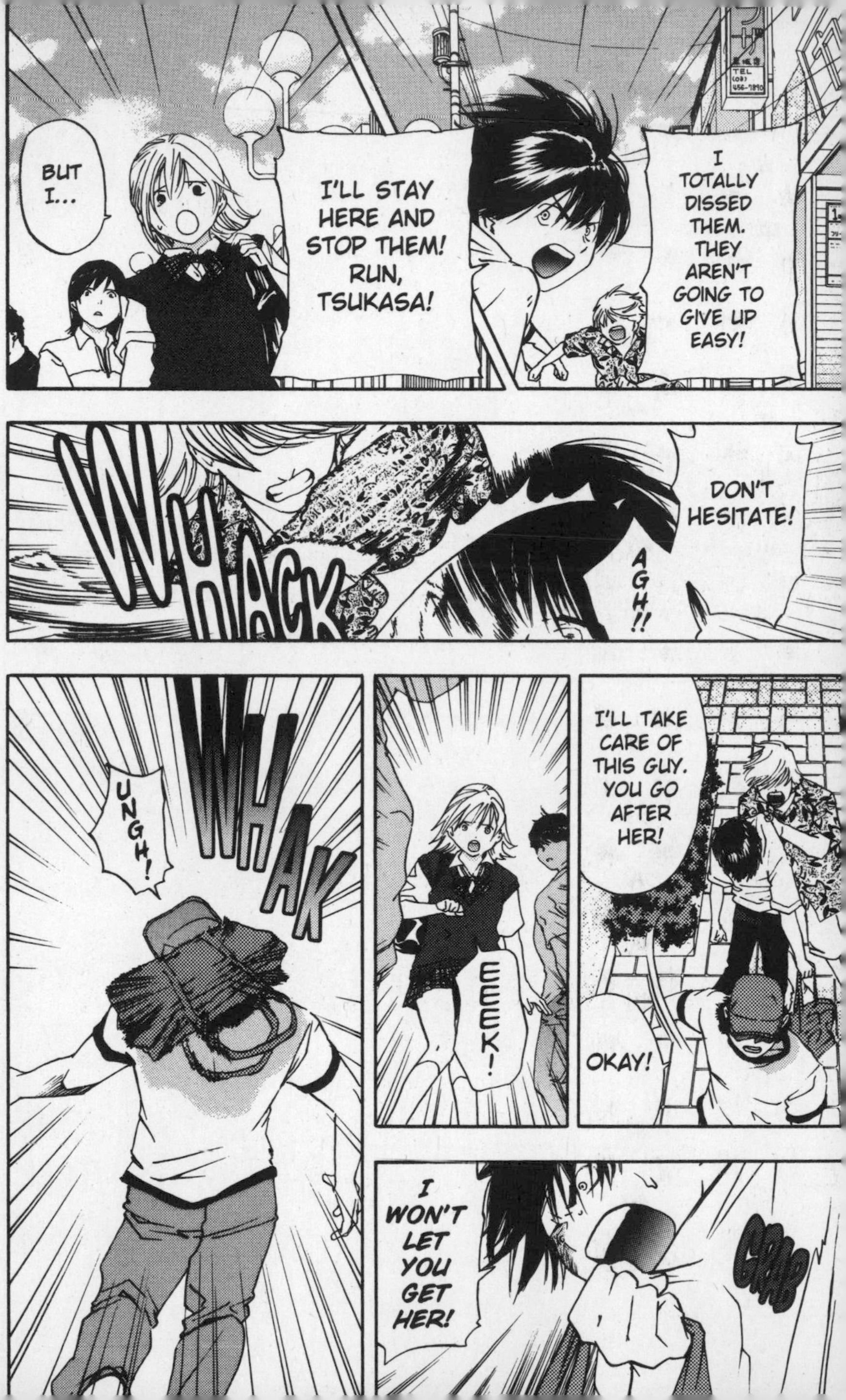
TEL
(03)
456-7890
I TOTALLY DISSED THEM. THEY AREN'T GOING TO GIVE UP EASY!
I'LL STAY HERE AND STOP THEM! RUN, TSUKASA!
BUT I...
DON'T HESITATE!
AGH!!
WHACK
I'LL TAKE CARE OF THIS GUY. YOU GO AFTER HER!
OKAY!
EEEK!
I WON'T LET YOU GET HER!
GRAB
WHAK
UNGH!

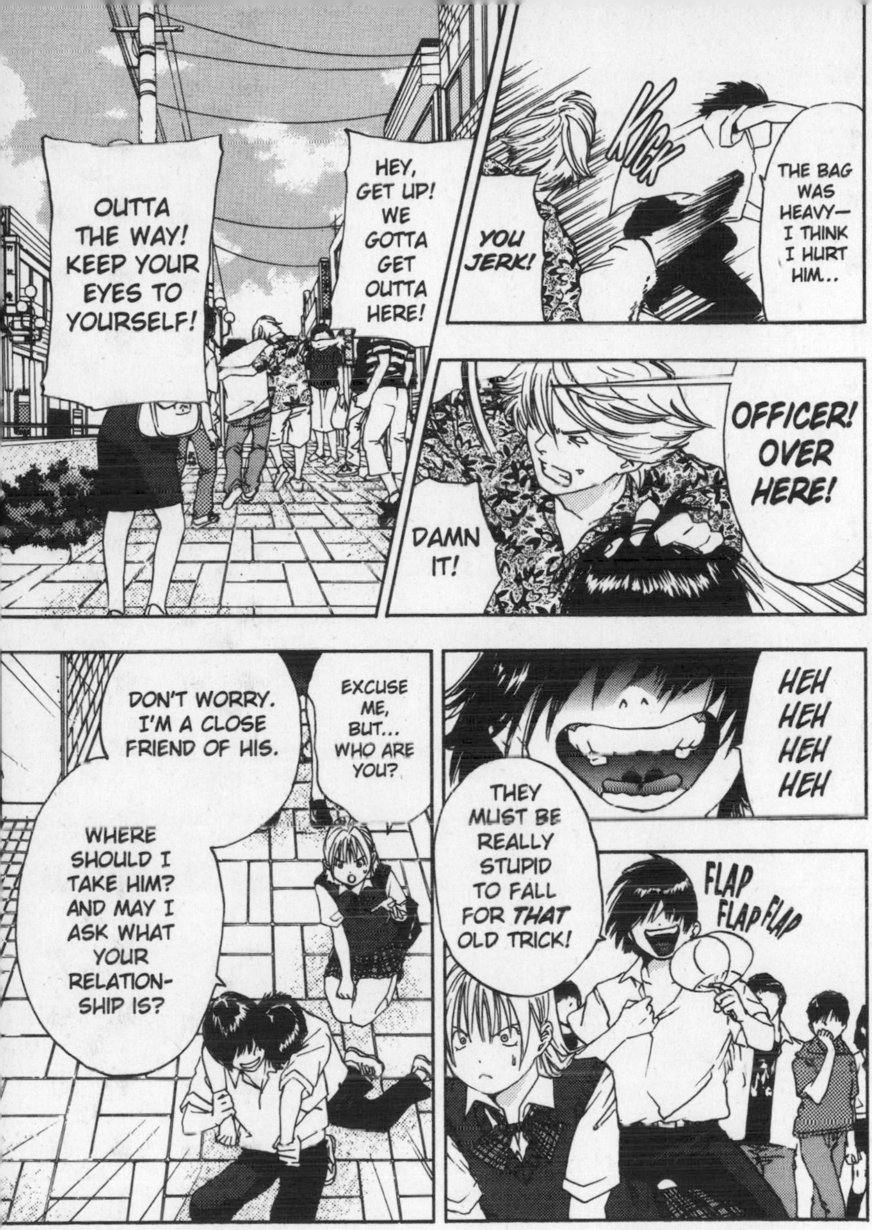
KICK
THE BAG WAS HEAVY— I THINK I HURT HIM..
YOU JERK!
OFFICER! OVER HERE!
DAMN IT!
HEY, GET UP! WE GOTTA GET OUTTA HERE!
OUTTA THE WAY! KEEP YOUR EYES TO YOURSELF!
HEH HEH HEH HEH
FLAP FLAP FLAP
THEY MUST BE REALLY STUPID TO FALL FOR THAT OLD TRICK!
EXCUSE ME, BUT... WHO ARE YOU?
DON'T WORRY. I'M A CLOSE FRIEND OF HIS.
WHERE SHOULD I TAKE HIM? AND MAY I ASK WHAT YOUR RELATIONSHIP IS?

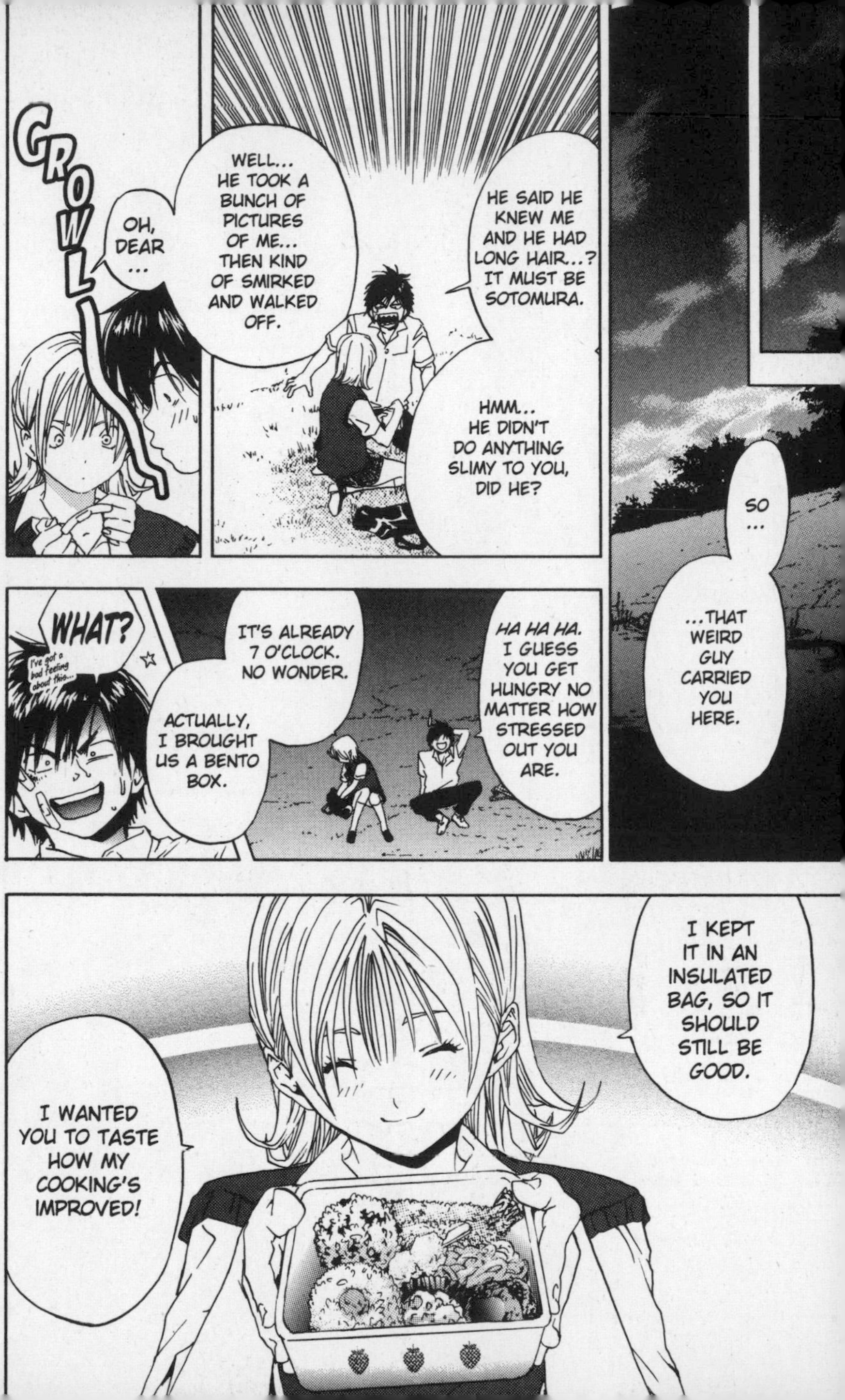
SO ...
...THAT WEIRD GUY CARRIED YOU HERE.
HE SAID HE KNEW ME AND HE HAD LONG HAIR...? IT MUST BE SOTOMURA.
HMM.. HE DIDN'T DO ANYTHING SLIMY TO YOU, DID HE?
WELL... HE TOOK A BUNCH OF PICTURES OF ME... THEN KIND OF SMIRKED AND WALKED OFF.
OH, DEAR ...
GROWL
HA HA HA. I GUESS YOU GET HUNGRY NO MATTER HOW STRESSED OUT YOU ARE.
IT'S ALREADY 7 O'CLOCK. NO WONDER.
ACTUALLY, I BROUGHT US A BENTO BOX.
WHAT?
I've got a bad feeling about this...
I KEPT IT IN AN INSULATED BAG, SO IT SHOULD STILL BE GOOD.
I WANTED YOU TO TASTE HOW MY COOKING'S IMPROVED!

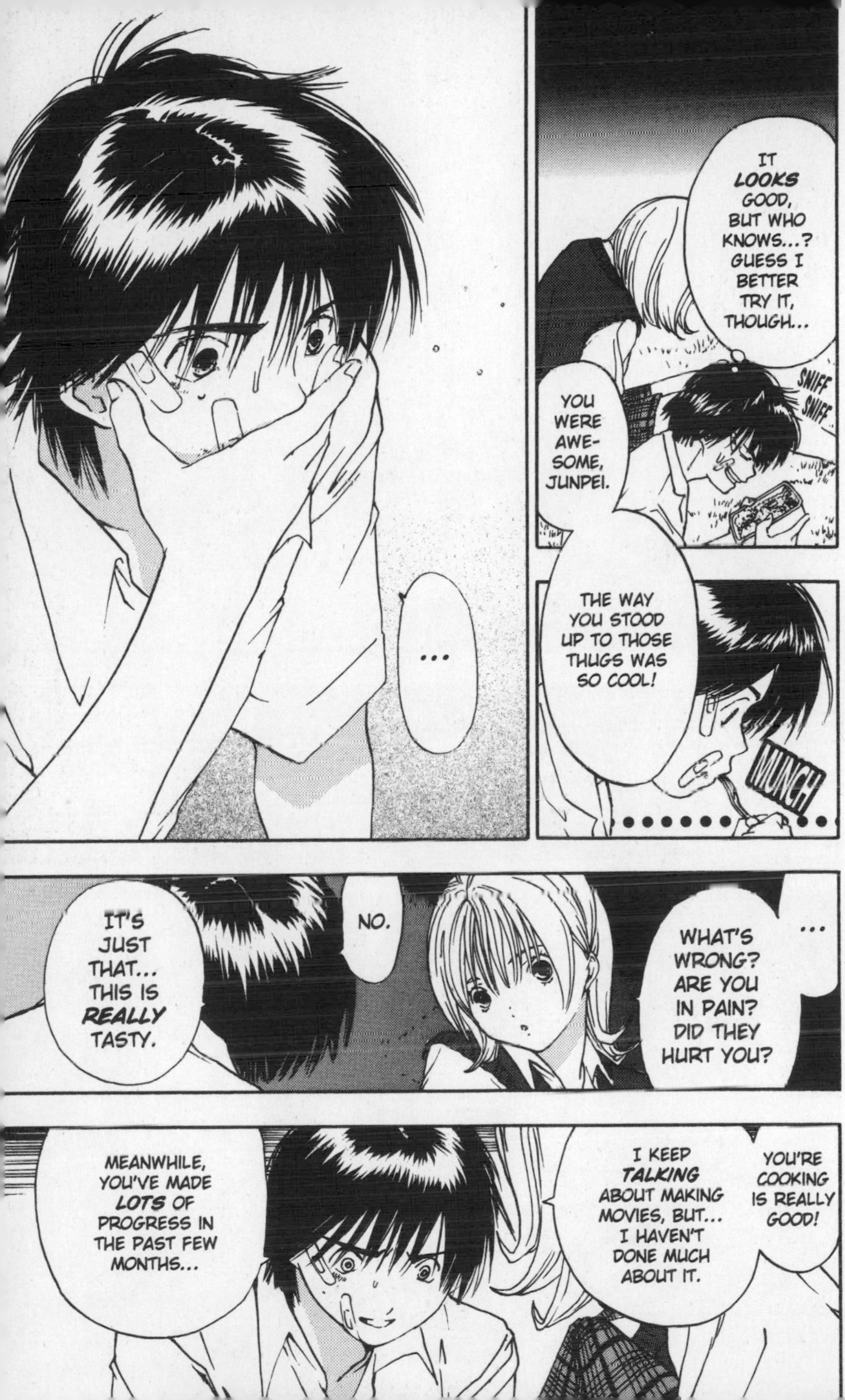
IT LOOKS GOOD, BUT WHO KNOWS...? GUESS I BETTER TRY IT, THOUGH...
SNIFF SNIFF
YOU WERE AWESOME, JUNPEI.
THE WAY YOU STOOD UP TO THOSE THUGS WAS SO COOL!
MUNCH
....
...
...
WHAT'S WRONG? ARE YOU IN PAIN? DID THEY HURT YOU?
NO.
IT'S JUST THAT... THIS IS REALLY TASTY.
YOU'RE COOKING IS REALLY GOOD!
I KEEP TALKING ABOUT MAKING MOVIES, BUT... I HAVEN'T DONE MUCH ABOUT IT.
MEANWHILE, YOU'VE MADE LOTS OF PROGRESS IN THE PAST FEW MONTHS...

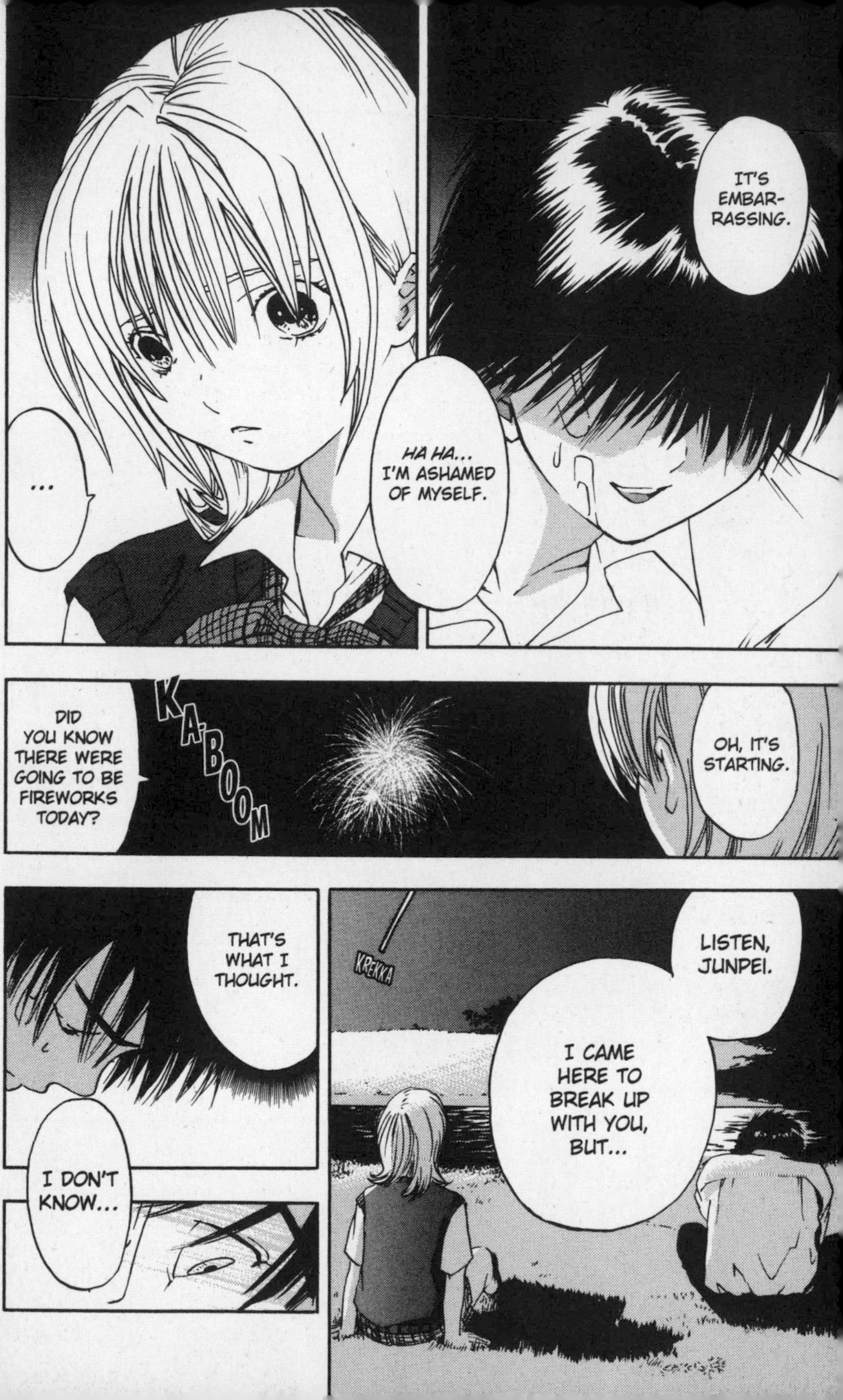
IT'S EMBAR-RASSING.
HA HA... I'M ASHAMED OF MYSELF.
...
OH, IT'S STARTING.
KABOOM
DID YOU KNOW THERE WERE GOING TO BE FIREWORKS TODAY?
LISTEN, JUNPEI.
KREKKA
I CAME HERE TO BREAK UP WITH YOU, BUT...
THAT'S WHAT I THOUGHT.
I DON'T KNOW...

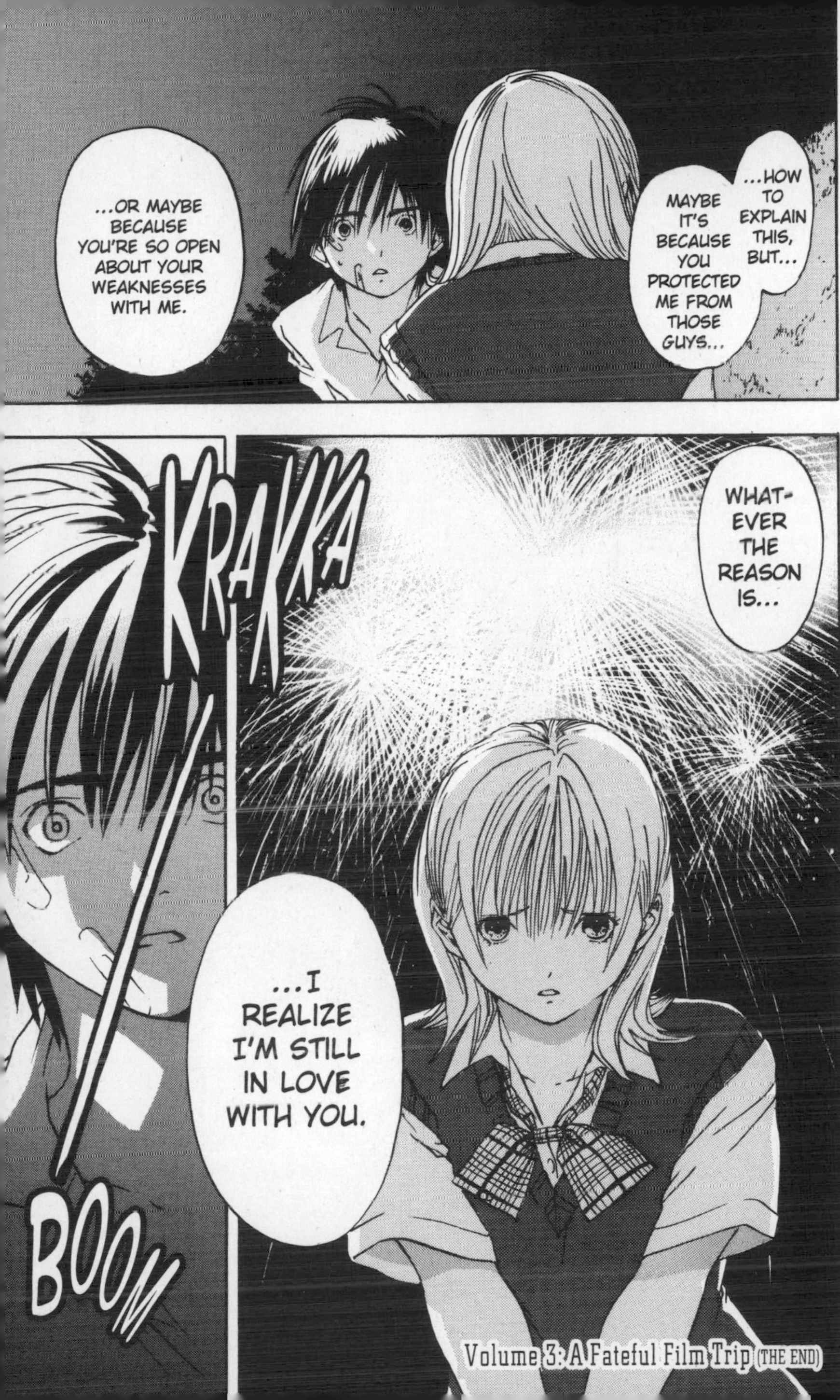
...HOW TO EXPLAIN THIS, BUT...
MAYBE IT'S BECAUSE YOU PROTECTED ME FROM THOSE GUYS...
...OR MAYBE BECAUSE YOU'RE SO OPEN ABOUT YOUR WEAKNESSES WITH ME.
WHAT-EVER THE REASON IS...
...I REALIZE I'M STILL IN LOVE WITH YOU.
KRAKKA
BOOM
Volume 3: A Fateful Film Trip (THE END)

A Sneak Peek at Volume 4!

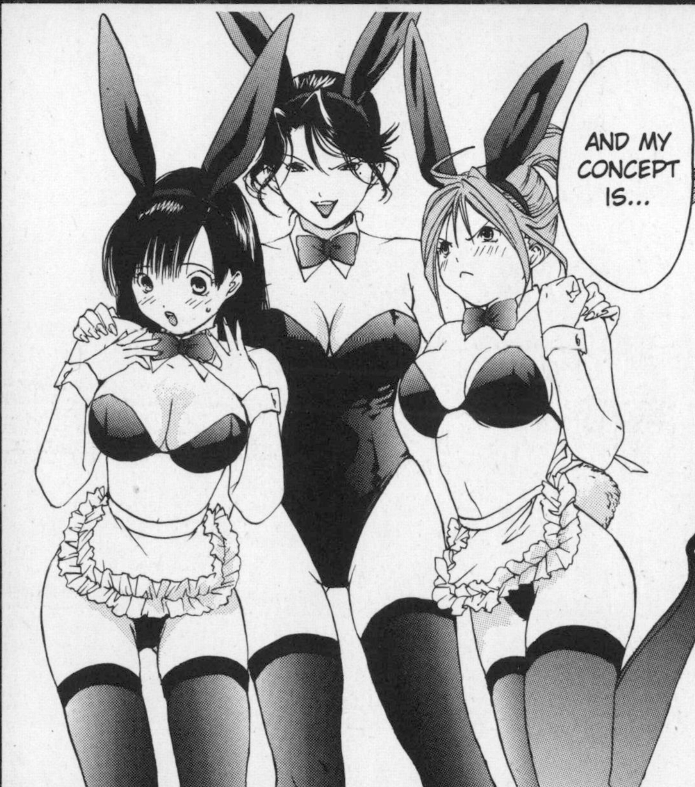
AND MY CONCEPT IS...

Junpei's in heaven when Aya collaborates on his first screenplay, Satsuki plays the star and Tsukasa plays his real-life girlfriend! But can Junpei play all three girls forever, or will they decide he's just a *player*...!?

AVAILABLE NOW!

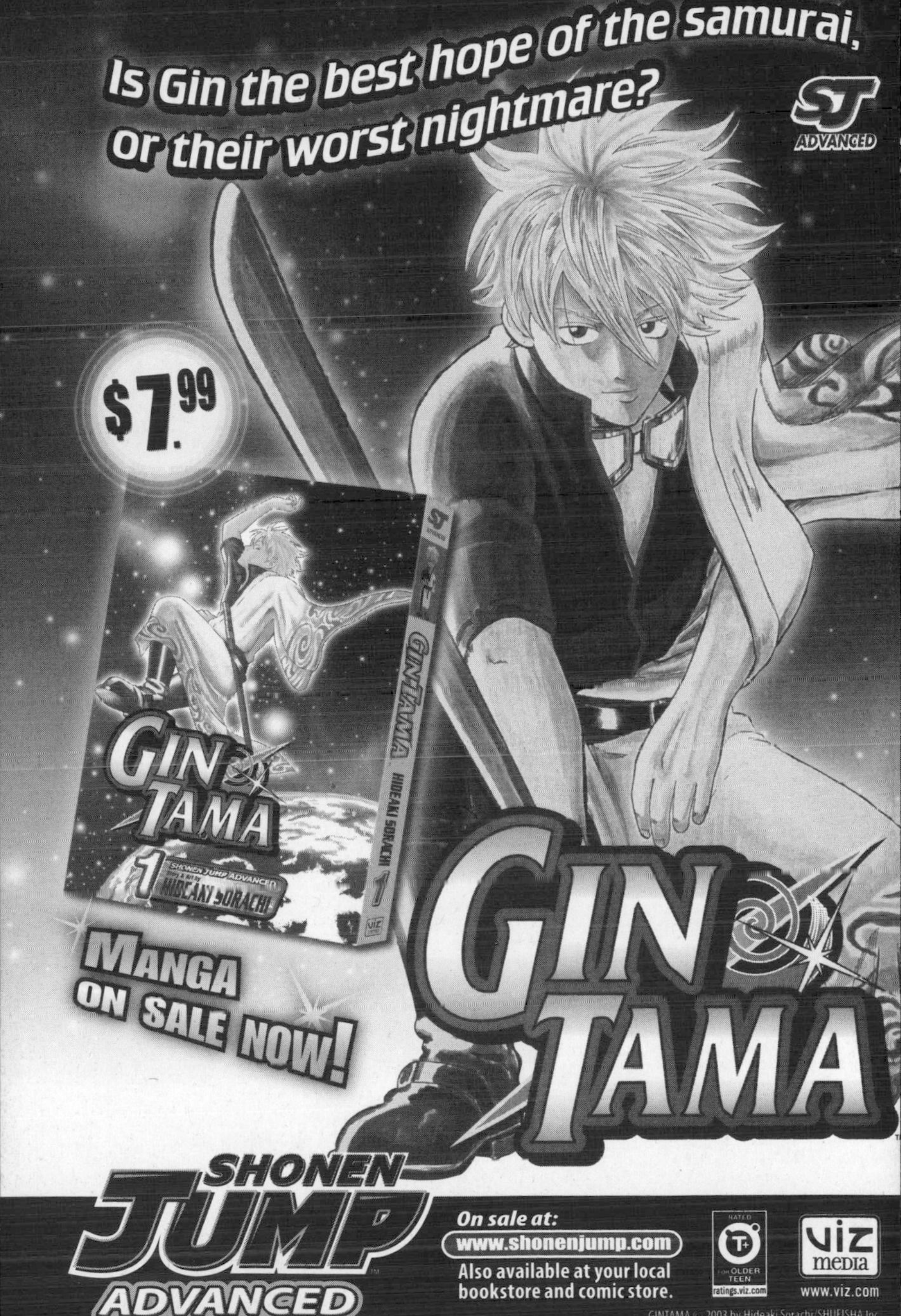

Is Gin the best hope of the samurai,
or their worst nightmare?
SJ ADVANCED
$7.99
GIN TAMA
1 SHONEN JUMP ADVANCED
HIDEAKI SORACHI
MANGA ON SALE NOW!
GIN TAMA
SHONEN JUMP ADVANCED
On sale at:
www.shonenjump.com
Also available at your local bookstore and comic store.
RATED T+ FOR OLDER TEEN
ratings.viz.com
viz media
www.viz.com
GINTAMA © 2003 by Hideaki Sorachi/SHUEISHA Inc.

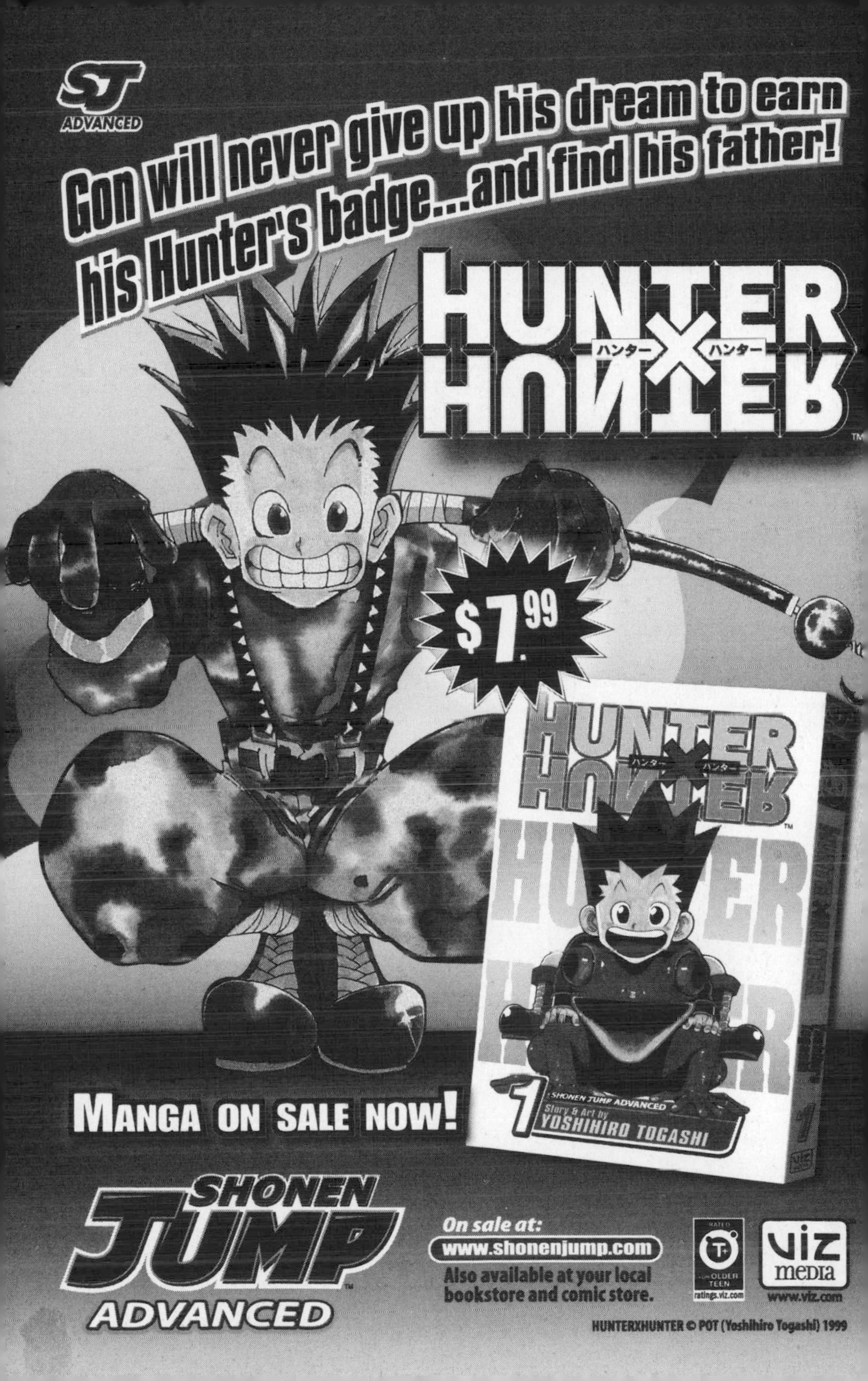

SJ ADVANCED
Gon will never give up his dream to earn his Hunter's badge...and find his father!
HUNTER×HUNTER
ハンター ハンター
$7.99
HUNTER×HUNTER
1
SHONEN JUMP ADVANCED
Story & Art by
YOSHIHIRO TOGASHI
MANGA ON SALE NOW!
SHONEN JUMP ADVANCED
On sale at:
www.shonenjump.com
Also available at your local bookstore and comic store.
RATED T+ FOR OLDER TEEN
ratings.viz.com
viz media
www.viz.com
HUNTERXHUNTER © POT (Yoshihiro Togashi) 1999

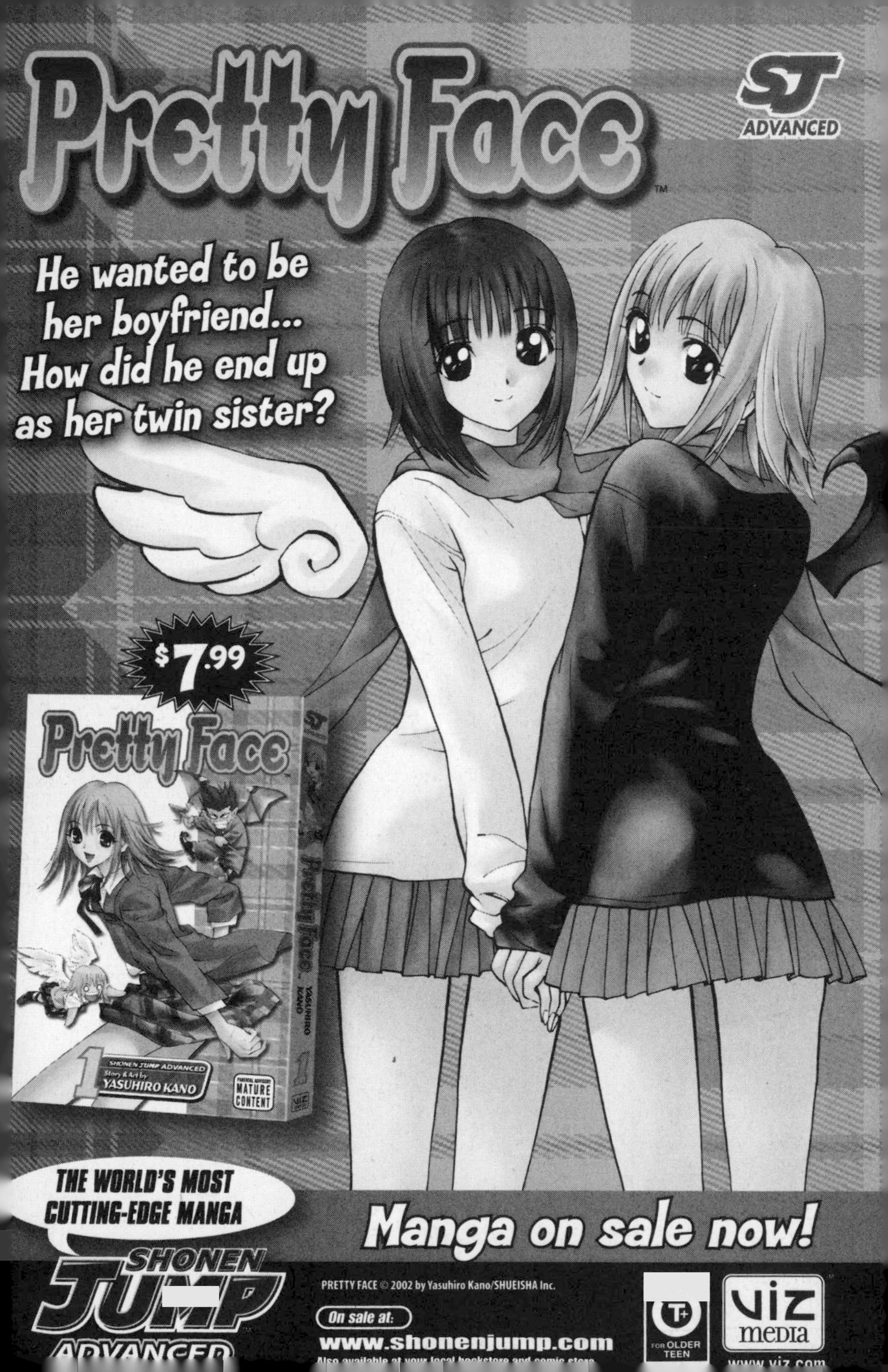
Pretty Face™
SJ ADVANCED
He wanted to be her boyfriend... How did he end up as her twin sister?
$7.99
Pretty Face
SHONEN JUMP ADVANCED
Story & Art by YASUHIRO KANO
PARENTAL ADVISORY MATURE CONTENT
THE WORLD'S MOST CUTTING-EDGE MANGA
Manga on sale now!
SHONEN JUMP ADVANCED
PRETTY FACE © 2002 by Yasuhiro Kano/SHUEISHA Inc.
On sale at:
www.shonenjump.com
T+ FOR OLDER TEEN
VIZ media
www.viz.com

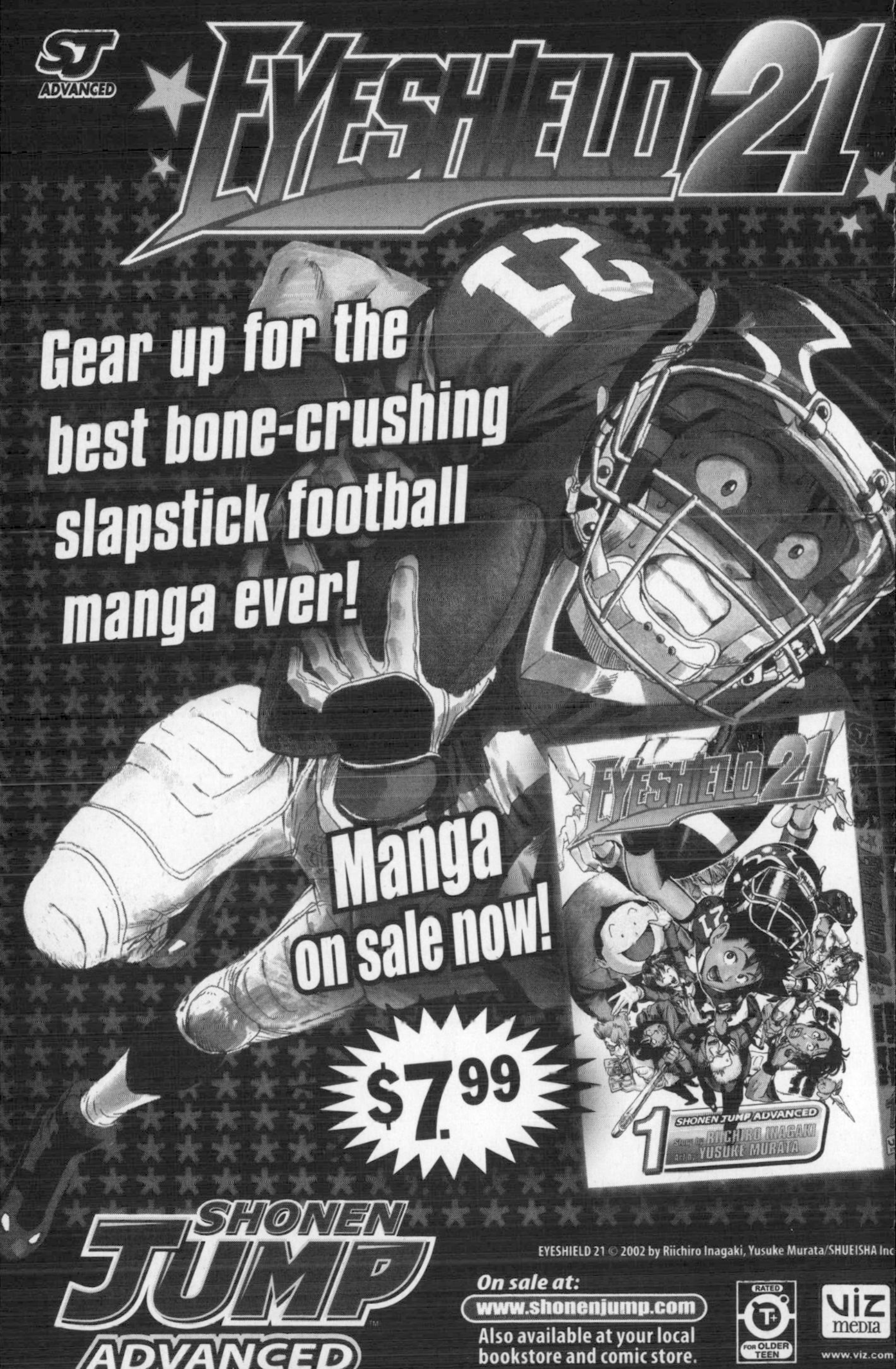

Tell us what you think about SHONEN JUMP manga!

Our survey is now available online.
Go to: **www.SHONENJUMP.com/mangasurvey**

Help us make our product offering better!

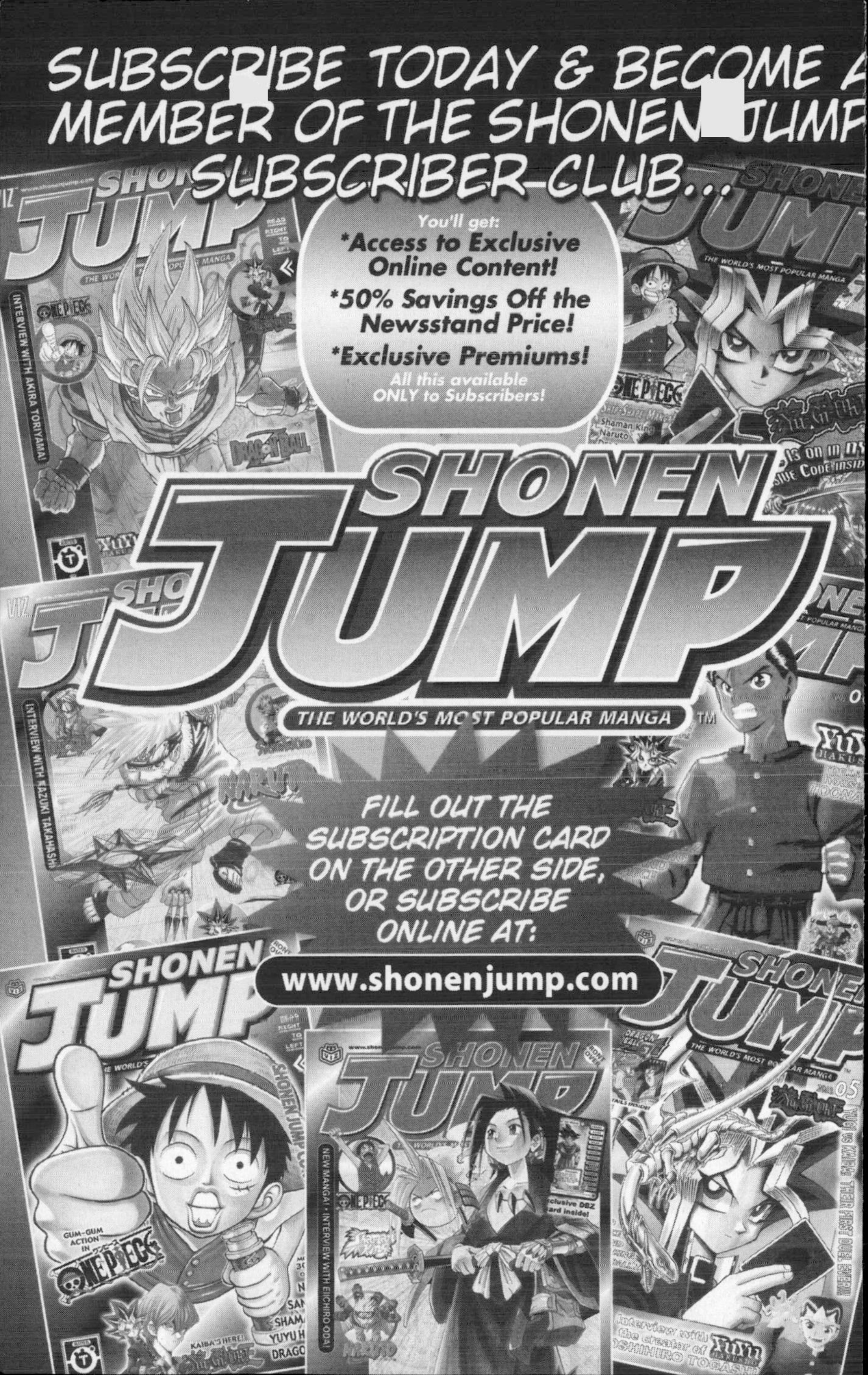
SUBSCRIBE TODAY & BECOME A
MEMBER OF THE SHONEN JUMP
SUBSCRIBER CLUB...
You'll get:
*Access to Exclusive Online Content!
*50% Savings Off the Newsstand Price!
*Exclusive Premiums!
All this available ONLY to Subscribers!
SHONEN JUMP
THE WORLD'S MOST POPULAR MANGA
FILL OUT THE SUBSCRIPTION CARD ON THE OTHER SIDE, OR SUBSCRIBE ONLINE AT:
www.shonenjump.com